INTERNATIONAL CORPORATE FINANCE

INTERNATIONAL

CORPORATE

FINANCE

MARKETS, TRANSACTIONS, AND FINANCIAL MANAGEMENT

Edited by

Harvey A. Poniachek

Boston
UNWIN HYMAN
London Sydney Wellington

Unwin Hyman Inc.,
8 Winchester Place, Winchester, Mass. 01890, USA

Published by the Academic Division of
Unwin Hyman Ltd
15/17 Broadwick Street, London W1V 1FP, UK

Allen & Unwin (Australia) Ltd,
8 Napier Street, North Sydney, NSW 2060, Australia

Allen & Unwin (New Zealand) Ltd in association with the
Port Nicholson Press Ltd,
Compusales Building, 75 Ghuznee Street, Wellington 1, New Zealand

First published in 1989

Library of Congress Cataloging-in-Publication Data

International corporate finance : markets, transactions, and financial
  management / [edited by] Harvey A. Poniachek.
      p. cm.
   Bibliography: p.
   Includes index.
   ISBN 0-04-445394-9 (alk. paper).

      1. International business enterprises—Finance. 2. International
finance. I. Poniachek, Harvey A.
   HG4027.5.I555   1989
   658.1′599—dc19   88-36651
                                                                          CIP

British Library Cataloguing in Publication Data

International corporate finance.
   1. International financial management
   I. Poniachek, Harvey A.
   658.1′5

ISBN 0-04-445394-9

Typeset by Mathematical Compositions Setters Ltd, Salisbury,
and printed by The University Press, Cambridge

*Dedicated with love to Shelley
and Dana, my daughters*

Contents

List of Figures

List of Tables

XiV

About the Editor and Contributors

HARVEY A. PONIACHEK is Senior Manager and Economist at Ernst & Whinney, and for the past six years, Adjunct Associate Professor of Finance and International Business at New York University Graduate School of Business Administration. He was previously Adjunct Professor of Economics and Finance at Pace University. During his professional career—including fourteen years with Bank America—he has had a range of responsibilities, with an increasing focus on international finance, currency and commodity markets and country risk assessment. His previous publications include *Monetary Independence under Flexible Exchange Rates* (1979), *Direct Foreign Investment in the United States* (1986), and chapters in *The International Business Handbook* (1988) and *The International Finance Handbook* (1983).

JOSEPH A. ARNETT is a vice president and trade finance and marketing officer at Bank of America, the North American Division, California Commercial Banking, Los Angeles. He has been with the bank since 1970 in the capacity of account officer for Latin American and European countries. From 1982 to 1985 he was with the bank's training department, where he conducted trade finance workshops throughout North America. Joseph Arnett holds a degree from the American Graduate School of International Management at Glendale, Arizona.

BRENDA BASKIN is a Ph.D. Candidate in Finance at Columbia University. In 1985–87 she was a summer inter in the World Bank, Bank of America and Chemical Bank, where she worked on subjects concerning international financial markets.

CRISTOPHER BOURDAIN earned a B.A. degree at Brown University in 1981. Trained on the foreign exchange advisory desk at Union Bank of Switzerland, New York Branch. Moved in 1983 to Crédit Lyonnais, New York branch as foreign exchange corporate advisor. Joined Bank America International, N.Y. as Vice-President and senior financial market advisor in 1986, servicing U.S. and European corporate accounts. Presently with Manufacturers

Hanover Trust of New York. Frequent lecturer on foreign currency options at the World Trade Institute and New York University, School of Continuing Education. Lectured on managing over-the-counter options portfolio at INSEAD, Fontainebleau, 1987.

CHARLES T. CRAWFORD is a senior manager with Price Waterhouse and director of that firm's Center for Transnational Taxation in New York. Mr. Crawford's writings include tax articles in the *Journal of Taxation*, *Tax Adviser*, *International Tax Institute*, *German-American Trade News*, *International Tax Journal*, *Euromoney*, *Yachting Magazine*, *Golf Journal*, and *Amerikahandel*, and "International Tax Planning and Execution" in the *Handbook of International Financial Management*. He earned B.S. and LL.B. degrees from the University of Kansas and an LL.M. degree from the University of Missouri. He is a member of the bars of New York, Kansas, and Missouri and is a certified public accountant. Mr. Crawford's principal outside activity in the financial area has been service as assistant treasurer, past treasurer, director, and member of the Executive Committee of the United States Squash Racquets Association.

SCOTT N. DILLMAN is vice-president and treasurer of Gulf International Bank. Previously he was vice-president and manager of the Global Options Trading Unit at Bank of America headquartered in New York. Before joining Bank of America, Mr. Dillman was the manager of currency and interest rate options at Marine Midland Bank, where he also handled bill futures arbitrage. Prior to that he marketed financial futures and worked in the economics department at Donaldson, Lufkin, and Jenrette. His experience also includes market analysis at the U.S. Treasury Department in Washington, D.C. Dillman graduated from Gettysburg College in 1979 with a B.A. in economics. His publications include "Rolling Thunder": *The Financial Futures Handbook*; "Delta: The Option Tool for Hedging and Trading"; "Life after Delta: Gamma" *Euromoney Supplement*; and "Corporate Foreign Exchange Management" in *Intermarket*.

ALEXANDER E. FLEMING is a senior economist in the financial policy and analysis department of the World Bank. Prior to that he served as economist in both the economic section and the overseas department of the Bank of England. He has also taught economics and finance at St. Andrews University in Scotland and has lectured and published widely on financial topics.

DAVID GOLD is a consultant to the United Nations Centre on Transnational Corporations. He holds a master of philosophy in economics from Columbia University (1974) and is completing requirements for a Ph.D. at the City University of New York. He was previously director of military research at the Council on Economic Priorities and has taught at Columbia University, the University of California, and the New School for Social Research. In addition to conducting his current research on international investment and the multinational corporation, Mr. Gold has published and spoken widely on macroeconomics issues and the economics of military spending.

RICHARD M. HAMMER, a partner at Price Waterhouse, is national director of international tax services of the U.S. firm, based in New York, and chairman of the Price Waterhouse World Firm's international tax services panel. He is also president of the International Fiscal Association; chairman of the fiscal committee of the business and industry advisory committee to OECD; chairman of the tax committee of the U.S. Council for International Business; chairman of the tax committee of the U.S. Business and Industry Advisory Committee to OECD; and member of the investment policy advisory committee of the U.S. Trade Representative.

Mr. Hammer is co-author of "Accounting for the Multinational Corporation" (Financial Executives Research Foundation, 1977), and his writings include tax articles in the *Tax Adviser*, *Journal of Taxation*, *NYU Tax Institute Proceedings*, *Practical Accountant*, *Tulane Tax Institute Proceedings*, and *British Tax Review*.

Mr. Hammer is a regular speaker at various tax institutes and other forums. He has a B.A. degree *cum laude* from Princeton and an M.B.A. from the Harvard Graduate School of Business. Mr. Hammer is a certified public accountant in New York and several other states.

JOHN HEIN has been director of international economics at the Conference Board, a New York-based not-for-profit organization, since 1967. Holder of three degrees from Columbia University, Mr. Hein previously served as economist and chief of the foreign research division at the Federal Reserve Bank of New York.

LAWRENCE M. KRACKOV currently holds the position of treasurer at CBS Records. Previously he was assistant treasurer at CBS, where he established a $200 million underwritten Euronote issuance facility, implemented the first foreign-currency-denominated debt and nine currency-debt swaps for a total of $200 million, and established a $1 billion annual foreign-exchange hedging program. Mr. Krackov has also held the position of director of acquisitions at CBS and previously performed a similar function as the assistant to the chairman of Coca-Cola of New York. His prior professional experience included diverse assignments in financial planning and analysis, including the position of director of financial planning and control at Monsanto.

He holds a bachelor of arts degree in economics from Cornell University and both juris doctor and M.B.A. degrees from Columbia University. He is also currently assistant professor at Pace University, where he has taught several different finance courses.

Mr. Krackov has made several presentations at professional conferences, including speeches on the international finance topics of "Euro Notes and Commercial Paper," "Foreign-Exchange Exposure Management," and "International Cash and Treasury Management." He is also co-author of the book *Financial Management: A Practical Approach to Avoiding Financial Bloomers*.

JOSEPH G. KVASNICKA is a Professor of Finance at DePaul University in Chicago, where he teaches graduate and undergraduate courses in international finance and banking. He also holds a position of an advisor and consultant to the Federal Reserve Bank of Chicago.

Prior to his joining the faculty of DePaul in 1987, he was, for the previous 25 years, a member the research staff of the Federal Reserve Bank of Chicago, most recently as a Vice President and the Head of the International Section of the bank's Research Department.

While on a leave-of-absence from the Fed, Dr. Kvasnicka spent two years on the White House staff as the Senior Economist with the President's Council of Economic Advisers in the President's Nixon and Ford administrations, and held several part-time positions as a Visiting Professor and Lecturer at the Graduate School of Banking at the University of Wisconsin, at Indiana University, the University of Pittsburgh, and at the Graduate School of Business at the University of Cape Town, South Africa.

Dr. Kvasnicka was the Editor of the Federal Reserve Bank of Chicago's *International Letter*, and has written numerous articles in the area of international finance. His most recent publication is the editorial authorship of a book, *Readings in International Finance*, published by the Federal Reserve Bank of Chicago in 1987.

FRANK RIBEIRO is a vice-president and director in the BankAmerica Capital Markets Group and is the head of the swap finance unit located in New York City. He has been active in currency and interest-rate swaps and capital market arbitrage since 1981. Prior to joining Bank of America, Mr. Ribeiro was in the international finance group at Exxon Corporation. He holds a master of arts degree in public and international affairs from Princeton University. He has served with the U.S. State Department as an economist at the U.S. Embassy in London and has been an advisor to the United Nations and several of its member countries on issues of international finance.

DAVID SPISELMAN is a management consultant and faculty member at New York University where he teaches cash management. He is a principal in the Tactical Finance Group, as well as president of David Spiselman and Company, Inc. His clients include most of the largest banks in Manhattan, as well as many of the *Fortune* 500 corporations that use their services. Mr. Spiselman is an expert in the areas of international treasury management, treasury automation, computer crime prevention, cash forecasting, and cash accounting. He has been quoted and published in journals, magazines, and books on such topics as treasury automation, float management, and computer crime and countermeasures. He is frequently a featured speaker at financial conferences and conventions.

Prior to starting his own company in 1980, Mr. Spiselman worked on the staffs of such companies as Time Inc., American Express, and Atlantic Richfield and for Security Pacific and Irving Trust. He also sits on the board of directors of NYU's Management Decision Laboratory and on the boards of several small corporations.

Mr. Spiselman earned an M.B.A. in finance from NYU. He also holds an M.A. in psychology from the New School for Social Research.

Preface

RAPID expansion of international trade and investment in the post-World War II period stimulated the growth and development of companies with substantial international business, known as international or multinational corporations (MNCs). MNCs are the most important actors in the world economy. They are heavily engaged in international trade and capital flows, and generate the bulk of direct international investment. The risks inherent in international operations are high, but so are the potential rewards. The ability to employ worldwide resources quickly in response to environmental conditions and market opportunities affords MNCs a distinct advantage over domestic companies.

International financial management is more complex than its domestic equivalent because management must cope with different financial markets, regulations and tax systems. Effective financial management has become more significant than ever before primarily for corporate success because of enhanced international competition, and greater risk and opportunities.

This book addresses the subject of corporate finance of multinational corporations and corporations with substantial international business. The standard theory of corporate finance is applicable to MNCs and corporations that are heavily engaged in international business. However, some adjustments are necessary because of the complexities of the international environment, or due to problems uniquely associated with international operations that require new formulations or special attention.

The book is organized in five parts. Part I sets the framework of international corporate finance. Part II addresses the international organization and financial markets, with particular emphasis on foreign exchange and the Eurocurrency markets. Part III examines international business—in terms of trade and investment—of the multinational corporation and the corporation with extensive international business. Part IV reviews subjects concerning financial management. Part V involves techniques of financial hedging operations. Finally, the book is accompanied by several appendixes.

The book provides the reader with a thorough examination of international financial management, and many of the ideas and techniques presented could provide valuable assistance to professional financial managers in the corporation, bank and government. The book provides valuable information and insight and can be used as a book of readings for students.

This book and the plan thereof grow out from a decade of teaching international corporate finance and international financial markets courses at New York University and at Pace University, and working in the financial market and with multinational corporations some fourteen years at Bank of America. I owe as editor a great intellectual debt to the contributing authors and many of my colleagues at the bank and the university.

Harvey A. Poniachek
New York City, March 1988

PART I

INTRODUCTION

1 The Framework of International Corporate Finance

HARVEY A. PONIACHEK

OVER the past forty years, most of the world's large manufacturing firms—both in the United States and elsewhere—have been transformed from strictly national or domestic to multinational or international enterprises. International business remains the domain of a relatively small number of large multinational corporations (MNCs) with an ever-growing market share. A common definition of a multinational company is one with investment and sales in two or more countries, or one with business activities in two or more countries. MNCs are positioned to take advantage of the complex marketplace, since they are relatively unconstrained in their global activities. International diversification reduces fluctuations in corporate earnings, and enhances their shareholders' value.

As the world economy becomes more integrated, MNCs' role is ever increasing, and new companies are joining their ranks. Competition among MNCs in many key industries has intensified in recent years. This phenomenon has been further aggravated by lower global economic growth and the emergence of MNCs from Japan and the newly industrialized countries, such as South Korea.

Operation and financial management of MNCs' international business occurs in an environment characterized by volatile foreign-exchange rates, a variety of restrictions on capital flows, various levels of country risk, different tax systems, and a wide spectrum of institutional settings. The principles of corporate financial management, however, generally apply for the multinational corporation or the corporation with extensive international business. Environmental and market complexities occasionally modify some of these principles. Moreover, some international financial management applications have no domestic counterparts and arise entirely because of a unique institutional setting.

Recent dramatic changes in the international financial markets have significant implications for corporate operation, financial management, survival, and competitive position. In this environment, management's

3

ability to seize opportunities and avoid unnecessary risk depends on its knowledge of the international environment and its proficiency in various management principles. By focusing on the international market environment and financial management issues, particularly of the MNCs, this book provides a comprehensive framework for international corporate finance and a balanced and integrated treatment of environmental and institutional settings, business transactions, and management aspects. It discusses the international financial and foreign-exchange markets, trade and investment, and issues concerning financial management and techniques for operating in the financial markets. Considerable attention is paid to financial innovations in funding and hedging methods through currency swaps and options.

MNCS AND THEIR ACTIVITIES

The involvement of multinational corporations in international business is growing. Of the more than 10,000 multinational corporations in the world, the fifty largest (of which about half are American) conduct about 50 percent of their operations abroad and account for 80 percent of global direct foreign investment and international production activities. The United States has about 3,500 MNCs (a multinational corporation is defined as having at least one operation abroad). Of these, about 300 corporations or, about 8.5 percent, are billion-dollar companies in terms of assets; they account for 80 percent of the total assets of the group.

The largest U.S. nonbank companies derive about 33 percent of their revenues from abroad and have the same proportion of assets there. The ratios are much higher for the largest companies. U.S. MNCs operate about 24,000 affiliates around the world, of which the 850 largest account for 53 percent of total assets.

About two-thirds of U.S. affiliates abroad are located in industrial countries, and the remaining third operate in the less developed countries (LDCs). Japan and the Asia Pacific region are likely to assume greater importance; they now host only 11 percent of U.S. subsidiaries.

The very high growth rate that U.S. MNCs and international transactions displayed between the mid-1960s and mid-1970s has now subsided, apparently because their positioning abroad has been largely completed. Price stability substantially deflated trade flows, and country risk and portfolio balance considerations suggest more subdued expansion. MNCs are the most important actors in the world economy. They are heavily engaged in international trade and capital flows, and generate the bulk of direct international investment. Japanese and European MNCs' foreign production and investment grew considerably faster in the current decade than foreign production and investment of U.S. based companies. The U.S. emerged as the largest host country to

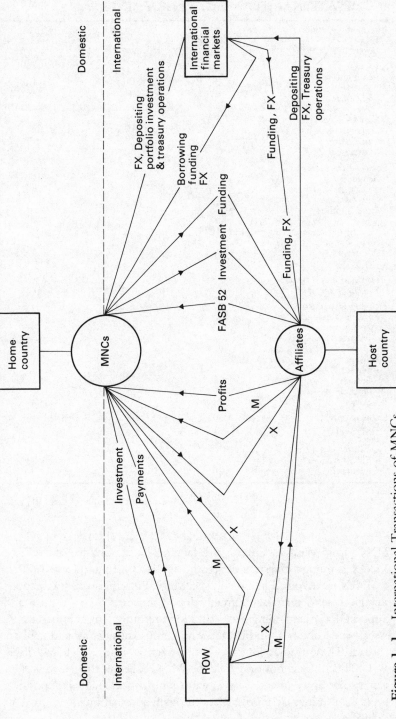

Figure 1-1. International Transactions of MNCs.

ROW = Rest of the World   I = Import
X = Export   FX = Foreign Exchange

Table 1-1.

INTERNATIONAL TRANSACTIONS OF MNCs.

International trade:
  Export
  Import

Services:
  Remittances:
    Dividends
    Royalties
    Fees
  Various services:
    Transportation
    Insurance
    Interest

Financial transactions:
  Banking:
    Deposits
    Loans
  Other funding:
    Notes-issuing facilities (NIFs)
    Revolving underwriting facilities (RUFs)
    Eurocommercial paper
  Payments

Investment:
  Portfolio investment
  Direct foreign investment

Hedging instruments:
  Foreign exchange:
    Forward markets
    Futures
    Options
    Swaps
  Interest:
    Futures
    Options
    Swaps

Financial markets:
  Home
  Host
  Offshore:
    Eurocurrency
    Eurobond

MNCs from Western Europe and Japan. The importance of the U.S. MNCs as foreign investors peaked in the late 1960s and early 1970s.

MNCs are involved in a broad spectrum of international transactions that give rise to financial intermediation. The average MNC exports and imports, has outstanding short- and long-term foreign-currency loans, assets, and liabilities, and operates numerous subsidiaries and affiliates abroad. These transactions are summarized in Figure 1-1 and Table 1-1. The unique position held by MNCs affords them access to a variety of capital markets to obtain competitive financing, position profits and minimize taxation, and diversify internationally in order to reduce risk.

FINANCIAL MANAGEMENT POLICIES

The objective of the MNCs is to maximize their shareholders' investments. To meet this objective. financial management addresses three major decisions concerning investment, financing, and dividend policy. An optimal combination of the three financial decisions that financial managers are concerned with are; 1. Capital budgeting decision, 2. Financing decision, and 3. Dividend policy decision. The capital budgeting on investment decision is concerned with how to allocate funds to competing projects and assets in such a way that shareholders' wealth is maximized. The financing decision involves generating funds either internally or from external sources at the least possible cost. The dividend policy involves decisions concerning the distribution of profit to stockholders and the level of retained earnings, which, in turn, affects liquidity, risk and the value of the firm. See Table 1–2.

Generally, corporate decisionmaking authority is decentralized, with substantial authority afforded to subsidiaries and affiliates abroad. There is, however, considerable variation among companies, depending on their size, experience, and type of business. Capital budgeting is usually controlled by the parent company, but it is not clear to what degree international treasury operations are centralized. Companies with advanced management information systems and efficient communications networks are likely to tightly manage treasury operations across geographic regions.

Table 1–2.
FINANCIAL DECISION PRINCIPLES

MNCs' objectives; maximizing the value of the firm, or stockholders' wealth

---

I Investment (capital budgeting)
@ assessment criteria and selection of assets
@ selection among competing projects
@ growth strategy—m&a, natural growth
@ assets management

II Financing (capital structure)
@ debt/equity
@ cost and risk

III Dividend policy
@ payout ratio
@ retained earnings
@ funding considerations

FINANCING AND FINANCIAL MARKET TRENDS

MNCs have access to a wide range of international sources of funds, of which the most important are the Eurocurrency and the Eurobond markets. In addition, MNCs have access to the capital markets of host

countries in which their affiliates are located and to their home
country's financial markets.

Because of the sharp acceleration in deregulation and development in
the global economy, dramatic changes have occurred in the capital
markets, financial institutions, and instruments. Major new financial
instruments—such as note-issuing facilities (NIFs), currency and
interest-rate options, and swaps—have been created, which provide
corporations with a broader and more flexible range of funding and
hedging of interest and currency exposure.

Currency swaps often are employed to lower borrowing cost, particularly by companies with high creditworthiness. These instruments
further diminish the barriers between domestic and international
markets and between different currency sectors and foster integration.
This high degree of international financial integration is providing
corporations with alternative sources and methods of financing.
Enhanced international integration has increased the portion of domestic financial intermediation being conducted via the international
markets. Technology also has enhanced integration by reducing transaction cost and facilitating the prompt dissemination of information.
Concurrent movements in interest rates and equity prices across
countries have increased significantly in recent years.

Financial markets have tended toward securitization. This phenomenon is reflected in a massive shift away from international bank credit
and toward acquiring international securities. U.S. corporations have
subsequently reduced their reliance on direct bank financing.

THE SCOPE AND NATURE OF THE BOOK

The applied approach of this book is based on the principles of
international corporate financial management. Contributions by corporate professionals and academics inform and interpret these issues for
both corporate executive and student.

The book is organized in five parts. Part I introduces the framework
of international corporate finance. Part II examines the international
monetary system, the foreign-exchange markets, the Eurocurrency
markets, and the institutional settings of the market. Part III examines
international transactions and business of the MNCs and reviews the
role of the MNCs, international trade and its financing, international
investment, and the balance of payments and its financing. Part IV
reviews issues concerning international corporate financial management: MNC funding, exposure management, cash management, and
MNC taxation. Finally, Part V is concerned with techniques of
operating in international financial markets, especially currency swaps
and currency options. The appendixes to the book discuss exposure
management, currency operation, artificial currency baskets, and
country risk assessment.

PART II

INTERNATIONAL FINANCIAL AND CAPITAL MARKETS

2 The Global Monetary and Financial System

HARVEY A. PONIACHEK

THE GLOBAL monetary system—which consists of exchange arrangements sponsored by the International Monetary Fund (IMF), international liquidity, and issues concerning balance-of-payments adjustments—went through a major restructuring in the early 1970s. It has grown rapidly, become large, efficient, and competitive, and gained in breadth, depth, and resiliency. It has developed a unique institutional setup, with markets and participants throughout the world. To date, the new system had performed unevenly—occasionally failing to provide sufficient exchange-rate stability and proper balance-of-payments adjustments. However, the system seems sufficiently stable to withstand several challenges posed by the external debt problems of the less developed countries (LDCs) since the early 1980s.

In the 1960s and early 1970s the rapid expansion of world trade and multinational corporations' activities, combined with the imposition of regulatory restrictions in many countries, provided a strong impetus for the expansion of the international financial market. The market's structure and operations were largely affected by the regulatory environments and economic developments around the world, which in turn shaped the evolution of the instruments, regulations, and performance.

The market is in a continuous state of evolution, and in recent years it has experienced profound changes. The international debt problems, disinflation and increased volatility of interest and exchange rates, deregulation of the financial services industry, and technological advancements brought several structural changes in the international financial markets.[1] These changes include the following:

1 Financial innovations were introduced in the form of financial techniques and instruments (such as interest and currency swaps). Innovations were designed to reduce the cost and risk associated with interest and exchange-rate volatility.
2 The distinction diminished between banks and nonbank financial intermediaries and between the domestic and the international markets. Financial institutions expanded their range of customers and financial service and entered into new business. There was an

11

increased substitutability of different types of instruments and
institutions, with a substantially expanded role of the commercial
banks as participants in the securities markets. These developments triggered a trend toward despecialization and globalization
in the industry.

3 The credit markets were securitized. This resulted in a decline of
traditional syndicated lending and a sharp expansion of the
securities market. This trend has been partly associated with the
evolution of a variety of instruments, such as Euronotes, that
serve as substitutes for traditional credit.

4 Policy independence of many countries was reduced by the
enhanced degree of international integration of financial and
goods markets. The pace of change, although not the same
everywhere, required national governments to maintain a stable
and sound environment and to coordinate national policies.

The international financial market, which is part of and operates
within the international monetary system, comprises the foreign-
exchange market, the Eurocurrency market, and the international bond
market. The market competes with and functions as a complement to
the national financial markets in many respects.

In the foreign-exchange markets, national monies are exchanged for
each other. The operation of these markets is largely influenced by the
international monetary system, particularly the exchange regime, which
is established by the Articles of Agreement of the International
Monetary Fund. The international money and credit markets (that is,
the Eurocurrency and international bond markets) have many linkages
with the domestic financial markets in many countries, which, in turn,
have contributed to international economic and financial integration.

In the Eurocurrency and international bond markets—the markets for
money, credit, and capital—funds denominated in foreign currencies are
deposited, lent, and borrowed, and international bonds are issued. The
distinction between international money markets and international
credit or capital markets is arbitrary and is based on the length of
maturity. Accordingly, transactions for maturities of up to twelve
months are classified as money-market activities, whereas transactions
beyond twelve months constitute credit or capital transactions.

The outlook for the international financial market is dominated by
the (1) evolution toward a multiple-currency international reserve
system and regional currency blocs; (2) changes in regulations in the
major countries; (3) development of new payment systems and procedures; (4) increased international and regional interdependence of
financial markets, and the need for a higher degree of coordinated
control and supervision; and (5) large LDCs' balance-of-payments
deficits, growing external financial requirements and debt burden.
These trends could (1) diminish the significance of the U.S. dollar in the

12

long run; (2) modify the relative competitive position of the major international financial centers and affect the location of transactions; (3) improve the efficiency of the international payments system; (4) increase the likelihood of supervision over Eurobanks and standardization of supervision across national borders, partly in an effort to eliminate competitive advantages originating from diversity in national regulations; and (5) contribute to balance-of-payments disequilibrium and growing external debt of less developed countries, requiring continuous intermediation by Eurobanks. However, commercial banks' reduced capacity to lend (because of increased risk of international lending, prudent behaviour, and regulatory requirements) also reduced their capacity to intermediate internationally. Under these circumstances, the reduced access of less developed countries to financial markets increases the risk of widespread default.

THE INTERNATIONAL MONETARY SYSTEM

As a result of unprecedented disturbances in the world economy, the international monetary system underwent profound changes in the early 1970s. The foreign-exchange regime of the Bretton Woods system was abandoned, and a hybrid international monetary system evolved. The world's monetary relations are currently conducted in the context of a heterogeneous system characterized by both flexible and fixed exchange rates and often described as the widespread floating of currencies. The system is still in a state of evolution, and three regional monetary blocs (the U.S. dollar, the European currencies, and the Japanese yen) and a multiple arrangements system are emerging.

The IMF's Articles of Agreement are the central legal framework of the international monetary system. They provide the basis for consistent purposes and principles together with rights and obligations accepted by all member countries. The second amendment of the Articles of Agreement entered into force on April 1, 1978.

The most important modifications of the articles deal with the exchange arrangements, gold, and special drawing rights (SDRs). The amended articles give legal recognition to a (new) system comprising a multiplicity of exchange rate practices that represent a complete departure from the central feature of the Bretton Woods articles, but they provide procedures for a possible future return to a par-value system. Although the system allows member countries to freely choose their exchange arrangements and allows rather loose exchange discipline, it emphasizes that underlying domestic economic and financial policies and conditions are the source of currency stability. Therefore, it puts more of the burden on domestic policies for the maintenance of balance-of-payments adjustment and exchange-rate stability than the par-value system did. In addition, the articles give the IMF powers of 13 surveillance over exchange-rate policies to ensure that no country manipulates exchange rates.

The monetary agreements embodied in the second amendment reflect both the profound changes that occurred in the global economic environment and the compromise on international monetary reform. The system, unlike the original Bretton Woods system, allows a greater degree of flexibility in members' behavior and permits international monetary relations to evolve through time. In essence, the monetary system represents only a phase of international monetary evolution and reform rather than a complete reform, and it allows the existing rules and regulations to evolve further in the future. The system provides an improvement over the original Bretton Woods system in terms of the three problem areas of the international monetary system—adjustment, liquidity, and confidence.

EXCHANGE-RATE SYSTEM

The second amendment of the IMF's Articles of Agreement gives legal validity to a new system of multiple exchange-rate practices by allowing members to choose their exchange arrangements. According to Article IV, Section 2(b), exchange arrangements may include "(i) the maintenance by a member of a value for its currency in terms of the special drawing right or another denominator, other than gold, selected by the member, or (ii) cooperative arrangements by which members maintain the value of their currencies in relation to the value of the currency or currencies of other members, or (iii) other exchange arrangements of a member's choice." Each member is required to notify the IMF of the exchange arrangements that it applies and of any subsequent changes that it intends to adopt in its exchange regime. Although members are free to apply the exchange arrangements of their choice, they are subject at all times to surveillance by the IMF. Moreover, each member is required to seek to promote exchange stability by pursuing orderly economic and financial conditions and to avoid manipulating exchange rates or the international monetary system. In essence, the system gives members freedom of choice of foreign-exchange arrangements but not freedom of behavior, and it emphasizes internal economic conditions, rather than exchange discipline, as the source of currency stability.

The IMF is required to oversee the international monetary system in order to ensure its effective operation and the observance by each member of its obligations. Accordingly, the Fund exercises surveillance over the exchange-rate policies of its members. The principles and procedures for surveillance may be modified from time to time according to experience and the circumstances of the international monetary system, but they must be consistent with the pursuit of orderly domestic economic and price stability, social and political conditions, and the freedom of members to choose their exchange arrangements.

To assist the IMF in fulfilling this objective, each member is required to provide it with the information necessary for such surveillance and, when necessary, to consult with it on the exchange-rate policy.

Consultations have stressed the need to discuss with member countries the medium-term implications of their policies, including their debt and the balance of payments, and the need for structural adjustment. A new procedure, referred to as enhanced surveillance, has been adopted for a few countries in the context of multiyear rescheduling arrangements. Periodic consultations, which provide the primary means for the exercise of surveillance, occur annually, but longer and shorter intervals are common. The annual cycle is used for countries whose policies have a substantial impact on other members, for countries with IMF stand-by or extended arrangements, and for countries for which there are questions concerning balance of payments viability. The 1985–86 consultations were concluded with 83 percent of the Fund membership.[2]

THE ROLE OF GOLD

Gold had a central role in the post–World War II monetary system of the Bretton Woods system, but the second amendment of the IMF's Articles of Agreement introduces changes designed to achieve a gradual reduction of the role of gold (and reserve currencies) in the international monetary system and to make the SDR the principal reserve asset. The most important changes in the amended articles include the removal of gold as the common denominator of the exchange rate and promoting the SDR; abolishing the official gold price of thirty five SDRs per ounce; abandoning any obligation to pay in gold by members to the IMF and by the IMF to members; allowing monetary authorities of member countries to deal in gold among themselves or in the free market at market-related prices; and agreeing to permit the disposal of some IMF gold holdings.

One-sixth of the original IMF gold holdings (or 25 million ounces) was sold through the IMF Trust Fund to the private market, and the profit was distributed among the neediest of the least developed countries. The sale was through public auctions over the four-year period that ended in May 1980. Another one-sixth of the IMF's original holdings was sold (restitute) to the member countries at the official price. The rest of the Fund's 100 million ounces of gold is to be held until its disposition is determined by an 85 percent majority of the total voting power.

Although the formal role of gold in the international monetary system has been diminished and the present IMF arrangements, to a large extent, demonetize it de jure, demonetization de facto will not be accomplished because gold continues to be held as an official reserve asset by member countries. In addition, the IMF Articles of Agreement

15

allow central banks to trade gold among themselves at market prices, which may thereby reverse the de facto demonetization that occurred in August 1971, monetize new gold, and give the metal a higher degree of liquidity than it had before.

The termination of gold transactions between the IMF and its members and the disposal of one-third (and perhaps ultimately all) of the gold originally held by the Fund are major steps in reducing the monetary role of gold, but the acquisition by countries of the gold sold by the Fund increases their gold reserves and enhances, rather than diminishes, its role in the system. The degree of gold demonetization, as it is now reflected in the IMF's Articles of Agreement, had to be compromised during the negotiations on monetary reform. In the real world, however, efforts to demonetize gold have been only partially successful, and it remains a significant component of central banks' reserves.

Despite its diminished official role and its immobile and not very productive nature, gold is presently a highly desired asset, and it has again achieved enhanced status in financial markets. Valuation of official gold holdings at market prices is widespread, and gold's reemerging monetary role is now well under way. In practice the valuation of official gold holdings at market prices and the higher reserve-adequacy ratios have little effect on financial behavior and balance-of-payments financing methods and produce little benefit to the countries involved. Higher valuations are inconsistent with the idea that the SDR should have an enhanced role in the international monetary system and should become a crucial element in liquidity control. A drastic reduction in the role of reserve currencies, particularly the dollar, is crucial to making SDRs a main reserve asset. (The consolidation of official foreign-exchange holdings by exchanging them against SDRs was proposed, but this kind of substitution account was rejected. This account would have enabled official holders of dollars to exchange them at the IMF for SDR-denominated assets and then to have the reserve-currency countries redeem the currencies by issuing long-term instruments to the Fund. The capabilities of this account would have been limited and at best could have provided a vehicle to diversify only some international currency holdings.)

The high price of gold (and the value of officially held gold reserves) provides strong impetus to those who would like to see it officially enhanced in the international system. Despite the high price of gold and the freedom of the monetary authorities to trade in it, gold is not used in international settlements, although central banks of small countries may sell some as a last resort in case of severe balance-of-payments problems when access to alternative credit is not available. In the mid-1970s Italy used official gold valued at 80 percent of market value to back up a big balance-of-payments loan from West Germany. The use

16

of gold as collateral in transactions among central banks remonetizes official gold holdings. In the past official gold reserves have been sold in the market only by countries in need of balance-of-payments financing (for example, Portugal, Zaïre, and India).

Whatever benefits are to be derived from higher gold prices, they are unequally distributed. The main beneficiaries are the industrial countries, whereas the less developed countries could be adversely affected. The latter's interest should be in promoting gold demonetization, further allocations of SDRs, expansion of IMF credit lines, and creation of an efficient mechanism for transfer of resources.

The official attitude toward the role of gold in the monetary system is inconsistent among the major countries, particularly between the United States and Western Europe. Although they all act within the legal context of the IMF Articles of Agreement, their behavior and intent differ substantially. Evidence of the increased significance of gold is reflected in the role of gold in the structure and operation of the European Monetary System (EMS), official gold valuation procedures, official acquisition/liquidation of gold holdings, and government and official attitudes.

Evidence of creeping remonetization is reflected in the design of the EMS. In March 1979 eight countries participating in the EMS (Belgium, Denmark, France, Germany, Ireland, Italy, Luxembourg, and the Netherlands) were issued SDR 14 billion European currency units (ECUs) against their deposit with the European Monetary Cooperation Fund (EMCF) of gold and U.S. dollars. In July 1979 the United Kingdom was also issued ECUs against its deposit with the EMCF of gold and U.S. dollars. (For these countries gold deposited with the EMCF is excluded from their official reserve holdings, but all ECU holdings are included in the foreign exchange.) Pooling reserve currencies and gold, against which ECUs were issued, implies a strong monetization of gold as well as an enhancement of the dollar, two assets of monetary significance that the IMF attempts to reduce.

The EMS has effectively monetized gold at approximately the market price and given it an enhanced monetary role. It provided for the conversion of some official gold reserves of its eight member countries and the United Kingdom into ECUs. The idea behind the plan was provided by Italy and France, the most gold-conscious countries of the EEC.

A new international macroeconomic policy approach formulated by the group of the seven major industrial countries (G7) considers the construction of an index by which to measure currency value. The index, in turn, will include gold and a number of other commodities. The inclusion of gold in this context is considered by some market observers as the possible resurrection of gold in the international monetary system.

THE SPECIAL DRAWING RIGHT

The special drawing right (SDR) is a basket of currencies with each component (as well as the basket itself) determined at spot exchange rates. Since January 1, 1981, it has been based on a basket of five currencies instead of the basket of sixteen that was in effect from mid-1978 to the end of 1980.[3] The currency weights are based on international trade statistics for the five-year period 1980 to 1984 and on other consideration (such as international investment and finance) as follows: U.S. dollar, 42 percent; deutsche mark, 19 percent; British pound, 12 percent; Japanese yen, 15 percent; and French franc, 12 percent (see Figure 2–1).

Presently, the role of the SDR is rather limited, remains confined to an official reserve status, and accounts for a very small proportion of global reserves. Commercial SDR-denominated transactions are conducted on a limited scale, but no transactions between governments and the private sector occur. Numerous changes in the characteristics of SDRs and expansion of its possible uses were designed to promote it to become the principal reserve asset of the international monetary system. Changes include the increase in its holdings and uses, the abrogation of the reconstitution requirement, the adoption of a simplified valuation system for the SDR, and the increases in interest rates paid by the IMF to members on their holdings of SDRs. (For more detail see Appendix A on artificial currency baskets.) Some of the most important changes that were introduced at the time of the amended Articles of Agreement and are as follows:

1   The amended Articles of Agreement require the value of the IMF's assets to be expressed and the currency holdings in the General Resources Account to be maintained in terms of SDRs.
2   The IMF is authorized to allocate SDRs to members that participate in the Special Drawing Rights Department when the world's need for additional liquidity arises.
3   The use of SDRs has been broadened by allowing participants to enter into transactions that include swap arrangements, spot and forward activities, loans, pledges, and donations by agreement, without requiring decisions by the IMF.
4   The IMF may authorize transactions in SDRs between participants that are not otherwise provided for by the Articles, subject to appropriate safeguards.
5   The IMF has raised (to eight) the number of institutions other than national treasuries, central banks, and the Fund that can hold SDRs.
6   The valuation of the SDR has been simplified.
7   The interest rate paid by the IMF to members on their holdings of SDRs has been increased from 80 percent to 100 percent of the weighted rate in the markets of the five countries whose currencies

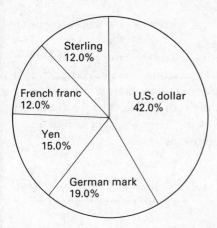

Figure 2–1. The Composition of the SDR, 1986.

are included in the SDR valuation basket. The same weighting system or basket is now used to determine both the value of and interest rate of the SDR.

8 The Fund decided in principle to abrogate the requirement that members maintain, over time, a minimum average level of SDR holdings.

FOREIGN-EXCHANGE ARRANGEMENTS

Some countries continuously adopt new exchange arrangements or modify their existing ones. These changes reflect the trend observed in recent years to adopt exchange practices best suited to each country's institutional circumstances and individual policies. Most of these changes consist of abandoning a pegged exchange rate in favor of a more flexible exchange regime. In recent years, there has been a reduction in the number of countries maintaining a fixed exchange rate.[4]

Increased flexibility in exchange arrangements has involved the use of wider margins in the pegging of a currency to a composite of other currencies. In addition, several countries have begun to declare official market exchange rates for up to one year in advance, based primarily on anticipated variations in inflation rates at home and abroad.

Since the breakdown of the Bretton Woods system of fixed exchange rates in early 1973, countries have adopted a broad spectrum of exchange-rate practices, ranging from independent floating rates with relatively little intervention to the maintenance of a fixed exchange rate in terms of a single currency. Although the heterogeneity of exchange-rate practices makes it difficult to define precisely the present exchange regime, it has come to be known as the system of widespread floating of currencies. The second amendment of the IMF's Articles of Agreement legalized the status quo of the wide spectrum of existing exchange 19 arrangements and in effect gave legal validity to a system comprising multiple exchange-rate practices.

A country that adopts a floating exchange rate either can float independently or in a group or can let its currency crawl. A country that adopts a fixed exchange rate can peg its currency rate either to a single foreign currency (such as the U.S. dollar or French franc) or to a basket of foreign currencies (such as SDR or a composite of currencies of countries with which trade is the most significant).

Table 2–1A.
EXCHANGE RATE ARRANGEMENTS, June 30, 1988.[1]

		Currency pegged to		
US Dollar	French Franc	Other currency	SDR	Other composite[2]
Afghanistan	Benin	Bhutan	Burma	Algeria
Antigua & Barbuda	Burkina Faso	(Indian	Burundi	Austria
Bahamas	Cameroon	Rupee)	Iran, I.R. of	Bangladesh
Barbados	C. African Rep.	Kiribati	Jordan	Botswana
Belize	Chad	(Australian Dollar)	Libya	Cape Verde
Djibouti	Comoros	Lesotho	Rwanda	Cyprus
Dominica	Congo	(South	Seychelles	Fiji
Ecuador	Côte d'Ivoire	African		Finland
El Salvador	Equatorial	Rand)		Hungary
Ethiopia	Guinea	Swaziland		Iceland
	Gabon	(South		
Grenada		African		Israel
Guatemala	Mali	Rand)		Kenya
Guyana	Niger	Tonga		Kuwait
Haiti	Senegal	(Australian		Malawi
Honduras	Togo	Dollar)		Malaysia
Iraq				Malta
Lao P.D. Rep.				Mauritius
Liberia				Nepal
Mozambique				Norway
Nicaragua				Papua New Guinea
Oman				Poland
Panama				Romania
Paraguay				São Tomé &
Peru				Príncipe
St. Kitts & Nevis				Solomon Islands
St. Lucia				Somalia
St. Vincent				
Sierra Leone				Sweden
Sudan				Tanzania
Suriname				Thailand
				Vanuatu
Syrian Arab Rep.				Western Samoa
Trinidad & Tobago				Zimbabwe
Uganda				
Venezuela				
Viet-Nam				
Yemen Arab Rep.				
Yemen, P.D. Rep.				
Zambia				

The exchange arrangements around the world in mid-1988 are shown in Table 2–1. The major industrial countries' currencies (including such currencies as the Canadian dollar, the Japanese yen, the British pound, and the U.S. dollar) float independently on the exchange markets, and their exchange rates are essentially determined by forces of supply and demand. The monetary authorities of each country intervene, to varying degrees, in their respective foreign-exchange markets in order to maintain orderly conditions.

Flexibility Limited in terms of a Single Currency or Group of Currencies		More Flexible		
Single currency[3]	Cooperative arrangements[4]	Adjusted according to a set of indicators[5]	Other managed floating	Independently floating
Bahrain	Belgium	Brazil	Argentina	Australia
Qatar	Denmark	Chile	China, P.R.	Bolivia
Saudi Arabia	France	Colombia	Costa Rica	Canada
United Arab Emirates	Germany	Madagascar	Dominican Rep.	Gambia, The
	Ireland	Portugal	Egypt	Ghana
	Italy		Greece	Guinea
	Luxembourg		Guinea-Bissau	Japan
	Netherlands		India	Lebanon
			Indonesia	Maldives
			Jamaica	New Zealand
			Korea	
				Nigeria
			Mauritania	Philippines
			Mexico	South Africa
			Morocco	Spain
			Pakistan	United Kingdom
			Singapore	
			Sri Lanka	United States
			Tunisia	Uruguay
			Turkey	Zaïre
			Yugoslavia	

Table 2–1A. *(continued)*

Classification status[1]	1982	1983	1984	1985
Currency pegged to				
US Dollar	38	33	34	31
French Franc	13	13	13	14
Other Currency	5	5	5	5
of which: Pound Sterling	(1)	(1)	(1)	(1)
SDR	15	12	11	12
Other currency composite	23	27	31	32
Flexibility limited vis-à-vis a single currency	10	9	7	5
Cooperative arrangements	8	8	8	8
Adjusted according to a set of indicators	5	5	6	5
Managed floating	20	25	20	21
Independently floating	8	8	12	15
Total[6]	146	146	148	149

[1]Excluding the currency of Democratic Kampuchea, for which no current information is available. For members with dual or multiple exchange markets, the arrangement shown is that in the major market.

[2]Comprises currencies which are pegged to various "baskets" of currencies of the members' own choice, as distinct from the SDR basket.

[3]Exchange rates of all currencies have ·hown limited flexibility in terms of the US dollar.

Source: IMF, *International Financial Statistics*, September 1988, p. 20.

Many of the less developed countries peg their exchange rates to the currencies of their major trading partners and fluctuate along with them, whereas some of the less developed countries' currencies are pegged to a weighted basket of major currencies, such as SDRs, or an especially constructed basket. In most of the developing countries, however, international transactions are subject to various exchange controls.

In terms of the number of countries in the various categories of exchange arrangements, the majority of the IMF members are classified as having pegged rates, which makes the system look like a fixed-rate system rather than a floating-exchange-rate system. However, most of the major currencies float independently, float jointly, or crawl, which implies that even currencies that peg their exchange rates against major floating currencies or weighted baskets are subject to fluctuations.

MULTIPLE CURRENCY PRACTICES, BILATERAL PAYMENT ARRANGEMENTS, AND CAPITAL CONTROLS

In recent years measures have been taken in a number of countries to abolish or simplify multiple currency practices and unify existing dual exchange-rate arrangements. Reliance on multiple currency practices by

					End of Period				
	1986				*1987*			*1988*	
QI	*QII*	*QIII*	*QIV*	*QI*	*QII*	*QIII*	*QIV*	*QI*	*QII*
31	31	31	32	33	34	35	38	39	38
14	14	14	14	14	14	14	14	14	14
5	5	5	5	5	5	5	5	5	5
(–)	(–)	(–)	(–)	(–)	(–)	(–)	(–)	(–)	(–)
12	10	10	10	10	10	9	8	7	7
32	33	31	30	27	27	27	27	29	31
5	5	5	5	5	4	4	4	4	4
8	8	8	8	8	8	8	8	8	8
5	5	6	6	6	5	5	5	5	5
21	21	20	21	22	24	24	23	21	20
16	18	20	19	20	19	19	18	18	18
150	151	151	151	151	151	151	151	151	151

[4]Refers to the cooperative arrangement maintained under the European Monetary System.
[5]Includes exchange arrangements under which the exchange rate is adjusted at relatively frequent intervals, on the basis of indicators determined by the respective member countries.
[6]Including the currency of Democratic Kampuchea.

the developing countries decreased. By definition, a multiple currency practice arises when the authorities create a spread of more than 2 percent between the buying and selling rates for spot exchange transactions or create a difference of more than 1 percent between spot exchange rates for different types of transactions (that is, a special exchange-rate regime for some or all capital transactions and/or some or all invisibles, an import rate different from an export rate, more than one rate for imports, and more than one rate for exports).[5]

In addition, there has been a further reduction in the number of bilateral payments arrangements both among Fund members and between members and nonmembers. The number of bilateral arrangements among members declined from ninety five in 1964 to about fifty at the end of 1985. The number of bilateral payments arrangements maintained by Fund members with nonmembers has also declined substantially over this period from 227 in 1964 to about 84 in early 1985. The value of trade between Fund members maintaining bilateral payments agreements represents about one-seventh of 1 percent of the value of world trade of Fund members.[6]

Liberalization of international capital movements continued to take place in recent years in both industrial and developing countries. Several of these programs were implemented within comprehensive exchange reforms that involved the adoption of a market-oriented floating exchange system. Capital controls are implemented in various forms, some implicit, others explicit. According to the IMF definition, the

Table 2–1B.
MEMBERSHIP OF CURRENCY AND TRADE AREAS,
December 30, 1983.

Sterling area:
  United Kingdom
  Channel Islands
  Gibraltar
  Isle of Man

US dollar area:
  United States, Puerto Rico,
    US Virgin Islands
  Bolivia
  Canada
  Colombia
  Costa Rica
  Dominican Republic
  Ecuador
  El Salvador
  Guatemala
  Haiti
  Honduras
  Liberia
  Mexico
  Micronesia
  Nicaragua
  Panama
  Philippines
  Venezuela

Franc zone:
  France (Metropolitan)
  Andorra
  Benin
  Cameroon
  Central African Republic
  Chad
  Comoros
  Congo, People's Republic
  Gabon
  Guadeloupe
  Guiana
  Ivory Coast
  Mali
  Martinique
  Mayotte
  Monaco
  Niger
  Polynesia (French)
  Réunion
  St. Pierre-et-Miquelon
  Senegal
  Togo
  Upper Volta
  Wallis-et-Futuna

European Economic Community:
  Belgium
  CFA Area (Associate)
  Denmark
  France
  Germany, West
  Greece

Ireland
Italy
Kenya (Associate)
Luxembourg
Malta (Associate)
Mauritius (Associate)
Morocco (Associate)
Netherlands
Nigeria (Associate)
Sudan (Associate)
Tanzania (Associate)
Tunisia (Associate)
Turkey (Associate)
Uganda (Associate)
United Kingdom

European Free Trade Association:
  Austria
  Finland (Associate)
  Iceland
  Norway
  Portugal
  Sweden
  Switzerland

Ruble-yuan area:
  Albania
  Bulgaria
  China, People's Republic
  Cuba
  Czechoslovakia
  Germany, East
  Hungary
  Korea (North)
  Mongolia
  Poland
  Romania
  USSR
  Viet Nam

Central American Common Market:
  Costa Rica
  El Salvador
  Guatemala
  Honduras
  Nicaragua

Latin American Free Trade Association:
  Argentina
  Bolivia
  Brazil
  Chile
  Colombia
  Ecuador
  Mexico
  Paraguay
  Peru
  Uruguay
  Venezuela

Caribbean Community and Common Market
  Anguilla
  Antigua & Barbuda
  Barbados
  Belize
  Dominica
  Grenada
  Guyana
  Jamaica
  Montserrat
  St. Kitts-Nevis
  St. Lucia
  St. Vincent & Grenadines
  Trinidad & Tobago

Organization of Petroleum Exporting Countries
  Algeria
  Ecuador
  Gabon
  Indonesia
  Iran
  Iraq
  Kuwait
  Libya
  Nigeria
  Qatar
  Saudi Arabia
  United Arab Emirates
  Venezuela

Independent countries

The following nations do not belong to any organized group. They generally administer their own currency and foreign trade, but for matters of convenience, some maintain monetary links to other major units.

Afghanistan
Andorra
Angola
Australia
Bahamas
Bahrain
Bangladesh
Bermuda
Bhutan
Botswana
Brunei
Burma
Burundi
Cape Verde
Cayman Islands
Cyprus
Djibouti
Egypt
Equatorial Guinea
Ethiopia
Fiji
Gambia, The
Ghana
Guinea
Guinea-Bissau
Hong Kong
India
Indonesia
Iran
Israel
Jamaica
Japan
Jordan
Kampuchea, Democratic
Korea (South)
Kuwait
Lao People's Dem. Rep.
Lebanon
Lesotho

Madagascar
Malawi
Malaysia
Maldives
Mauritania
Mauritius
Morocco
Mozambique
Nepal
Netherlands Antilles
New Zealand
Oman
Pakistan
Papua New Guinea
Rwanda
São Tomé e Príncipe
Seychelles
Sierra Leone
Singapore
Solomon Islands
Somalia
South Africa
Spain
Sri Lanka
Sudan
Suriname
Swaziland
Syria
Taiwan
Thailand
Tonga Islands
Vanuatu
Western Samoa
Yemen Arab Republic
Yemen Peo. Dem. Rep.
Yugoslavia
Zaire
Zambia
Zimbabwe

Source: Philip P. Cowitt, editor, *1984 World Currency Year Book* Brooklyn, N.Y.: International Currency Analysis, Inc., 1985.

following types of controls are most common:[7]

1 Restrictions on payments in respect to current transactions;
2 Restrictions on payments in respect to capital transactions;
3 Prescription of currency;
4 Bilateral payments arrangements with members;
5 Bilateral payments arrangements with nonmembers;
6 Import surcharges;
7 Advance import deposits;
8 Required surrender of export proceeds.

Table 2–2.

OFFICIAL HOLDINGS OF RESERVE ASSETS, END OF YEAR 1982–87 AND END OF MARCH 1988[1] (In Billions of SDRs)

	1982	1983	1984	1985	1986	1987	March 1988
All countries							
Total reserves excluding gold							
Fund-related assets							
Reserve positions in the Fund	25.5	39.1	41.6	38.7	35.3	31.5	30.7
SDRs	17.7	14.4	16.5	18.2	19.5	20.2	20.5
Subtotal, Fund-related assets	43.2	53.5	58.0	56.9	54.8	51.7	51.1
Foreign exchange	285.1	308.4	349.0	343.3	363.9	454.8	465.6
Total reserves excluding gold	328.3	361.9	407.1	405.3	418.7	506.4	516.7
Gold[2]							
Quantity (millions of ounces)	949.2	947.8	946.8	949.4	949.1	944.5	946.2
Value at London market price	393.1	345.4	297.8	282.6	303.3	322.3	311.6
Industrial countries							
Total reserves excluding gold							
Fund-related assets							
Reserve positions in the Fund	17.1	25.6	27.2	25.2	23.0	20.4	19.9
SDRs	14.1	11.5	13.4	14.9	16.1	16.4	16.8
Subtotal, Fund-related assets	31.1	37.1	40.6	40.1	39.1	36.8	36.7
Foreign exchange	153.2	167.9	183.9	187.3	209.8	283.3	288.6
Total reserves excluding gold	184.4	205.0	224.5	227.4	248.9	320.1	325.3
Gold[2]							
Quantity (millions of ounces)	787.3	786.6	786.0	786.5	785.7	781.4	783.6
Value at London market price	326.1	286.6	247.2	234.1	251.1	266.6	258.1
Developing countries							
Total reserves excluding gold							
Fund-related assets							
Reserve positions in the Fund	8.4	13.6	14.3	13.5	12.4	11.1	10.8
SDRs	3.7	2.9	3.1	3.3	3.4	3.8	3.6
Subtotal, Fund-related assets	12.1	16.5	17.4	16.9	15.8	14.9	14.4
Foreign exchange	131.9	140.5	165.1	161.0	154.1	171.5	177.0
Total reserves excluding gold	143.9	156.9	182.5	177.9	169.8	186.4	191.4
Gold[2]							
Quantity (millions of ounces)	161.8	161.2	160.8	162.9	163.4	163.1	162.6
Value at London market price	67.0	58.7	50.6	48.5	52.2	55.7	53.5
Capital importing developing countries							
Total reserves excluding gold							
Fund-related assets							
Reserve positions in the Fund	2.7	3.4	2.8	2.6	2.4	2.2	2.0
SDRs	2.4	1.8	1.9	2.1	2.3	2.6	2.4
Subtotal, Fund-related assets	5.1	5.2	4.7	4.7	4.8	4.8	4.4
Foreign exchange	86.2	100.7	128.6	123.8	124.8	141.8	148.6
Total reserves excluding gold	91.5	105.9	133.3	128.5	129.5	146.6	153.0
Gold[2]							
Quantity (millions of ounces)	139.1	138.3	137.6	139.9	140.6	140.4	139.8
Value at London market price	57.6	50.4	43.3	41.6	44.9	47.9	46.1

Table 2–2. (continued)

	1982	1983	1984	1985	1986	1987	March 1988
Capital importing developing countries with debt-servicing problems							
Total reserves excluding gold							
Fund-related assets							
Reserve positions in the Fund	1.2	1.3	1.0	0.8	0.8	0.6	0.4
SDRs	0.7	0.5	0.5	0.7	0.7	1.2	1.1
Subtotal, Fund-related assets	1.9	1.8	1.5	1.5	1.4	1.8	1.6
Foreign exchange	23.1	28.0	43.8	39.5	29.9	28.9	30.0
Total reserves excluding gold	25.1	29.9	45.3	41.1	31.4	30.6	31.6
Gold[2]							
Quantity (millions of ounces)	47.7	46.7	47.7	47.9	47.9	47.9	47.7
Value at London market price	19.8	17.0	15.0	14.3	15.3	16.3	15.7

Source: International Monetary Fund, *Annual Report*, 1987.

[1]'Fund-related assets' comprise reserve positions in the Fund and SDR holdings of all Fund members and Switzerland. Claims by Switzerland on the Fund are included in the line showing reserve positions in the Fund. The entries under 'Foreign exchange' and 'Gold' comprise official holdings of those Fund members for which data are available and certain other countries or areas, including Switzerland.

[2]One troy ounce equals 31.103 grams. The market price is the afternoon price fixed in London on the last business day of each period.

INTERNATIONAL RESERVES AND LIQUIDITY

The international reserves of a country are composed of monetary authorities' holdings of SDRs, reserve position in the IMF, which consists of members' subscriptions paid in reserve assets, credit extended by the Fund to its members through the sale of other members' currencies, and the credit extended to the Fund by members under various borrowing arrangements—foreign exchange, gold, and since 1979 ECUs. There are five ways by which international reserves may be created:

1 New SDR allocation by the IMF;
2 Increased reserve position in the IMF through expansion of quotas and the Fund's use of countries' currencies;
3 Increased foreign exchange through international borrowing, particularly from the Eurocurrency markets, through an autonomous capital inflow of reserve currencies and through intervention in the foreign-exchange markets;
4 Purchases of nonmonetary gold by monetary authorities, which thereby monetizes it, or valuing official gold holdings at or near market price;
5 Creation and distribution of ECUs by the EMS.

International reserves are liquid assets that are immediately available (for liquidation at or near market price) to smooth out fluctuations in foreign-exchange earnings needed to finance imports of goods and services and cover temporary balance-of-payments deficits. The IMF maintains that an adequate level of reserves is essential to the smooth

27

Table 2-3
INTERNATIONAL RESERVE ADEQUACY,
1981 AND 1987

	Reserves/Imports (Percentage)		Reserves/Monthly Imports (Ratio)	
	1987	1981	1987	1981
Region/Country				
World	48.3	42.7	5.8	5.1
Industrial Countries	45.7	44.4	5.5	5.3
United States	37.5	51.3	4.5	6.2
Japan	61.2	27.5	7.3	3.3
Germany	54.2	53.4	6.5	6.4
Developing Countries	45.5	39.0	5.5	4.7
Africa	30.8	22.7	3.7	2.7
Asia	32.3	28.9	3.9	3.5
Korea	9.1	10.8	1.1	1.3
Europe	34.5	29.3	4.1	3.5
Middle east	81.0	62.9	9.7	7.5
Egypt	15.2	20.9	1.8	2.5
Western hemisphere	64.8	43.2	7.8	5.2
Brazil	44.9	32.1	5.4	3.8
Mexico	107.3	21.8	12.9	2.6
Oil-Exporting Countries	95.0	63.5	11.4	7.6
Non-Oil Exporting Countries	36.0	30.6	4.3	3.7

Source
Calculations were performed by Harvey Poniachek based on data from the IMF, International Financial Statistics (September 1988).
Notes
Adequacy is measured in terms of international reserves as a percentage of imports. Alternatively, adequacy is defined as the number of months that imports can be financed by international reserves. International reserves include gold valued at year end prices.

functioning of the international economy.[8] International reserves allow countries to avoid abrupt adjustments in their economic policies in response to adverse international payments positions. International reserves provide buffers that countries can draw down and replenish as their international receipts fluctuate relative to their payments needs. (See Tables 2–2 and 2–3 and Figures 2–2 and 2–3.)

Whether a given level of international reserves is sufficient to ensure the satisfactory functioning of the world economy is determined by whether the level of global reserves is a crucial factor in the functioning of the world economy. This view maintains that slow growth or decline in reserves could lead many countries to adopt restrictive economic policies out of concern about external financing difficulties.[9]

Although the term *international reserves* usually refers to actual official holdings, a country's international liquidity includes its official international reserves, its ability to borrow from financial markets, and conditional borrowing available at the IMF. Under the present international monetary arrangements the stock of international reserves is more a reflection of the economic policies and reserve preferences of individual countries than an exogenous constraint on countries' policies.[10] The importance of the level of reserves as a constraint on policy has declined for countries with access to international financial markets and, in particular, for the reserve-currency countries.

Creditworthy countries have been able to borrow reserves at competitive terms in international financial markets. The net cost of these borrowed reserves equals the difference between the cost of borrowed

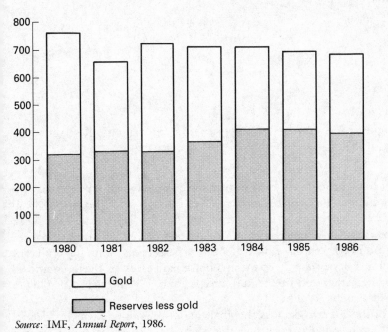

Gold

Reserves less gold

Source: IMF, *Annual Report*, 1986.

Figure 2–2. International Reserves, 1980–86.

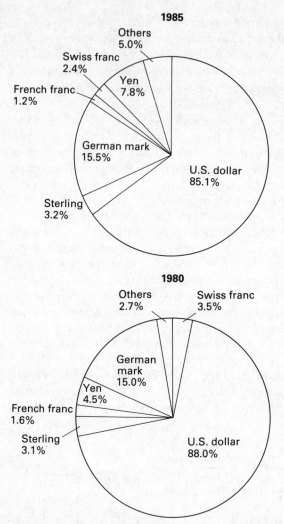

Source: IMF, *Annual Report*, 1986.

Figure 2–3. Currency Composition of International Reserves, 1980 and 1985.

funds and the return earned on reserve assets valued on deposit.[11] In addition to the acquisition of reserves through actual borrowing from private markets and intervention in the foreign-exchange markets, countries can arrange for lines of credit from either private financial institutions, central banks, or other official institutions. A significant number of developing countries do not have access to the international credit market and can acquire reserve primarily through a surplus in their current accounts.

In the last two decades the financing of balance-of-payments deficits has been less dependent on the availability of reserves than on the creditworthiness of the countries.[12] Moreover, the adoption of floating exchange rates reduced the need for monetary reserves because there is no longer any obligation to defend fixed parities by using monetary reserves. At the same time, the international financial markets have become a major source of reserve growth, through provision of credits, or because the debts incurred by the deficit countries are reflected in increased reserves in the surplus countries, as was the case after the various oil price hikes. These structural shifts reduced the significance of global reserves as a constraint on the development of the world economy.

The IMF suggests that the demand for international reserves has not been significantly reduced by the advent of floating exchange rates. [13] Countries have continued to hold reserves as a precaution against unanticipated shocks, as a means of demonstrating creditworthiness, and for exchange-market intervention. The existence of a stable demand for reserves is reflected in both the relative stability of the ratios of nongold reserves to imports for most country groups and the willingness of countries to maintain reserve holdings even under adverse circumstances. During the 1980s, the industrial countries have maintained their reserves at 19 percent of their imports, while for the developing countries, the ratio was 33 percent. Furthermore, their reserves to monthly imports ratios were 2.3, while the developing countries' ratios averaged 3.5 to 4.0.

Although gold has conspicuously lacked high liquidity since August 1971, this has changed recently. The high price of gold and freedom to trade gold by monetary authorities could increase its liquidity and monetary role. Monetary authorities who value their gold holdings at market-related prices cannot be sure, however, that in case of need they can liquidate their gold at those prices. The effective gold holding at liquidation might, depending on market conditions, be below the market price but above the official price.

Higher gold prices and official gold valuation at market prices affect the global distribution and the nominal level of international reserves. Accordingly, reserve distribution shifts in favor of the industrial countries, which possess 83 percent of total official gold (the Western European countries, Canada, and the United States), but away from the less developed countries, which hold only 6 percent of the total.

The international reserve adequacy indicator—measured in terms of the ratio of international reserves to annual imports and expressed as a percentage—shows that (with gold valued at market price) global reserve remained stable throughout the 1980s. The valuation of gold at the market price overstates reserves, but it is probably closer to economic reality than valuation at the official price. The proper economic evaluation of international reserves requires that gold be valued at a price somewhat below its market price but above the official price.

The bulk of international reserve and international financial assets are denominated in dollars, and the dollar's value determines the value of those holdings. The desire to minimize exchange-rate losses has contributed in recent years to currency diversification by official and private foreign-exchange holders. The diversification of the currency composition of foreign-exchange reserves has occurred since the mid-1970s. The share in foreign-exchange reserves of reserve assets denominated in the U.S. dollar fell by five percentage points, to 65 percent, whereas the share of almost all other currencies increased. There are significant differences in the pattern of currency diversification between industrial and developing countries. The industrial countries have experienced greater diversification of reserve holdings than developing countries.[14]

Central banks play a major role in the foreign-exchange market through their holdings of foreign-exchange reserves. The process of exchange diversification could have profound effects on future developments in the foreign-exchange markets and could encourage the evolution of a multiple-reserve currency system. This trend is an inevitable development that reflects the changing distribution of global economic power and the consequent responsibilities accompanying it. Indeed, the monetary authorities of the major currencies are now more willing to assume a relatively larger key-currency role. In a multi-currency reserve system, there is an important role for artificial units (such as the ECU and SDR). In this context a dollar substitution account could be beneficial. Important steps have recently been taken to enhance the SDR, but its development into a fully accepted reserve asset and unit of account will take a long time.

In summary, the distinction between changes in official monetary reserves and international liquidity has diminished due to both international borrowing and also relatively easy access to, and widespread use, of the Eurocurrency market. This development has had several effects. It reduced the optimum level of reserves, diminished the link between a country's reserve position and its willingness and ability to run balance-of-payments deficits and made necessary a revision of the concept and estimation of reserve adequacy whereby access to international capital markets and use of borrowings have to be considered.

INTERNATIONAL DEBT

The international debt crisis since 1982 modified significantly the international financial markets and reduced the growth of sovereign syndicated lending to many LDCs. It required wide-scale rescheduling and financing negotiations between the major debtor countries and the banks under the auspices of the IMF. These agreements usually involved adjustment programs of the indebted countries, restructured loan agreements, and often the provision of new loans. More specifically, the framework of restructuring foreign debt is associated with economic policy reform, deferments of amortization payments, bridge financing, and financing modalities. The latter includes currency denomination options, onlending and relending, trade and credit facilities, cofinancing with multilateral institutions and debt conversion into bonds and equity.[15]

The IMF has played a central role in the management of the debt crisis by assisting developing countries in the design of economic programs and by helping to mobilize the necessary financial resources in support of these programs. The Fund's strategy is based on a case-by-case approach involving coordinated efforts by debtor and creditor countries, commercial banks, and multilateral financial institutions. Creditor governments have also facilitated financial flows to developing countries through the Paris Club. The Paris Club has agreed to successive annual rescheduling in a number of cases and to multiyear rescheduling agreements.

Although the international debt problem appears to have been managed successfully, conditions remain fragile and a matter of concern to the major commercial banks, governments and multilateral institutions. Some indebted countries have made progress by improving their economic structures through the elimination of various distortions and tax systems. However, the heavily indebted countries did not make sufficient progress and their debt/export ratio, an indicator of creditworthiness, deteriorated further in 1986, from about 300 to 370.

By reducing debt-servicing burdens to more manageable proportions, the restructuring packages are designed to provide relief to debtor countries and to benefit the creditor banks themselves. Restructuring modified borrowing conditions: The LIBOR-based interest rates tended to be abandoned in favour of lower benchmarks, contractual fees narrowed, maturities lengthened to encompass even some "perpetual" notes, and new kinds of options, tailored to the specific needs of borrowers and investors, were introduced.

After the crisis management stage and the difficult negotiations on adjustment programs, the task today—in a third stage—is to achieve a long-term consolidation of outstanding debts and thus make it easier for the debtor countries to resume growth on a durable basis. A sustainable external balance cannot be achieved by the most heavily indebted countries by relying solely on positive current-account developments. These countries need a favorable inflow of capital funds that would not add to the external interest burden. Furthermore, a necessary condition for a market-oriented solution of the international debt problem is a favorable economic environment in the industrial countries themselves. By providing sufficient scope for the growth of debtor countries' export markets, they could meet their debt-service obligations without retrenchment.

The realization that the international debt problem remains serious led to the formulation of a new international debt strategy by U.S. Treasury Secretary James Baker in October 1985, which was presented at the IMF-World Bank Annual Meeting in Seoul as "a program for sustained growth."[15]

The new debt strategy aims at defusing the international debt crisis through structural reform and a resumption of economic growth in the debtor countries. The success of this strategy depends on the co-operation of the debtor countries and the commercial banks, increased financial assistance from the international development institutions, an adequate economic growth, and an openness to developing countries' exports in the industrial countries themselves.[16]

The Baker plan foresees a 50 percent increase (amounting to $3 billion on an annual basis) in new lending by the World Bank and its affiliated institutions to the principal problem debtor countries and a total $20 billion of additional new lending by the commercial banks over the next three years. Access to these sources will be conditional on the adoption of growth-oriented structural adjustment programs to be worked out by the debtor countries in close cooperation with the IMF and the World Bank.

Baker's plan[17] stressed the continued validity of the case-by-case approach and emphasized three elements. Debtor countries need to implement structural adjustments by increasing reliance on the private sector to help increase employment, production, and efficiency; mobilize domestic savings and facilitate efficient investment; and encourage foreign direct investment and capital inflows, including trade liberalization. The Fund should continue to play a central role in managing the debt problem, and the role of multilateral banks, particularly the World Bank, should be enhanced by increased and more effective structural adjustment lending. Table 2–4 shows external debt by the main indebted countries.

Table 2–4.
REPORTING BANKS' EXPOSURE TO SELECTED DEVELOPING COUNTRIES.[a]

Country	Dec. 1981	Dec. 1982	Dec. 1983	Dec. 1984	Dec. 1985	June 1986
Algeria	6.9	6.5	7.8	7.8	9.8	11.2
Argentina	22.9	22.2	27.3	26.1	28.9	30.6
Brazil	49.6	56.1	71.2	76.9	76.9	77.4
Chile	9.6	10.4	13.0	13.6	14.3	14.0
Ecuador	4.2	4.1	5.1	4.9	5.2	5.1
Indonesia	4.5	6.2	13.7	14.1	15.2	15.8
Malaysia	3.2	4.6	11.4	11.2	11.2	10.9
Mexico	55.5	58.9	72.0	72.1	74.5	74.0
Morocco	3.3	3.6	4.4	4.4	4.8	5.1
Nigeria	4.7	7.0	9.3	8.1	9.1	9.1
Peru	4.3	5.2	6.5	5.7	5.6	5.4
Philippines	7.2	8.3	13.7	13.8	13.4	14.1
South Korea	16.9	18.8	29.3	30.9	34.4	35.0
Taiwan	5.5	5.2	6.8	6.0	5.5	6.0
Venezuela	22.3	22.7	28.3	25.0	25.8	25.9
Total	220.6	239.8	319.8	320.6	334.6	339.6
Memorandum item: Total as a percentage of banks' aggregate external claims on all countries	14.2	14.2	15.2	14.8	13.0	12.3

Source: BIS, *International Banking and Financial Market Developments* October 1986.
[a]External claims in domestic and foreign currency of banks reporting to the BIS.
Note: Data since December 1983 are not comparable with those of previous periods due to the widening of the coverage of banks reporting to the BIS. For details, see BIS, *International Banking Developments*, Third Quarter 1984.

Total commercial bank lending to the world's 15 most indebted countries is some $1,400 billion, of which the major U.S. banks account for $70 billion. The banking industry lacks confidence that most LDC debtors will be able to restore their creditworthiness. Therefore, banks are reducing their outstanding credit to the LDCs by selling these loans in the secondary market at approximately 50 percent discount, or through debt/equity conversion. The latter program—amounts to the exchange of LDCs' loans held by banks into equity of cooperation in these countries—resulted to date in a $6 billion conversion, or about 2 percent of the outstanding debt of the 11 most indebted LDCs.[19]

NOTES

1. Bank for International Settlements, *Fifty-fifth Annual Report* (Basle: BIS, June 1985). Bank for International Settlements, Recent Innovations in International Banking, April 1986.
2. International Monetary Fund, *Annual Report 1986* (Washington, D.C.: IMF, 1986).
3. The IMF unified and simplified effective January 1, 1981, the currency basket that determines the value of, and the interest rate on, the SDR. Until mid-1974 the SDR was fixed in terms of gold. Since July 1, 1984, the IMF has been using a new method of valuing the SDR in terms of currencies. From mid-1978 to the end of 1980, a sixteen-currency basket based on sixteen countries that had the largest share in the world export of goods and services in the five-year period from 1972 to 1976 had been used for the valuation of the SDR. The currency composition of the basket will be adjusted at five-year intervals.

   At noon each business day, the Fund values the currency components of this basket at their U.S. dollar middle rates in the London exchange market and in the case of yen at the Tokyo rate. The sum of the U.S. dollar equivalents of the currency components yields the rate for the SDR in terms of the U.S. dollar. Exchange rates for the SDR in terms of other currencies, as used in Fund operations and transactions, are ascertained by the IMF from the "representative" market exchange rates of these currencies for the U.S. dollar.
4. IMF, "Exchange Arrangements & Exchange Restrictions." *Annual Report 1986 and 1988.*
5. *Ibid.*
6. *Ibid.*
7. *Ibid.*
8. IMF, *Annual Report 1986*, note 2 above.
9. Deutsche Bundesbank (1985).
10. IMF, *Annual Report 1986*, note 2 above.
11. *Ibid.*
12. Deutsche Bundesbank, note 9 above.
13. IMF, *Annual Report 1986*, note 2 above.
14. *Ibid.*

International
Corporate
Finance

. Maxwell Watson *et al.*, *International Capital Markets; Developments and Prospects*, Chapter IV, IMF, Washington, D.C., January 1988.
16. *Ibid.*
17. IMF, *Annual Report 1986*, note 2 above.
19. Watson, op. cit., p 50.

36

3 The Foreign-Exchange Market

HARVEY A. PONIACHEK

THE MARKET for foreign exchange facilitates the exchange of different national monies across national borders. The exchange rate is a key price, particularly for very open economies and for firms and individuals involved in international business. Since early 1973 the world has operated under a hybrid exchange-rate system: the major currencies are floating and have no central par values; some currencies are fixed in terms of a specially designed basket of currencies or the special drawing right (SDR); and some have fixed rates in terms of a major currency.

The foreign exchange is a major aspect of the international environment with no domestic counterpart. The implications of foreign-currency volatility for corporate earnings, funding, and investment are considerable. Financial decisionmaking by MNCs requires high proficiency in the foreign-exchange market. This chapter reviews the characteristics of the currency markets and examines exchange-rate determination theories and models and discusses currency management and performance. The appendix, written by a market practitioner, discusses how to operate in the currency market.

TYPES OF FOREIGN-EXCHANGE TRANSACTIONS

SPOT, FORWARD, SWAP, FUTURES AND OPTIONS

There are several types of foreign-exchange transactions: spot, forward, swap, futures, and options. In spot transactions, the most common in the foreign-exchange market, currencies are bought or sold for immediate delivery. In practice, however, paperwork must be processed, and settlement or value date is usually two business days after the transaction is originated. Exchange transactions for next-day value, one business day after the transaction is originated, are conducted for spot Canadian dollar against the U.S. dollar transactions in North America. Trading for "value today" requires an adjustment of the spot rate to reflect the interest-rate differential between the two currencies involved 37 for the two days between today and the value day for spot transactions.[1] Tables 3–1, 3–2, and 3–3 provide quotations on various types of foreign-exchange transactions.

In (outright) forward transactions currencies are purchased or sold for future delivery beyond two working days. In a swap contract an

Table 3–1.
CURRENCY SPOT AND FORWARD RATES.

12/10 314	12:45 EST EURO-DOLLAR 12:44 EST			[NOONAN, ASTLEY, PEARCE (212) 504 2900] EURO CD(TOPS) : 12:43 EST BID		FED FUNDS : 12:43 EST DT		PAGE 314 FRA'S : 12:43 EST DT :	
O/N	5 13/16 – 5	15/16	1MO	6.23	BID	5 3/4		1 × 4	5.97 – 6.07
T–N	5 7/8	–6	3MO	6.01	ASK	5 7/8		2 × 5	5.93 – 6.03
	5 7/8	–6	6MO	5.95	LST	5 13/16		3 × 6	5.89 – 5.99
1WK	6	–6 1/8	1YR	6.01	OPN	5 7/8		4 × 7	5.89 – 5.99
				EURO CD(JPN)		TERM		5 × 8	5.89 – 5.99
1MO	6 5/16 – 6	7/16	1MO	6.33	1MO	6 5/16 – 6	7/16	6 × 9	5.90 – 6.00
2MO	6 1/8 – 6	1/4	2MO	6.18	2MO	6 1/8 – 6	1/4	7 × 10	5.93 – 6.03
3MO	6 1/16 – 6	3/16	3MO	6.10	3MO	6 1/16 – 6	3/16	9 × 12	6.02 – 6.12
4MO	6	–6 1/8	4MO	6.08	4MO	6	–6 1/8	1 × 7	5.98 – 6.08
5MO	6	–6 1/8	5MO	6.04	5MO	6	–6 1/8	2 × 8	5.96 – 6.06
6MO	6	–6 1/8	6MO	6.01	6MO	6	–6 1/8	3 × 9	5.94 – 6.04
9MO	6	–6 1/8	9MO	6.03	9MO	6	–6 1/8	4 × 10	5.94 – 6.04
1YR	6	–6 1/8	1YR	6.04	1YR	6	–6 1/8	6 × 12	5.97 – 6.07

12/10	12:46 EST EURO-STERLING 12:44 EST	[NOONAN, ASTLEY, PEARCE (212) 504 2900] EURO-YEN 12:44 EST	EURO-MARKS 12:44 EST	12/10 12:44 315 EURO-SWISS 12:44 EST
O;N	–	–	–	–
T/N	11 – 11 1/4	4 1/4 – 4 3/8	4 3/4 – 4 7/8	1 3/8 – 1 5/8
S/N	11 – 11 1/4	4 3/8 – 4 1/2	4 7/8 – 5	1 3/8 – 1 5/8
1WK	11 – 11 1/4	4 7/16 – 4 9/16	5 – 5 1/8	1 1/4 – 1 1/2
1MO	11 1/16 – 11 3/16	4 5/8 – 4 3/4	5 3/16 – 5 5/16	4 1/2 – 4 5/8
2MO	11 1/4 – 11 3/8	4 1/2 – 4 5/8	5 1/16 – 5 3/16	4 5/16 – 4 7/16
3MO	11 3/8 – 11 1/2	4 3/8 – 4 1/2	4 15/16 – 5 1/16	4 1/4 – 4 3/8
4MO	11 3/8 – 11 1/2	4 3/8 – 4 1/2	4 7/8 – 5	4 1/4 – 4 3/8
5MO	11 3/8 – 11 1/2	4 5/16 – 4 7/16	4 13/16 – 4 15/16	4 3/16 – 4 5/16
6MO	11 3/8 – 11 1/2	4 5/16 – 4 7/16	4 13/16 – 4 15/16	4 1/8 – 4 1/4
9MO	11 3/8 – 11 1/2	4 1/4 – 4 3/8	4 3/4 – 4 7/8	4 1/8 – 4 1/4
1YR	11 3/8 – 11 1/2	4 1/4 – 4 3/8	4 3/4 – 4 7/8	4 1/8 – 4 1/4

[NAP NEW DOLLAR, FRA'S AND CD'S LOCATED ON PAGE 314]

12/10	12:46 EST ECU DEPOSITS 12:44 EST	[NOONAN, ASTLEY & PEARCE (212) 504 2900] EURO-LIRA 12:44 EST	EURO-CANADA 12:44 EST	PAGE 316 EURO-GUILDER 12:44 EST
O;N	–	–	–	–
T/N	–	–	–	–
S/N	–	–	–	–
1WEEK				
1MO	8 1/16 – 8 3/16	–	8 1/4 – 8 1/2	6 1/8 – 6 1/4
2MO	8 1/16 – 8 3/16	–	8 1/8 – 8 3/8	6 – 6 1/8
3MO	8 – 8 1/8	–	8 1/8 – 8 3/8	5 15/16 – 6 1/16
4MO	–	–	–	–
5MO	–	–	–	–
6MO	7 13/16 – 7 15/16	–	8 1/8 – 8 3/8	5 13/16 – 5 15/16
9MO	–	–	–	–
1YR	7 1 /16 – 7 13/16	–	8 1/4 – 8 1/2	5 11/16 – 5 13/16

Source: Telerate December 10, 1986.

Table 3–2.
CURRENCY FUTURES.

0947 INTERNATIONAL MONETARY MARKET CHICAGO CURRENCY FUTURES IMMX
TX 255123   CH1 312 930 3048   NY 212 363 7000 · LDN 01 920 0722

DATA	TAS OF VOLUME	CLOSE OP INT	6	FEB VOLUME	5 OP INT	1987	VOLUME	OP INT
BPH	6613	24551	RPM	146	1689	BPU	41	362
CDH	6717	16026	CDM	772	5700	CDU	143	1513
DMH	28796	48862	DMM	813	4154	DMU	60	444
FRH	0	341	FRM	0	2			
JYH	9403	28198	JYM	117	2280	JYU	0	85
SFH	25612	32409	SFM	886	2443	SFU	62	356
ECH	0	6	ADH	177	1556	ADM	2	102
CFH	1740	15364	PFH	1839	20204			
P								

S2-K2-2   REUTER MONITOR   1331

Source: Reuter Monitor February 9, 1987.

Table 3–3.
CURRENCY OPTIONS, THE SWISS FRANC AND DEUTSCHE MARK.

02/09   14:29 EST   [PHLX OPTIONS ON SWISS FRANC] (XSF)   PAGE 15087

	CALL	TIME	BID	ASK	LAST	PUT	TIME	BID	ASK	LAST
DEC 58	FLB	11:27	8.98	9.08		FXB	11:23	10.97	11.05	
DEC 59	FLF	11:27	8.23	8.33		FXF	13:00	11.06	11.14	1.12
DEC 60	FLJ	11:27	7.52	7.62		FXJ	10:08	1.38	1.46	
DEC 61	FLN	11:27	6.50	6.60		FXN	13:36	1.48	1.56	1.63
DEC 62	FLR	11:27	6.18	6.28		FXR	12:31	1.75	1.85	
DEC 63	FLV	11:27	5.56	5.66		FXV	10:09	2.35	2.45	
DEC 64	FLC	12:32	5.10	5.20		FXC	14:26	2.42	2.52	
DEC 65	FLG	12:32	4.57	4.67		FXG	14:26	2.85	2.95	
DEC 66	FLK	12:32	4.07	4.17		FXK	14:26	3.33	3.43	
DEC 67	FLO	09:57	3.37	3.47		FXO	14:24	3.85	3.95	
DEC 68	FLS	12:32	3.17	3.22		FXS	11:24	4.70	4.80	
DEC 69	FLW	13:01	2.75	2.85		FXW	10:10	5.53	5.63	
DEC 70	FLD	12:33	2.17	2.27		FXD	10:10	6.22	6.32	
DEC 71	FLX	09:58	2.01	2.11		FXX	10:11	6.96	7.06	

02/09 14:29 EST [PHLX OPTIONS ON DEUTSCHE MARK] (XDM) PAGE 15088

	CALL	TIME	BID	ASK	LAST	PUT	TIME	BID	ASK	LAST
FEB 46	MBW	14:24	9.18	9.28		MNW	12:54		0.01	
FEB 47	MBD	14:23	8.18	8.28		MNW				
FEB 48	MBH	14:23	7.18	7.28		MNH	12:55		0.01	
FEB 49	MBL	14:24	6.18	6.28		MNL	12:55		0.04	
FEB 50	MBP	14:24	5.12	5.22		MNP	13:50		0.01	0.02
FEB 51	MBT	14:24	4.12	4.22		MNT	12:55	0.01	0.02	
FEB 52	MBA	14:23	3.12	3.22		MNA	12:55	0.01	0.05	
FEB 53	MBE	14:23	2.33	2.43	2.30	MNE	14:27	0.02	0.05	0.03
FEB 54	MBI	14:26	1.34	1.42	1.39	MNI	14:19	0.07	0.10	0.08
FEB 55	MBM	14:20	0.60	0.65	0.62	MNM	13:52	0.27	0.31	0.29
FEB 56	MBQ	14:22	0.18	0.22	0.20	MNQ	14:24	0.77	0.85	
FEB 57	MBU	14:07	0.05	0.08	0.05	MNU	14:24	1.69	1.79	
FEB 58	MBB	12:03		0.02	0.01	MNB	14:24	2.64	2.74	
MAR 40	MCV					MOV	08:06		0.01	
MAR 41	MCC					MOC	08:06		0.01	
MAR 42	MCG					MOG	08:06		0.01	

Source: Telerate, February 9, 1987.

institution buys or sells a currency for one maturity and sells or buys the equivalent amount for a later date. In a futures contract a company buys or sells a standardized amount of foreign currency on an organized futures exchange for delivery on one of several standardized future dates. In a foreign-exchange options contract a company buys or sells the right—but not the obligation—to receive or deliver a specified amount of foreign currency at a specified price on or before a specified future date. Banks trade standardized foreign-currency options on organized exchanges and also write and trade custom-tailored options outside organized exchanges.

Foreign-exchange rates are quoted in terms of the buying, or bid, rate and the selling, or the offer or ask, rate. Accordingly, quotes are stated with two numbers: The first indicates the price at which the trader is willing to purchase the foreign currency in terms of local currency; the second shows the price at which the trader is willing to sell foreign currency in terms of local currency. The difference between the buying and selling rates is the spread. The spread fluctuates according to the stability in the market, the currency involved, the location of the market, and the volume of transactions in a particular currency. Higher spreads are caused by great uncertainty, low volumes of trade, and a relatively small market. Conversely, narrower spreads occur with stable conditions, high volumes of trade, and an actively traded currency.

Spot exchange rates can be quoted in terms of (1) the number of foreign units to one local unit (the indirect or European method) and (2) the number of local units to one or 100 units of foreign currency (the direct or U.S. method). In London sterling against foreign currencies is quoted according to the European method. In New York the dollar against the foreign currencies used to be quoted in U.S. terms, but in mid-1978 the European method of quotations was adopted, except for sterling quotations.

In the forward exchange market, currencies are bought or sold now for future delivery (value dates are more than two days in the future). A forward exchange contract is an agreement to deliver a specified amount of one currency for a predetermined amount of another currency at a given rate at an agreed time. Although payment is in the future, the exchange rate is agreed on in the present. Each maturity has a specific exchange rate that almost always differs from today's spot exchange rate.

Forward transactions are usually for one month or a multiple thereof from the spot value date at the time of the transaction. Forward exchange rates for the major trading currencies are normally quoted with a buying and a selling rate for periods of one, two, three, six, nine, and twelve months. Up to these maturities the market is very active, and trading does not lead to wide exchange-rate fluctuations. Beyond these maturities the market is thin, and trading usually leads to wide exchange-rate fluctuations. At a higher cost, contracts can be arranged for a specific date in the future that does not indicate a number of full months, that is, an odd date.

When the forward exchange rate is higher than the current spot rate, the currency is trading at a premium for that forward maturity. If the forward rate is below the spot rate, then the currency is trading at a discount.

Forward exchange-rate quotations are stated in three different ways: (1) in terms of discounts or premiums expressed in points, where the forward rate is calculated by subtracting or adding the points from or to the spot rate; (2) in terms of outright forward buying and selling rates, derived by subtracting the corresponding points from spot buying and selling rates; and (3) in terms of the forward discounts or premiums expressed in percentages, which should be converted into points and subtracted or added to the spot rates.

Under ideal market conditions the forward discount or premium on a currency in terms of another currency is determined by and related to the difference in interest rates that prevail in the two countries: That is, the forward market is determined by international interest-rate differentials, and the difference between spot and forward quotations generally reflects the difference between the costs of borrowing the two currencies for the relevant time period. Accordingly, the currency of the higher-interest-rate country is at a discount in terms of the currency of the lower-interest-rate country, whereas the currency of the lower-interest-rate country is at a premium in terms of the higher-interest-rate currency.

The forward contract is the most important method available for eliminating exchange risk that arises because of future foreign-exchange-rate fluctuations. The demand for forward transactions arises because exchange rates fluctuate and the risk of an exchange-rate appreciation or depreciation must be hedged. In addition, forward exchange contracts allow the exact value of a scheduled international transaction to be determined, which assists corporate business planners.

The activities of arbitrageurs ensure a simultaneous process of rate determination in foreign-exchange and money markets, so that the interest-rate differential is just offset by the discount or premium on forward exchange. This is the point at which interest parity holds, or at which the covered interest differential—the nominal interest-rate differential adjusted for the forward premium or discount—is zero. In this case, the forward exchange rate is also said to be at interest parity: The interest differential and the forward discount or premium, expressed in percentage per annum, are equal.

According to interest parity theory the forward premium or discount on a currency in terms of another currency equals but is opposite in sign to the interest-rate differentials between the two countries. The country with the higher interest rate has a forward discount on its currency, and the country with the lower interest rate will be at a forward premium. Under interest parity conditions, it is not possible to realize any profits

41

from covered arbitrage. Interest-rate parity results from use of covered-interest arbitrage, which induces capital flows that tend to enforce interest-rate parity. If a net return was possible from borrowing in one currency and investing in another with a cover in the forward market, there would be an incentive for covered-interest arbitrage to take place.

The relationship between the spot and forward rates and interest rates can be approximated in the following formula:

$$Rd = Rf + \frac{\text{forward} - \text{spot}}{\text{spot}}$$

where Rd and Rf are the domestic and foreign short-term interest rates in percentage per period, forward is the forward price of foreign currency for delivery at the end of the period, spot is the spot price (forward − spot)/spot.

Interest-rate parity holds among currencies only when interest-rate arbitrage is accessible to participants. These rates are the net of costs associated with taxes, exchange controls, reserve requirements, and so forth. Except for the Eurocurrency interbank market, national financial markets are usually not completely free, and strict interest-rate parity does not hold. In these cases the forward discounts and premiums reflect other factors, such as country risk, in addition to interest differentials.

Large deviations between interest-rate differentials and forward exchange-rate discounts or premiums are usually evident when exchange rates are under pressure and speculation is rampant. In practice, interest parity is often achieved in international markets, but deviations from interest-rate parity are common because (1) exchange restrictions may impede the flow of arbitrage funds; (2) the cost of transacting foreign exchange and securities is not a negligible factor and reduces capital mobility and movements; (3) there is a commercial and country risk of default; and (4) the supply of arbitrage funds is limited and not infinitely elastic. Interest parity is more likely attained in the offshore Eurocurrency market because of the absence of restrictions and the resulting high mobility of funds from one Eurocurrency to another (see Figure 3.1 for Eurocurrency interest rates and forward discounts and premiums for the corresponding currencies).

The relationship between the interest-rate differential and the exchange rate is expressed by the following equations:

Forward premium or discount, percent per annum (indirect quote or European terms)

$$= \left(\frac{\text{spot} - \text{forward}}{\text{forward}} \right) \times \frac{12}{\text{number of months}} \times 100$$

Forward premium or discount, percent per annum (direct quote or American terms)

$$= \left(\frac{\text{forward} - \text{spot}}{\text{spot}}\right) \times \frac{12}{\text{number of months}} \times 100$$

Spot is spot exchange rate, and forward is forward exchange rate.

A swap transaction is one in which a currency is bought and sold simultaneously, but the delivery dates for the purchase and sale are different. In a swap transaction, the amount purchased always equals the amount sold, and the parties' net exchange position remains unchanged. If there is a change in the exchange rate of the currencies, there will not be a foreign-exchange gain or loss as a result of a swap transaction.

The swap rate is the difference between the spot exchange rate and a related forward exchange rate expressed on an annual percentage basis, in terms of forward discount if the forward rate is lower than the spot rate and forward premium if the forward rate is higher than the spot rate. This rate is the link between the spot rate and the forward rate or the link between two forward rates for two different maturity dates, and it is directly related to the interest-rate differential between the two relevant currencies. Swap rates are not true exchange rates and may not be reciprocated to change the terms in which they are expressed. These rates may be determined by several factors that affect both spot and forward exchange rates.

The two value dates in a swap transaction can be any pair of future dates. However, in practice, markets exists only for a limited number of standard maturities—that is, exactly one week, one month, two months, and so on—that are called even dates. Maturities such as one month and six days are called odd dates. Active trading in the interbank market is usually limited to even dates for maturities longer than a week. A common swap transaction is called a spot-against-forward swap, in which the trader buys or sells a currency for the ordinary spot value date and simultaneously sells or buys it back for a value date one week, one month, or three months later. Another type of swap transaction is called a tomorrow-next swap or a rollover, in which the dealer buys or sells a currency for value the next business day and simultaneously sells or buys it back for value day after. Yet a more elaborate type of swap is called a forward-forward, where the dealer buys or sells a currency for one future date and sells or buys it back for another future date.

Banks conduct swap transactions among themselves and with some of their corporate customers. The parties to the contract do not incur any foreign-exchange-rate risk because the bank contracts are both to pay and to receive the same amount of currency at specified rates. A swap transaction, which can be considered as if it were a simultaneous borrowing and lending operation, provides several functions: (1) It allows the use of a currency for a period in exchange for another currency that is not needed during that time; (2) it offers an attractive investment vehicle for temporarily excess funds of corporations; and (3) it provides a mechanism for a bank to accommodate the outright forward transactions conducted with customers or to bridge gaps in the maturity structure of its outstanding spot and forward contracts.

Covered interest-rate differential is the difference between interest rates on comparable financial instruments in two different currencies, adjusted for the relevant swap rate. A covered interest-rate differential implies that the interest obtainable on the foreign-currency investment is without exchange risk. Uncovered interest arbitrage occurs when an investor transfers funds from one currency to another and ignores the fact that currencies with high interest rates tend to be prone to devaluation.

Arbitraging involves the simultaneous buying and selling of currencies to take advantage of a price and yield differential in the market. A trader or investor may compare the premium or discount with currency money-market interest rates in different currencies to determine whether profitable investment opportunities exist. If the interest differential in favor of a given currency is higher (lower) than the discount in the forward market on that currency, then there is an incentive to swap one currency for another, invest the funds in the high- (low-)interest-rate currency, and cover the investment in the forward market.

Whether or not it is profitable to move short-term funds from one market to another depends not only on the nominal interest rate that might be gained by so doing but also on the relation of the two currencies in the spot and forward markets. The comparison between covered and uncovered yield differentials determines which one the investor will choose. Covered interest arbitrage is a transaction in which an investor transfers funds and takes out a corresponding forward contract that guarantees against exchange risk. A more refined method of determining the costs and benefits of moving funds internationally would have to consider foreign-exchange-rate margins between buying and selling rates and interest-rate margins between ask and bid rates, as well as transactions costs. In practice, such costs factors are likely to represent important barriers to covered arbitrage operations.

Besides forward exchange contracts, the alternative methods of hedging foreign-exchange risk are (1) using currency composites (such as SDRs and ECUs); (2) leads and lags, by speeding up or delaying payments and receipts proceeds from international transactions; (3) matching income and outlays; (4) changing the currencies in which transactions are invoiced; and (5) using money-market transactions. A brief description of how to operate in the inter-bank foreign-exchange market is provided in the appendix to this chapter.

FOREIGN-EXCHANGE FUTURES

Trading in foreign-exchange futures contracts for standardized currency amounts, and maturities not tailored to the exact requirements of individual parties or selected value dates, has been conducted in the International Monetary Market (IMM) in Chicago since 1972 and in the Commodity Exchange (COMEX) in New York since 1980. Regulated by the Commodities Future Trading Commission, the markets provide an alternative method for hedging foreign-currency positions as well as for speculations.

Futures foreign-exchange contracts are usually settled before the value dates by payment or receipt of the difference between the contract and present prices rather than by actual delivery of the currency traded. Daily limits are placed on the allowed exchange fluctuations: That is, on the increases or decreases in the prices of foreign currencies from one day to the next. Buyers and sellers pay brokerage fees on transactions; the fees actually replace the spread between buying and selling rates, and they are required to establish a margin or security deposit for each contract bought or sold. After a transaction has been arranged, the buyer and seller each make a separate contract with each other.

CURRENCY OPTIONS

In the past few years, currency options have become popular as hedging instruments, particularly for management of tentative commitments, e.g., international bids. Options are available from organized exchanges, like the Chicago Mercantile Exchange, and from commercial and investment banks. Currency options have similar characteristics to stocks and other financial assets. An option gives the holder the right but not the obligation to buy (call) or sell (put) a currency at a fixed price and date. The seller of a call or put must sell or purchase the currency if the buyer of the call or put so desires. In turn, the seller is compensated by receiving a payment, know as premium.

Currency options are available for the major currencies. The options are available in European and American terms, where the former cannot be exercised till maturity, while the latter can be closed out prior to maturity. The currency option market is most suitable for hedging of tentative commitments, where the need to use currency is uncertain.

FOREIGN-EXCHANGE MARKETS AND TRADING

The global market for foreign exchange consists of numerous domestic markets that are closely linked through an efficient communication network and arbitrage. The market has acquired breadth, depth, and resilience from (1) a wide spectrum of participants, currencies, and

45

types of transactions, combined with (2) the ability to absorb large transactions without excessive price movements, and (3) the ability to recover quickly from a price distortion resulting from a large transaction.

A market for foreign exchange consists of individuals, corporations, banks, and brokers who buy or sell currencies. Currency trading in each country is conducted through the intermediation of foreign-exchange brokers, who match currency bids and offers of banks and also trade directly among themselves internationally. Banks in each country and throughout the world are linked by telephones, telexes, and the Reuter and Telerate monitors. The monitors are telecommunication systems that allow market participants to display the exchange rates at which they deal and to transmit other news and market information. All subscribers have their own monitors and access to the price information that is provided. Through the Reuter and Telerate monitors and other means of rapid communication, there is quick and wide dissemination of exchange-rate information and quotations. This in turn contributes to a worldwide market with narrower spreads for nonbank participants.

The foreign-exchange market for any currency consists of all the financial centers around the world (London, New York, and so forth) where the currency is traded. However, local banks often benefit from closer access to national currency, although this advantage is not absolute.

Although the market is global, the exchange market in each country has its own identity and institutional and regulatory framework. An efficient communication system can substitute for participants' need to convene in a specific location (bourse). Indeed, the U.K.-U.S. type of market is based on communication networks, whereas the European approach remains traditional, based on the physical meeting of the participants, usually at the bourse. Daily meetings take place in some markets such as those in Frankfurt, Paris, and so forth, where representatives of commercial banks and the central bank meet and determine a rate, known as the fixing rate. In those countries, the posted fixing rate serves as a guide for pricing small- to medium-sized transactions between banks and their customers. Among major industrial countries, Japan, Germany, France, Italy, and the Scandinavian and the Benelux countries have a daily fixing. The United Kingdom, Switzerland, Canada, and the United States do not.[2]

Foreign exchange is traded in a twenty-four-hour market. As the market in the Far East closes, trading in Middle Eastern financial centers has been going on for a couple of hours, and the trading in Europe is just beginning. At noon in London, the New York market is opening; as London closes, the market in San Francisco opens and trades with the East Coast of the United States and the Far East as well.

Banks, including central banks, dominate the foreign-exchange market, with 90 percent of foreign-exchange trading constituting interbank trading. Nonbank participants in foreign-exchange trading include commodities dealers (45 percent of total nonbank trading), multinational corporations (30 percent), nonbank financial institutions (10 percent), and oil corporations (10 percent).[3]

The foreign-exchange market performs three major functions: (1) It is part of the international payments system and provides a mechanism for exchange or transfer of the national money of one country into the money of another country, thereby facilitating international business; (2) it assists in supplying short-term credits through the Eurocurrency market and swap arrangements; and (3) it provides foreign-exchange instruments for hedging against exchange risk.

Foreign-exchange trading expanded sharply under the floating-exchange-rate system, and the number of banks participating in the market increased significantly as they entered the market to service their corporate clients. Increased hedging by companies of their cash flows and balance sheets was accompanied by the entrance of new corporate participants into the market. In addition, to some extent, the growth of spot and forward business resulted from the increase in Eurocurrency lending and speculative activity.

The demand for a particular currency in the foreign-exchange market depends on the need that participants have to settle international transactions involving current-account and capital transactions of each country or third countries. The major determinants for a currency choice in trade contracts are (1) exchange-rate stability, (2) financial expediency, and (3) tradition and habit in commodity-market trading.[4]

The various currencies used in global trade appear to conform to the following pattern: (1) Exports of industrial commodities tend to be denominated in the currency of the exporting country; (2) trade in raw materials tends to be quoted and denominated in U.S. dollars; (3) when export invoicing is not in the country's currency, the importing country's currency or the dollar is usually used, although the former is preferred; and (4) the existence of forward markets is a precondition for the use of that currency in trade contracts.

The dollar is used in 52 percent of world exports, whereas the U.S. share of global trade is about 12 percent, which implies that 40 percent of world trade is denominated in dollars as a third currency. In 1977 the German and Swiss trade shares were 11 percent and 1.5 percent, respectively, but about 3 percent and 0.5 percent of world exports were contracted in deutsche marks and Swiss francs, respectively, as third currencies. There is no use of the deutsche mark for third-country trade, but the Swiss franc is widely used. The use of other currencies as third currencies is negligible. These proportions of third-country uses in global trade are similar to those of the Eurocurrency market, where the dollar consists of three-quarters of the market.[5]

The daily average volume of worldwide foreign-exchange trading—defined as dollar turnover of all purchases, spot, forward, and swap contracts—was estimated at $195 billion in 1986, or $60 trillion for the whole year. (World trade during the year was about $2.1 trillion; see Table 3–4 for global currency trading.)[6]

Although most commercial banks handle foreign-exchange transactions for their clients, many banks also act as market-makers, with each prepared to deal with other banks at any time. This activity constitutes the interbank market, where portfolio positions are adjusted and exchange rates are determined.

The most important exchange markets are located in London, New York, Paris, Frankfurt, Amsterdam, Milan, Zurich, Toronto, Brussels, Bahrain, and Tokyo. There are significant differences among various markets in size and type of transactions.

As Table 3–5 and Figure 3–1 on worldwide foreign-exchange trading show, some 90 percent of all foreign-exchange activity consists of

Table 3–4A.

DAILY AVERAGE FOREIGN-EXCHANGE TURNOVER, SPOT AND FORWARD (billions of US dollars).

Market[a]	1973	1979	1986
Frankfurt	19–20	15	20
London	4–5	10–12	89
Zurich	5–6	5	7
Paris	1	3–4	5
New York			55
Tokyo			19
Total	29–32	33–36	195

Source: Group of Thirty, *Foreign Exchange Market under Floating Rates* (New York: Group of Thirty, 1979), p. 80; 1986 data were estimated by H. Poniachek.
[a]Central bank estimates in each center.

Table 3–4B.

INTERBANK TURNOVER AS A PROPORTION OF TOTAL SPOT AND FORWARD TURNOVER, 1979 and 1986 (percentage).

Market	1979[a]	1986
London	90	90
Frankfurt	75–90	75–90
Zurich	90[b]	90
Paris	85–90	85–90
New York		85
Tokyo		65

Source: See Table 3–4A.
[a]Central bank estimates.
[b]In Zurich the proportion is estimated at 80 to 85 percent excluding interbank deposit business between Swiss banks, which is conducted through the US dollar in the absence of a domestic money market.

Table 3–4C.
PROPORTION OF FOREIGN-
EXCHANGE TRANSACTIONS
VIA THE DOLLAR, 1979[a] and
1986 (percentage).

Market	1979	1986
London	90	95
Frankfurt	90	90
Zurich	95–99	95–99
Paris	60[b]	60
New York		100
Tokyo		75

Source: See Table 3–4A.
[a]Central bank estimates.
[b]In Paris about 15 percent of turnover is in deutsche
marks, about 10 percent each in Swiss francs and sterling, and the residual 5 percent in other currencies. The
proportion going through the US dollar has declined
from about 80 percent in 1970.

interbank trading for speculative and arbitrage purposes among a few
currencies. The bulk of trading is through the dollar, which remains the
dominant currency through which foreign-exchange transactions are
executed. Nondollar trading is dominated by the deutsche mark, the
pound sterling, and the Swiss franc, which far exceed their propor-
tionate role in international trade and investment. Their main attrac-
tions are well-developed markets and wide institutional support,
combined with relative freedom from exchange controls.

Following London, New York is the second-largest and fastest-
growing foreign-exchange market. A great number of currencies are

Table 3–5A.
GROWTH IN FOREIGN EXCHANGE TURNOVER AMONG
BANKING INSTITUTIONS IN THE UNITED STATES, April
1983 to March 1986 (millions of US dollars).

	Banks Represented on Both Surveys			All Banks Represented on either Survey		
	April 1983	March 1986	Change %	April 1983[a]	March 1986	Change %
German marks	216,662	427,136	97.1	228,643	452,843	98.1
Japanese yen	145,540	261,301	79.5	154,694	304,677	97.0
British pounds	109,992	222,548	102.3	116,995	246,012	110.3
Swiss francs	83,902	122,817	46.4	85,994	127,981	48.8
Canadian dollars	49,717	65,862	32.5	52,655	68,352	29.8
French francs	30,605	42,732	39.6	30,830	48,103	56.0
Dutch guilders	10,271	18,416	79.3	11,194	18,517	65.4
Other currencies	20,961	57,184	172.8	22,980	58,852	156.1
Total	667,650	1,217,996	82.4	702,499	1,325,337	88.3
Sample size	106	106		119	123	

[a]Individual currencies do not add to total. The total excludes $1.5 billion of cross-currency trans-
actions, in which a foreign currency is purchased or sold directly against another foreign currency
rather than against dollars.

Table 3–5B.

TURNOVER SURVEY OF 123 BANKING INSTITUTIONS, March 1986, Aggregate Results (millions of US dollars).

Transaction Category	German Marks	Japanese Yen	British Pounds
Outright spot transactions			
Interbank:			
Direct with banks in US	56,898	30,870	49,711
Direct with banks abroad	76,790	32,512	44,242
Through brokers	155,201	77,110	69,400
Customer:			
Nonfinancial institutions	10,655	6,158	6,000
Financial institutions	18,293	15,874	8,423
Swap transactions			
Maturity one year or less:			
Interbank			
Direct with banks in US	11,407	14,499	7,509
Direct with banks abroad	21,602	27,823	9,054
Through brokers	57,609	71,409	28,489
Customer			
Nonfinancial institutions	4,592	2,143	2,276
Financial institutions	6,969	8,612	4,445
Maturity greater than 1 year:			
Interbank	1,627	1,066	617
Customer			
Nonfinancial institutions	64	151	68
Financial institutions	23	169	97
Outright forward transactions			
Interbank	10,263	7,068	6,391
Customer:			
Nonfinancial institutions	5,655	3,047	2,698
Financial institutions	2,942	2,004	2,068
Currency futures and options			
Futures contracts	7,395	2,287	2,806
Options contracts:			
Purchased:			
Over-the-counter	836	424	416
On an exchange	1,190	512	324
Sold			
Over-the-counter	838	448	320
On an exchange	1,994	491	658
Total spot	317,837	162,524	177,776
Total swap	103,893	125,872	52,555
Total forward	18,860	12,119	11,157
Total options	4,858	1,875	1,718
Total interbank:			
Direct with banks in the US	68,305	45,369	57,220
Direct with banks abroad	98,392	60,335	53,296
Through brokers	212,810	148,519	97,889
Unspecified	11,890	8,134	7,008
Total	391,397	262,357	215,413
Total customer:			
Nonfinancial	20,966	11,499	11,042
Financial	28,227	26,659	15,033
Total	49,193	38,158	26,075
Total turnover	452,843	304,677	246,012
Currency share %	34.2	23.0	18.6
Number of deals	119,319	69,531	67,495
Average deal size	3.7	4.3	3.6

Swiss Francs	Canadian Dollars	French Francs	Dutch Guilders	All Other	All Currencies
13,820	3,988	4,222	2,341	6,817	168,667
21,562	9,422	9,502	3,426	9,726	207,182
30,910	17,755	11,785	4,792	10,546	377,499
2,667	2,574	890	327	1,870	31,141
4,735	3,611	738	268	1,343	53,285
4,359	3,085	2,226	1,078	3,655	47,818
8,508	6,254	5,525	2,320	9,510	90,596
22,532	12,242	9,150	2,359	6,977	210,767
1,555	719	641	192	432	12,550
2,160	3,056	764	250	1,646	27,902
550	73	132	49	247	4,361
18	23	19	3	73	419
14	8	32	2	259	604
5,150	1,699	1,248	798	3,588	36,205
1,025	2,362	622	178	1,255	16,842
829	452	248	125	558	9,226
5,247	512	0	0	156	18,403
580	119	137	0	67	2,579
601	163	15	0	9	2,814
450	35	193	9	118	2,411
709	200	14	0	0	4,066
73,694	37,350	27,137	11,154	30,302	837,774
39,696	25,460	18,489	6,253	22,799	395,017
7,004	4,513	2,118	1,101	5,401	62,273
2,340	517	359	9	194	11,870
18,179	7,073	6,448	3,419	10,472	216,485
30,070	15,676	15,027	5,746	19,236	297,778
53,442	29,997	20,935	7,151	17,523	588,266
5,700	1,772	1,380	847	3,835	40,566
107,391	54,518	43,790	17,163	51,066	1,143,095
5,265	5,678	2,172	700	3,630	60,952
7,738	7,127	1,782	645	3,806	91,017
13,003	12,805	3,954	1,345	7,436	151,969
127,981	68,352	48,103	18,517	58,852	1,325,337
9.7	5.2	3.6	1.4	4.4	100.0
30,286	27,984	20,503	9,243	34,615	378,976
4.0	2.4	2.3	2.0	1.7	3.4

Table 3–5C.

TURNOVER SURVEY OF THIRTEEN NONBANK
FINANCIAL INSTITUTIONS, March 1986,
Aggregate Results (millions of US dollars).

Transaction Category	German Marks	Japanese Yen	British Pounds
Outright spot transactions			
With a bank counterparty			
Direct with banks in US	14,152	7,743	9,898
Direct with banks abroad	8,493	5.939	5,947
Through brokers	18,673	8,752	8,758
Customer			
Nonfinancial institutions	5,339	3,896	2,466
Financial institutions	7,435	4,206	4,120
Swap transactions			
Maturity one year or less:			
With a bank counterparty:			
Direct with banks in US	5,541	10,547	7,783
Direct with banks abroad	4,390	8,139	5,977
Through brokers	1,440	1,267	1,589
Customer:			
Nonfinancial institutions	684	1,144	778
Financial institutions	3,486	2,400	1,809
Maturity greater than one year			
With a bank counterparty	7	112	0
Customer:			
Nonfinancial institutions	2	83	39
Financial institutions	2	95	0
Outright forward transactions			
With a bank counterparty	2,173	3,534	1,913
Customer:			
Nonfinancial institutions	1,778	964	1,077
Financial institutions	712	505	757
Currency futures and options			
Futures contracts	12,645	10,361	5,252
Options contracts:			
Purchased:			
Over-the-counter	98	143	75
On an exchange	2,182	4,507	811
Sold:			
Over-the-counter	130	106	83
On an exchange	2,349	3,759	913
Total spot	54,092	30,536	31,189
Total swap	15,552	23,787	17,975
Total forward	4,663	5,003	3,747
Total options	4,759	8,515	1,882
Total interbank:			
Direct with banks in the US	19,693	18,290	17,681
Direct with banks abroad	12,883	14,078	11,924
Through brokers	20,113	10,019	10,347
Unspecified	2,180	3,646	1,913
Total	54,869	46,033	41,865
Total customer:			
Nonfinancial	7,803	6,087	4,360
Financial	11,635	7,206	6,686
Total	19,438	13,293	11,046
Total turnover	91,711	78,202	60,045
Currency share %	31.5	26.8	20.6
Number of deals	15,540	10,834	12,200
Average deal size	4.8	5.5	4.3

Swiss Francs	Canadian Dollars	French Francs	Dutch Guilders	All Other	All Currencies
2,605	1,270	795	233	1,777	38,473
4,330	665	219	111	911	26,615
6,970	1,320	316	171	486	45,446
1,107	734	360	180	295	14,377
2,851	357	398	56	411	19,834
2,107	1,882	666	372	1,029	29,927
2,272	533	108	48	1,156	22,623
747	574	51	33	229	5,930
358	350	106	4	109	3,533
1,374	564	411	96	287	10,427
24	10	0	0	0	153
75	0	0	0	96	295
107	0	0	0	96	300
1,128	722	156	54	901	10,581
154	123	68	24	178	4,366
229	245	142	9	350	2,949
6,885	1,689	3	0	27	36,862
1,704	607	12	0	1	2,640
281	55	83	0	0	7,919
9	301	12	0	0	641
409	118	79	0	0	7,627
17,863	4,346	2,088	751	3,880	144,745
7,064	3,913	1,342	553	3,002	73,188
1,511	1,090	366	87	1,429	17,896
2,403	1,081	186	0	1	18,827
4,712	3,152	1,461	605	2,806	68,400
6,602	1,198	327	159	2,067	49,238
7,717	1,894	367	204	715	51,376
1,152	732	156	54	901	10,734
20,183	6,976	2,311	1,022	6,489	179,748
1,694	1,207	534	208	678	22,571
4,561	1,166	951	161	1,144	33,510
6,255	2,373	1,485	369	1,822	56,081
35,726	12,119	3,985	1,391	8,339	291,518
12.3	4.2	1.4	0.5	2.9	100.0
5,487	1,948	1,361	411	3,468	51,249
4.8	4.8	2.8	3.4	2.4	4.6

Table 3–5D.

TURNOVER SURVEY OF NINE FOREIGN-EXCHANGE BROKERS, March 1986, Aggregate Results (millions of US dollars).

Transaction Category	German Marks	Japanese Yen	British Pounds
Outright spot transactions			
Between two banks in the US	82,722	35,077	27,305
Between two banks abroad	5,397	556	539
Between a bank in the US and a bank abroad	44,689	11,548	13,126
Involving a nonbank counterparty	16,797	12,350	7,945
Swap transactions			
Maturity one year or less:			
Between two banks in US	29,813	36,671	17,447
Between two banks abroad	378	489	194
Between a bank in the US and a bank abroad	17,632	11,839	14,090
Involving a nonbank counterparty	6,824	8,845	6,597
Maturity greater than one year	412	163	278
Outright forward transactions			
Between two banks in US	124	1,306	538
Between two banks abroad	58	17	18
Between a bank in the US and a bank abroad	172	346	579
Involving a nonbank counterparty	102	347	152
Total spot	149,605	59,531	48,915
Total swap	55,059	58,007	38,606
Total forwards	456	2,016	1,287
Total between two banks in US	112,659	73,054	45,290
Total between two banks abroad	5,833	1,062	751
Total between a bank in the US and a bank abroad	62,493	23,733	27,795
Total involving a nonbank counterparty	23,723	21,542	14,694
Total turnover	205,120	119,554	88,808
Currency share (%)	37.7	22.0	16.3
Number of deals	64,373	26,814	26,270
Average deal size	3.2	4.5	3.4

traded there, but about a half dozen major currencies account for the bulk of the volume. A 1986 survey of the Federal Reserve Bank of New York[7] showed that daily foreign-currency transactions net of double counting in the United States were $84.4 billion per day in March 1986.

Net foreign-currency transactions reported by banking institutions, foreign-exchange brokers, and nonbank financial institutions averaged $50 billion, $25.9 billion, and $8.5 billion, respectively, per day in March 1986. The average size of all foreign-currency transactions reported by banks, brokers, and nonbanks was $3.4 million, $3.6 million, and $4.6 million, respectively. The market share of the three major currencies—deutsche mark (34 percent), Japanese yen (23

Swiss Francs	Canadian Dollars	French Francs	Dutch Guilders	All Other	All Currencies
9,956	7,738	4,511	2,497	5,163	174,969
390	2,729	436	0	89	10,136
6,402	5,889	4,729	2,396	3,587	92,366
5,893	1,477	135	1	1,044	45,642
5,681	6,025	5,681	975	3,548	105,841
321	7,193	20	200	128	8,923
8,665	9,833	2,342	845	3,577	68,823
1,070	2,255	3,963	60	1,875	31,489
10	101	60	0	22	1,046
45	0	43	0	12	2,068
19	126	0	0	0	238
223	0	1	0	20	1,341
0	0	106	0	0	707
22,641	17,833	9,811	4,894	9,883	323,113
15,747	25,407	12,066	2,080	9,150	216,122
287	126	150	0	32	4,354
15,682	13,763	10,235	3,472	8,723	282,878
730	10,048	456	200	217	19,297
15,290	15,722	7,072	3,241	7,184	162,530
6,963	3,732	4,204	61	2,919	77,838
38,675	43,366	22,027	6,974	19,065	543,389
7.1	8.0	4.1	1.3	3.5	100.0
10,040	6,130	6,108	2,338	8,113	150,186
3.9	7.1	3.6	3.0	2.3	3.6

percent), and British pound (19 percent)—dominates the market, while the market share of the four other currencies—Swiss franc, Canadian dollar, French franc, and Dutch guilder—accounts for the balance.

In 1986, 63.2 percent of all foreign-exchange trading reported by banks was in spot contracts, and 29.8 percent was in swap contracts. Trading in outright forward contracts by banks was 4.7 percent. Trading in foreign-currency futures and in foreign-currency options, both exchange traded and over the counter, was 2.3 percent in 1986 (see Figure 3–1).

Brokers' spot contracts rose to 59.4 percent in 1986, and swap activity fell to 39.8 percent. For nonbank financial firms, trading in spot, swap, and forward contracts represented 49.7 percent, 25.1

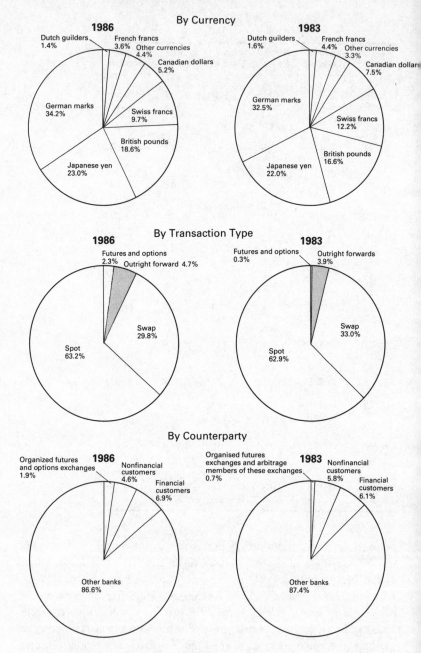

Distribution of foreign exchange turnover reported by banks

By Currency

1986
- Dutch guilders 1.4%
- French francs 3.6%
- Other currencies 4.4%
- Canadian dollars 5.2%
- German marks 34.2%
- Swiss francs 9.7%
- British pounds 18.6%
- Japanese yen 23.0%

1983
- Dutch guilders 1.6%
- French francs 4.4%
- Other currencies 3.3%
- Canadian dollars 7.5%
- German marks 32.5%
- Swiss francs 12.2%
- British pounds 16.6%
- Japanese yen 22.0%

By Transaction Type

1986
- Futures and options 2.3%
- Outright forward 4.7%
- Swap 29.8%
- Spot 63.2%

1983
- Futures and options 0.3%
- Outright forwards 3.9%
- Swap 33.0%
- Spot 62.9%

By Counterparty

1986
- Organized futures and options exchanges 1.9%
- Nonfinancial customers 4.6%
- Financial customers 6.9%
- Other banks 86.6%

1983
- Organised futures exchanges and arbitrage members of these exchanges 0.7%
- Nonfinancial customers 5.8%
- Financial customers 6.1%
- Other banks 87.4%

Note: Due to rounding some totals may not add up to 100%

Figure 3–1A. Distribution of Foreign-Exchange Turnover Reported by Banks, 1983 and 1986.

Distribution of foreign exchange turnover
reported by nonbank financial firms

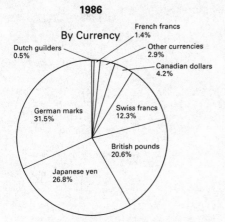

1986

By Currency

French francs 1.4%

Dutch guilders 0.5%

Other currencies 2.9%

Canadian dollars 4.2%

German marks 31.5%

Swiss francs 12.3%

British pounds 20.6%

Japanese yen 26.8%

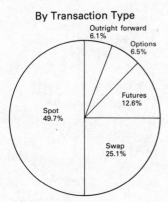

By Transaction Type

Outright forward 6.1%

Options 6.5%

Futures 12.6%

Spot 49.7%

Swap 25.1%

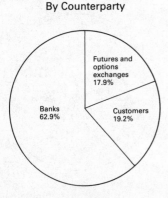

By Counterparty

Futures and options exchanges 17.9%

Banks 62.9%

Customers 19.2%

Note: Due to rounding some totals may not add up to 100%

Figure 3–1B. Distribution of Foreign-Exchange Turnover Reported by Nonbank Financial Firms, 1986.

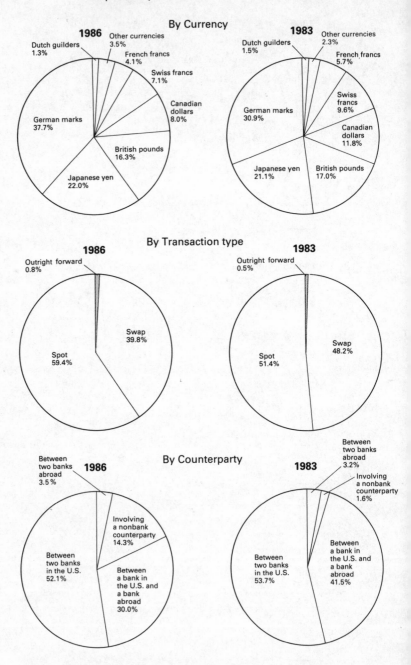

Distribution of foreign exchange turnover reported by brokers

By Currency

1986

- Dutch guilders 1.3%
- Other currencies 3.5%
- French francs 4.1%
- Swiss francs 7.1%
- Canadian dollars 8.0%
- German marks 37.7%
- British pounds 16.3%
- Japanese yen 22.0%

1983

- Dutch guilders 1.5%
- Other currencies 2.3%
- French francs 5.7%
- Swiss francs 9.6%
- German marks 30.9%
- Canadian dollars 11.8%
- Japanese yen 21.1%
- British pounds 17.0%

By Transaction type

1986

- Outright forward 0.8%
- Swap 39.8%
- Spot 59.4%

1983

- Outright forward 0.5%
- Swap 48.2%
- Spot 51.4%

By Counterparty

1986

- Between two banks abroad 3.5%
- Involving a nonbank counterparty 14.3%
- Between two banks in the U.S. 52.1%
- Between a bank in the U.S. and a bank abroad 30.0%

1983

- Between two banks abroad 3.2%
- Involving a nonbank counterparty 1.6%
- Between a bank in the U.S. and a bank abroad 41.5%
- Between two banks in the U.S. 53.7%

Note: Due to rounding some totals may not add up to 100%

Figure 3–1C. Distribution of Foreign-Exchange Turnover Reported by Brokers, 1983 and 1986.

Currencies in the other currency column

Banking Institutions

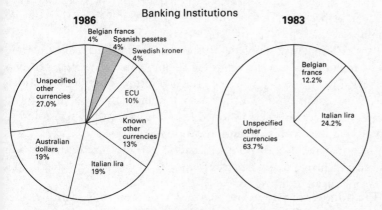

1986

Belgian francs 4%
Spanish pesetas 4%
Swedish kroner 4%
Unspecified other currencies 27.0%
ECU 10%
Known other currencies 13%
Australian dollars 19%
Italian lira 19%

1983

Belgian francs 12.2%
Italian lira 24.2%
Unspecified other currencies 63.7%

Nonbank Financial Institutions
1986

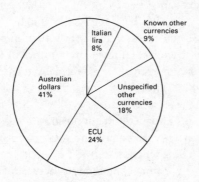

Italian lira 8%
Known other currencies 9%
Australian dollars 41%
Unspecified other currencies 18%
ECU 24%

Brokers

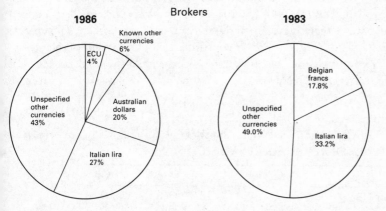

1986

Known other currencies 6%
ECU 4%
Unspecified other currencies 43%
Australian dollars 20%
Italian lira 27%

1983

Belgian francs 17.8%
Unspecified other currencies 49.0%
Italian lira 33.2%

Note: Due to rounding some totals may not add up to 100%

Figure 3–1D. Currencies in the Other Currency Column, 1983 and 1986.

percent, and 6.1 percent, respectively, of their total volume. Foreign-currency options and futures accounted for 6.5 percent and 12.6 percent, respectively, of total turnover—considerably more than for the commercial banks.

Bank trading with nonbank customers declined to 11.5 percent, while trading between the banks fell to 86.6 percent between the two surveys. Trading on organized options and futures exchanges expanded to 1.9 percent in 1986. For the surveyed nonbank financial institutions nearly 63 percent of their 1986 total volume was with banks. Another 19 percent was with nonbank institutions, of which 7.7 percent was with nonfinancial institutions. Trading on organized futures and options exchanges was 18 percent of the total volume reported by the nonbank financial firms.

The turnover in forward-market business is now only slightly higher than it was in 1973; its increase has been much less than the growth in spot-exchange transactions or in the value of total international transactions. This is explained partly by the fact that part of the increased need for forward cover has been handled through alternative methods. In addition, most countries regulate forward transactions in order to deter speculation, thereby reducing the number of forward contracts.

The London foreign-exchange market daily turnover is estimated at $90 billion in 1986.[8] The major share of trading was between the U.S. dollar and sterling (30 percent), followed by U.S. dollar/deutsche mark (28 percent). A substantial volume of business occurs between the U.S. dollar and the yen (14 percent of the total), Swiss franc (9 percent), U.S. dollar and the French franc (4 percent), lira (2 percent), and Canadian dollar (2 percent). Transactions between the U.S. dollar and other currencies amounted to only 7 percent of the total. Business not involving the U.S. dollar (cross-currency) was quite small (3 percent) and was largely between sterling and the deutsche mark (1 percent). ECU-denominated turnover constituted about 1 percent of the market.

Spot transactions accounted for 73 percent of the total, and forward contracts, 26 percent. Less than 1 percent of total market turnover was

Table 3–6.
TOTAL FOREIGN EXCHANGE TURNOVER IN
THE TOKYO MARKET, March 1986.[a]

		All Currencies	US dollar
Interbank	Ⓐ	639 (312)[b]	492 (204)
Direct with banks in Japan		60 (37)	46 (24)
Through brokers in Japan		247 (101)	224 (81)
Direct with banks abroad		228 (111)	150 (63)
Through brokers abroad		104 (63)	72 (36)
Customers	Ⓑ	321 (173)	291 (146)
Total	Ⓐ+Ⓑ	960 (485)	783 (350)

Source: Bank of Japan.
[a]Outright spot plus outright forward plus swaps; in billion of US dollars equivalent.
[b]Figures in parentheses are except swaps.

represented by forward maturities of more than one year. Foreign-currency options contracts and foreign-currency futures contracts were insignificant (well under 1 percent of business in total). Activity in the foreign-exchange market over the survey period was predominantly interbank. Banks' business directly with customers accounted for 9 percent of total turnover. Foreign-exchange trading in Tokyo is summarized in Table 3–6.

THE ROLE Of THE FOREIGN-EXCHANGE RATE

Foreign-exchange-rate considerations play a significant role in financial management of international business. Exchange rates are the prices of one country's money in terms of other countries' money. Through exchange rates, domestic prices are effectively translated into foreign prices, and vice versa. Close links exist between exchange rates and key economic variables (such as inflation, interest rates, capital flows, and the balance of payments), and depending on the openness of the economy, the exchange rate could become a key price that affects a wide range of economic activity.

The exchange rate affects prices and costs, particularly of tradeable goods, and plays a significant role in the economy. The immediate effect of a currency depreciation is to increase the prices of imports to domestic buyers and to reduce the prices of exports to foreign buyers. Changes in relative prices promote domestic balance-of-payments adjustments along the lines of traditional analysis. A devaluation-induced increase in the domestic price levels reduces the country's real income and thereby gradually reduces domestic demand. The contractionary effect results in lower import demand and reduced demand for domestically produced goods, releasing some of these goods for the export market.

The exchange rate has an important, but by no means decisive, role in solving balance-of-payments problems. Often exchange-rate changes are ineffective in promoting balance-of-payments adjustments because domestic developments neutralize these changes. Reasonable domestic policies are the essential prerequisites on which exchange-rate policy can be solidly based. The exchange rate is not a panacea and cannot replace responsible monetary, fiscal, and income policies. Exchange-rate changes must be accompanied by appropriate fiscal and monetary policies if they are to be effective, otherwise a depreciation can be inflationary. In the short run, depreciation usually worsens the trade balance through the J-curve effect—that is, the terms of trade initially worsen, exports decline, and imports may increase. Normally the favorable effects of currency change take time to become effective. The impact of exchange-rate movements on domestic prices, production, and employment depends on the state of the economy. When the economy is at full capacity, currency depreciation could be inflationary, thereby diminishing international competitiveness that might have resulted from the initial exchange-rate decline.

EXCHANGE-RATE DETERMINATION

The international monetary system sets the stage for foreign-exchange arrangements and currency behavior. The operation of the foreign-exchange markets is largely affected by the international monetary system, which, in turn, is established by the International Monetary Fund's (IMF's) Articles of Agreement.

There is no consensus on how exchange rates are determined. The interpretations vary widely among the various theories, ranging from the traditional approach of trade-oriented demand-and-supply factors to the modern approach of the asset-market mechanism and expectations. The analysis of currency determination is complicated by the interdependence of the exchange rates, by monetary and other economic policies, and by factors affecting economic and financial performance.

The various theories of exchange-rate determination can be reconciled, however, in terms of the time horizon that they are addressing (that is, short, medium, and long) or in terms of monetary or nonmonetary approaches. Some explanations, however, are actually subsets of the major theories. Various indexes have been identified and developed as proxies for exchange-rate determination and behavior. These indexes could be identified as proxies or reduced forms of the various exchange-rate theories. Technical analysis, which is commonly used in commodity and stock prices analysis, is also applied to foreign-currency projections.

Exchange-rate policy and intervention are widespread and play a significant role in foreign-exchange determination in the short run. Currency management policies attempt to affect the demand for, and supply of, the domestic currency in the foreign-exchange market and alter the expectations of market participants with regard to future exchange rates and their preference for assets denominated in various currencies.

The foreign-exchange market have been subject to considerable volatility and to erratic movements in recent years, thus making currency-rate forecasting both difficult and significant for multinational corporations' foreign-exchange-exposure management. Some have suggested that exchange-rate behavior is more akin to stock market prices than to the traditional versions of the purchasing-power-parity theory.

Foreign-Exchange Arrangements

Foreign-exchange-rate determination is affected by (1) the exchange regime or arrangement to which each country or group of countries adheres under the IMF Articles of Agreement or outside it, (2) market forces, and (3) official management. In 1988 the following types of currency arrangements were practiced by IMF members and other countries:[9]

1 A currency may be pegged to a single currency, SDR, a currency composite, or a basket of currencies.
2 Limited flexibility may be exercised in terms of a single currency (that is, the U.S. dollar) or a group of currencies
3 Cooperative exchange arrangement of the European Monetary System (see Tables 3–7 and 3–8).
4 Flexibility may be increased by adjusting the rate according to a set of indicators (or managed floating rate) or by floating independently.
5 Multiple currency practices and dual exchange-rate arrangements may be employed. By IMF definition, a multiple-currency practice arises when the authorities create a spread of more than 2 percent between the buying and selling rate for spot exchange transactions, or when they create a difference of more than 1 percent between spot exchange rates for different types of transactions (that is, special exchange-rate regimes for some or all capital transactions and/or some or all invisibles; import rates different from export rates; more than one rate for imports; and more than one rate for exports).

Table 3–7.
EUROPEAN MONETARY SYSTEM.

	Belgium (DFR)	Denmark (DCR)	France (FF)	Ireland (IR£)	Italy (LIT)	Netherlands (HFL)	West Germany (DM)
100 DFR.		1872.15	16.6310	1.8510	37.1020	5.5870	4.959
	—	1859.52	16.1476	1.78209	35.1459	5.3777	4.7866
Belgium		1789.85	15.8990	1.7695	32.9090	5.3415	4.740
100 DCR.	553.00		89.925	10.0087	200.620	30.2100	26.810
	544.39	—	87.906	9.70150	191.331	29.276	26.058
Denmark	528.70		85.970	9.56830	177.940	28.8825	25.630
100 FF	628.97	116.32		11.3830	228.170	34.3600	30.495
	619.29	113.758	—	11.0362	217.654	33.304	29.643
France	601.295	111.20		10.8825	202.380	32.8475	29.150
1 IR £	56.5115	10.4511	9.1890		2050.03	3.0878	2.740
	56.1138	10.3077	9.0611	—	1972.17	3.0176	2.6360
Ireland	54.025	9.9913	8.7850		1818.34	2.9510	2.619
100 LIT.	3.0387	0.5620	0.4941	0.05499		0.1660	0.1473
	2.8453	0.5227	0.4594	0.05071	—	0.1530	0.1362
Italy	2.6953	0.4985	0.4383	0.04877		0.14725	0.1306
100 HFL.	18.9143	346.24	304.44	33.8868	679.120		90.770
	18.3692	341.580	300.269	33.1384	653.546	—	89.008
Netherlands	18.0831	331.020	291.04	32.3939	602.410		86.780
100 DM	2109.50	390.16	343.05	38.1825	765.400	115.235	
West	2089.15	383.762	337.349	37.2306	734.253	112.349	—
Germany	2016.55	373.00	327.92	36.4964	678.650	110.167	
ECU-Parity[b] =	42.4582	7.85212	6.90403	0.768411	1483.58	2.31943	2.05853

Source: Union Bank of Switzerland, *Foreign Exchange News* January 1988.
[a]Central rates and intervention points between the currencies participating in the European monetary system.
[b]as of September 28, 1988.
Note: Upper line: ceiling. Middle line: central rate. Lower line: floor.

Table 3–8.

THE CALCULATION OF ECU RATES, November 3, 1986.

	National currency component (A)	Exchange rate against US$ (B)	Components of ECU (C)	Currency per ECU (D)	Weights 17 Sept. 1984 (E)
German mark	0.719	2.0645	0.348268	1.945228	32.01
French franc	1.31	6.7352	0.194501	6.346088	19.03
Sterling	0.0878	1.4115	0.062203	0.751905	14.98
Italian lira	140	1424.5	0.098280	1342.20	10.13
Dutch guilder	0.256	2.3305	0.109848	2.195860	10.11
Belgian franc	3.85	42.84	0.089869	40.3650	8.52
Danish krone	0.19	7.775	0.024437	7.325816	2.7
Irish punt	0.00871	1.3208	0.006594	0.803539	1.3
Greek drachma	1.15	139.8	0.008226	131.72	1.2
dollar/ecu			0.94222708		100.00

The dollar exchange rate from London and Dublin is the number of dollars per currency unit rather than the number of currency units per dollar. Column (C) is found for each of these two currencies by multiplying the value in column (A) by that in column (B); and column (D) by dividing the dollar equivalent of the ecu (C) by the rate in column (B).

6   Non-IMF members, including the East bloc and other Communist countries, have various exchange arrangements, fixed rates being the most common.

(The IMF's 151 members exchange arrangements are shown in Table 2–1A in Chapter 2. Table 2–1B shows membership of currency and trade areas around the world.)

Foreign-Exchange-Rate Determination

Foreign-exchange-rate determination under currency arrangements 1, 2, 4, and 5 is, to a great extent, predetermined, and these currency rates tend to depend primarily on the stability of the major currencies. By pegging to a basket of currencies (or the SDR), countries are often more sensitive to fluctuations in certain bilateral exchange rates than in others. Because of import or export relations or currency denomination of international trade, these currencies are more heavily weighted in the basket. Under the arrangements in which currencies are pegged to other currency composites or baskets of currencies, the composites of the basket are usually not made public, but its structure usually reflects the composite of the countries' major trading partners. Under the third arrangement the use of a set of indicators requires knowledge of the indicators and the mechanics of exchange adjustment in order to predict how authorities determine a change in the exchange rate.

Currencies in the EMS have fixed but adjustable cross-exchange rate vis-à-vis each other, but they fluctuate jointly against the currencies of the rest of the world. Exchange-rate determinations under arrangement 4 are largely determined by market forces and official policies. The major currencies are included in these two arrangements.

The theory of exchange-rate determination has changed considerably in recent years. It recognizes that currency-rate determination is a complex and an interactive process that cannot be fully explained by any limited set of explanatory variables. Foreign-exchange rates can more adequately be explained by the various factors that affect international transactions in goods, services, and financial assets, as well as domestic monetary and financial conditions and expectations.

There is a wide spectrum of exchange-rate theories and models, and within this spectrum each model emphasizes a different cause and effect and different transmission channels. Some theories of exchange-rate determination can be classified according to whether they are short-, medium-, or long-term and by theoretical underlying of the model. Some theories are rivals, extensions, or complements of others. Although there is no one generally accepted theory or model of exchange-rate determination, there are several main approaches or theories that provide a general framework for analysis of exchange rates. These theories can be classified in terms of the time horizon and in several groups along the following three features.

1   The traditional approach of exchange-rate determination is based on Keynesian economic theory. It considers foreign-exchange rates as prices that clear supply of and demand for goods in international transactions and in turn, in foreign-exchange markets, in a process that simultaneously determines many other variables in the economy. The analysis emphasizes the effects of development in the current account. Deteriorating balance-of-trade or currency-account deficits are likely to lead to exchange-rate depreciation, whereas improving conditions have an opposite effect. The currency-account balance does not explain exchange-rate developments very satisfactorily. Most of the short-term variations in exchange rates have little to do with balance-of-payments performance, and even over longer periods of time the relationship is loose.

2   Monetary and asset-market theories of exchange-rate determination include the monetary approach to exchange-rate determination; the quantity theory models; the asset-market theories of exchange-rate determination; and the purchasing power parity (PPP) theory. The monetary theory of exchange-rate determination emphasizes the role that markets for money and securities play in the determination process; views the exchange rate as a relative price of two national assets or monies, rather than relative prices of different national outputs and as determined primarily by the demand for and supply of the stocks of various national monies and expectations; considers the exchange rate as endogenously determined by stock equilibrium conditions in markets for

national monies; and maintains that the equilibrium currency rate is attained when the existing stocks of the two national monies are willingly held. The monetary theory assumes that there are free capital mobility and perfect substitutability between foreign and domestic assets denominated in different currencies; expectations of future exchange rates strongly affect rates; an efficient market prevails; perfect arbitrage conditions imply purchasing power parity; and interest-rate parity. Under free and efficient markets, future spot-exchange rates, interest-rate and inflation differentials, and forward discounts and premiums are simultaneously determined. Changes in one of these variables will affect all the others, creating a new equilibrium level.

According to the asset-market view the exchange rate is the relative price of two national monies, or two assets, and the price of a particular currency is determined mainly by the relative supplies of and demands for these monies or assets. Alternatively, the exchange rate represents an equilibrium between the desire to hold stocks of assets denominated in that currency and the available supply of such assets. Like other asset prices, exchange rates are affected by changes in supply of and demand for money and (financial) assets; economic and financial conditions and developments (such as interest rates and inflation); monetary and fiscal policy; market expectations; and efficient market behavior (where new information concerning the future is reflected immediately in current prices, thereby precluding unexploited profit opportunities from arbitrage). The theory implies that the exchange rate, like the prices of other assets, is much more sensitive to expectations concerning future events than the national price level. At times exchange rates demonstrate random fluctuations in response to new information that modifies the expectations of the markets about conditions that could influence exchange rates. Indeed, in periods that are dominated by news that alters expectations, exchange rates are likely to be much more volatile than national price indexes, and departures from PPP are likely. The exchange rate can be affected by monetary policy and the market's expectations of its future course. Modifications in policies or expectations thereof could induce shifts in the demand for assets denominated in different currencies. A significant factor that affects the relative attractiveness of currencies is interest rates, but the relationship between exchange and interest rates is not tight. The asset-market approach is relevant for countries that have well-developed capital and money markets coupled with relatively free exchange markets where arbitrage between domestic and foreign assets is allowed. In countries where such arbitrage is limited or nonexistent, the exchange rate is determined by supply and demand in goods markets and official intervention.

3 The general equilibrium and portfolio balance theory considers the exchange-rate determination as part of the general (real and monetary) equilibrium of the system. The equilibrium exchange rate can change with an accompanying change in the money supply or in the real money demand or both. The portfolio approach is a synthesis of both the traditional and monetary theories and considers exchange-rate determination as a simultaneous process of adjustments and asset valuation induced by monetary and real factors. Exchange-rate movements change the real value of the money stock or the relative supplies of domestic and foreign assets.

Changes in the relative return and risk of foreign-currency-denominated assets will affect their prices and the exchange rate. In addition, changes in wealth will affect the demand and supply of foreign assets over time and, in turn, the exchange rate. It is through growth of wealth via the currency account that the real sector affects foreign exchange rates. The portfolio model assumes perfect capital mobility and high substitutability between domestic and foreign assets.

The exchange rate in the short run is determined in the asset market, since the asset market adjusts more quickly than the goods markets. The exchange rate can (in the short run) be inconsistent with both goods and bond market equilibrium, but in the long run, both markets must be in equilibrium at the same exchange rate.

Purchasing Power Parity (PPP)

The purchasing power parity theory maintains that any divergence of the exchange rate from the equilibrium price levels in different countries will set in motion corrective forces to restore equilibrium, which can take time.[10] Alternatively, the PPP theory maintains that exchange rate changes would offset over time divergent movements in national price levels. Accordingly, a country that experiences higher inflation will experience a corresponding depreciation of its currency, while a country with a lower inflation rate will experience an appreciation. Evidence suggests that the theory is correct only as a long-run approximation of reality, except under conditions of hyperinflation, since traded goods do not flow instantaneously from one market to another to equalize prices.

The PPP theory has two versions. In its absolute version the theory states that the equilibrium exchange rate between domestic and foreign currencies equals the ratio of domestic to foreign price levels, or that equilibrium exchange rates would be those that make price levels equal everywhere. Mathematically, the PPP theory can be stated as follows:

Rate of change
of the exchange rate = Rate of change in relative price levels

or

Expected rate of change
of the exchange rate = Expected inflation rate differential

The relative version of the PPP theory relates equilibrium changes in exchange rates to change in the ratio of domestic to foreign price index ratios. In essence it asserts that a change in the exchange rate that would retain the original level of the relative price of tradeable to nontradeable goods in the economy also would establish an equilibrium rate of exchange. The relative hypothesis states that the exchange rate between the currencies of any pair of countries should be a constant multiple of the ratio of general price indexes of the two countries or, equivalently, that percentage changes in the exchange rate should equal percentage changes in the ratio of the price index. For instance, the exchange rate of country A's currency should change to maintain equilibrium in the same direction and same proportion as the change in country A's prices over the change in country B's prices.

Thus, if e_o is the current equilibrium exchange rate (that is, if one unit of foreign currency equals e_o units of the home currency), p_h the home country price level, and p_f the foreign price level, then $e_o = p_h/p_f$, or $p_f e_o = p_h$. In other words, a unit of home currency should have the same purchasing power around the world.

A critical feature of this approach is that internationally traded goods are arbitraged so that the exchange rate equals the price of traded goods, in common currency, in different countries. Although this phenomenon remains correct for traded goods, there is no reason to expect the price of nontraded goods to be equal everywhere.

The PPP theory is valid under four conditions: (1) if changes in the economy originate in the monetary sector; (2) when the internal relative price structures remain relatively stable; (3) if relative prices are unchanged as a result of changes in the real sector; and (4) when no structural changes occur in the economy (such as a change in tariffs, a change in autonomous capital inflows, changes in technology, or a change in taste). In the real world, however, these conditions are not likely to hold. They might either be set off by events that are independent of monetary developments or be influenced by those developments. Therefore, at least in the short run, exchange-rate fluctuations would not be matched by corresponding fluctuations of aggregate price levels.

The PPP theory does not successfully explain short-term movements in exchange rates that can result from uncertainties and lags in the adjustment process, flows of capital, or current-account imbalance. Most observers of PPP conclude that the theory holds up in a loose and

approximate fashion and that the matching between inflation differentials and depreciation is not close. Empirical evidence shows that during the 1970s and 1980s short-term changes in exchange rates bore little relationship to short-run differentials in national inflation rates, and frequent divergences from purchasing power parities have resulted. Evidence of the purchasing power parity theory shows that disparities between relative prices and exchange rates exist in the short run but that the theory holds over the long run.

The PPP does not specify the channels or mechanisms through which prices and exchange rates are interactive or the conditions that must prevail for PPP to hold. Therefore, it should not be viewed as a theory of exchange-rate determination. The usefulness of the PPP model in estimating divergences between the actual exchange rate and the long-term equilibrium rate depends on the choice of a base period, the choice of the relevant price indexes, and the projection of the price indexes for the forecast period. Capital flows cause most deviations from PPP. If differences in inflation rates between countries are small, their influence on competitiveness is likely to be swamped by other factors, such as the balance-of-payments performance, capital flows, and the like. In that case, comparison of the inflation differential does not explain exchange-rate variations.

4. Additional or alternative theories or hypotheses are either derived from or based on the above three approaches or are limited to using a single variable or multiple factors to explain exchange-rate behavior.

Indexes Reflecting Exchange-Rate Behavior

One approach to exchange-rate forecasting specifies a structural model of the economy where the spot rate can be expressed as a function of lagged endogenous and exogenous variables. The function is first estimated and then used to forecast rates. Alternatively, various indicators or indexes are used to assess and forecast exchange rates. These indicators (or factors) are subsets of and proxies for the various theories of exchange-rate determination and, in a sense, are applied as reduced forms of these theories or models. Indicators are used by the IMF, the BIS, central and commercial banks, and other market participants. The indexes can be classified into several groups:

1 Effective and real effective exchange rates,
2 Current account balance of the balance of payments,
3 Short-term interest rates,
4 Inflation (consumer price indexes, wholesale prices indexes),
5 Growth rate of the monetary aggregates,
6 Capital account balance of the balance of payments,
7 Economic and exchange-rate policy and intervention, and
8 Forward exchange rates.

These indexes can be organized along the exchange-rate theories (identified earlier) as follows:

Indexes 1, 2, and 4 belong to the traditional approach to exchange-rate
   determination;
Indexes 1 and 4 reflect the PPP theory, which could be classified in the
   context of the traditional and the monetary and asset-market
   theories;
Indexes 3, 5, and 6 are derived from the monetary and asset-market
   framework to the exchange-rate;
Indexes 7 and 8 also operate through the channels outlined by the
   monetary theory and asset-market approach to the exchange rate.

The present exchange system encourages use of effective exchange
rates and not bilateral rates. The effective exchange rate measures a
currency's value in terms of weighted average of the currencies of its
major trading partners. The weights reflect the relative significance of
the major trading partners in a country's trade. The weights are based
on countries' bilateral and multilateral shares of trade in manufactures,
and they also take into account the relative size of countries' economies.

A more useful index of measuring exchange-rate changes is in terms of
real effective rates, wherein the trade-weighted exchange-rate changes
are adjusted for past inflation differentials. Real exchange-rate indexes
are particularly useful in assessments of how past exchange-rate changes
and domestic price changes affect a country's competitive position with
its trading partners. [11] An increase in these indexes denotes a loss of
competitiveness; a decrease denotes an improvement. (See Table 3–9
for effective and real effective exchange-rate indexes.)

The effective exchange-rate indexes have several shortcomings in
terms of accuracy and international comparability:

1 The indexes relate only to the manufacturing sector;
2 The choice of the weights contains an element of arbitrariness;
3 Relative costs and prices, although very important, are not the only
   factors that determine competitiveness;
4 Nonprice factors can justify exchange-rate movements that are not
   in line with the development of a country's relative costs and
   prices;
5 The choice of the base period affects whether exchange rates were
   out of line with relative costs and prices at the beginning of the
   period.

Because of these shortcomings, changes in countries' international
competitive positions would not necessarily indicate a movement away
from equilibrium. Substantial divergences in the index, however,
indicate a significant change in a country's international competitive
position.

Changes in current account balances affect exchange rates in two
ways: through their direct impact on the demand and supply of the

currencies concerned in the exchange market, and through the changes that they usually induce in the market's views about the equilibrium exchange-rate of currencies. The resultant exchange-rate movements themselves can temporarily amplify currency payments imbalances. The initial increase in the surplus and the later swing into substantial deficit are due partly to the initially perverse J-curve effects of exchange rate changes. Countries' current account balances do respond quite strongly, although usually with a considerable time lag, to changes in international competitive positions.

Changes in interest rate differentials influence exchange rates through their induced effects on international flows of funds. Usually, an inflow of funds from one country to another will involve switching currencies from one denomination into another. This, in turn, will increase demand for the currency with the higher interest rate and appreciate its value. The reverse process occurs in the currency of the country with the lower interest rate.

Inflation differentials exert a significant impact on exchange rates, particularly over the medium or longer term. Exchange rates tend over time to reflect purchasing power parity relationships. The country that has the lowest rate of inflation (measured, for instance, by the consumer price indexes) has also the most steadily appreciating exchange rate. However, deviations from purchasing power parity can sometimes prove substantial, because of, for instance, relatively substantial current account surplus or deficit and high inflation. Countries with relatively better price performance that experience a serious deterioration of their current account balance of payments and much lower nominal interest rates are likely to experience substantial depreciation.

Different rates of monetary expansion affect exchange rates through a process that involves such factors as changes in the income velocity of money, interest rate differentials, and price expectations. In the short term, exchange rate developments are significantly influenced by financial markets (i.e., capital account transactions). These markets are affected by interest rates or by the relative yields on various types of money market assets in each country.

Governments' policies affect the environment of the foreign exchange markets. Exchange rates can be strongly influenced by the adoption of more vigorous anti-inflationary policies as well as by exchange rate intervention. These policies rely heavily on tighter domestic monetary conditions and they usually exert upward pressure on the level of domestic interest rates, thus widening interest rate differentials in favor of the countries pursuing them.

Alternatively, forecasting can rely on forward exchange rates. However, the interest rate parity conditions suggest that forward exchange rates are determined by interest rate differentials between countries. Therefore, the forward rate is not an efficient indicator of the future spot rate.

71

Table 3–9A.

EFFECTIVE AND REAL EFFECTIVE EXCHANGE RATES, INDUSTRIAL COUNTRIES

	United States	Canada	Japan	Australia	France	Germany	Italy
Nominal against 15 other industrial-country currencies							
1983	114.2	100.8	107.8	92.0	87.3	107.5	90.3
1984	122.3	97.3	112.9	94.2	84.4	107.3	86.7
1985	127.0	92.8	115.9	76.3	85.5	107.8	82.1
1986	106.0	87.6	150.1	61.4	87.4	116.1	82.9
1987	94.1	89.6	164.4	58.3	87.1	122.0	82.3
1987							
August	95.7	90.0	162.7	59.8	86.8	121.3	81.5
September	93.9˙	90.3	165.4	60.5	86.9	121.5	81.8
October	93.4	90.7	165.1	58.9	86.7	121.3	81.7
November	90.0	89.3	171.2	54.3	86.7	123.6	81.2
December	87.4	89.4	178.6	55.1	87.0	123.8	81.4
1988							
January	87.4	91.0	179.8	55.1	87.2	123.4	81.3
February	88.2	92.6	179.3	56.0	86.8	122.9	81.0
March	86.8	93.7	180.7	57.0	86.3	122.8	80.5
April	85.8	94.6	183.2	57.5	85.9	122.6	80.1
May	86.1	94.5	183.7	60.0	86.1	122.1	79.7
June	87.6	96.6	182.0	63.7	86.1	121.5	79.4
July	90.1	98.1	177.4	65.0	85.6	120.7	79.2
June 24	87.8	97.5	181.5	65.2	86.0	121.2	79.3
July 1	89.7	97.4	177.2	64.6	85.9	121.1	79.3
8	89.7	97.9	176.7	64.5	85.9	121.0	79.2
15	90.3	98.1	177.2	64.7	85.6	120.7	79.2
22	90.0	98.7	177.5	65.5	85.4	120.5	79.1
29	90.1	98.0	178.5	65.5	85.3	120.3	79.2
August 5	90.6	98.4	178.2	65.6	85.1	120.1	79.2
Real against 15 other industrial-country currencies							
1983	112.7	102.6	96.8	101.8	94.7	101.0	101.1
1984	119.6	100.1	97.8	106.4	97.0	98.0	101.8
1985	121.7	96.3	99.0	88.9	100.4	96.6	100.2
1986	100.9	93.3	122.1	78.3	103.7	103.6	102.5
1987	90.2	96.4	127.9	80.3	105.1	106.7	103.2
1988							
February	85.5	100.2	135.9	79.8	103.9	107.0	104.2
March	84.2	101.7	136.7	81.5	103.6	106.9	103.0
April	83.3	103.0	137.6	82.6	103.2	106.5	102.2
May	83.7	103.0	137.4	86.6	103.5	106.3	102.0
June	85.4	104.7	135.6	92.5	103.6	105.8	101.6
July	88.1	106.3	131.6	94.8	103.1	105.0	101.2
Real against 18 other industrial-country and 22 LDC currencies							
1983	114.9	104.6	100.4	102.0	94.4	100.6	100.8
1984	120.8	102.6	102.4	106.7	96.4	96.8	101.0
1985	123.3	99.0	104.2	89.6	99.9	95.6	99.7
1986	106.4	94.3	126.7	80.2	104.2	104.7	103.8
1987	96.3	96.5	131.6	81.9	106.2	109.0	105.7
1988							
February	90.9	99.6	138.7	81.1	104.7	108.9	106.6
March	89.5	100.9	139.3	83.0	104.4	108.7	105.3
April	88.7	102.1	140.1	84.1	103.9	108.2	104.3
May	89.0	102.1	140.0	87.8	104.0	107.8	103.9
June	90.5	104.0	138.6	93.4	103.9	107.0	103.3
July	92.8	105.9	134.8	95.5	103.3	105.8	102.5

Source: Morgan Guaranty Trust Company, *World Financial Markets*, August 1988
Note: Index numbers, 1980–82 average = 100.

United Kingdom	Austria	Belgium	Netherlands	Spain	Switzerland	Denmark	Norway	Sweden
91.6	103.6	90.0	105.0	78.4	111.5	96.4	99.5	82.2
88.1	103.6	88.9	103.9	77.4	110.5	93.9	97.8	84.3
88.2	104.2	89.6	104.0	75.6	109.5	95.1	95.6	83.9
80.7	107.8	92.9	110.3	73.4	118.1	99.7	89.2	81.6
79.0	110.8	95.6	114.6	73.1	123.1	102.8	85.7	80.1
78.9	110.1	95.2	114.1	73.6	122.6	101.3	87.3	80.2
79.6	110.1	95.3	114.4	74.6	122.7	101.0	87.4	79.7
80.0	115.7	95.1	114.5	75.9	122.3	101.3	87.0	79.6
81.5	110.9	95.6	115.9	75.6	125.4	102.5	85.2	79.2
81.9	110.8	95.8	115.9	75.2	126.9	103.0	83.5	78.9
81.2	110.7	95.6	115.8	74.8	126.5	103.0	84.6	79.1
80.8	110.7	95.4	115.6	75.0	125.1	102.8	85.4	79.7
83.5	110.7	95.2	115.4	75.5	123.9	102.3	85.1	79.9
85.2	110.6	94.9	115.3	76.2	123.6	101.5	86.1	80.1
85.4	110.4	94.8	115.0	76.0	122.2	101.2	87.1	80.4
83.4	110.1	94.5	114.3	75.6	121.8	101.6	87.1	80.3
83.2	109.7	93.9	113.3	74.8	121.2	100.9	86.3	80.5
83.5	109.9	94.2	113.9	75.4	121.9	101.4	87.3	80.3
82.4	109.8	94.2	113.7	74.9	122.0	101.4	86.7	80.7
82.7	109.9	94.0	113.8	74.8	121.5	101.1	86.6	80.6
82.4	109.7	94.0	113.4	74.8	121.5	100.8	86.5	80.6
83.5	109.7	93.9	113.2	74.7	121.1	100.7	86.1	80.4
84.3	109.7	93.8	112.9	74.8	120.7	100.7	86.2	80.3
84.3	109.6	93.6	112.7	74.9	120.2	100.5	86.2	80.2
93.1	102.0	88.6	100.8	88.8	105.1	100.4	102.0	90.8
90.2	103.0	85.9	97.8	91.0	100.1	99.2	100.5	96.0
92.8	103.2	85.3	96.5	92.3	97.9	101.2	99.3	96.9
87.2	106.3	84.5	101.2	93.8	105.4	107.3	96.9	95.9
87.4	110.0	84.2	104.3	95.7	109.3	111.5	100.3	95.2
90.5	109.5	82.3	102.3	101.1	109.9	112.5	101.8	96.6
93.7	109.6	81.9	102.7	99.9	109.1	112.4	101.4	97.2
96.0	109.1	81.6	102.8	101.3	108.4	111.5	103.1	97.3
96.3	108.3	80.9	102.5	100.7	106.8	111.8	104.7	97.8
94.1	109.5	80.5	101.9	100.2	106.2	111.9	104.0	97.7
93.7	110.2	79.7	101.4	99.1	105.1	110.6	103.1	97.9
93.1	102.1	88.2	99.5	89.2	105.1	100.3	101.9	91.0
89.7	102.6	85.0	95.9	91.2	99.8	99.0	100.5	95.8
92.2	102.8	84.5	94.8	93.0	97.7	101.1	99.7	96.7
88.0	107.1	85.0	101.1	96.2	107.2	107.8	97.7	96.6
88.9	111.5	85.4	105.2	99.2	112.2	112.4	101.2	96.5
91.9	110.9	83.4	103.0	104.5	112.6	113.3	102.8	97.7
95.2	110.9	82.9	103.3	103.2	111.7	113.2	102.4	98.3
97.5	110.3	82.5	103.4	104.5	110.7	112.3	104.1	98.4
97.6	109.3	81.8	102.9	103.7	108.9	112.6	105.7	98.8
95.3	110.4	81.2	102.0	103.0	108.2	112.6	104.8	98.6
94.6	110.9	80.2	101.1	101.5	106.8	111.2	103.9	98.7

Table 3-9B.
REAL EFFECTIVE EXCHANGE RATES, DEVELOPING COUNTRIES

	Argentina	*Brazil*	*Chile*	*Colombia*	*Mexico*	*Peru*	*Venezuela*
1983	71.6	86.0	89.3	104.9	79.0	98.5	117.3
1984	80.2	85.7	90.1	99.6	91.9	105.8	85.9
1985	71.0	84.8	79.5	85.3	90.4	96.5	92.7
1986	60.8	74.2	68.4	67.4	65.0	96.3	85.4
1987	53.3	73.6	65.1	63.1	66.7	107.7	60.2
1987							
August	54.6	71.2	66.1	63.5	69.6	120.0	64.3
September	53.5	71.1	65.3	62.8	71.5	121.1	64.6
October	53.9	73.3	64.3	62.2	73.6	120.0	65.0
November	49.3	73.9	61.7	60.4	73.6	104.9	64.2
December	49.0	74.7	61.4	60.1	67.3	80.2	63.3
1988							
January	49.4	76.9	59.1	61.6	72.6	76.6	62.9
February	50.9	78.0	60.7	67.2	79.0	85.9	62.9
March	51.7	76.9	59.8	66.8	80.1	104.2	62.7
April	52.3	78.3	59.1	66.3	79.7	121.4	62.2
May	55.1	78.0	60.0	64.9	80.0	131.7	62.4
June	57.0	80.7	60.3	65.2	81.4	145.0	63.2
July	61.1	80.7	62.7	66.3	83.9	193.3	64.2

Source: Morgan Guaranty Trust Company, *World Financial Markets*, August 1988.
Note: Index numbers, 1980-82 average = 100.

Technical Analysis

Technical analysis—long used in commodity trade and the stock market—investigates the behavior of currency price movements based on historical trends and by using graphical techniques.[12] The analysis does not explain reasons for an exchange rate level, but indicates the expected trend.

Technical analysis assumes that prices contain all the available information, they do not move randomly, but according to definite trends, thus future prices will not differ much from the past, and price movements over period of time occur in cycles of varying sizes. Historic price development is generally represented in the form of a line graph, a bar-chart, or a point and figure chart. A distinction is made between longer-term trends that can last a year or more, and short-term trends. Chart reading is based on experience in interpreting various types of graphs rather than on science.

In forecasting, analysts search for support and resistance levels by using various confirmation indicators. Support and resistance levels are price levels that have formed the lower and upper boundaries in earlier price movements and will probably continue to do so in the shorter term. In addition, there are the momentum and the overbought/oversold indicators. Momentum indicators can give a good indication of when an exchange rate is an overbought or oversold level. In this respect, it fulfills the same function as an overbought/oversold indicator (percentage differential between actual rate and a moving average).

74 Technical models generate buy and sell signals. In its simplest form,

Hong Kong	Indonesia	Korea	Malaysia	Phillippines	Singapore	Taiwan	Israel	Turkey
95.0	96.2	97.6	113.9	96.1	101.8	94.6	120.8	94.2
99.5	96.0	96.5	119.7	107.9	102.5	97.1	119.5	89.6
103.3	93.7	88.7	115.7	114.1	95.2	94.3	106.5	88.8
93.3	70.6	82.0	94.0	89.8	79.8	88.4	100.7	70.6
89.2	53.9	84.0	87.9	86.5	73.3	93.4	97.2	62.6
89.5	55.1	86.1	88.5	88.3	74.3	97.4	99.7	63.2
90.2	54.0	85.0	88.4	87.1	73.6	97.4	99.8	61.7
90.0	54.3	85.7	87.1	89.2	73.1	98.1	100.6	60.8
89.1	52.8	85.3	84.9	87.4	72.0	94.9	99.3	58.7
87.2	51.1	84.4	82.8	87.8	70.2	96.0	99.0	62.4
85.8	51.0	85.4	81.5	87.5	70.1	95.6	100.2	62.9
85.9	51.7	88.0	80.8	87.6	70.8	96.2	101.4	63.4
86.5	50.9	89.1	80.2	87.4	70.3	95.0	102.0	64.4
86.6	50.5	89.3	79.7	86.4	70.3	94.6	102.5	65.1
88.5	50.8	90.4	79.4	87.8	70.3	94.3	104.5	64.7
90.2	51.8	92.5	80.8	90.8	70.6	93.0	105.5	65.0
90.8	53.4	95.4	81.6	94.5	71.5	94.9	109.1	66.1

the filter rule for technical models states: Sell if the exchange rate has fallen by more than x percent since its last peak and buy if the rate has climbed x percent above the last low point.

Short- and Long-Term Models

The short-run, or liquidity, view of the exchange rate emphasizes the role of asset (or money) markets' equilibrium, expectations, and the high degree of capital mobility. Some models view the exchange rate's short-term effects on expectations and capital flows and its long-term effects on competitiveness. A long-term view of exchange-rate determination is formulated in terms of monetary and real factors. Here the critical assumptions are that (1) real as well as monetary factors are important in determining the behaviour of exchange rates and (2) purchasing power parity restores equilibrium in traded goods and the monetary sectors.

Over time the exchange rate is determined by the interaction between goods markets and asset markets. The approach does not preclude the role of real monetary factors because these must enter as determinants of the demand for cash balances, thus exerting an effect on the exchange rate. The long-run equilibrium of exchange rates requires that all markets clear: that is, money stock and goods markets are in equilibrium, and purchasing power parity holds. Any of these conditions might not hold in the short run, and exchange rates therefore can depart from long-run equilibrium. See Figure 3–2.

75

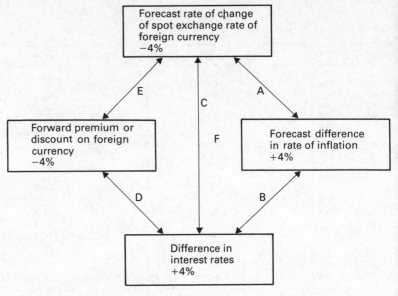

Source: David Eiteman and Arthur Stonehill, *Multinational Business Finance*, fourth edition (Reading, Mass.: Addison-Wesley, 1986).

Assumptions:

1. Spot exchange rate today: £1.00 = $1.4000.
2. Forward exchange rate (one year): £1.00 = $1.3440.
3. Forward discount on pound = $[(1.3440 - 1.4000)/1.4000] \times 100 = -4\%$.
4. Forecast spot exchange rate in one year: £1.00 = $1.3440.
5. Forecast rate of change of spot exchange rate for pound: -4%.
6. Forecast rate of inflation for one year: U.S. = 4%; U.K. = 8%.
7. Forecast difference in rate of inflation: +4%.
8. Interest rates on one-year government maturities: U.S. = 7%; U.K. = 11%.
9. Difference in interest rates: +4%.

Five theories underlie the relationships illustrated

1. The Theory of Purchasing Power Parity (Relationship A).
2. The Fisher Effect (Relationship B).
3. The International Fisher Effect (Relationship C).
4. The Theory of Interest Rate Parity (Relationship D).
5. The forward rate as an unbiased predictor of the future spot rate (Relationship E).

Figure 3–2. Theoretical Relationship among Spot Exchange Rates, Forward Rates, Interest Rates, and Inflation Rates.

Foreign-Exchange Management

Since March 1973 the exchange-rate system has been floating but managed to varying degrees by the monetary authorities, both through direct and indirect intervention. Different countries attach varying degrees of importance to exchange-rate stability and, in turn, exercise different exchange-rate policies. These diverging policies stem, in part, from differences among countries in the degree of their openness (that is, relative share of imports in GNP, which affects the importance of the exchange rate as a price that influences the economy).

Four main objectives are met by foreign-exchange market intervention: (1) to prevent disorderly markets by resisting short-term currency rate changes; (2) to counteract medium- and long-term variations in the exchange rate in order to affect trends in the currency rate; (3) to establish either a moving or fixed exchange-rate target or to intervene if the exchange level is not consistent with official monetary policy or if the exchange level does not appropriately reflect future trends because private market participants do not have sufficient information; and (4) to speed up real adjustments in the balance of payments and the economy, to affect domestic money supply, or to affect international reserves.

Intervention involves four major methods: (1) purchases or sales of foreign exchange in the market by a central bank or monetary authority; (2) official or quasi-official borrowing or lending denominated in foreign currencies; (3) various forms of controls on foreign transactions and payments; and (4) indirect intervention through monetary and fiscal policy measures. The first intervention method is the most common, while the last exerts a major influence on the exchange market by affecting short-term capital flows.

The case for intervention becomes stronger as the potential cost of wide exchange-rate fluctuations increases. Exchange management is necessary if the free-market forces could lead in the short run to excessive fluctuations. Intervention seeks to reduce the expected volatility of exchange rates. Exchange intervention targets may be stated in terms of bilateral rates or effective or weighted-average rates, or in relation to predetermined central rates. Intervention requires that the monetary authorities act as sellers (or buyers) of foreign exchange and buyers (or sellers) of domestic currency. Intervention is most likely to occur when disorderly market conditions develop: The market becomes extremely one-sided, large exchange-rate movements take place on little trading volume, traders are unwilling to make quotations for certain currencies, bid-offer quotations widen for a given currency, and rate movements tend to accumulate in one direction. When traders are unwilling to acquire a given currency, disorderly markets could move exchange rates without regard for underlying economic conditions and thus impede normal commercial and financial transactions.

Yet in other cases the authorities are committed to intervene in their exchange markets under international or regional agreements (such as pegged exchange-rate arrangements or agreements within the European Monetary System). The European Monetary System is a regionally fixed but adjustable exchange-rate system that floats against the rest of the world. Members of the EMS have fixed central cross-exchange rates and intervene to maintain their parities. Intervention is conducted in dollars and each other's currencies.

Since 1973 intervention in the foreign-currency market has been an important feature of the exchange system, although its nature and pattern varies from country to country. Evidence shows that active exchange-rate policy management does not necessarily ensure exchange-rate stability or desired exchange level, but policy becomes more effective when it is accompanied by fiscal and monetary measures. Current exchange markets are characterized by active exchange-rate management and substantial currency rate movements.

In most countries, information about direct official intervention in foreign-exchange markets is not made public. The magnitude of intervention generally can be assessed only through an examination of changes in international reserves, although this measure of intervention has several limitations.

The United States Intervention System

When a foreign central bank intervenes by selling dollars and buying domestic currency, for example, it finances the dollar sales from its international reserve holdings or obtains financing by borrowing from a variety of sources—from private financial institutions, from official institutions (such as the IMF), or under swap networks (such as the Federal Reserve and the EMS). By contrast, when a central bank intervenes by buying foreign-exchange shares and selling its own currency, it creates domestic liquidity and accumulates international reserves.

In the case of the United States, almost all the Federal Reserve (the Fed) borrowing for intervention has been through the swap network, which enables the Fed and its participating countries to acquire foreign currencies needed for market intervention. The network is a set of short-term reciprocal currency agreements of $30 billion that the Federal Reserve maintains with fourteen foreign central banks and the Bank for International Settlements (BIS). Each agreement allows the Federal Reserve and the foreign bank short-term access to the other's currency up to a specified limit. Since 1973 the Federal Reserve and other central banks have used the swap lines on numerous occasions to finance exchange-market interventions. See Table 3–10.

The U.S. Treasury has also established temporary swap lines to facilitate operations of the Exchange Stabilization Fund (ESF). The Treasury, with the Federal Reserve Bank of New York acting as the agent, can participate with the Federal Reserve in its intervention activities. The Treasury can also obtain foreign exchange by borrowing from the International Monetary Fund, by selling foreign-denominated securities, and by selling gold and special drawing rights.

U.S. intervention is conducted mainly through the swap system, under which drawings can be held only by mutual consent. A drawing usually will be initiated by a telephone call, followed by an exchange of cables specifying terms and conditions. Technically, a swap consists of a spot and a forward foreign-exchange transaction. The Federal Reserve

Table 3–10.
FEDERAL RESERVE RECIPROCAL CURRENCY
ARRANGEMENTS, (millions of dollars).

Institution	Amount of Facility, April 30, 1988	Amount of Facility, January 31, 1980
Austrian National Bank	250	250
National Bank of Belgium	1,000	1,000
Bank of Canada	2,000	2,000
National Bank of Denmark	250	250
Bank of England	3,000	3,000
Bank of France	2,000	2,000
German Federal Bank	6,000	6,000
Bank of Italy	3,000	3,000
Bank of Japan	5,000	5,000
Bank of Mexico	700	700
Netherlands Bank	500	500
Bank of Norway	250	250
Bank of Sweden	300	300
Swiss National Bank	4,000	4,000
Bank of International Settlements:		
Swiss francs/dollars	600	600
Other authorized European currencies/ dollars	1,250	1,250
Total	30,100	30,100

Source: Federal Reserve Bulletin July 1988.

sells dollars spot for the currency of the foreign central bank and simultaneously contracts to buy back the dollars forward for the same amount of foreign currency on or before the maturity date three months later. Drawings can be rolled over for additional three-month periods by mutual agreement.

The agreements establishing swap lines are limited to one year but have been renewed annually, by mutual consent, for additional one-year periods. Swaps mature in ninety days. They are retired by repurchasing the foreign bank's dollars. The Federal Reserve gives the foreign central bank a dollar amount equal to the size of the intervention and receives sufficient foreign exchange to cover its dollar purchase. The foreign bank's dollars are then invested in a nonnegotiable U.S. Treasury certificate or indebtedness until the swap is retired.

U.S. intervention is carried out on a day-to-day basis by officers at the foreign-exchange desk at the Federal Reserve Bank of New York, under authorization and a directive from the Federal Open Market Committee (FOMC), which consults closely with the U.S. Treasury. Intervention is conducted indirectly through the brokers' market via commercial bank agents and directly through commercial banks.

The techniques of central bank foreign-exchange intervention vary from country to country. For countries in which foreign-exchange brokers operate, some central banks actively participate and intervene in the broker market. Others deal directly with commercial banks. A few central banks approach the brokers' market indirectly through a 79 commercial bank that acts as agent. This approach enables the central bank to limit the visibility of its operations.

In January 1985 the finance ministers and central bank of the Group of Five (G5) countries (France, the Federal Republic of Germany, Japan, the United Kingdom, and the United States) reaffirmed their commitment to undertake coordinated intervention as necessary. At a meeting at the Plaza Hotel in New York on September 22, 1985, the finance ministers and central bank governors of the five major industrial countries agreed that the currency levels did not reflect underlying economic conditions and that a further appreciation of the nondollar currencies against the dollar would be desirable. Accordingly, the G5 intervened in the foreign-exchange markets toward that end. [13] Absence of a coherent framework for macroeconomic coordination reduced the effectiveness of currency management, however, and on February 22, 1987, the six major industrial countries, or the Group of Six (G6), convened at the Louvre in Paris against the background of increased volatility in the international financial markets and reached an agreement to promote adjustment and to stabilize the exchange rates. [14] For the first time the agreement covered both economic policy and exchange rates.

Experience with Floating Exchange Rates

The foreign-exchange markets have been characterized by considerable volatility and uncertainty since the adoption of floating rates in 1973. Both divergent economic performance by the major countries and currency diversification contributed to unsettled conditions that can be measured by several criteria. First, exchange-rate movements were at times far greater than the corresponding movements in domestic price levels. Markets at times overreacted to changing circumstances and moved exchange rates beyond underlying equilibrium levels. Second, exchange markets have not been reasonably accurate in anticipating short- or medium-term trends in the exchange-rate movements.

In the 1980s currencies experienced short-term volatility in terms of variability and size of standard deviation of the daily exchange-rate movements. In April 1985, for example, day-to-day movements of the dollar/deutsche mark rate exceeded 1 percent on half of the working days, and those of the dollar/sterling rate on two-thirds of the working days. Daily movements of the dollar/yen rate also became larger during February and April 1985 but not to the same extent as for the deutsche mark and sterling. See Table 3–11 for more information.

There are substantial economic costs when exchange rates fluctuate widely over the short run: (1) Transaction costs associated with covered interest arbitrage increase compared with the previous periods, and (2) market spreads between the bid and offer quotations widen, reflecting

Table 3–11.
DAILY VARIABILITY OF SELECTED DOLLAR EXCHANGE
RATES.[a]

Periods	Deutsche Mark	Japanese Yen monthly figures	Pound Sterling
1982 (average)	3 (0.66)	4½ (0.76)	2 (0.59)
1983 (average)	2 (0.55)	1 (0.52)	1½ (0.53)
1984			
January-July (average)	3 (0.66)	1 (0.42)	2 (0.55)
August	3 (0.71)	– (0.50)	2 (0.60)
September	7 (1.41)	– (0.43)	7 (1.19)
October	4 (0.74)	1 (0.40)	4 (0.70)
November	3 (0.84)	– (0.41)	2 (0.83)
December	– (0.51)	– (0.30)	1 (0.49)
1985			
January	1 (0.48)	– (0.31)	5 (0.71)
February	3 (1.21)	4 (0.70)	6 (1.09)
March	7 (1.07)	2 (0.54)	8 (1.48)
April	11 (1.30)	3 (0.67)	14 (1.53)
May	9 (1.13)	0 (0.40)	5 (0.99)
June	6 (0.83)	0 (0.30)	5 (0.94)
July	7 (0.87)	2 (0.57)	8 (0.99)
August	3 (0.70)	0 (0.28)	9 (1.28)
September	9 (1.64)	3 (1.43)	9 (1.79)
October	4 (0.63)	2 (0.74)	2 (0.50)
November	1 (0.53)	2 (0.81)	2 (0.60)
December	2 (0.53)	0 (0.35)	3 (0.64)
1986			
January	3 (0.68)	2 (0.61)	6 (0.86)
February	5 (0.76)	8 (1.07)	9 (1.06)
March	6 (0.88)	4 (0.069)	6 (1.04)
April	6 (1.09)	5 (0.92)	5 (0.74)

[a]Variability is measured by the number of days within a month on which exchange exceed 1 percent. Figures in brackets are the standard deviations of day-to-day percentage changes in exchange rates.
Source: Bank for International Settlements, *Fifty-sixth Annual Report* Basle, 1986.

the higher risk involved in doing business at that time. The greater the risk perceived, the wider the bid–offer spread.

The floating exchange rates often require substantial official exchange-rate intervention to create stable conditions. Opponents of flexible rates argue that the instability of floating rates contributes to poor economic performance in the world, whereas proponents maintain that the volatility and instability of exchange rates are primarily symptoms of the instability of the underlying economic and financial fundamentals.

Floating exchange rates have not solved the underlying international financial problems that led to their adoption, nor have they completely freed countries from the effects of those problem. The evidence to date shows that despite substantial nominal as well as real exchange-rate movements, large balance-of-payments imbalances persist, raising doubts about how efficient the flexible-exchange-rate system is in facilitating international adjustments. It seems, however, that the limited impact of the recent exchange-rate changes on the balance-of-payments adjustment mechanism is attributable to two main factors: the inadequate application of domestic policies and short- and medium-term lags in the major industrial economies. Exchange-rate changes can induce a balance-of-payments adjustment over a short- and medium-term period only if domestic policies are applied in the same direction. In the absence of appropriate domestic policies, currency adjustment fails to improve the balance of payments, and in some cases it can aggravate the rate of inflation.

Relative price changes brought by exchange-rate movements have a strong effect on the volume of foreign trade, but only after a considerable time lag. The evidence suggests that divergent cyclical economic trends have had a larger effect on the currency-account performance than changes in nominal or real exchange rates. Exchange-rate movements have been offset by inadequate domestic policies, by lagged responses—both short- and medium-term—to relative price changes, and by divergent cyclical developments in different countries.

Reconciliation of the Various Exchange-Rate Theories

There is no single theory of exchange-rate determination, but the determination of equilibrium exchange rate, although difficult, is useful as an analytical concept. Different theories or factors explain alternative aspects of currency-rate movements that can be reconciled as explaining an interactive process that needs to be viewed as a whole. Although an interdependent and comprehensive approach to exchange-rate determination is the most appropriate, various exchange-rate theories could apply to different time horizons or involve different variables, reflecting different views of exchange-rate determination and different economic theories.

There is no generally accepted theory or model of exchange-rate determination, but four main approaches provide a general framework for analysis of exchange rates: (1) traditional income expenditure theory; (2) asset-market and monetarist theory; (3) general equilibrium and portfolio theory; and (4) subsidiary theories and subsets of the major theories.

As a complete and exclusive analysis of foreign exchange, some regard the traditional theories as incomplete or faulty. However, each of these theories has a strong and valid element under well-defined circumstance and appropriate interpretation.

In the short term, exchange rates are determined mainly by the monetary asset-market mechanism and expectations. The exchange rate is considered the relative price of different national currencies, rather than national output, and it is determined mainly by demand for and supply of different national monies and financial assets (stocks and flows). The currency rate is influenced by expectations of future exchange rates or real and monetary economic factors and policies that determine the trade balance and relative prices. The asset-market model "extends the monetary model because one does not have to rely on shifts in money demand or supply as sole determinants of exchange-rate movements but rather can consider shifts between domestic and foreign assets as motivated by, for instance, expectations."[15]

In the long-term context, both monetary and real factors jointly affect the exchange rate. The monetary expansion is matched by a price increase so that real balances and interest rates are unchanged, and spot and forward rates depreciate in the proportion as increases in the nominal quantity of money—that is, according to quantity-theory PPP principles. Exchange rates respond to changes in real economic conditions that require adjustments in the relative prices of different national outputs, as well as to changes in monetary conditions. Therefore, the PPP does not provide a guide for day-to-day fluctuations of exchange rates but can be valid in the long run if the economy does not experience structural change that require adjustments of relative prices. However, it takes considerable time for improved competitiveness in the goods markets to be fully reflected in trade flows.

Financial and monetary markets can adapt to changes in circumstances more rapidly than goods markets. Indeed, for the short run the exchange rate is dominated by the asset markets and specifically by capital mobility and money-market equilibrium. Arbitrage of traded goods prices and goods markets equilibrium is attained only over time. In the short run, the scope for goods arbitrage can be limited, and accordingly the purchasing power parity might apply only to a limited set of commodities. "Under these conditions, it is useful to abstract altogether from the detail of goods markets and view exchange rates as being determined entirely in the asset market."[16]

The currency account of the balance of payments determines the evolution of the exchange rate over time. A surplus implies accumulation of net external assets that leads to an appreciating exchange rate. The longer the time horizon being considered "the greater the potential size and importance of cumulative flows of assets, and the stronger influence of current account factors on the equilibrium value of the currency."[17]

The asset-market approach suggests that an analysis of exchange rates should be conducted in a general macroeconomic framework. An integrated exchange-rate model assumes relationships among exchange rates, interest rates, and relative prices. Accordingly, in equilibrium under perfect conditions, interest rates, prices, and forward and spot exchange rates are interdependent in a manner such that the purchasing power parity, interest-rate parity, and the expectations of the forward exchange rate are determined.

Finally, reconciliation of the various theories of exchange-rate determination can be attempted by applying them to various time horizons. For instance, elements of the traditional approach are implicitly integrated in the general equilibrium and portfolio models. This is in essence a long-term framework of currency-rate determination. The asset-market framework and monetary theory relate primarily to the short term. An alternative but less effective method of reconciliation of the various exchange-rate theories classifies the various theories along monetary and nonmonetary type models. Finally, statistical indicators can be derived from the various theories and applied in an ad hoc manner. Figure 3–2 provides practical interpretation of exchange-rate determination.

SUMMARY

Throughout the 1980s, international capital flows have dominated developments in exchange rates and produced excessive currency movements that significantly affect the international competitiveness and trade flows of the major countries. Exchange-rate fluctuations over the past ten years have been much larger than could be reasonably explained by changes in underlying conditions. Misaligned exchange rates and balance-of-payments disequilibrium have increased protectionist pressures and the debt-servicing problems of developing countries. These problems lead some to question the adequacy of the international monetary system and to propose policies to improve its functioning and diminish exchange-rate volatility. The successful operation of the EMS is often cited as a model for a more stable exchange-rate system.

There is a broad consensus that the functioning of the floating exchange-rate system needs to be improved, but two recent official studies ruled out any return to a fixed exchange-rate system.[18]

The Group of Ten concluded that the floating exchange-rate system functioned reasonably well in facilitating balance-of-payments adjustment, insulated economies from external shock, and helped maintain a free trading system. The group rejected fundamental reform of the international monetary system but suggested that improvements could be made within the present framework, largely through national policies, international coordination, and strengthened IMF surveillance.

The Group of Twenty-four report concluded that the present system of exchange rates has not been satisfactory because of excessive currency volatility, large and persistent misalignment of exchange rates, lack of discipline and coordination in the conduct of macroeconomic policy in the major countries, and divergent economic performance among them.

Three types of proposals for improving the functioning of the existing system have emerged:[19]

1 Adopting target zones for key currency exchange rates;
2 Introducing objective indicators or quantitative targets for macroeconomic policy and performance into multilateral IMF surveillance;
3 Using the consultation mechanisms within the existing system.

The first two proposals would move the system toward automaticity and centralization in adjustment and coordination. The third proposal retains the discretionary decentralized character of the exchange system but relies on cooperation among member countries.

The Group of Twenty-four expressed the view that target zones could help achieve the objective of exchange-rate stability and sustainable external equilibrium. The group also considered the adoption of a set of indicators or targets in the conduct of surveillance. It accorded a high priority to maintaining a reasonable degree of exchange-rate stability and called for improved' international policy coordination and a strengthening of the surveillance role of the IMF. The Group of Twenty-four also recommended a trigger mechanism that, in the event of excessive instability or serious misalignment, would automatically give rise to consultation procedures. The report envisioned a greater role for official exchange-market intervention.[20]

NOTES

1. An eligible value date must be a business day in the home countries of the currencies transacted. For a spot transactions on Monday, value date would be Wednesday, on Tuesday it would be Thursday, and so forth. Whenever there are ineligible days such as weekends, the value date moves forward to the next eligible business day. For a spot transaction on Thursday the value date would be Monday, and on Friday it would be Tuesday.
2. R. M. Kubarych, *Foreign Exchange Markets in the United States*, revised edition (New York: Federal Reserve Bank of New York, 1983).
3. I. H. Giddy, "Measuring the World Foreign Exchange Market," *Columbia Journal of World Business* 14(4) (1979): 36–48.
4. T. Nakamura, "The Test of a Currency Is Who Trades in It," *Euromoney* (1980): 168–72.
5. H. R. Heller, "International Role of the Dollar: An Analysis of Long-Term Trends," Bank of America memo, San Francisco (May 1980).
6. I. H. Giddy and Group of Thirty, *Foreign Exchange Markets under Floating Rates* (New York: Group of Thirty, 1980). Alternative estimates by commercial and official banking sources suggested that global foreign-exchange trading in 1977 amounted to $30 to $50 trillion. Heller suggested a $60 to $70 trillion trade volume for 1978.
7. Federal Reserve Bank of New York, *Summary of Results of U.S. Foreign Exchange Market Turnover Survey Conducted in March 1986* (New York: Federal Reserve Bank, 1986).
8. Bank of England, "The Market in Foreign Exchange in London," Press Notice (August 20, 1986).
9. IMF, *International Financial Statistics* (September 1988).
10. P. Isard, *Exchange Rate Determination: A Survey of Popular Views and Recent Models*, Princeton Studies in International Finance No. 42 (Princeton, N.J.: International Finance Section, Department of Economics, Princeton University, 1978).

11. The effective exchange rate is an index that shows the change in any currency against its major trading partners. It measures a currency's performance in relation to other currencies and reflects trends in international competitiveness. Effective exchange rates have gained broad acceptance in official exchange rate policies. Effective exchange indexes have been developed by the IMF, U.S. Treasury, Federal Reserve Board, Morgan Guaranty Trust Company, U.K. Treasury, and others. The various indexes vary in the number of countries and their statistical approach.

A weighted-average index involves the multiplication of index numbers by weights and a summation of these components. Indexes of effective exchange rates are based on weights for the various currencies that approximate the relative importance of the partner currencies. The most widely used weighting systems are the multilateral system, in which each currency is weighted in proportion to the partner country's share in world trade or trade among the industrial countries, and the bilateral system, in which the weights are proportional to each partner's bilateral share of the country's trade. For instance, calculations of the effective exchange rates based on the IMF's multilateral exchange-rate model (MERM) considers the implicit weight structure of the relative importance of a country's trading partners in its bilateral relationship.

An additional index of interest is the real effective exchange-rate index, which is calculated by adjusting the effective exchange index by the weighted inflation rate (that is, inflation differentials weighted by the same weights that are used in deriving the effective exchange rates), where

EM = the weighted average of percentage changes in the dollar cost of individual foreign currencies

$\$/FCI$ = the percentage of change in the dollar cost of foreign currency i

$MI/\Sigma M$ = U.S. imports from country i, as a proportion of total U.S. imports from all countries in the set

The next equation is used to calculate a trade-weighted average of changes in the foreign-exchange cost of dollars:

$$Ex = \Sigma \left(\frac{\Delta fci}{\$}\right)\left(\frac{xi}{Ex}\right)$$

where

Ex = the weighted average of percentage changes in the foreign currency cost of dollars

= the percentage change in the foreign currency i cost of dollars

= U.S. exports to country i, as a proportion of total U.S. exports to all countries in the set

The following equation combines the above export-weighted and import-weighted averages to provide an overall measure of exchange-rate change:

$$E = -(Em)\frac{m}{m+x}(Ex)\frac{x}{m+x}$$

where

$m/(m + x) =$ U.S. imports as a proportion of total trade with all countries in
   the set

$x/(m + x) =$ U.S. exports as a proportion of total trade with all countries in
   the set. The countries in the set are Australia, Austria, Belgium-
   Luxembourg, Canada, Denmark, Finland, France, Germany, Greece,
   Iceland, Ireland, Italy, Japan, the Netherlands, New Zealand,
   Norway, Portugal, Spain, Sweden, Switzerland, Turkey, United
   Kingdom

For further discussion of the index see Morgan Guaranty Trust Company,
"Dollar Index Confusion," *World Financial Markets* (October–November
1986), and Manufacturing Hanover Economic Report, *Why Our Trade
Gap Persists* (September 1986).

12. ABN Bank, "Forecasting the U.S. Dollar, Part II: Using Technical
   Analysis," *ABN Economic Review* (October 1985).
13. Bank for International Settlements (BIS), *Fifty-sixth Annual Report* (Basle:
   BIS, 1986).
14. International Monetary Developments, *OECD Economic Outlook* 41 (June
   1987): 55–61.
15. Dornbusch, R., "Monetary Policy Under Exchange Rate Flexibility," in
   Frenkel, J. A. and H. G. Johnson (Eds). *Managed Exchange Rate Flexibility:
   The Recent Experience*, Federal Reserve Bank of Boston. Conference Series
   No. 20, Boston, 1978.
16. *Ibid.*
17. Crockett, A., "Determinants of Exchange Rate Movements: A Review."
   Finance and Development, March 1982.
18. Andrew Crockett and Morris Goldstein, *Strengthening the International
   Monetary System: Exchange Rates, Surveillance, and Objective Indicators*, Occasional Paper 50 (Washington D.C.: IMF, February 1987).
19. *Ibid.*, pp. 1–3.
20. *Ibid.* See also William Williamson, *Target Zones and the Management of the
   Dollar*, Brookings Papers on Economic Activity 1 (1986), pp. 165–74.

APPENDIX:

Foreign-Exchange Formulas and How to Operate in the Currency Market

CHRISTOPHER S. BOURDAIN

HOW RATES ARE QUOTED

The quotation of foreign-exchange rates is always expressed as a bid–ask spread: the price one is willing to pay for a unit of currency and the price at which one is willing to sell a unit of the same currency. Most currencies are commonly quoted against the U.S. dollar in indirect, or European terms—that is, in units of foreign currency bid or asked for one dollar. One might see the going dollar/deutsche mark rate quoted as

$$\$/DM: 1.7400/1.7410 \; \textit{or} \; 1.7400/10 \; \text{(European terms)}$$

One can just as easily quote this exchange relationship in direct, or U.S. terms—that is, dollars bid or asked per unit of foreign currency. All that is required is to reverse the bid/ask order and take the reciprocals:

$$\frac{1}{1.7410} \; \frac{1}{1.7400} = 0.5744/0.5747 \; \text{(U.S. terms)}$$

Currency futures and listed options contracts in the United States, along with retail (banknote) exchange, would commonly quote deutsche mark/dollar in this way.

· Elsewhere, some currencies, primarily those of the United Kingdom and many former dependencies, are commonly quoted against the U.S. dollar in U.S. terms. For example, a sterling/dollar quote of 1.7140/50 shows that £1 = \$1.7140/50. The rate expresses dollars bid/asked for one pound sterling.

CALCULATION OF SPOT CROSS-RATES

For those based in the United States, a cross-rate means the exchange rate of one nondollar currency against another nondollar currency. Whether one or both foreign currencies are quoted in U.S. or European terms, the logic of cross-rates remains the same: One must take the selling rate of one currency against the buying rate of the other to arrive at a correct dealing quotation.

Cross-rates for two currencies quoted in European terms against the dollar can always be quoted two ways. For example, if $/DM is 1.7400/10 and $/FFr is 5.9025–75, one can quote the cross-rate as follows:

$$\text{DM/FFr:} \underbrace{\frac{\overbrace{5.9025}^{\text{(FFr sale rate)}}}{\underbrace{1.7410}_{\text{(DM buy rate)}}}}_{} \Bigg/ \underbrace{\frac{\overbrace{5.9075}^{\text{(FFr buy rate)}}}{\underbrace{1.7400}_{\text{(DM sale rate)}}}}_{} = 3.3903/51$$

$$\text{FFr/DM:} \frac{1.7400}{5.9075} \Bigg/ \frac{1.7410}{5.9025} = 0.2945/50$$

If one of the two currencies in a cross-rate is quoted in U.S. terms against the dollar, one has only to multiply the buying rate of the one against the selling rate of the other, and so forth. Sterling/DM would thus be calculated as follows:

$$\text{£/DM: } 1.7140 \times 1.7400/1.7150 \times 1.7410 = 2.9824/58$$

FORWARD SWAPS, PREMIUMS, AND DISCOUNTS

All currency transactions involving exchange or settlement on a future date imply the existence of a swap transaction. A swap is basically a currency repurchase agreement, whereby a party might exchange a currency at a set rate for settlement at one date, with simultaneous agreement to reverse the transaction on some future date at another set rate.

As with all other types of repo, each party in a currency swap is effectively lending one currency and borrowing the other against it. Swap pricing will act similarly to bond pricing in certain respects: The party who is to buy and/or hold the higher-interest-rate currency for the duration of the swap pays a premium to the party who is to hold the lower-interest-rate currency. This premium should exactly neutralize the former's seeming interest advantage and bring the latter back to parity with what he could have earned by keeping his funds in the higher-interest-rate currency all along. If this adjustment were not the case, then anyone with a chance to borrow would borrow in a low-interest currency, sell it out, and buy high-interest rate currencies for set periods via swaps. Swap prices adjust exchange rates to maintain interest-rate parity over time, neutralizing potential distortions in financial markets.

All forward exchange premiums/discounts then really reflect the annualized interest-rate differential between currencies to be exchanged, generally based on the Euro-interest rate for each currency. The actual pricing for a swap is expressed as an absolute quantity of a currency, quoted in points, or ten-thousandths of a unit of currency in most cases. The points will either be added to or subtracted from the rate used for the initial part of the swap (generally, the spot rate), depending on how the exchange rate is quoted and on which currency carries the higher interest rate.

The most easily comprehensible way to calculate a swap rate for a three-month sale and repurchase of DM against dollars would be to set up a simple model: What would be the total amount reimbursed if one were to place DM on deposit for three months, as against the total amount to reimburse if one were to borrow the equivalent amount in dollars for three months? The three-month forward rate for $/DM must equalize whatever these two amounts come out to be.

For this model, one must use the simple interest formula:

$$\frac{\text{Principal} \times \text{Days} \times \text{Interest rate per annum}}{360 \text{ (or 365)}} = \text{interest}$$

With spot $/DM at 1.7400, three-month Euro-DM at 4 percent (bid), three-month Euro-$ at $7\frac{5}{8}$ percent (offered), and a ninety-three-day run from spot until the three-month date, the model would look like this for a notional amount of DM 17,400,000.00:

	DM 17,400,000.—	@1.7400			= $ 10,000,000.00
Interest at 4% for 93 days	= DM 179,800.—		Interest at $7\frac{5}{8}$% for 93 days	= $	196,979.17
DM reimbursement:	17,579,800	(@1.7240)	Dollar reimbursement:		10,196,979.17

Swap = – 0.0160

The three-month forward $/DM rate must render the two theoretical reimbursement amounts equal. Therefore, the rate must be the DM amount divided by the dollar amount (for a forward rate in European terms). As shown in the model, this works out to be 1.7240. The three-month $/DM swap rate as it would be quoted would then be the difference between the forward rate and the spot rate. In the above case, it would work out as DM – 0.0160. or – 160 points. If one were to look at the entire model in U.S. terms, spot would be 0.5747, the forward rate would be 0.5800, and the swap would therefore be $ + 0.0053, or

53 points. In either case, the party selling and buying the low-interest-

rate DM and holding the high-interest-rate dollars for the term of the The Foreign- swap receives a less favorable rate for the forward end of the swap. In Exchange Market this way, he pays the compensatory premium to the forward seller of DM. This is also referred to as "paying the points."

The swap model above is a perfectly proper way to calculate a swap rate and/or forward rate when one knows the Euro-interest rates, the number of days, and the spot rate for a currency. In reality, however, the model does not accurately represent what is occurring under a swap. Under a swap, one of the two currency amounts remains constant, while the other changes only to the extent of the annualized interest rate differential. Adapting the swap model to take this factor into consideration and reducing it algebraically, one arrives at a simple formula for calculating swap rates. From this formula, a host of others derives.

S = Spot rate
D = Number of days
E = Base currency interest rate
I = Foreign currency interest rate

SWAP RATE FORMULA, FOR CURRENCY QUOTED IN EUROPEAN
  TERMS:

$$\frac{S \times D(I - E)}{360 + (D \times E)} = \text{Swap rate} \qquad (3.1)$$

SWAP RATE FORMULA, FOR CURRENCY QUOTED IN U.S. TERMS:

$$\frac{S \times D(E - I)}{360 + (D \times I)} = \text{Swap rate} \qquad (3.2)$$

SWAP RATE FORMULA, WHEN ONE CURRENCY TRADES ON A
  365-DAY BASIS:

$$\frac{S(D \times I) - 365/360 \times S(D \times E)}{365 + (D \times I)} = \text{Swap rate} \qquad (3.3)$$

Staying with currencies trading on a 360-day basis, one can use the basic formulas in different forms depending on which pieces of information are given and which ones one is seeking:

INTEREST RATE DIFFERENTIAL REPRESENTED BY A SWAP
  (SWAP RATE = R):

$$\frac{R(360 + D \times E)}{S \times D} = E - I(\% \text{ p.a.}) \qquad (3.4)$$

SWAP COST/EARNING:

$$\frac{\text{Swap} \times 360}{\text{Spot} \times \text{Days}} = \text{Swap cost} (\% \text{ p.a.}) \qquad (3.5)$$

91

FINDING EURO-RATE I, KNOWING SPOT, THE SWAP, AND
EURORATE E:

$$E - \frac{R(360 + D \times E)}{S \times D} = I(\text{in \% p.a.}) \tag{3.6}$$

It might prove useful to verify all the above formulas with the \$/DM
swap information provided earlier:

$$\frac{1.7400 \times 93 \ (0.04 - 0.07625)}{360 + (93 \times 0.07625)} = -0.0160 \tag{3.1a}$$

$$\frac{0.5747 \times 93 \ (0.07625 - 0.04)}{360 + (93 \times 0.04)} = +0.0053 \tag{3.2a}$$

$$\frac{0.0160 \ (360 + 93 \times 0.07625)}{1.7400 \times 93} = 0.0363 \ \text{(previous figures/rates rounded)} \tag{3.4a}$$

$$\frac{0.0160 \times 360}{1.7400 \times 93} = 0.0356 \ \text{(or, 3.56\%)} \tag{3.5a}$$

$$0.07625 - \frac{0.0160 \ (360 + 93 \times 0.07625)}{1.7400 \times 93} = 0.03995 \tag{3.6a}$$
(previous figures rounded)

A forward outright transaction is one where two parties agree today to
exchange currencies at a set rate on some future date. In appearance, no
swap is involved. In reality, however, there is both a spot transaction
and a swap underlying the "outright" sale or purchase. What the two
parties are in effect doing is a spot exchange transaction and then an
extension of credit in the currency due. A forward outright buyer of
DM is buying DM from the seller, then in effect giving the seller DM
financing, allowing the seller to postpone delivery and use the DM in
the meantime. Meanwhile, the DM buyer does not have to come forth
with the dollar countervalue right away either: He is able to benefit
from the effective dollar credit terms given by the DM seller. The
adjustment that the two parties will make to the spot price is precisely
the swap price as previously illustrated. Because ultimately the exchange
is a one-way trade, however, the spot price used for an outright
transaction must be a correct market bid or offer, not merely an
approximate market-level rate as one might use for the first part of a
swap. If spot \$/DM were quoted as 1.7400–10, and the three-month
\$/DM points as 160/155, then a three-month forward outright DM
quote whereby one could arrange to lock in a DM purchase or sale
would be 1.7240/55. A forward outright buyer of DM in this example
is really buying DM spot at 1.7400, then simultaneously doing a
three-month swap, selling DM spot at 1.7400, and buying them back
forward at 1.7240. Because he benefits from the use of dollars in the
meantime, the outright rate is less favorable for him than the spot rate.

CALCULATING FORWARD CROSS-RATES

The simplest way to calculate forward cross-rates is to work backwards from the forward outright rates in the two currencies concerned. The procedure might appear cumbersome, but the entire calculation can be performed in under a minute. Continuing on the example shown above, one might wish to calculate three-month forward DM/FFr.

Spot $/DM = 1.7400/10
3-month $/DM = 160/155
(swap)
Spot $/FFr = 5.9025/75
3-month $/FFr = 200/300
(swap)

As shown previously, the spot cross-rate for DM/FFr comes out as 3.3903/51. Meanwhile, the three-month points for $/FFr, quoted in European terms, are ascending, indicating that the nondollar currency (FFR) has a higher interest rate than dollars. The points must then be added to the spot rate to derive the forward outright rate. (Descending points, for quotes in European terms such as the $/DM 160/155 quote above, indicate that the nondollar currency has lower interest rates than the dollar: The swap points will therefore be a negative adjustment to the spot rate.)

$$3\text{-month outright } \$/DM = 1.7240/55$$
$$3\text{-month outright } \$/FFr = 5.9225/5.9375$$

$$3\text{-month outright DM/FFr} = \frac{5.9225}{1.7255} / \frac{5.9375}{1.7240} = \underline{3.4323/3.4440}$$

To find out what three-month DM/FFr swap points are worth, one has only to take the difference between the spot cross-rate and the forward outright cross-rate. In the example above, the swap points equal 420/489. Because these cross-rates are using the DM as the base currency, showing FFr bid/asked for one DM, one can determine from the ascending forward swap points that FFr interest rates are higher than the base currency (DM) interest rates.

To determine forward cross-rates when one currency is quoted in U.S. terms, such as sterling against DM, the procedure is much the same: The spot £/DM calculation is illustrated earlier in this appendix.

QUOTING FORWARD RATES FOR "ODD DATES"

Forward swap points are generally quoted in the interbank market for the so-called straight periods over the spot date: One, two, three, six, and twelve months. Dates falling between these periods are known as odd dates, and the calculation of a forward rate for such a date is a fairly simple prorating exercise.

If three-month DM (ninety-three days over spot) is quoted at 160/155, and six-month DM (182 days over spot) is quoted at 290/285, one might figure out the swap rate for 115 days over spot using one of two methods.

1   Figure out how many points there are per day between the three- and six-month dates, the number of days between the three-month date and the odd date, and thus how many points to add to the three-month swap rate.

There are 130 points between the three-month and six-month swap rates on both the bid side and the ask (offered) side. Meanwhile, there are eighty-nine days in this period. $130 \div 89 = 1.46$ points per day between three and six months. 115 days is twenty-two days over the three-month date. Therefore, one must add 1.46×22, or 32 points, to the three-month swap rate to get a 115-day swap rate. One can thus quote 115-day $/DM as 192/187.

2   Divide a nearby straight date swap rate by the number of days in that period, and multiply by the number of days to the odd date.

This method is less precise, although it can work when the yield curves for the two currencies involved are parallel. In the above example, a three-month swap rate of 160/155 implies that there are 1.72/1.67 points per day over the ninety-three-day period. Multiplied by 115, one comes up with a 115-day swap rate of 198/192. This rate is different enough from the rate calculated under the more precise method to cause concern. In fact what is demonstrated is that the $/DM interest-rate differential narrows somewhat between three months and six months because the points per day are greater over the first three-month period than during the three-month against six-month period.

DETERMINING IMPLICIT PROFIT AND LOSS

The liquidation value of outstanding foreign-exchange positions at current rates determines the implicit profit or loss on such positions. If one had bought DM 17,500,000 forward at 1.7500 and could now liquidate this position at a rate of 1.7240, one would have an implicit dollar profit of $150,812.06 (DM amount ÷ transaction rate *minus* DM amount ÷ current available rate).

Profits and losses on positions that one actually closes out are realized on the settlement date of the offsetting transactions. Thus, if in October one bought DM for delivery in February, and then in November one sold the DM back for the same date in February, the profit or loss would be booked in February.

One might have several different outstanding positions in a currency all falling on the same settlement date. Before revaluing at current rates in such a case, one must first determine the net position and the average exchange rate of this position.

For example, one might have the following outstanding positions, all settling three months from spot:

Purchase of DM 30,000,000 at 1.9000 = $15,789,473.68
Purchase of DM 15,000,000 at 1.7500 = $8,571,428.57
Sale of   DM 20,000,000 at 1.8100 = $11,049,723.76
Purchase of DM 30,000,000 at 1.7800 = $16,853,932.58

The net position shown will be long DM 55,000,000 or short $30,165,111.07. Dividing the net DM position by the net dollar position, one arrives at the average rate (in European terms) for the outstanding position: 1.8233. It is this net position at the average rate that will then be revalued at currently available rates for the three-month date. If the holder of the above net position could sell DM 55,000,000 three months forward at today's outright of 1.7255, then his implicit profit on his outstandings revalues as $1,709,707.82.

CANCELLATIONS AND ASSIGNMENTS

Corporations on occasion wish to realize profits or losses from foreign exchange positions before they actually are due to settle; or they might wish to cut down trading limit utilization with a particular counter-party. In such cases they might choose to ask their counterparty to cancel the outstanding exchange contracts; or they might ask a third party to step in and take the outstanding positions from them. Both cancellations and assignments generally require specific legally documented recognition by the parties concerned of what has been done. Meanwhile, calculation of what kind of settlement must be made is nothing more than determining the present value of the outstanding position.

For example, a corporation long DM 55,000,000 with bank *A* for settlement in three months, and with an implicit profit of $1,709,707.82 on the position, might assign the entire position to bank *B*. Bank *B*, then, must determine the present value of the contract(s) it will be taking onto its books. Present value can be determined using the following equation:

$$\frac{\text{Future amount}}{1 + (\text{Interest rate} \times \text{Days}/360)} = \text{Present value}$$

In the three-month example above, if the three-month dollar lending rate is at $7\frac{5}{8}$ percent p.a. and the period in question is ninety-three days long, then present value of $1,709,707.82 will be $1,676,677.28. This is the amount that bank *A* would pay to cancel the outstanding three-month contracts; and this is the amount that bank *B* would pay to take on the contracts as substitute counterparty for bank *A*.

For present valuation beyond one year, yearly compounding must be taken into consideration. The equation for present valuation of an amount due to settle sometime between one and two years forward would thus look like this:

$$\frac{\text{Future amount}}{(1 + (\text{Interest rate} \times \text{Days}/360)) \times (1 + (\text{Interest rate} \times \text{Days}/360))} = \text{Present value}$$

Each additional year would require one more compounding.

4 The International Money and Capital Markets

HARVEY A. PONIACHEK

THE INTERNATIONAL money and capital markets include the Eurocurrency and international bond markets. The markets are parallel to and interdependent with the traditional international domestic money and capital markets, and they are closely linked to the corresponding national markets. These markets differ from both the traditional international and domestic capital markets in regulation, institutional structure, interest-rate determination, flow of funds, and lending and borrowing practices. The Eurocurrency market is closely interdependent with the foreign-exchange market, but the two markets are distinct in function.

The Eurocurrency market is an international financial market for bank deposits and loans denominated in foreign currency. The international bond market—the long-term capital market—is composed of foreign and Eurobond segments. The market is not subject to various national regulations and extends throughout the world.

Yields on Eurocurrency and Eurobond transactions are normally closely related to those prevailing in the national domestic markets unless exchange controls or other factors inhibit arbitrage. However, the international money and capital market has an independent international interest-rate structure, which mirrors the interest rates in the correspondent national financial markets and is greatly affected by them.

The theoretical interpretations of the Eurocurrency market vary considerably and have different implications concerning the market's control. The Euromarkets are frequently alleged to cause excessive monetary creation and to threaten the stability of the international financial system.

Innovations and subsequent changes have reduced the differences between the various sectors of the Euromarket (such as the money, credit and capital markets), between the various currencies, and between the world's important financial centres. There has been an increased integration of international capital markets. The Eurocurrency and international bond markets' growth and expansion depend on demand for their services and on their competitiveness relative to the respective domestic markets. Competitiveness in turn is derived from

97

differences in the regulatory environments (reserve requirements, ceilings on interest payments, and from fiscal incentives, particularly tax) and in operational efficiencies (economies of scale).

Since 1982 the pattern of international financial markets has changed considerably. Syndicated bank lending has declined, and a major shift has occurred toward securitization, with a substantial expansion in the volume of international capital-market issues. The trend toward securitization will continue, with the result of further erasure of demarcation lines between the various sectors of the Euromarket. Banks remain active as intermediaries and large-scale buyers and issuers of securities.

International bank lending continues to be characterized by a substantial amount of both "involuntary" lending to LDCs under officially sponsored credit packages and lending to industrial countries. The market issued increasing volumes of securitized debt instruments of Eurobonds and Euronotes, and new borrowing instruments were developed to accommodate individual requirements.

New financial facilities—together with new techniques that keep refinancing costs low, such as currency and interest-rate swaps and option and futures contracts—tend to further obscure the differences between short- and long-term financing, between credits and bonds, as well as between different credit currencies.

THE EUROCURRENCY MARKET

Eurocurrencies or Eurocurrency deposits (and loans) are bank deposits (and loans) denominated in currencies other than those of the countries in which the issuing banks are located; the Eurocurrency market is the market for these deposits and loans. For instances, a Eurodollar deposit is a time deposit denominated in dollars in a bank outside the United States, and a Eurodollar loan is a dollar-denominated loan issued by a bank located outside the United States. Likewise, Euro-deutsche mark deposits (and loans) and Euro-Swiss franc deposits (and loans) are deutsche mark- and Swiss franc-denominated deposits (and loans) made outside Germany and Switzerland, respectively.

The Eurocurrency market comprises Eurobanks that are located worldwide, and not in a geographically defined area. Despite the domestic connotation, the market is not located in Europe, although the main market is located there. Other rapidly growing Eurocurrency markets exist in Canada, Japan, the Bahamas, the Cayman Islands, Panama, Hong Kong, Singapore, and Bahrain.

Eurocurrency deposits are created when a domestic company places them on deposit offshore. For instances, a Eurodollar deposit arises when the owner of a dollar-denominated deposit in the United States deposits it abroad in a foreign bank (or in a U.S foreign branch). Although the latter receives title ownership of the original deposit and issues a claim (deposit) against itself denominated in dollars, the dollars are never physically removed from the United States. The Eurocurrency deposits are usually in the form of large short-term time deposits, including negotiable certificates of deposits (CDs), which are issued to banks and nonbanks, resident and nonresident. All Eurocurrency transactions are unsecured credits. Business in the Eurocurrency market is conducted in large sums; the common unit for Eurodollar transactions is $1 million, although smaller amounts of $200,000 to $250,000 are exchanged. The funds offered on the market range in maturity from twenty-four hours to several years.

A Eurocurrency does not necessarily involve a foreign-exchange transaction but involves a transaction in a foreign currency. Nevertheless the transfer of a Eurodeposit is often accompanied by a foreign-exchange transaction, in which the proceeds are switched into some other currency.

The Eurocurrency market constitutes a money market that is parallel to the respective domestic money markets and provides services that compete with and complement those markets. Apart from their location, Eurocurrency deposits (and loans) are essentially identical in characteristics to the deposits (and loans) of a bank in the corresponding domestic markets. Accordingly, Eurodollars (or say, Euro-deutsche mark) deposits (or loans) are not special types of dollars or deutsche mark instruments, and there is nothing to distinguish then from ordinary dollars or deutsche mark deposits (or loans) when they are used for spending purposes.

The Eurocurrency banks are not subject to disadvantaged domestic banking regulations (such as reserve requirements and interest-rate restrictions) and benefit from various fiscal incentives (such as low tax rates) and economies of scale. These factors give Eurobanks a competitive advantage over their domestic counterparts and enable them to attract business from domestic banks by offering better terms to both borrowers and lenders (that is, higher deposit rates and lower lending rates than the corresponding domestic rates). The margin between deposit and lending rates is narrower than the margin in the corresponding domestic money market.

Transactions in the Eurocurrency market involve substantial interbank deposits. For example, a European bank holding a deposit in a U.S. bank may make a Eurodollar deposit with another European bank, which in turn may deposit the proceeds with another bank, and so on. Each redeposit transfers ownership of the original deposit at the U.S. bank and creates new Eurodollar-deposit liabilities on the books of the foreign banks involved. The total Eurodollars so created may be several times the amount of the original claim on the U.S. bank.

Factors Affecting the Markets

The Eurocurrency market emerged primarily because Eurobanks could avoid costs and restrictions that existed in the domestic market and because efficient offshore financial service was needed. Participants can obtain and employ funds that are not subect to the additional costs and regulatory restrictions that the various countries apply. The benefit associated with avoiding reserve requirements, interest-rate restrictions, and higher tax rates yielded an interest advantage shared among the Eurobanks, depositors, and borrowers and the freedom from foreign-exchange restrictions contributed to the development of the Eurocurrency market.

The conditions required for proper functioning of the Eurocurrency market (or any other external financial markets) are (1) freedom from foreign-exchange controls; (2) ability to offer competitive deposits and loan rates; and (3) demand for offshore financial services. These conditions did not exist until the post–World War II recovery of the global economy and the restoration of convertibility of major European currencies in 1958.

The origin of the Eurocurrency market in its present form is traced back to the early 1950s, when the Eastern bloc countries, particularly the Soviet Union, sought to deposit their dollar assets outside the United States to avoid the risk of a seizure of their funds by the United States if East–West relations worsened. Accordingly, they transferred their dollar assets from U.S. to European banks. This move set the initial stage for the creation of the Eurodollar market. Later they were gradually joined by U.S. multinational corporations, individuals, and other governments with sizable dollar holdings that for a variety of reasons wished to keep their holdings outside the United States.

Several major events provided further impetus for the vigorous development of the Euromarket: (1) The pound sterling crisis of 1957, (2) the introduction in 1958 of convertibility for Europe's major currencies, (3) substantial U.S. balance-of-payments deficits, which led to monetary and balance-of-payments controls, and (4) various balance-of-payments policies in the industrial countries.

Relatively large and persistent balance-of-payments deficits led to the impositions of U.S. capital controls, which were in effect from 1963 to 1973 and consisted of (1) the Interest Equalization Tax (IET), (2) the Foreign Direct Investment Program (FDIP), and (3) the Voluntary Foreign Credit Restraint (VFCR) program. These controls blocked foreign borrowers and U.S. multinational corporations from the U.S. money markets and drove them into the Eurocurrency market.

In addition to capital controls, the Federal Reserve System's Regulations Q and D played a significant role in the Eurodollar development and stimulated the growth of the market. These regulations increased the cost of funds and reduced the banks' ability to compete with foreign banks. These factors induced, to a large part, the establishment of overseas branches of U.S. banks and, in turn, promoted the growth of the Eurocurrency market in order to secure funds exempted from these limitations.

Regulation Q established a ceiling on interest rates on time deposits in the United States and forbade member banks to pay interest on deposits with maturities of less than thirty days. Regulation Q was originally designed to protect savings and loans associations from excessive competition from commercial banks. The thrift institutions were considered to be the weaker institutions and to deserve this competitive edge so that they could continue to channel most of their resources into long-term home mortgages.

By contrast, the Euromarket interest rates were determined by market forces of supply and demand and were free of any national regulations. Therefore, the Eurocurrency market provided an alternative to U.S. investors by offering higher interest rates than those prevailing domestically. However, overseas branches of U.S. banks were not subject to Regulation Q.

The Eurodollar banks' ability to offer higher rates than the banks in the United States greatly increased their attractiveness to investors, particularly when domestic money rates were above Regulation Q ceilings. On several occasions, as U.S. interest rates rose, member banks experienced a runoff in deposits from domestic offices due to their inability to compete effectively for domestic funds. Consequently, they turned to their foreign branches, which were not subject to interest-rate ceilings and thus were able to compete for funds. Deposits received at overseas branches were transferred back to the U.S. for use by the domestic offices. Effective in September 1969 the Federal Reserve Board imposed a 10 percent marginal reserve requirement on any increase in the net liabilities of U.S. offices of member banks to their overseas branches above their May 1969 levels, thus reducing the attractiveness of Eurodollar funds. The Monetary Control Act of 1980 gradually phased out and ultimately eliminated all limitations on the maximum rates of interest and dividends that may be payable on deposits and accounts by depository institutions.

Deposits for less than thirty days at U.S. commercial banks that are members of the Federal Reserve System were classified until recently as demand deposits, subject to Regulation D reserve requirements. The Monetary Control Act of 1980 modified Regulation D. It defines a new type of time deposit with a minimum maturity of fourteen days to help improve the ability of domestic banks to compete with Eurocurrency markets. Reserve requirements increase the effective cost of funds. Eurobanks, as well as foreign branches of U.S. banks, are not subject to Regulation D, and this amounts to a substantial cost savings on their sources of funds. Eurobanks are able, on the one hand, to bid for funds by offering competitive rates and maturities tailored to depositors' needs and, on the other hand, to relend or offer these funds at slightly higher rates. Consequently, Eurocurrency deposit rates are normally higher and loan rates lower than those in the domestic market for the corresponding currency. For instance, the Eurodollar rate is largely affected by U.S. interest rates, and it moves jointly with it.

In summary, in the 1960s and early 1970s capital controls and monetary policies sharply curtailed the ability of banks in the United States to lend abroad. These regulations drove U.S. corporations to the Eurodollar market, not only to finance their capital expenditures abroad but also to cover the required repatriation of foreign earnings. Despite the removal of several of the factors that contributed to the growth and development of the Eurocurrency market, the market still contains several characteristics that make it unique and advantageous: (1) U.S. overseas branches are not subject to Regulation D member-bank reserve requirements or to fees of the Federal Deposit Insurance Corporation: and (2) the market could continue to benefit from the geographic, political, and structural advantages—that is, different time zones, lower tax rates, and its wholesale nature.

Characteristics

The Eurocurrency market centers in London and is composed of additional financial centers in Western Europe, the Caribbean, Asia, the United States, and Canada. According to the Bank for International Settlements, the narrow definition of the Eurocurrency market includes the external assets or liabilities denominated in foreign currencies of banks in fifteen reporting European countries, which account for 59 percent of the global market. Table 4–1 shows the market's geographic composition and magnitude.

There has been a secular change in the currency composition of the Eurocurrency market. The U.S. dollar in 1987 accounted for 64 percent of all foreign liabilities of European banks, down from 68 percent in 1986. See Table 4–2 and Figure 4–1.

The gross size of the Eurocurrency market—measured in terms of the external liabilities of banks in the European reporting countries and of the branches of U.S. banks in the offshore centers of the Caribbean and Far East—reached a total of $2,772 billion in 1986. The gross size includes the total foreign-currency liabilities of banks in the above countries vis-à-vis banks and nonbank residents and nonresidents, outside and within the reporting area. The narrowly defined Eurocurrency market—defined in terms of the total assets or liabilities of the reporting European area—reached $1,293 billion, of which 65 percent was denominated in U.S. dollars and 35 percent was denominated in European currencies. Following the U.S. dollar, the deutsche mark was the second most significant currency in the market, amounting to 13 percent of the entire market.

The broadest definition of the gross Eurocurrency market measures The International
the external assets or liabilities denominated in foreign currencies of *Money and*
banks in the reporting European countries, the United States, Canada, *Capital Market*
and Japan, as well as the foreign branches of U.S. banks in the
Caribbean and the Far East. This market reached about $2,772 billion
in June 1986, of which the fifteen reporting European countries
accounted for 61 percent, and the offshore centers for 27 percent—the
second largest center, after London. The market size of each financial
center is shown in Tables 4–1 and 4–2.

The estimated sources and uses statement of the Eurocurrency market
shows the volume of new funds intermediated in the market. This
aggregate is also known as the net size of the Eurocurrency market
because it excludes interbank deposits in the reporting area but makes
allowance for the banks' use of foreign-currency funds for domestic
lending. See Table 4–3.

Suppliers of funds to the Euromarket are commercial banks, central
banks, governments, international monetary institutions, nonfinancial
institutions, and individual investors. Borrowers of funds in the market
include commercial banks, securities brokers and dealers, government
agencies, international corporations, exporters and importers. Industrial countries provide some 70 percent of the sources, and use about
60 percent of the uses; while the rest of the world accounts for the
balance.

There are two fundamental questions regarding the Eurocurrency
market and the conventional definition of national money stock: Is
Eurocurrency money? Whose money is it? All concepts of the U.S. and
European money stock exclude Eurocurrency deposits. However, a case
can be made for treating these deposits as money on the grounds that
they fit into a broad definition of money.

The bulk of Eurocurrency liabilities are time deposits that are
excluded from narrowly defined domestic money supplies. Regardless of
maturity date and unlike demand deposits in domestic currency, the
Eurocurrency deposits cannot be used directly as payments mediums.
Eurocurrency deposits do not constitute money in its narrowly defined
sense of a means of payment and cannot be compared with the narrowly
defined money stock M1.

In fact, the same qualification about the degree of near money of
domestic time and savings deposits and money-market paper applies to
Eurocurrency deposits. These assets have to be liquidated first to
facilitate a payment. Eurodollars have to be converted into a demand
deposit with a bank in the United States to facilitate payments. (These
characteristics make Eurocurrency deposits more likely candidates for
inclusion in the broader monetary aggregates such as M2 and M3 than
in M1.)

Moreover, national money supply usually excludes all interbank
deposits, the bulk of the Eurocurrency market. A large portion of the 103

Table 4-1.

EXTERNAL POSITIONS OF BANKS IN INDIVIDUAL REPORTING COUNTRIES,
IN FOREIGN CURRENCIES AND ECUs (billions of US dollars).

Reporting countries	Amounts outstanding							
	1985 Dec	1986 Sept	1986 Dec I	1986 Dec II	1987 March	1987 June	1987 Sept	1987 Dec
	Assets							
European countries								
Austria	25.9	33.0	35.3	35.3	37.1	37.8	39.2	41.9
Belgium	87.5	105.9	117.6	117.6	127.7	132.3	133.8	155.3
Luxembourg	106.5	128.2	138.3	138.3	147.3	151.4	155.3	178.8
Denmark	10.9	11.3	11.1	11.1	13.0	13.4	14.0	15.7
Finland	5.7	7.7	7.6	7.6	7.3	7.9	8.7	8.4
France	144.4	151.9	167.7	167.7	177.4	188.3	196.1	219.7
Germany	27.5	39.7	41.8	41.8	43.5	46.9	52.0	58.1
Ireland	2.8	3.5	3.4	3.4	3.7	4.3	4.3	5.2
Italy	46.8	42.1	52.1	52.1	50.6	52.6	51.7	58.7
Netherlands	55.8	67.4	68.3	68.3	75.3	79.9	78.9	91.1
Norway	3.8	3.8	5.2	5.2	4.8	5.3	5.3	6.6
Spain	17.4	20.2	20.8	20.8	20.8	20.0	20.9	21.8
Sweden	7.5	10.7	9.2	9.2	12.5	13.6	16.8	14.7
Switzerland	36.6	46.0	46.4	46.4	52.2	54.8	56.3	63.8
United Kingdom	549.7	648.9	666.1	666.1	693.1	715.1	738.6	803.4
Sub-total	1,128.9	1,320.2	1,391.0	1,391.0	1,466.2	1,523.8	1,571.8	1,743.1
Other industrial countries								
Canada	42.8	45.1	49.6	49.6	48.4	46.0	45.9	49.2
Japan	120.9	163.5	207.4	207.4	230.5	253.9	278.1	288.3
(JOM)	–	–	–	69.5	81.2	97.4	111.2	122.9
(Others)	120.9	163.5	207.4	137.9	149.3	156.5	166.9	165.4
United States	16.2	24.4	26.5	26.5	34.5	34.0	41.0	50.7
(IBFs)	8.9	17.2	18.3	18.3	25.5	25.7	30.4	39.9
(Others)	7.3	7.2	8.2	8.2	9.1	8.3	10.6	10.8
Sub-total	179.9	233.0	283.4	283.4	313.5	333.9	365.0	388.2
Other reporting countries[a]	575.8	651.8	705.6	705.6	719.3	753.2	809.1	873.9
Grand Total	1,884.6	2,205.1	2,379.9	2,379.9	2,499.0	2,610.9	2,745.8	3,005.1
	Liabilities							
European countries								
Austria	35.4	43.4	46.9	46.9	48.5	49.7	51.4	57.0
Belgium	98.9	119.5	132.3	132.3	145.0	148.9	149.2	174.6
Luxembourg	98.2	119.3	128.6	128.7	137.0	141.7	145.9	166.1
Denmark	10.8	11.6	10.9	10.9	12.8	13.2	14.2	15.8
Finland	10.4	13.0	13.7	13.7	15.8	17.7	20.0	21.6
France	172.6	188.8	199.4	199.4	208.5	218.8	226.9	250.8
Germany	27.5	37.4	37.8	39.5	39.2	41.9	45.0	51.0
Ireland	4.3	5.4	5.9	5.9	6.4	7.0	6.7	8.0
Italy	57.5	59.2	70.5	70.5	72.2	73.8	72.1	85.6
Netherlands	53.3	65.1	67.3	67.3	74.4	77.1	77.1	85.4
Norway	9.9	12.8	14.3	14.3	14.8	16.3	17.1	18.8
Spain	16.1	17.5	18.3	18.3	19.3	20.9	23.1	24.6
Sweden	17.3	22.0	20.9	20.9	27.9	29.8	33.8	34.0
Switzerland	35.1	42.9	45.6	45.6	50.2	49.9	52.7	56.7
United Kingdom	575.1	679.9	697.9	697.9	728.3	759.1	776.3	833.6
Sub-total	1,222.4	1,437.7	1,510.1	1,511.9	1,600.2	1,665.7	1,711.5	1,883.7
Other industrial countries								
Canada	61.9	61.6	65.5	65.5	64.3	61.8	62.1	67.2
Japan	129.8	192.9	254.5	254.5	269.9	319.3	333.9	368.2
(JOM)	–	–	–	69.7	79.2	100.0	110.2	133.1
(Others)	129.8	192.9	254.5	184.8	190.7	219.3	223.7	235.1
United States	15.4	29.5	29.7	29.7	38.2	38.5	45.2	55.0
(IBFs)	10.2	20.8	22.4	22.4	28.0	30.2	33.9	44.4
(Others)	5.2	8.7	7.3	7.3	10.2	8.2	11.3	10.6
Sub-total	207.0	284.1	349.7	349.7	372.3	419.5	441.2	490.4
Other reporting countries[a]	551.2	624.1	665.4	665.4	686.1	719.9	775.9	829.5
Grand Total	1,980.6	2.346.0	2,525.2	2,527.0	2,658.6	2,805.1	2,928.6	3,203.6

Source: BIS, *International Banking and Financial Market Developments*, May 1988, p. 4.
[a]Except for Hong Kong, includes also the position in domestic currencies

				Estimated exchange rate adjusted changes					
1985 Q4	1986 Q1	1986 Q2	1986 Q3	1986 Q4	1987 Q1	1987 Q2	1987 Q3	1987 Q4	Reporting countries

Assets

1985 Q4	1986 Q1	1986 Q2	1986 Q3	1986 Q4	1987 Q1	1987 Q2	1987 Q3	1987 Q4	Reporting countries
									European countries
2.1	0.5	1.7	2.0	1.9	0.3	1.0	1.5	-1.4	Austria
2.7	2.1	-2.0	10.4	11.0	5.2	5.3	1.6	9.2	Belgium
5.9	-0.4	5.1	2.9	7.4	2.3	5.3	4.2	7.2	Luxembourg
2.8	-0.7	2.1	-2.2	-0.4	1.6	0.4	0.6	0.5	Denmark
-0.1	0.4	0.6	0.7	-0.1	-0.5	0.6	0.8	-0.7	Finland
6.5	-7.1	2.1	2.4	14.4	4.3	11.8	7.9	9.4	France
3.7	0.6	2.6	7.2	2.0	0.7	3.6	5.1	3.6	Germany
0.1	0.3	0.1	0.3	-0.2	0.1	0.7	-0.1	0.5	Ireland
11.7	-12.4	4.4	-0.1	9.5	-3.4	2.3	-0.9	2.4	Italy
1.7	1.9	3.2	0.7	0.2	4.0	5.0	-0.9	4.8	Netherlands
1.0	-0.3	-0.4	0.6	1.3	-0.5	0.6	-0.1	1.1	Norway
0.4	0.4	1.0	0.8	0.5	-0.3	-0.7	0.9	–	Spain
-0.6	1.1	-0.6	2.3	-1.5	3.0	1.1	3.2	-2.9	Sweden
2.8	2.6	3.0	1.6	-0.1	4.5	2.9	1.5	4.1	Switzerland
9.3	9.7	11.9	42.2	14.9	10.6	24.5	23.8	21.9	United Kingdom
50.1	-1.5	34.7	71.7	60.8	32.0	64.3	48.9	59.7	Sub-total
									Other industrial countries
1.5	3.6	-1.6	-0.3	4.3	-1.4	-2.4	-0.1	2.8	Canada
11.2	11.4	2.4	25.6	43.3	21.3	23.6	24.2	4.8	Japan
–	–	–	–	–	11.7	16.2	13.8	11.7	(JOM)
11.2	11.4	2.4	25.6	43.3	9.6	7.4	10.4	-6.9	(Others)
0.1	2.4	0.4	2.3	2.1	6.2	-0.2	7.0	2.9	United States
0.2	4.1	0.5	1.7	1.1	5.9	0.4	4.7	4.3	(IBFs)
-0.1	-1.7	-0.1	0.6	1.0	0.3	-0.7	2.3	-1.4	(Others)
12.8	17.4	1.2	27.6	49.7	26.2	21.0	31.1	10.5	Sub-total
24.3	3.5	20.5	44.1	53.7	8.4	33.4	55.9	49.5	Other reporting countries[a]
87.2	19.4	56.4	143.4	164.3	66.5	118.7	135.9	119.7	Grand Total

Liabilities

1985 Q4	1986 Q1	1986 Q2	1986 Q3	1986 Q4	1987 Q1	1987 Q2	1987 Q3	1987 Q4	Reporting countries
									European countries
3.1	-0.1	2.1	1.6	2.8	-0.5	1.5	1.8	0.4	Austria
2.9	2.4	-0.7	9.4	11.7	7.1	4.7	0.4	11.0	Belgium
6.2	1.2	4.4	3.7	7.0	2.2	5.8	4.5	5.0	Luxembourg
2.8	-0.2	1.8	-1.6	-0.9	1.5	0.5	1.0	0.6	Denmark
0.5	0.2	0.6	1.0	0.7	1.6	1.9	2.3	0.2	Finland
5.9	-3.5	2.3	5.1	8.7	2.7	11.2	8.2	8.0	France
3.6	-0.3	1.1	7.6	0.3	-1.0	2.8	3.0	3.6	Germany
–	0.9	0.1	-0.1	0.4	0.2	0.5	-0.3	0.6	Ireland
8.0	-7.6	5.9	-1.7	10.3	-0.9	2.1	-1.6	7.1	Italy
1.8	1.4	3.4	1.7	1.5	4.2	3.2	0.1	1.5	Netherlands
1.7	0.6	0.6	1.1	1.4	0.1	1.6	0.8	0.7	Norway
-0.3	-0.1	-0.2	1.1	0.7	0.7	1.7	2.1	0.5	Spain
-0.7	2.5	-0.6	1.9	-1.3	6.6	1.9	4.1	-1.9	Sweden
3.1	1.8	2.6	1.5	2.3	3.5	-0.1	2.8	0.8	Switzerland
17.5	9.0	13.7	49.1	15.9	14.5	33.3	17.5	15.3	United Kingdom
56.0	8.1	37.0	81.4	61.7	42.4	72.6	46.7	53.4	Sub-total
									Other industrial countries
1.0	2.8	-1.1	-2.6	3.8	-1.6	-2.5	0.3	4.3	Canada
9.3	16.5	8.9	31.8	61.0	12.1	49.9	14.9	24.1	Japan
–	–	–	–	–	9.5	20.8	10.2	22.9	(JOM)
9.3	16.5	8.9	31.8	61.0	2.6	29.1	4.7	1.2	(Others)
1.6	4.9	1.7	3.8	0.4	6.2	0.6	6.7	2.2	United States
2.1	3.6	0.3	4.0	1.7	3.9	2.5	3.6	4.6	(IBFs)
-0.5	1.3	1.5	-0.2	-1.4	2.4	-1.9	3.1	-2.4	(Others)
11.9	24.2	9.6	33.0	65.1	16.8	48.0	21.9	30.7	Sub-total
26.2	2.9	17.8	43.8	41.3	15.0	33.4	56.0	38.6	Other reporting countries
94.1	35.3	64.4	158.3	168.1	74.2	154.1	124.6	122.6	Grand Total[a]

Table 4–2.

CURRENCY BREAKDOWN OF REPORTING BANKS EXTERNAL POSITIONS, ALL SECTORS (billions of US dollars).

Currencies	Amounts outstanding							
	1985 Dec	1986 Sept	1986 Dec I	1986 Dec II	1987 March	1987 June	1987 Sept	1987 Dec
Assets								
Banks in industrial reporting countries								
A) foreign currencies								
Dollars	863.0	972.3	1,051.8	1,051.8	1,064.0	1,147.3	1,191.4	1,238.
Others	406.2	529.4	566.9	566.9	650.9	648.0	680.4	814.
of which:								
Deutsche mark	167.1	200.7	212.6	212.6	238.0	234.3	243.5	297.
Swiss francs	81.5	104.0	111.5	111.5	126.3	117.4	115.2	139.
Yen	51.4	82.2	85.2	85.3	101.1	108.9	121.7	147.
Sterling	23.5	28.1	32.6	32.6	38.6	40.3	43.5	48.
French francs	14.5	17.0	19.0	19.0	22.3	21.2	23.3	27.
Guilders	11.0	13.4	14.9	14.9	16.5	16.1	16.1	19.
Belgian francs	7.4	9.6	10.4	10.4	11.5	11.8	11.7	13.
Italian lire	4.0	7.2	9.3	9.3	11.6	10.7	10.4	11.
Unallocated[a]	45.7	67.4	71.2	71.2	85.0	87.4	95.0	109.
B) ECUs	39.5	51.5	55.6	55.6	64.8	62.4	64.9	78.
C) domestic currency								
Dollars	401.6	417.6	444.7	444.7	417.5	435.8	447.1	458.
Other	286.6	409.8	442.8	442.8	510.1	537.7	576.6	689.
D) Total (A + B + C)	1,997.0	2,380.6	2,561.9	2,561.9	2,707.3	2,831.2	2,960.5	3,278.
Banks in other reporting countries	579.9	656.6	710.2	710.2	723.7	757.7	813.9	878.
Grand Total	2,576.9	3,037.3	3,272.2	3,272.2	3,431.0	3,588.9	3,774.4	4,157.
Liabilities								
Banks in industrial reporting countries								
A) foreign currencies								
Dollars	970.9	1,093.7	1,181.0	1,181.8	1,182.8	1,290.8	1,329.5	1,377.
Other currencies	421.5	582.8	629.6	630.6	732.2	738.5	766.0	926.
of which:								
Deutsche mark	163.1	215.3	237.6	237.6	273.5	272.2	278.0	338.
Swiss francs	91.2	124.4	134.4	134.6	153.4	147.2	145.9	181.
Yen	49.2	83.3	83.5	83.7	99.5	106.1	112.2	137.
Sterling	29.0	34.7	39.8	39.8	49.5	52.0	56.8	67.
French francs	17.8	20.5	23.1	23.1	27.6	25.5	27.4	35.
Guilders	13.9	16.1	17.7	17.7	18.8	19.0	18.7	22.
Belgian francs	7.6	9.8	11.0	11.0	11.8	11.7	11.7	13.
Italian lire	4.7	7.9	8.2	8.2	9.1	9.0	10.4	12.
Unallocated[a]	45.1	70.7	74.3	74.9	89.1	95.9	104.9	119.
B(ECUs	37.0	45.2	49.2	49.2	57.5	55.9	57.1	69.
C) domestic currency								
Dollars	350.9	379.9	414.0	414.0	404.5	418.2	452.5	477.
Other	207.2	272.5	299.4	299.0	361.2	379.8	423.3	517.
D) Total (A + B + C)	1,987.5	2,374.2	2,573.3	2,574.6	2,738.3	2,883.2	3,028.5	3,368.
Banks in other reporting countries	553.1	626.7	667.9	667.9	688.6	722.9	779.2	832.
Grand Total	2,540.6	3,000.9	3,241.2	3,242.5	3,426.8	3,606.1	3,807.7	4,201.

Source: BIS, *International Banking and Financial Market Developments* May 1988, p. 5.
[a]Includes the total foreign currency positions of banks in the United States for which no currency breakdown is available.

			Estimated exchange rate adjusted changes						
1985 Q4	1986 Q1	1986 Q2	1986 Q3	1986 Q4	1987 Q1	1987 Q2	1987 Q3	1987 Q4	Currencies
			Assets						
									Banks in industrial reporting countries
									A) foreign currencies
22.6	8.2	20.3	80.8	79.5	12.1	83.3	44.1	46.8	Dollars
36.2	4.3	14.9	17.3	28.9	40.8	3.6	33.2	19.7	Other
									of which
10.2	−2.7	4.3	−4.3	3.8	9.4	−0.5	10.2	14.7	Deutsche mark
9.3	−1.9	0.1	3.0	6.6	6.1	−7.8	−1.5	1.4	Swiss francs
14.5	0.1	1.2	13.6	5.9	8.1	8.6	12.3	1.9	Yen
2.2	1.0	2.1	1.6	4.1	3.1	1.6	2.7	−1.6	Sterling
0.7	1.6	−0.2	−1.1	1.6	1.9	−0.8	2.2	1.2	French francs
−	−0.4	1.1	−0.6	1.0	0.5	−0.3	0.1	0.3	Guilders
0.3	0.4	0.2	−	0.5	0.2	0.5	−	−0.1	Belgian francs
0.1	0.4	2.6	−0.9	2.0	1.8	−0.6	−0.2	−0.1	Italian lire
−1.2	5.9	1.4	6.0	3.5	9.7	3.0	7.4	1.9	Unallocated[a]
4.0	3.4	0.7	1.2	2.1	5.2	−1.6	2.7	3.7	B) ECUs
									C) domestic currency
10.7	−5.1	8.8	12.3	27.2	−27.3	18.3	11.3	11.1	Dollars
23.3	21.7	16.5	22.3	29.6	31.2	32.5	38.4	11.4	Other
96.8	32.4	61.2	133.9	167.3	62.1	136.1	129.7	92.6	D) Total (A + B + C)
									Banks in other reporting countries
24.8	3.8	20.5	44.6	53.6	8.2	33.5	56.2	49.4	
121.6	36.2	81.8	178.5	220.8	70.3	169.6	185.9	142.0	Grand Total
			Liabilities						
									Banks in industrial reporting countries
									A) foreign currencies
23.5	−0.9	35.3	88.4	87.3	1.0	107.9	38.8	48.4	Dollars
42.1	30.4	9.6	28.6	37.3	53.4	13.6	28.5	32.2	Other
									of which:
11.8	8.1	4.7	2.5	13.5	18.1	2.3	7.0	15.7	Deutsche mark
9.0	2.0	−0.5	7.1	8.9	8.3	−4.8	−0.4	7.0	Swiss francs
15.6	4.6	2.8	10.7	3.1	8.2	7.4	5.6	2.7	Yen
2.2	0.9	2.1	2.8	4.6	6.1	2.4	4.2	1.7	Sterling
1.6	3.8	−2.8	−0.7	2.1	2.9	−1.7	1.9	3.6	French francs
0.8	−0.3	0.9	1.3	0.9	−0.2	0.4	−0.2	1.0	Guilders
−	1.2	−0.8	0.3	0.8	−	−	−	−0.4	Belgian francs
0.4	0.8	1.0	0.4	0.1	0.4	0.1	1.4	0.3	Italian lire
0.7	9.5	2.2	6.9	3.5	9.7	7.3	9.0	0.7	Unallocated[a]
2.4	2.9	1.7	−2.5	2.2	4.7	−0.8	1.3	3.5	B) ECUs
									C) domestic currency
18.3	1.2	1.1	26.6	34.1	−9.4	13.7	34.3	24.9	Dollars
13.5	6.0	7.8	14.8	24.3	37.9	21.6	42.3	21.5	other
99.8	39.6	55.5	155.9	185.2	87.6	155.9	145.2	130.5	D) Total (A + B + C)
									Banks in other reporting countries
26.6	3.1	17.9	44.2	41.2	15.0	33.9	56.3	38.6	
126.4	42.7	73.4	200.1	226.4	102.6	189.8	201.5	169.1	Grand Total

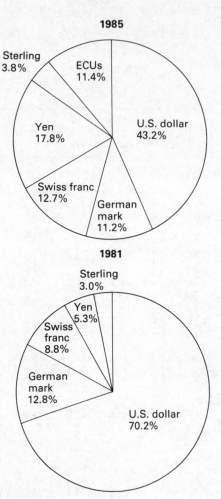

1985

Sterling 3.8%

ECUs 11.4%

Yen 17.8%

U.S. dollar 43.2%

Swiss franc 12.7%

German mark 11.2%

1981

Sterling 3.0%

Yen 5.3%

Swiss franc 8.8%

German mark 12.8%

U.S. dollar 70.2%

Source: BIS, *Annual Report*, 1986.

Figure 4–1. Eurocurrency Market Currency Composition, 1981 and 1985.

net market size is already counted in some countries' domestic money supplies. Thus there is substantial overlap between net Eurocurrency liabilities and domestic aggregates. The only portion of the net size of the Eurocurrency market that does not overlap national money supplies and is strictly comparable with them is the nonbank portion. In summary, whether the Eurocurrency market consists of banks or of financial intermediaries that do not create money but only increase the efficiency with which it is used, they offer assets that are near money.

Functions

The Eurocurrency market is primarily an international interbank deposit market through which the world's major banks (1) adjust their

Table 4–3.
ESTIMATED SOURCES AND USES OF INTERNATIONAL
BANKING FUNDS (billions of US dollars).

			Exchange Rate Adjusted Flows						Stocks at end of 1987
	1980	1981	1982	1983	1984	1985	1986	1987	
Uses:									
Reporting area	88	93	42	53	76	77	138	235	1,385
Outside area	68	66	39	28	14	19	14	7	726
Unallocated	4	6	14	4	–	4	13	13	109
Total	160	165	95	85	90	100	165	255	2,220
Sources:									
Reporting area	104	137	93	80	62	83	136	172	1,541
Outside area	52	17	-12	1	29	16	-2	50	490
Unallocated	4	11	14	4	-1	1	31	33	189
Total	160	165	95	85	90	100	165	255	2,220
Net:									
Reporting area	-16	-44	-51	-27	14	-6	2	63	-156
Outside area	16	49	51	27	-15	3	16	-43	236
Unallocated	–	-5	–	–	1	3	-18	-20	-80

Source: BIS, 56th *Annual Report* (1986), and 58th Annual Report, 1988.

overall liquidity positions in both domestic and foreign currencies by
bidding for (borrowing) and offering (lending, depositing) excess
balances, (2) conduct foreign-exchange hedging and arbitrage
operations, and (3) recycle or intermediate funds through bank loans
and international bond issuing, from surplus to deficit countries.

Eurocurrency business is conducted vis-à-vis financial and
nonfinancial entities, but interbank transactions account for the bulk of
the market's assets and liabilities—75 percent and 85 percent,
respectively. The interbank market allows banks to adjust their liquidity
positions to some degree in an analogous manner to the interbank
Federal Funds market in the United States. It also provides a
mechanism by interbank lending and borrowing to obtain foreign
exchange to cover forward foreign-exchange commitments and to
conduct covered interest-rate arbitrage.

The Eurocurrency market is closely linked to the foreign-exchange
market, but the two markets are distinct in function. In the foreign-
exchange market one currency is exchanged for another, but in the
Eurocurrency market deposits and loans are usually made in the same
currency. The Euromarkets enhance substitutability among currencies
and link foreign-exchange markets (forward and spot) closely to
domestic markets.

Eurocurrency transactions are often linked with foreign-exchange
activities because (1) many of them occur solely for the sake of swapping
funds into the local currency or into a third currency; (2) they often
form part of arbitrage activity that can be conducted only in the
foreign-exchange market; and (3) their activities lead to a considerable
amount of various foreign-exchange transactions. For instances, Eurobanks in temporary need of, say, deutsche marks may prefer to borrow

109

them in the form of Euro-deutsche mark deposits rather than buy them or obtain them through swap transactions. Conversely, mismatched maturity dates of Eurocurrency deposits may be more conveniently rectified with the aid of swap or uncovered spot transactions instead of Eurocurrency transactions.

Like domestic bank deposits, Eurocurrency deposits are usually in the form of interest-bearing time deposits that are issued by banks to banks and nonbanks, residents and nonresidents, and their maturities are accommodated to depositors' needs. The degree of transformation conducted by the Eurocurrency market is reflected by several indexes: (1) The ratio of transformation (that is, the ratio of each net position in absolute terms to the sum of total foreign-currency assets and liabilities), (2) the maturity profile of assets and liabilities (that is, percentage of each maturity category as a percentage of total assets and liabilities), and (3) the net credit creation measured by assigning various coefficients of liquidity to both assets and liabilities based on maturities (such as 10 to cash, 9 to time deposits up to one month, and so forth).

The evidence shows that the maturity structure of interbank activity is highly balanced and a relatively small amount of transformation is undertaken in trading among Eurobanks. Over 70 percent of total liabilities mature in less then three months, whereas some 65 percent of the assets mature in less than three months.

Substantial transformation occurs vis-à-vis the nonbank sector. The data show that the average term to maturity of loans to nonbanks (assets) exceeds that of deposits (liabilities). Whereas 77 percent and 90 percent of total liabilities mature within three and six months, respectively, 57 percent and 63 percent of claims mature within one year and over and six months to several years, respectively.

Transactions in the Eurocurrency market involved substantial interbank deposits. For example, a European bank holding a deposit in a U.S. bank may make a Eurodollar deposit with another European bank, which in turn may deposit the proceeds with another bank, and so on. Active wholesale Eurocurrency markets exist for most major currencies. This interbank transaction may continue through several banks, which function as intermediaries between the original depositor and the ultimate borrower. Each depositing bank charges a small profit or spread above the London Interbank Offering Rate (LIBOR). The margins usually range from one thirty-second to one-fourth of 1 percent for prime means. The lending bank typically uses a broker, who disguises the names of the potential transactors until the deal is near conclusion in order to secure the best offer of an interbank-deposit rate of interest.

The Theoretical Interpretations of the Eurocurrency Market

The theoretical interpretation of the credit-creating potential of the

Euromarket is a controversial issue that arises from the diversity of the theoretical interpretations of the market's growth and mechanism. The competing hypotheses or interpretations of the Eurocurrency may be classified in terms of (1) the money-and-credit-multiplier model, (2) the nonbank financial intermediaries, and (3) supply and demand of the Eurocurrency markets. The rapid growth of the Eurocurrency market is often explained in the context of a multiple credit-and-deposit-expansion mechanism, similar to what prevails in a national commercial banking system.

Accordingly, an initial reserve injection into the Eurobanking system could, through the chain of lending and depositing in the market, expand credit by some multiple of the initial cash added. This interpretation, though inappropriate, serves as a basis for many of the exaggerated estimates of the Euromarket's potential credit creation.

Applications of the commercial bank deposit and credit-multiplier model is inappropriate for several reasons. First, only in a system where the liabilities of the financial intermediaries also serve as the means of payment can there be multiple expansion of money and credit. Second, Eurocurrency deposits are not money because they do not serve as a means of payment. They are near money and function as a short-term store of value fitted into broadly defined money concepts. Because Eurobanks' deposits do not serve as a medium of exchange and do not hold stable or fixed ratios of reserves to deposits (because they are not subject to reserve requirements), there is no clearly defined base money for Eurobanks; the Eurobanks are more like nonbank financial intermediaries than like commercial banks.

The Eurocurrency market exists largely because of its competitiveness, which is derived both from regulatory practices of national monetary authorities and also from the more profitable nature of the wholesale market. Banks are able to offer higher rates of interest to depositors and lower lending rates to borrowers than prevail in domestic money markets. This competitive edge is derived from freedom from a number of regulatory practices of national monetary authorities.

International Interest Rates

The Eurocurrency market has developed an international interest-rate structure that is determined mainly by the corresponding interest rates in each country's currency. Although Euromarket interest rates are dominated by domestic rates, they also influence these rates. Interest rates in national markets and the corresponding Eurocurrency sectors are closely linked and may be largely determined by the degree of capital controls and the degree of freedom for arbitrage and capital flows.

The interest-rates structures for equal maturities in the Eurocurrency market and the corresponding national market are closely linked, but rate differentials exist because of reserve requirements on domestic deposits and higher operating costs. Accordingly, the Eurocurrency market offers higher deposit rates and lower loan rates.

Under free-market conditions, arbitrage keeps interest rates in the domestic market and the corresponding Eurocurrency market closely linked. The Euromarket rate can fall to a level at which it becomes profitable to place funds in the domestic market. Below that level the rate is unlikely to fall as long as arbitrage activity continues. Similarly, the Euromarket cannot rise vis-à-vis the corresponding domestic market beyond the level at which it becomes profitable to move funds from the domestic to the Eurocurrency market.

Although Eurodollar rates are influenced by interest rates in the United States, they reflect a different interest-rate structure from that prevailing in the U.S. market. The different exists because of reserve requirements and FDIC fees on U.S. deposits of member banks. But both interest-rate structures are closely linked. For instance, at times three-month Eurodollar rates may move more in line with three-month U.S. CD rates, which would indicate that the CD arbitrage channel has become the most active one; at other times U.S. nonbank borrower arbitrage on a three-month basis may become more important, which would affect the CD differential between the U.S. and the Eurodollar market.

The above interest-rate relationship is also observed in other sectors of the Eurocurrency market. For instance, in Germany, where there are no impediments to international interest arbitrage, Euro-deutsche mark rates are unlikely to rise above domestic interbank market rates. However, they may decline below those rates because of the cost effect of minimum-reserve requirements on nonresident deposits. The higher the reserve ratios, the wider Euro-deutsche mark rates deviate from domestic interbank rates. Thus as long as Euro-deutsche mark rates are in line with domestic interbank rates, the differential between domestic money-market interest rates in Germany and the United States will determine the swap rate and the uncovered differential between Euro-dollar and Euro-deutsche mark rates. However, as Euro-deutsche mark rates decline below the domestic rates, the swap rate will then determine the uncovered interest-rate differential.

The high degree of global integration of financial markets has been further enchanced in the United States by the abolition of the withholding tax in 1984. It brought about a narrowing of yield differentials between domestic and Euro-issues as well as tighter price formulas. Yields on new issues in the international securities markets are being quoted less in terms of the Euromarket and more in terms of yields on U.S. government paper.[1]

There are close relationships between Euromarket interest rates and the corresponding national rates and spot and forward foreign-exchange rates. In general, spot exchange rates, forward discounts or premiums, and Eurocurrency interest rate differentials are determined simul-

Table 4-4A.
EUROCURRENCY INTEREST RATES.

12/10	12:44	[NOONAN, ASTLEY & PEARCE INC.—NEW YORK]				PAGE 311
	STERLING 12:38 EST	*LIRE* 12:42 EST	*D/MARK* 12:40 EST	*CANADIAN $* 12:03 EST	*YEN* 12:43 EST	*SWISS FRANC* 12:43 EST
SPOT	1.4250 −60 QUOTE	139000 −200 LIRE/MARK	2.0080 −90 QUOTE	1.3790 −93	162.50 −55 QUOTE	1.6795 −10
IMM	−	69260−69275	2.7−2.2	−	4−3.5	11−9.5
T/N	1.90−1.80	8−15	0.45−0.3	0.8−0.9	0.85−0.8	2.3−2.1
S/N	6−5.8	50−55	1.6−1.3	−	2.4−2.1	2.1−1.9
1WK	13.4−13	110−125	3.75−3.25	5.3−5.8	5.4−5.2	15.0−14.0
1MO	57.5−56.5	550−585	18.5−17.75	24−26	24.5−24	27−24
2MO	119−117	1150−1200	38−37	48−51	48.5−47.5	756−53
3MO	177−176	1650−1700	57−56	73−76	70−69	77−74
4MO	242−239	2200−2300	77−74	100−106	92−90	106−101
6MO	360−356	3200−3250	115−112	156−161	135−132	160−155
9MO	524−520	4300−4500	177−170	240−250	205−200	250−240
1YR	675−667	5650−5950	235−228	315−330	272−267	330−320

12/10	12:44 EST	[NOONAN, ASTLEY & PEARCE INC.—NEW YORK]				PAGE 312
	NETHERLANDS 12:31 EST GUILDER	*SPAIN* 12:27 EST PESETA	*AUSTRIA* 12:42 EST SCHILLING	*SWEDEN* 12:23 EST KRONA	*DENMARK* 12:33 EST KRONE	*NORWAY* 12:32 EST KRONE
SPOT	2.2725 −35	135.45 −55	14.12 −13	6.9380 −00	7.5935 −60	7.5350 −75
T/N	2−1	1.34−2.25	−2−+1	6−7	−	34−36
S/N	−	6.3−6.5	−2−+1	−	−	−
1WK	−	13−18	10−D	47−51	−	220−240
1MO	3−2	65−75	60−10	208−218	230−260	880−920
2MO	6−4.5	130−150	125−25	415−430	475−505	1665−1705
3MO	9−7	190−220	175−25	615−635	745−775	2250−2290
6MO	31−27	370−410	300−D	1150−1190	1640−1700	4300−4360
1YR	95−85	670−750	550−+70	2125−2200	3125−3250	7450−7600
X/DM	113.03−04	67.42−47	7.0355−60	N.A.	3.7765−75	N.A.
			TEL. 504−2800	TLX. 3766527		

[SEE PAGE 313 FOR OTHER EXOTIC CURRENCIES

12/10	12:45 EST	[NOONAN, ASTLEY & PEARCE INC.—NEW YORK]				313
	AUSTRALIA 12:18 EST DOLLAR	*NEW ZEALAND* 11:16 EST DOLLAR	*HONG KONG* 12:43 EST DOLLAR	*SINGAPORE* 12:43 EST DOLLAR	*MALAYSIA* 12:43 EST RINGGIT	*SPOTS* 12:43 EST INDIA
SPOT	0.6527 −32	0.5030 −40	7.7940 −60	2.1905 −15	2.5930 −45	0.0759 −61 SO. AFRICA
T/N	1.85−1.75	1.95−1.75	6.5−4.5	1.9−1.6	−	.4456−76
1WK	12.75−12	−	43−38	12−10		MEXICO
1MO	52−50	63−58	200−180	42−38	10−30	880−885
2MO	105−103	121−115	310−280	83−79	50−75	VENEZUELA
3MO	152−150	172−162	410−380	123−119	90−120	21.10−70
6MO	294−289	333−323	750−700	230−223	260−200	PORTUGAL
1YR	555−545	—AUSS DESK TEL.−504−2891/95 TLX−3712621				150−151
2YR	1020−980	AS RANGES 12/10[NOTES:]				BELGIUM
3YR	1350−1280	SYD .6508−.5623[] 21 MONTH AUS				41.98−03
4YR	1610−1530	LDN .6520−.6533[] 905−885				EC/US$
5YR	1850−1775	NYK .65 −.65 []				1.0353−58
		[OTHER EXOTIC CURRENCIES—PAGE 312 TEL 504-2800]				

Source: Telerate December 10, 1986.

Table 4-4B.

EUROCURRENCY DEPOSIT RATES AND INTERNATIONAL BOND YIELDS[a]

	1985 Dec	1986 Dec	1987 Dec	Jan	Feb	Mar	1988 Apr	May	Jun	Jul
Eurodollar										
overnight	12.25	22.00	6.75	6.69	6.69	6.75	6.88	7.31	7.44	7.56
one month	8.00	6.50	7.06	6.69	6.69	6.69	7.00	7.44	7.69	8.00
three months	7.88	6.25	7.37	6.81	6.69	6.81	7.19	7.63	7.81	8.31
six months	7.88	6.12	7.50	6.87	6.75	7.06	7.44	7.81	7.94	8.50
twelve months	7.94	6.12	7.81	7.25	7.12	7.44	7.88	8.31	8.25	8.75
Euro-Canadian dollar										
one month	9.00	8.00	8.00	8.50	8.25	8.25	8.44	8.81	8.69	9.00
three months	9.00	8.12	8.12	8.37	8.37	8.37	8.75	8.94	9.06	9.38
six months	9.00	8.19	8.44	8.50	8.37	8.62	8.88	9.19	9.31	9.63
twelve months	9.00	8.31	8.87	8.75	8.75	9.00	9.25	9.63	9.63	10.00
Euro-French franc										
one month	12.50	10.12	8.75	7.50	7.25	7.81	8.00	7.31	7.25	7.13
three months	13.00	10.37	9.00	8.00	7.75	8.31	8.25	7.50	7.38	7.38
six months	13.13	9.75	9.25	8.25	8.19	8.44	8.38	7.63	7.63	7.75
twelve months	12.25	8.75	9.25	8.50	8.50	8.56	8.50	8.00	7.88	8.06
Euromark										
one month	4.75	5.12	3.25	3.19	3.31	3.25	3.31	3.31	4.25	5.00
three months	4.75	4.87	3.37	3.25	3.31	3.31	3.44	3.56	4.38	5.06
six months	4.75	4.81	3.50	3.31	3.37	3.37	3.63	3.81	4.50	5.31
twelve months	4.81	4.81	3.75	3.56	3.50	3.56	3.81	4.19	4.69	5.50
Euro-Dutch guilder										
one month	5.75	6.31	4.50	3.94	3.94	3.87	3.88	3.81	3.94	5.00
three months	5.75	6.00	4.62	4.00	4.00	3.87	3.94	3.94	4.31	5.25
six months	5.81	5.87	4.69	4.12	4.06	4.06	4.06	4.13	4.56	5.44
twelve months	5.88	5.81	4.81	4.37	4.12	4.19	4.19	4.44	4.81	5.50
Euro-Swiss franc										
one month	3.88	3.94	2.50	1.25	1.37	1.62	2.06	2.81	3.38	3.44
three months	4.00	3.94	3.00	1.81	1.69	1.87	2.25	2.88	3.44	3.88
six months	4.00	3.87	3.19	2.37	2.12	2.19	2.44	2.94	3.56	4.13
twelve months	4.06	3.87	3.25	2.87	2.69	2.62	2.75	3.13	3.63	4.25
Eurosterling										
one month	11.69	11.12	8.56	8.44	9.00	8.44	8.06	7.38	9.38	10.38
three months	11.81	11.12	8.81	8.69	9.31	8.56	8.31	7.75	9.94	10.81
six months	11.81	11.06	9.00	8.87	9.50	8.69	8.69	8.25	10.06	10.88
twelve months	11.69	11.06	9.31	9.25	9.75	9.00	9.06	8.81	10.25	11.00
Euroyen										
one month	7.13	4.56	4.00	4.06	4.37	4.00	3.81	4.06	4.13	4.38
three months	6.56	4.50	4.12	4.12	4.19	4.00	3.94	4.06	4.38	4.63
six months	6.50	4.37	4.12	4.12	4.19	4.12	4.13	4.25	4.56	4.75
twelve months	6.38	4.31	4.12	4.19	4.19	4.19	4.25	4.31	4.69	4.75
European currency unit										
one month	9.63	8.56	6.62	5.87	6.12	6.19	6.13	5.63	5.06	6.94
three months	9.63	8.44	6.75	6.19	6.31	6.37	6.38	6.00	6.44	7.25
six months	9.63	8.06	6.87	6.37	6.44	6.44	6.50	6.31	6.69	7.56
twelve months	9.63	7.31	7.00	6.62	6.62	6.62	6.69	6.56	6.94	7.69
International bond yields[b]										
United States companies										
Eurodollar	9.68	8.67	9.99	10.95	10.41	10.21	10.31	10.24	9.79	9.78
Euromark	6.73	6.62	6.82	6.87	7.04	6.74	6.69	6.54	6.27	6.33
Swiss franc	5.49	5.70	5.43	5.50	5.83	5.56	5.71	5.57	5.66	5.61
European governments										
Eurodollar	10.52	9.91	11.41	11.81	11.63	11.63	11.64	11.48	11.38	11.50
Euromark	7.03	6.77	6.65	6.76	6.61	6.61	6.21	6.23	6.07	6.06
Swiss franc	4.91	4.51	4.38	4.39	4.54	4.15	4.11	4.05	3.71	3.88
European currency unit	10.23	10.20	10.43	10.46	11.10	11.06	10.84	10.85	10.56	10.35

Source: Morgan Guaranty Trust Company, *World Financial Markets*, August 1988.
Notes:
[a]prime banks' bid rates, at or near end of month.
[b]average yield of several actively traded, high quality issues with a maturity of seven to twelve years at or near end of month.

taneously in such a way as to ensure that the interest-rate differential will be equal to the discount or premium on the forward exchange rate. See Table 4–4 for interest rates.

The Euromarket provides an efficient mechanism for almost perfect covered-interest-rate arbitrage. Under normal conditions, covered interest differentials are reduced or nonexistent—that is, there is no scope for making profits by borrowing one currency for investment and another on a covered basis. This implies that interest-rate differentials between Eurocurrencies should correspond to the swap rates of the forward premium/discount between the respective currencies (that is, the difference between spot and forward exchange rates expressed on an annual percentage basis).

The equilibrium between interest rates on different Eurocurrencies and the corresponding swap rates is brought about by a continuous process of arbitrage by the Euromarket operators. When interest-rate parity does not hold exactly, discrepancies will be particularly great when there are large movements in relative rates and prices.

Interest rates and swap rates may temporarily get out of line, but market participants will discover any incentives for covered-interest-rate arbitrage opportunities, thereby rectifying the disequilibrium in the market. The cost of foreign-exchange transactions may, however, be a considerable barrier to covered-interest-rate arbitrage operations within the Euromarket, thereby allowing an attractive covered-interest-rate differential to persist for a while. Sometimes investors would be better off if they stayed in their positions rather than switching into another one on a covered basis, while in other instances borrowers of a specific currency are better off if they borrow the desired currency directly rather than borrowing the other currency on a swap basis.

International Financial Centers

The international financial market is composed of traditional international financial centers and offshore centers. An international financial center may provide several services, some of which are usually conducted by the domestic financial market:

1 Traditional international financial transactions between foreign and domestic entities. These transactions include clearing of international payments, foreign-exchange business, short-term credit supply, and so forth.
2 Facilitation of financial transactions between foreign entities. This is defined as entrepot finance services (or offshore banking), in which the financial center merely intermediates by providing banking services to third parties.
3 Offshore banking. The distinction between major international financial centers (such as London and New York) and offshore centers (such as the Bahamas, Luxembourg, and Singapore) is to

some extent an arbitrary one. For example, New York offers many of the same advantages for Eurocurrency business, in terms of freedom from reserve requirements and interest withholding taxes, that the Bahamas does.

A financial center (such as London, or New York) has a highly developed commercial infrastructure and a great concentration of financial institutions where the national or regional financial transactions are conducted. Prior to the emergence of the Eurocurrency markets, traditional financial centers provided a broader range of financial services (loans, foreign-exchange transactions, letters of credit, and underwriting of international securities). With development of the Euromarket, entrepot and offshore financial transactions became significant. Entrepot financial centers provide the services of their domestic financial institutions to both domestic and foreign entities and may or may not be capital exporters.

Offshore centers may be of two types, either shell or functional. A shell center acts as a location of records, but little or no actual banking transactions are carried out there, whereas a functional center is one at which financial transactions are conducted. Functional centers serve as significant links between Eurocurrency markets, helping to intermediate funds around the world, from major international financial centers to end users. Shell centers are commonly used by international banks and nonbanks to minimize taxes and other costs.

Offshore banking centers attract international banking business (nonresident, foreign-currency denominated assets, and liabilities) by reducing or eliminating restrictions on operations as well as lowering taxes and other levies. Over a dozen centers qualify under this definition (see Table 4–5). More specifically, the following five advantages of offshore centers can be observed:

1 Absence of central-bank regulations, particularly of reserve requirements on Eurocurrency deposits;
2 Absence of restrictions on interest paid on deposits;
3 Fiscal incentives where taxes and levies on offshore business are actually nonexistent, in sharp contrast to the situation at domestic locations, and license fees are usually low;
4 Local capital requirements are low or nonexistent and entry is relatively easy;
5 Offshore centers allow a reduction of country risk.

The Asian and North American currency markets are of particular interest. The Asian currency market is the pool of dollars and other foreign-currency-denominated assets and liabilities of banks located in Asia. The market was created in Singapore in 1968, when the government licensed a branch of Bank of America to establish a special international department to handle transactions of nonresidents. All

Table 4–5.
SELECT OFFSHORE BANKING CENTERS.

	Number of Offshore Banks	Assets $ billions
Anguilla	100	
Bahamas	263	110.5
Bahrain	37	15.3
Cayman Islands	260	125.7
Hong Kong	74	238.6
Jersey	33	
Luxembourg	92	
Netherlands Antilles	43	12.5
New Hebrides	13	
Panama	66	32.2
Philippines	17	13.3
Singapore	66	144.2
United Arab Emirates	55	7.5

Source: International Monetary Fund, *Finance and Development*, 16 4 (1979); 46, and BIS, International Banking and Financial Market Developments, August 1988.

banks that were granted such licenses were required to set up a special account for nonresident transactions—namely, the Asian Currency Unit (ACU). Banks that operate in this market receive fiscal incentives and exemptions from various bank restrictions.

The Asian currency market developed vigorously in Singapore and Hong Kong, growing from $0.1 billion in 1968 to $383 billion in assets in early 1988. The market performs several functions:

1 It intermediates between Asian and Eurocurrency markets and within Asia.
2 It provides arbitrage facilities.
3 It is a channel for funds flowing into Asian projects and mobilizes funds for the region.

The growth of the North American Eurocurrency market has been influenced by the same general factors that affected the Eurocurrency market and other offshore centers. An additional consideration is that the Caribbean branches operate during the same hours as their parents and other U.S. banks on the East Coast. Most Caribbean branches are shell branches managed and staffed at the head offices of the parents rather than locally. Loans and deposits are negotiated at non-Caribbean centers (such as New York, and San Francisco) but are booked at the Caribbean branches, particularly for tax considerations. The increasing importance of these centers has led to slower growth in Euromarket transactions in London.

During the 1970s an increasing share of business was captured by various offshore banking centers. The volume of business transacted through offshore centers has increased with the growth of Eurocurrency, and by 1986 it accounted for some 27 percent of the global Euromarket. The striking increase in the importance of offshore centers largely reflects the advantages they offer vis-à-vis more traditional centers. Host countries' benefits from offshore banking are derived through salaries, other expenditures, fees, and some taxes.

International Banking Facilities

The International Banking Facilities or free monetary zones in the United States were first established in December 1981 by Edge and Agreement Corporations and by the U.S. branches and agencies of foreign banks. Their assets were 266 billion in early 1988. An IBF operates primarily as a recordkeeping entity similar to an offshore shell branch. The Board of Governors of the Federal Reserve System has amended its regulations regarding reserve requirements and payment of interest on deposits to permit the establishment of IBFs in the United States. The IBFs' state and city tax treatment varies among the various states, but they might ultimately be exempt from those taxes and thus benefit from lower effective tax rate and greater competitiveness. In May 1979 New York became the first state to adopt legislation that allowed the establishment of IBFs in New York City. Since then many other states have expressed interest in this type of banking and adopted similar legislation.

IBFs can accept deposits exempted from reserve requirements (Reserve D) and can make loans to foreign borrowers. These activities may be denominated in United States dollars and/or in foreign currencies. More specifically, subject to restrictions concerning eligible holders of deposits and loans, maturity and size of deposits and loans, IBFs may conduct the following transactions:

1 Accept deposits from and make loans to bank and nonbank customers located abroad only if that supports the customers' non-U.S. operations;

2 Extend credit to other IBFs or to an IBF parent institution in the United States (however, funds received by U.S. offices of IBFs' parent institutions are subject to reserve requirements on Euro-currency liabilities);

3 Offer to foreign nonbank residents time deposits with a minimum maturity or required notice period prior to withdrawal of two business days; such deposit accounts require minimum deposits and withdrawals of $100,000;

4 Offer time deposits to foreign offices of U.S. depository institutions or foreign banks, to other IBFs, or to the parent institution of an IBF with a minimum one-day (overnight) maturity.

The IBFs eliminated some of the disadvantages in the regulatory and tax environments that prevailed in New York City as well as in other financial centers in the United States vis-à-vis the Eurocurrency market and enhanced the international competitive position of banking institutions in the United States. However, the Federal Reserve Board has introduced several restrictions designed to reduce the likelihood that these facilities will circumvent interest-rate restrictions or reserve requirements and reduce the effectiveness of monetary policy. These measures will not allow the IBFs to enjoy the full advantages that offshore Eurocurrency centers have.

The Payments System

The bulk of Eurocurrency payments are settled through book entries in correspondent bank accounts in the countries where the particular currency is the legal tender and, to a lesser extent, through branch networks, rather than through the central banks' clearing and settlement facilities. The final net-net sums are settled through the central banks.

International transactions denominated in dollars are cleared in the United States through the New York CHIPS, SWIFT, the Fedwire, and proprietary communication networks of the major banks with their main international branches. Dollar clearings are performed for a variety of transactions, including payments for foreign trade in goods and services, direct and portfolio investment, Eurodollar market activity, and foreign-exchange and arbitrage transactions. The daily volume of the CHIPS system is presently about $200 billion. A substantial amount of international payments is settled through book entries in correspondent-bank accounts.

The dollar payments have the following characteristics and trends: (1) The bulk of daily dollar payments and settlements arise from Eurodollar and foreign-exchange transactions (53 to 58 percent and 39 to 45 percent of the market, respectively), while the aggregate contribution of trade, services, and investment (2.5 to 3.0 percent) is relatively small and declining. The significance of trade, services, and investment in global daily dollar payments diminishes between 1980 and 1990 by about 1.5 percentage points, while the Eurodollar market's contribution expands by some 3.0 percentage points, and the foreign-exchange market's share declines by 2.0 percentage points.

The geographic pattern of payments shows that North America and the United Kingdom are the major sources of dollar payments (about 30 percent each), followed by Continental Europe (26 percent), Asia Pacific (14 percent) and Latin America (2.5 percent). The regional pattern of payments is only slightly modified by 1990, with the United Kingdom, North America, and the Pacific gaining 1.5 to 3.0, 0.5, and 1.5 to 2.5 percentage points, respectively, while Continental Europe and Latin America lose 4.0 to 6.0 and 0.8 percentage points, respectively. See Table 4–6 and Figure 4–2.

New developments in the international payments system, both in

119

Table 4–6.

GLOBAL DAILY DOLLAR PAYMENTS BY TYPE OF TRANSACTION AND GEOGRAPHIC LOCATION, 1984 and 1990 (billions of US dollars).

	United Kingdom		Continental Europe		North America	
	1984	1990	1984	1990	1984	1990
Trade	0.10	0.11	0.85	0.90	1.20	1.32
Services	0.06	0.07	0.48	0.50	0.90	1.00
Investment	0.12	0.14	0.27	0.30	0.46	0.53
Euro$	56.09	143.60	43.35	84.66	41.43	108.37
F.X.	20.00	55.00	30.00	60.00	42.00	90.00
	50.00	110.00	30.00	60.00	42.00	90.00
Total	76.37	198.92	74.95	146.36	85.99	201.22
	106.37	253.92	74.95	146.36	85.99	201.22

Source: Harvey Poniachek, *NAD Economics* March 11, 1985.
Notes: Data for the United Kingdom's foreign exchange transactions were not readily available; estimates suggest about $20 billion, while some market sources indicate a possible $50 billion. Estimates for others are designed to capture the rest of the world.

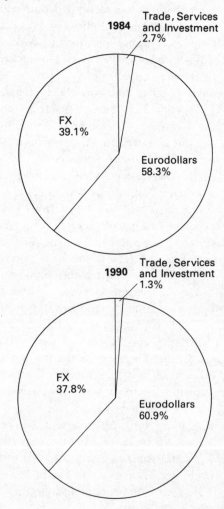

1984
Trade, Services and Investment 2.7%
FX 39.1%
Eurodollars 58.3%

1990
Trade, Services and Investment 1.3%
FX 37.8%
Eurodollars 60.9%

Figure 4–2A. Global Daily Dollar Payments, 1984 and 1990 (by type of transaction). Lower Range Estimates.

Latin America		Pacific Rim		Others		Total	
1984	1990	1984	1990	1984	1990	1984	1990
0.30	0.31	1.20	1.44	1.27	1.40	3.65	4.08
0.26	0.30	0.96	1.15	0.90	0.99	2.66	3.02
0.13	0.14	0.27	0.32	0.45	0.50	1.25	1.43
3.26	5.48	21.36	59.64	3.00	7.71	165.49	401.75
3.00	4.50	16.00	40.00	2.00	4.50	111.00	249.50
3.00	4.50	16.00	45.00	2.88	6.32	141.00	309.50
6.95	10.73	39.79	102.55	7.62	15.10	284.05	659.78
6.95	10.73	39.79	107.55	8.50	16.92	314.05	719.78

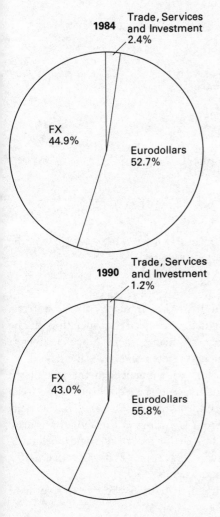

1984

Trade, Services and Investment 2.4%

FX 44.9%

Eurodollars 52.7%

1990

Trade, Services and Investment 1.2%

FX 43.0%

Eurodollars 55.8%

Figure 4–2B. Global Daily Dollar Payments, 1984 and 1990 (by type of transaction). Higher Range Estimates.

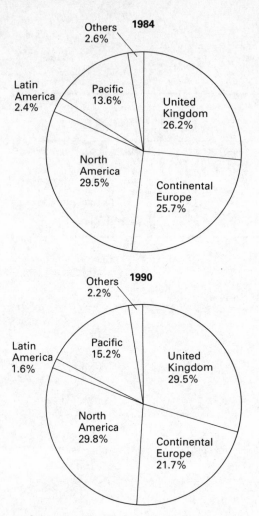

Figure 4–2C. Global Daily Dollar Payments, 1984 and 1990 (by geographic location). Lower Range Estimates.

terms of operating procedures and the development of new systems, could improve efficiency and significantly affect the operation of the banking industry and international cash management. Since October 1, 1981, the CHIPS system settlements are on a one-day value date basis, the same as the Fedwire and in line with practices in the rest of the world. This has eliminated overnight and weekend arbitrage between U.S. money markets and the Eurodollar market. The $200 billion daily clearing through the CHIPS system is facilitated through three main mechanisms: (1) Working balances of foreign banks held with U.S. correspondent banks, particularly in New York; (2) daylight overdrafts; and (3) matching of payments and receipts.

The adoption of same-day settlement reduces the risk of overnight

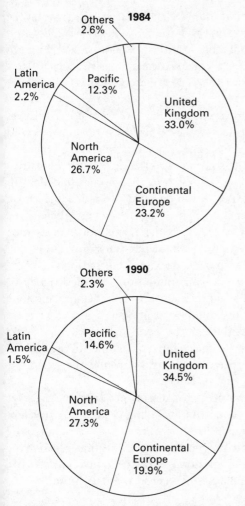

Figure 4–2D. Global Daily Dollar Payments, 1984 and 1990 (by geographic location). Higher Range Estimates.

overdraft and default, however, daylight overdraft is significant. CHIPS clearings are tenfold the working balances maintained with U.S. banks.

It is possible to arrange for delivery beyond the customary settlement date, subject to negotiation. There is no regular forward market in Eurocurrency deposits (not even Eurodollars). Such deals, which in fact amount to deferred loans to Eurodollars, can be arranged, even though such transactions are not very frequent.

In addition to the above changes, modification in the structure of the system is also underway. For instance, a proposal to set up a wholesale dollar clearing system in London was discussed during 1986. The proposal calls for the establishment of a central facility in London where dollar payments would be exchanged between participants each working day to a given cut-off time. Items eligible for exchange would be dollar payments made between participating banks in London, and capable of being netted out and settled in London. The London clearing house would transmit the net settlements instructions to New York, through SWIFT and/or the Federal Reserve Bank, for ultimate settlement.

The creation of this system could affect the pattern of dollar balances because smaller working balances would be held by overseas banks with their New York correspondents. The major disadvantage of the proposed facility is the risk of exposure to clearing default of participants, settling and nonsettling, as well as to their correspondents. (In the CHIPS system, credit exposure can be large, and individual banks, often relatively small, experience high daylight clearing liabilities.) If credit exposures cannot be avoided to the maximum extent, then wholesale London dollar clearing would merely transform to London the credit risk which New York banks are now confronting.

SWIFT provides an electronic communication system designed to transmit instructions speedily and efficiently. In the medium and long term, additional developments could occur in SWIFT, which operates in over twenty-five countries through the world and serves some 1,000 major banks. It is becoming the major impetus behind the standardization of the international operations of banks around the world. As SWIFT transactions grow, pressure will build for it to add a net settlement mechanism or multiple mechanisms in countries that have high transactions in foreign countries, including dollars. The development of a central Eurocurrency settlement mechanism would require the cooperation of central banks or multilateral institutions (such as the BIS), in order to reduce the enormous credit risk involved. Such a development is, however, unlikely to occur in the near future.

EUROCURRENCY LENDING

Market Size and Characteristics

The international market for bank loans, or the syndicated Eurocurrency bank-loan market, emerged in the late 1960s and developed rapidly in the 1970s to become the most important source of international bank credit and balance-of-payments financing. However, the relative importance of bank lending has diminished since the early 1980s because of the debt problems of the LDCs. Loans expanded from about $5 billion in 1970 to $88 billion in 1987, providing more than 26 percent of the medium- and long-term borrowing in international capital markets (international bonds account for about 53 percent, and Euro-note facilities for 21 percent). Syndicated Eurocurrency loans involve the making of bank loans or extending of credits by a group, or syndicate, of international banks, with each bank providing a part of the loan.

The syndicated loan market is a substantial segment of the Eurocurrency market and bank lending as a whole, although it has declined rapidly. Outstanding loans, about $2,220 billion in 1987, represent about 74 percent of the Eurocurrency market. These loans have become a significant activity and source of income for international commercial banks.

In the aftermath of the sharp oil-price increases and the consequent worldwide balance-of-payments disequilibriums, the need for large balance-of-payments financing generated growing demand for Eurocredits. The Eurocurrency market has performed an enormous task of recycling OPEC surpluses, channeling them to oil-importing countries (in the form of deposits and loans) to finance balance-of-payments deficits. Since the 1982 international debt crisis, lending to LDCs has declined considerably. See Tables 4–7 and 4–8 and Figures 4–3 and 4–4.

Syndicated Loans

The most common type of syndicated loan is a term loan under which the funds can be drawn down by a borrower within a specified period (the drawdown period) after the loan agreement has been signed and repayment is usually per an amortization schedule, which can begin anytime starting from drawdown but generally not later than the first five or six years of the loan. Another type of loan, less frequently used, is a revolving-credit where the borrower is given a line of credit that can be drawn and repaid with more flexibility than the term loan. This is

Table 4–7.
BORROWING ON THE INTERNATIONAL CAPITAL
MARKETS (millions of US dollars).

				January–March	
Instruments	1985	1986	1987	1987	1988
Bonds	169.1	228.1	177.3	57.7	54.1
Equities	2.7	11.7	18.2	2.8	0.7
Syndicated Loans	43.0	52.8	88.8	13.3	32.8
Note Issuance Facilities	34.4	24.8	28.1	5.3	7.5
Other Back-Up Facilities	8.5	4.5	1.8	0.6	0.5
A. Total Securities and Committed Facilities	257.7	321.9	314.2	79.7	95.6
Euro-commercial Paper Programmes	12.6	59.0	55.3	12.2	17.1
Other Non-Underwritten Facilities	10.6	8.6	14.3	2.4	5.5
B Total Uncommitted Borrowing Facilities	23.2	67.6	69.6	14.6	22.6
Grand Total (A + B)	280.9	389.5	383.8	94.3	118.2

Source: Financial Market Trends, 40, May 1988, p.5.

Table 4–8A.

INTERNATIONAL FINANCIAL MARKET ACTIVITY, BY MARKET SECTORS AND BORROWERS (billions of US dollars).

Borrowers	United States	Japan	Other industrial reporting countries	Other developed countries	Eastern Europe	Developing countries (incl. OPEC)	Other[a]	Total
Market sectors								
International bond issues								
1982	15.3	5.9	34.4	4.0	0.0	3.1	11.6	74.3
1983	7.9	11.3	34.3	3.6	0.0	1.8	14.9	73.8
1984	24.8	15.8	45.4	6.1	0.1	2.8	13.4	108.4
1985	40.6	20.0	67.8	9.4	0.4	6.1	20.2	164.5
1986	41.6	31.8	109.5	15.4	0.6	2.9	19.7	221.5
1987	22.6	42.3	76.7	11.9	0.6	2.0	19.5	175.6
1988, first quarter	3.0	9.4	35.7	3.4	0.4	0.9	6.7	59.5
Euro-note facilities[b]								
1982	0.4	0.0	0.9	0.4	0.0	0.5	0.2	2.4
1983	0.4	0.6	1.0	1.0	0.1	0.2	0.0	3.3
1984	3.0	0.2	9.4	4.8	0.1	0.6	0.7	18.8
1985	16.5	0.5	21.1	9.7	0.1	1.2	1.2	50.3
1986	19.0	10.4	27.6	11.0	0.1	1.3	1.7	71.1
1987	15.0	10.0	31.6	11.8	0.0	1.3	0.5	70.2
1988, first quarter	4.1	0.0	15.1	2.1	0.1	0.4	0.4	22.2
Total securities markets								
1982	15.7	5.9	35.3	4.4	0.0	3.6	11.8	76.7
1983	8.3	11.9	35.3	4.6	0.1	2.0	14.9	77.1
1984	27.8	16.0	54.8	10.9	0.2	3.4	14.1	127.2
1985	57.1	20.5	88.9	19.1	0.5	7.3	21.4	214.8
1986	60.6	42.2	137.1	26.4	0.7	4.2	21.4	292.6
1987	37.6	52.3	108.3	23.7	0.6	3.3	20.0	245.8
1988, first quarter	7.1	9.4	50.8	5.5	0.5	1.3	7.1	81.7
Syndicated bank loans[c]								
1982	7.0	0.1	22.9	12.5	0.8	53.5	2.6	99.4[d]
1983	3.4	0.1	13.6	5.6	0.8	26.6	1.7	51.8[d]
1984	3.6	0.3	8.3	4.2	2.5	17.1	0.6	36.6[d]
1985	2.1	0.0	5.1	2.4	3.6	7.8	0.1	21.1[d]
1986	3.8	0.3	10.6	3.5	2.0	16.4	1.2	37.8[d]
1987	15.8	0.5	52.0	7.8	1.9	8.9	1.0	87.9[d]
1988, first quarter	3.4	0.0	15.5	2.6	0.2	2.2	0.0	23.9[d]

Source: BIS, 58th *Annual Report*, June 1988, p. 123.
Notes:
[a]Offshore centres, international institutions plus unallocated items.
[b]Covers all Euro-note facilities including underwritten facilities (NIFs, RUFs and multi-component facilities with a note issuance option) and non-underwritten or uncommitted facilities, mostly in the form of Euro-commerical paper (ECP) programmes.
[c]Excludes existing loans newly negotiated where only spreads are changed.
[d]Includes the following amounts of lending under officially sponsored credit packages: $11.2 billion in 1982, $13.7 billion in 1983, $6.5 billion in 1984, $2.3 billion in 1985, $8 billion in 1986 and $4.7 billion in 1987. In the first quarter of 1988 such lending amounted to $1.7 billion.

similar to the term loan, but the borrower must pay a fee for the undrawn portion of the credit line. A combination of term loan and revolving-credit facility is also available, along with other variations tailored to the borrower's requirements. The amounts of individual loans vary from under $10 million to over $1 billion; maturities extend from over one year to fifteen years.

Banks that provide syndicated loans acquire funds for these financings primarily by borrowing in the form of short-term deposits from other banks (that is, they perform maturity transformation). For this reason

Table 4–8B.

ESTIMATED NET LENDING IN INTERNATIONAL MARKETS: INTER-
NATIONAL BANK LENDING AND SECURITIES ISSUES (billions of US dollars).

	Changes, excluding exchange rate effects[a]						Stocks at end of 1987
	1982	1983	1984	1985	1986	1987	
Total cross-border claims of reporting banks[b]	180.5	105.7	124.1	233.5	517.3	567.8	4,157.2
minus: double-counting due to redepositing among the reporting banks[b]	85.5	20.7	34.1	128.5	352.3	312.8	1,937.2
A = Net international bank lending[c]	95.0	85.0	90.0	105.0	165.0	255.0	2,220.0
Euro-bond and foreign bond issues	74.3	73.8	108.4	164.5	221.5	175.6	
minus: redemptions and repurchases	15.8	15.8	25.4	39.5	65.5	71.6	
B = Net international bond financing	58.5	58.0	83.0	125.0	156.0	104.0	984.0
C (A + B) = Total bank and bond financing	153.5	143.0	173.0	230.0	321.0	359.0	3,204.0
minus: double-counting[d]	8.5	13.0	28.0	55.0	76.0	44.0	284.0
D = Total net bank and bond financing	145.0	130.0	145.0	175.0	245.0	315.0	2,920.0

Source: BIS, 58th *Annual Report*, June 1988, p. 109.

Notes:

[a]The yearly changes in banking claims represent the sum of the quarterly changes, computed in the case of non-dollar assets at the exchange rates prevailing at the end of the respective quarter. Unless otherwise mentioned this method is used throughout the rest of this chapter. Non-dollar bonds are converted into dollars at rates ruling on announcement dates.

[b]Up to 1983 the reporting area includes banks in the Group of Ten countries, Luxembourg, Austria, Denmark and Ireland, plus the offshore branches of US banks in the Bahamas, the Cayman Islands, Panama, Hong Kong and Singapore. As from 1984 the reporting area includes in addition Finland, Norway and Spain as well as non-US banks engaged in international business in the Bahamas, the Cayman Islands, Hong Kong and Singapore, all offshore units in Bahrain and all offshore banks operating in the Netherlands Antilles.

[c]In addition to direct claims on end-users, these estimates include certain interbank positions: firstly, claims on banks outside the reporting area, the assumption being that these 'peripheral' banks will not, in most cases, borrow the funds from banks in the financial centers simply for the purpose of redepositing them with other banks in these centers; secondly, claims on banks within the reporting area, to the extent that these banks switch the funds into domestic currency and/or use them for direct foreign currency lending to domestic customers; thirdly, a large portion of the foreign currency claims on banks in the country of issue of the currency in question, e.g. dollar claims of banks in London on banks in the United States; here again the assumption is that the borrowing banks obtain the funds mainly for domestic purposes and not for re-lending abroad; a deduction is made, however, in respect of working balances and similar items.

[d]International bonds taken up by the reporting banks, to the extent that they are included in the banking statistics as claims on non-residents; bonds issued by the reporting banks mainly for the purpose of underpinning their international lending activities.

there are difficulties in financing long-term syndicated loans on a floating basis, subject to periodic interest adjustments (that is, on a rollover basis).

Syndicated Eurocurrency loans are rollover credits under which a bank agrees to make funds available for up to fifteen years. The price of rollover credits to the borrower has *three* components: A floating interest rate, a spread and various fees. The interest rate charged on most syndicated loans is floating, usually computed by adding a spread or margin to the London Interbank Offered Rate. The later is the rate at which banks lend funds to other banks operating in the Euromarket, adjusted every three or six months as market rates change. The new base rate is calculated two days prior to the rollover date as the average of the offer rates of several reference banks in the syndicate. This procedure enables the lending banks to obtain the funds they need in the market at all times at the prevailing terms and conditions.

The size of the spread depends on the market's assessment of the creditworthiness of the borrower, the maturity of the loan, and market

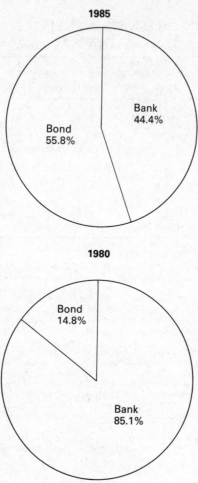

Source: BIS, Annual Report, 1986.

Figure 4–3. Lending in International Markets, 1980 and 1985.

conditions. The spread is negotiated with the borrower and either remains constant over the life of the loan, changes after a number of years, or is floating and is adjusted periodically. The higher the perceived risk associated with a borrower, the wider the spread that would be required. Evidence shows that the spreads on syndicated loans tend to narrow if the level of interest rates increases, the volatility of rates declines, or the maturities on loans are shortened.

For the lending bank, LIBOR represents the cost of the funds lent; the spread together with the fees constitute its net revenue, which offsets the cost of funds and intermediation risk. Interest on syndicated loans is charged in the same way that the banks have to pay interest to attract the deposits to make these loans—that is, every three or six months—and there is no interest-rate transformation. The floating-loan pricing method is attractive to both borrowers and lending banks; it

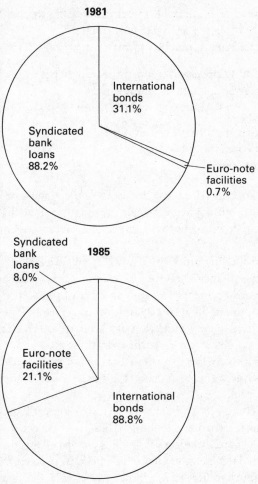

Source: BIS, *Annual Report*, 1986.

Figure 4–4. Funds Raised on International Markets, 1981 and 1985.

avoids being locked into paying more or receiving less than current interest rates when rates change, thereby reducing the risk associated with the interest-rate and maturity transformation.

The cost of arranging a syndicated loan is relatively low. In addition to the interest costs on a Eurocurrency loan, there are also commitment fees, front-end management fees, and occasionally an annual agent's fee. Commitment fees of 0.5 percent are charged against the undrawn amount of the loan and apply on both term loans and revolving credits. Front-end fees include participation fees and management fees and usually range between 0.5 and 1 percent of the value of the loan. Lending banks are paid participation fees depending on the size of their individual participation and managers are paid underwriting fees on the amount of their initial committed participation. All interest payments are paid free of any taxes. Similarly, if reserve requirements are raised or non–interest-bearing deposits are imposed, thereby increasing the cost of funds, the borrower has to pay the higher cost of credit.

The charges on syndicated loans may be summarized as follows:[2]

Annual payments = LIBOR + Spread × Amount of loan drawn
+ Commitment fee × Amount of loan undrawn
+ Tax adjustment (if any) + Annual agent's fee (if any)

Front-end charges = Participation fee × Face amount of loan
+ Management fee × Face amount of loan
+ Initial agent's fee (if any)

Syndicated Eurocredits contain advantages for both lenders and borrowers. They allow banks, both large and small, to share large credits with other banks, participate in many transactions, and diversify their risks.

Loan syndication increases the amount of bank credit available to borrowers without necessarily increasing the risk to individual lenders. It allows for the efficient arrangement of a larger amount of funds than any single lender can feasibly supply relatively quickly and cheaply. The underwriting procedure used in the syndication of Eurocurrency credits may allow the borrower to obtain better terms than those that would otherwise be available. For many sovereign-state borrowers, particularly the less developed countries, the loan market is one of the major international financing options.

The syndication procedure allows banks to diversify some of the unique risks that arise in international lending. These risks reflect, to some degree, the heavy concentration of lending to public-sector borrowers, approximately 70 percent of the total. The legal protection available to a bank is much different if a private borrower defaults compared with the situation when a public borrower defaults. In the former case, creditors can pursue various legal steps. When commercial banks lend to public-sector borrowers, there is much more uncertainty about legal recourse because some public-sector borrowers are covered by sovereign immunity.

Moreover, syndication allows banks to reduce sovereign risk by giving them the opportunity to diversify their international loans geographically, and it provides more protection against selective defaults. The syndication process tends to increase the penalty associated with selective defaults—that is, if a public-sector borrower chooses not to repay loans from individual banks or a group of banks in a particular country. Banks include a cross-default clause in the loan agreement that states that if one public borrower defaults, the loans of other public borrowers from that country may be called into default as well. In that case, the loans of those borrowers become due and payable.

In summary, a syndicated Eurocurrency loan, compared with a fixed-rate credit arranged by an individual bank, minimizes the various

Table 4–9.
RISK-REDUCTION STRATEGIES IN SYNDICATED LENDING.

Risk	Source of risk	Risk-reduction strategy
Country risk	Ability and willingness of borrowers within a country to meet their obligations	Syndication of the credit and diversification of bank's loan portfolio
Credit risk	Ability of an entity to repay its debts	Syndication of the credit and diversification of bank's loan portfolio
Interest risk	Mismatched maturities coupled with unpredictable movements in interest rates	Matching assets to liabilities by pricing credits on a rollover basis
Regulatory risk	Imposition of reserve requirements or taxes on the banks	A clause in the contract that forces the borrowers to bear this risk

risks that financial institutions participating in the market would otherwise face, through the strategies described in Table 4–9.[3] Syndicated Eurocurrency loans are usually unsecured, nonnegotiable, and generally remain on a bank's books until maturity. However, some loan agreements may allow banks to transfer or assign participants to their branches or other banks.

Syndicated loans are arranged by a manager or lead manager, which is usually a commercial bank, or a merchant or investment bank that has a mandate to handle the financing. Most loans are led by one or two major banks that negotiate to obtain a mandate to raise funds for the borrower. Often a potential borrower will set a competitive bidding procedure to determine which lead bank or banks will receive the mandate to organize the loan.

The lead manager of a syndicated loan negotiates its terms and conditions with the prospective borrower and is responsible for arranging the syndicate, preparing loan documentation, and organizing the signing of the loan agreement by the borrower and all participating lenders. After the management group has been formed with other banks that will underwrite part or all of the loan, the lead manager begins syndication by offering banks a chance to participate in amounts usually smaller than the manager's commitments. During syndication, a placement memorandum—which includes a summary of the terms, a description of the borrower's financial conditions, and other relevant information—is prepared and distributed among participants.

The lead bank is normally expected to underwrite a share at least as large as that of any other lender, but in a successful syndication the manager's own participation may be reduced. Because other banks are willing to participate in smaller credits to frequent borrowers during periods of uncertainty, club loans are often arranged in which the lead bank and managers fund the entire loan and no placement memorandum is necessary.

When the loan is fully syndicated—that is, when banks have agreed to provide funds for the entire loan—the loan agreement is signed by the borrower and all the participants. If the loan cannot be underwritten on the initial terms, it must be renegotiated or the lead manager must be willing to take a larger share into its own portfolio than originally planned. After signing the loan, the lead bank usually serves as agent to compute the interest-rate charges, to receive service payments, to disburse these to individual participants, and to inform them if there are any difficulties with the loan.

THE INTERNATIONAL BOND MARKET

Definitions

Borrowing in the international bond market takes place either through public or private issuing of Eurobonds (also known as international or external bonds) and foreign bonds. In contrast to the decline in international bank lending, the international bond market has increased sharply.

Bonds, floating rate notes (FRNs), and Euronotes have assumed a much greater importance relative to syndicated loans. The 1987 gross volume of new issues reached $245 billion, an amount three times as high as in 1982. Especially marked was the rise in floating rate note issues to $70 billion.

The international bond and Euro-note facilities market expanded from $4.5 billion in 1970 to $176 billion in 1987, of which $140 billion or about 80 percent was international bonds, and $70 billion or 20 percent was note issuance facilities. A summary of foreign and international Eurobond issuing by borrowing country or area, type of borrower, type of placement, market country, type of bond, purpose of borrowing, and currency denomination and maturity is given in Table 4–10 and Figure 4–5.

A Eurobond, or international bond, is a long-term security under-

Table 4–10A.
NEW EXTERNAL BOND OFFERINGS (billions of US dollars).

Instruments	1985	1986	1987	1987[a]	1988[a]
Straight bonds	94.8	141.5	123.8	48.7	44.8
Floating-rate issues	58.7	51.2	10.7	2.1	2.2
Equity-related	11.3	26.9	39.3	5.1	6.4
Zero coupons	1.9	3.1	1.7	1.0	0.1
Other	2.4	5.4	1.8	0.8	0.6
Total	169.1	228.1	177.3	57.7	54.1
Memorandum item:					
International bonds	136.6	187.7	140.5	48.4	40.4
Total issues at constant (end of 1986) exchange rates	191.4	233.4	166.2	56.2	48.1

Source: OECD, *Financial Market Trends*, 40, May 1988, p. 58.
Note:
[a] First quarter

written by an international syndicate of banks (commercial, investment, or merchant) and marketed internationally in countries other than the country of the currency in which it is denominated. The issue is not subject to any national restrictions.

A Eurobond is denominated in a currency that is not necessarily that of either the borrower or the investors. Most bonds have been denominated in U.S. dollars, but in contrast to the Eurocurrency market, nondollar issues are important. Many investors prefer issues in a strong currency, presumably in the belief that the lower interest rate on issues will be more than compensated for by the appreciation in capital value as the currency appreciates.

Eurobonds are issued in units of, or are equivalent to, $1,000 each

Table 4–10B.
EXTERNAL BOND OFFERINGS (billions of US dollars).

Borrowers	1985	1986	1987	1987[a]	1988[a]
OECD	148.2	213.3	164.2	54.2	51.0
Australia	5.7	10.0	6.0	2.2	1.7
Austria	2.4	3.7	4.5	1.6	2.9
Belgium	2.5	4.3	4.0	1.0	1.3
Canada	9.7	16.8	8.7	2.5	2.8
Denmark	2.9	9.1	4.1	2.7	1.0
Finland	1.4	3.3	3.0	1.0	1.5
France	11.6	13.6	8.9	3.9	4.1
Germany	3.1	11.8	10.5	4.8	3.1
Greece	0.7	0.2	0.5	0.1	—
Ireland	1.5	2.2	1.0	0.1	0.4
Italy	5.4	5.3	7.2	0.7	1.6
Japan	21.6	34.4	43.5	9.6	8.8
Netherlands	1.4	3.0	3.2	1.2	1.3
New Zealand	1.6	4.8	3.4	1.0	0.5
Norway	2.3	5.8	4.0	2.8	2.2
Portugal	0.3	0.5	0.6	0.1	0.5
Spain	1.4	1.7	0.6	—	0.6
Sweden	6.2	5.8	4.6	1.8	2.4
Switzerland	0.9	2.2	1.1	0.4	—
United Kingdom	15.6	19.6	12.4	4.4	6.3
United States	40.1	44.1	21.6	8.0	3.4
EEC Institutions	6.5	7.8	6.3	2.7	2.8
Other	3.4	3.3	4.5	1.6	1.8
Developing countries	7.2	4.3	2.5	0.5	0.9
Algeria	0.5	0.1	—	—	0.1
China	1.0	1.4	1.1	0.2	0.1
Hong Kong	0.1	0.3	0.1	—	0.1
India	0.4	0.3	0.3	0.2	0.1
Indonesia	—	0.3	—	—	—
Malaysia	2.0	—	0.2	—	0.2
South Korea	1.7	0.8	0.3	—	—
Thailand	0.9	0.1	—	—	—
Other LDCs	0.6	1.0	0.5	0.1	0.3
International Development Organizations	11.0	9.2	9.8	2.6	1.8
Other	2.7	1.3	0.8	0.4	0.4
of which:					
Hungary	0.4	0.3	0.5	0.3	0.3
South Africa	0.8	—	—	—	—
Total:	169.1	228.1	177.3	57.7	54.1

Source: OECD, *Financial Market Trends*, 40, May 1988, p. 95.
Note:
[a]First quarter.

133

Table 4–10C.

STRUCTURE OF CAPITAL DEMAND ON THE MARKETS
FOR EXTERNAL BOND ISSUES (percentage).

	1984	1985	1986	1987	1988[a]
OECD area	88.6	87.7	93.5	92.6	94.3
Oil exporters	0.5	0.5	0.2	0.1	0.6
Other developing countries	2.8	3.8	1.7	1.3	1.0
International development organisations	7.0	6.5	4.0	5.5	3.4
Other	1.1	1.5	0.6	0.5	0.7
Total	100.0	100.0	100.0	100.0	100.0
Memorandum item: Total issues in $ billion	111.5	169.1	228.1	177.3	54.1

Source: OECD, *Financial Market Trends*, 40, May 1988, p. 63.
Note:
[a]First quarter.

Table 4–10D.

CURRENCY DISTRIBUTION OF EXTERNAL
BOND OFFERINGS (percentage).[a]

	1985	1986	1987	1988[b]
US dollar	54.0	53.9	37.9	35.2
Yen	9.1	10.4	13.9	7.4
Swiss franc	11.3	10.7	13.0	15.6
Deutsche mark	8.5	8.0	8.4	13.0
Sterling	4.0	4.6	8.0	10.3
Australian dollar	1.6	1.5	5.1	2.8
ECU	5.2	3.4	4.1	3.4
Canadian dollar	1.6	2.3	3.4	6.2
French franc	1.1	1.7	1.3	0.9
Dutch guilder	1.3	1.3	1.2	1.4
Other	2.3	2.2	3.7	3.8
Total	100.0	100.0	100.0	100.0
Memorandum item: Total issues in US$ billion equivalent	191.4	233.4	166.2	192.3[c]

Source: OECD, *Financial Market Trends*, 40, May 1988, p. 68.
Note:
[a]All currencies converted into US dollar at constant (end of 1986) exchange rates.
[b]First quarter.
[c]At annual rate.

and are always available in bearer form, thus preserving anonymity of ownership. Interest is paid free of taxes. In general, bonds tend to have longer maturity than Eurocurrency loans. Bond issues are for over one to fifteen years' life to maturity at fixed and floating rate of interest, whereas Eurocurrency loans are available mainly for shorter maturities, primarily at floating interest rates, which vary every three to six months.

A foreign bond is a long-term security issued by a borrower in the national capital market of another country (as distinct from a Euro-bond, which is marketed internationally). Underwritten by a syndicate from one country alone and sold on that country's capital market, the

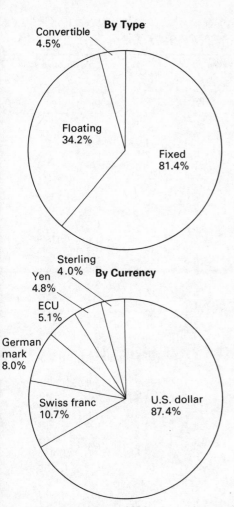

Source: BIS, *Annual Report*, 1986.

Figure 4–5. The International Bond Market, 1985.

bond is denominated in the currency of the country in which it is sold. Foreign bonds are usually available in bearer form, preserving anonymity of ownership. Normally interest is paid free of withholding tax to bond holders (not resident in the country of issue).

Dollar bonds issued by foreigners in New York are called Yankee bonds. These bonds are underwritten by an international syndicate managed by U.S. banks and placed in the United States. They are subject to U.S. law and have to be registered with the SEC. Most Yankee bonds are sold in the United States, but anyone can acquire them.

Eurobond Market Characteristics

The market's sharpest expansion occurred in the late 1950s and early

135

Table 4–10E.

DEBT OUTSTANDING AND NEW BORROWING IN THE INTERNATIONAL BON MARKETS BY NATIONALITY OF ISSUERS (billions of US dollars) ALL ISSUERS.

Country	Amount outstanding (end of period)					Changes in 1986		
	Dec 1982	Dec 1985	Dec 1986	Dec 1987	Mar 1988	gross new issues	net new issues	exchan rate effect
BIS Reporting area								
Austria	7.6	12.6	17.5	23.8	25.6	3.7	2.6	2
Belgium	1.9	6.5	10.9	13.9	13.9	4.2	3.7	0
Luxembourg	0.8	1.5	2.0	2.6	2.5	0.4	0.3	0
Canada	41.4	56.9	73.0	81.7	81.0	17.3	13.0	3
Denmark	5.4	12.3	20.1	26.8	26.6	8.0	6.2	1
Finland	3.6	6.5	9.9	14.2	14.4	3.4	2.2	1
France	18.4	39.0	48.2	58.0	59.5	13.1	5.6	3
Germany	3.1	10.8	23.0	35.3	36.9	10.6	10.3	1
Ireland	1.9	5.2	7.7	8.3	8.3	2.2	1.8	0
Italy	4.7	14.3	18.8	26.6	26.2	5.4	3.3	1
Japan	17.6	63.6	100.1	152.5	154.1	31.0	26.9	9
Netherlands	3.9	7.3	12.0	16.1	16.2	4.2	3.3	1
Norway	6.4	8.7	14.4	18.6	19.4	5.5	4.6	1
Spain	2.4	6.1	6.2	6.4	6.3	1.7	−0.7	0
Sweden	11.0	21.0	25.7	29.9	30.8	6.7	2.7	2
Switzerland	1.7	4.1	5.4	6.8	6.6	1.8	1.2	0
United Kingdom	11.1	29.9	48.0	63.9	68.9	19.5	17.2	1
United States	36.0	100.3	140.0	162.4	159.4	42.1	34.0	5
Hong Kong	0.2	1.3	1.9	2.0	2.1	0.6	0.5	-
Singapore	0.4	0.5	0.6	0.9	0.9	0.2	0.1	-
Other	0.4	0.6	0.7	0.8	0.7	—	—	-
Total	179.9	409.1	586.2	751.4	760.5	181.7	138.8	38
Other Developed Countries								
Australia	6.4	17.2	27.0	35.5	35.9	10.0	7.9	1
Greece	0.1	1.2	1.2	1.8	1.9	0.1	−0.1	0
Iceland	0.3	0.6	0.7	0.8	0.7	—	—	-
New Zealand	3.2	7.1	11.2	15.4	15.0	4.6	3.1	1
Portugal	0.1	0.9	1.5	2.5	2.9	0.4	0.4	0
South Africa	1.5	3.2	3.5	3.7	3.4	—	−0.2	0
Turkey	—	0.1	0.2	0.6	0.9	0.1	0.1	-
Other	0.1	0.2	0.2	0.3	0.4	—	—	0
Total	11.9	30.5	45.6	60.8	61.3	15.2	11.2	3
Eastern Europe								
Hungary	0.1	0.5	1.1	1.9	2.2	0.5	0.5	0
Other	0.5	0.5	0.6	0.5	0.5	0.1	0.1	-
Total	0.6	1.0	1.7	2.4	2.7	0.6	0.6	0
OPEC Countries								
Algeria	0.9	1.3	1.4	1.3	1.5	0.1	—	-
Indonesia	0.4	0.6	0.9	0.9	0.9	0.3	0.3	-
Trinidad/Tobago	0.1	0.4	0.5	0.7	0.8	—	—	0
Venezuela	1.1	1.1	1.0	1.1	1.1	—	−0.2	0
Other	0.3	0.6	0.6	0.4	0.2	—	—	-
Total	2.8	4.0	4.4	4.4	4.5	0.4	0.1	-
Non-OPEC LDCs								
Argentina	0.8	0.7	0.6	0.6	0.6	—	−0.2	0
Brazil	2.3	2.0	2.1	1.8	1.8	—	−0.3	0
China	0.1	1.1	2.5	4.2	4.4	1.2	1.2	0
India	0.4	0.8	1.3	1.8	1.8	0.4	0.3	0
Israel	2.7	2.3	2.0	1.5	1.5	0.1	−0.3	-
Korea (South)	0.3	2.8	4.0	4.9	4.4	0.8	0.8	0
Malaysia	0.9	5.4	5.8	6.5	6.7	—	—	0
Mexico	5.6	5.2	4.8	4.3	4.1	0.1	−0.6	0
Phillippines	0.9	1.0	0.9	0.9	0.8	—	−0.2	0
Thailand	0.2	1.4	1.4	1.6	1.5	—	−0.1	0
Other	1.0	1.1	1.1	1.1	0.8	—	−0.2	0
Total	15.2	23.9	26.6	29.4	28.6	2.6	0.4	2
International institutions	48.8	89.8	112.5	141.6	139.9	18.5	8.4	14
Grand Total	259.1	558.4	777.1	990.1	997.5	219.1	159.6	59

Source: BIS, International Banking and Financial Market Developments, August 1988, p. 26.

Changes in 1987			Changes in Q1 1987			Changes in Q4 1987			Changes in Q1 1988		
gross new issues	net new issues	exchange rate effects	gross new issues	net new issues	exchange rate effects	gross new issues	net new issues	exchange rate effects	gross new issues	net new issues	exchange rate effects
5.5	2.8	3.5	1.6	1.1	1.1	1.5	0.8	2.6	3.2	2.5	-0.7
4.2	1.9	1.2	1.0	0.6	0.2	0.8	—	1.0	1.0	0.3	-0.3
0.4	0.2	0.4	—	—	0.1	0.3	0.3	0.3	—	—	-0.1
9.0	3.1	5.6	1.8	0.5	2.0	2.2	1.2	3.8	1.9	-0.1	-0.5
5.1	3.6	3.1	3.3	2.9	1.0	0.6	0.3	2.3	0.9	0.2	-0.5
3.1	2.2	2.1	1.1	1.0	0.5	0.9	0.8	1.4	1.0	0.5	-0.3
9.3	3.4	6.4	3.9	2.0	1.9	1.2	0.1	4.7	3.1	2.5	-1.0
9.4	8.2	4.1	3.4	3.1	1.2	1.4	1.0	3.0	2.8	2.4	-0.8
0.4	-0.5	1.0	0.1	-0.2	0.3	—	-0.3	0.8	0.5	0.2	-0.2
6.3	5.1	2.7	0.4	0.3	0.8	3.9	3.7	2.0	1.7	0.5	-0.9
43.2	36.6	15.8	9.0	7.3	4.3	6.6	4.5	12.3	8.8	5.8	-4.2
3.6	2.0	2.1	1.5	1.3	0.7	0.3	-0.3	1.6	1.2	0.6	-0.5
4.3	2.1	2.2	2.0	1.5	0.6	0.2	-0.2	1.6	1.7	1.1	-0.3
0.6	-0.8	1.0	0.1	-0.3	0.3	0.1	-0.2	0.7	0.4	0.1	-0.2
4.2	0.9	3.2	1.5	0.8	1.0	0.6	-0.3	2.3	2.3	1.5	-0.5
1.4	0.9	0.5	0.6	0.5	0.1	0.3	—	0.4	0.1	-0.1	-0.1
11.7	9.5	6.4	3.1	2.6	2.1	2.6	1.9	4.4	5.6	5.2	-0.1
24.1	11.9	10.5	7.0	5.5	3.1	2.5	-2.4	7.5	2.0	-1.3	-1.6
0.1	0.1	0.1	—	—	—	—	—	0.1	0.2	0.1	—
0.2	0.2	—	0.1	—	—	0.1	0.1	—	—	—	—
0.1	—	0.1	—	—	0.3	—	—	0.3	—	0.1	-0.2
146.3	93.3	71.9	41.5	30.5	21.6	26.1	10.8	53.1	38.4	22.1	-13.0
6.7	4.3	4.2	1.9	1.2	1.2	0.6	-0.2	2.8	1.6	0.9	-0.5
0.4	0.3	0.2	0.1	0.1	0.1	—	—	0.2	0.2	0.2	-0.1
0.1	—	0.1	0.1	0.1	—	—	—	0.1	—	—	—
3.6	2.4	1.8	0.9	0.8	0.5	1.4	0.9	1.3	0.3	-0.2	-0.2
0.7	0.6	0.4	0.1	0.1	0.1	—	—	0.3	0.4	0.5	-0.1
—	-0.4	0.6	—	-0.1	0.2	—	-0.2	0.4	—	-0.1	-0.1
0.2	0.2	0.1	0.1	0.1	—	0.1	0.1	0.1	0.4	0.4	—
0.1	0.1	0.2	0.1	0.1	0.1	—	0.1	0.1	—	-0.1	-0.1
11.7	7.6	7.6	3.3	2.4	2.2	2.3	0.7	5.3	2.9	1.6	-1.1
0.6	0.5	0.2	0.3	0.3	—	0.3	0.3	0.2	0.3	0.3	—
—	—	—	—	-0.1	0.1	—	—	—	0.1	0.1	—
0.6	0.5	0.2	0.3	0.2	0.1	0.3	0.3	0.2	0.4	0.4	—
—	-0.1	0.1	—	—	—	—	—	0.1	0.1	0.2	—
—	-0.1	—	—	—	—	—	-0.1	—	—	—	—
0.1	0.1	0.1	—	—	—	0.1	0.1	0.1	0.1	0.1	—
—	-0.2	0.2	—	-0.2	0.1	—	—	0.2	0.1	0.1	—
—	-0.2	0.1	—	0.1	0.1	—	-0.2	-0.1	—	-0.2	-0.1
0.1	-0.5	0.5	—	-0.1	0.2	0.1	-0.2	0.3	0.3	0.2	-0.1
—	-0.1	0.1	—	—	—	—	—	0.1	—	—	—
—	-0.7	0.4	—	-0.1	0.2	—	-0.3	0.3	—	—	—
1.0	1.0	0.7	0.2	0.2	0.2	0.4	0.4	0.5	0.2	0.2	-0.1
0.3	0.2	0.3	0.2	0.2	0.1	0.1	0.1	0.2	—	—	—
—	-0.5	—	—	-0.1	—	—	-0.1	—	—	-0.1	—
0.3	0.2	0.7	—	—	0.2	—	—	0.5	—	-0.4	-0.1
0.2	0.1	0.6	—	—	0.2	—	—	0.4	0.2	0.2	-0.1
—	-0.8	0.3	—	-0.3	0.1	—	-0.3	0.2	—	-0.2	—
—	-0.1	0.1	—	—	—	—	—	0.1	—	-0.1	—
—	—	0.1	—	—	—	—	—	0.1	—	—	—
0.1	0.2	—	—	-0.1	0.1	—	-0.1	—	0.1	-0.1	-0.1
1.9	-0.5	3.3	0.4	-0.2	1.1	0.5	-0.3	2.4	0.5	-0.5	-0.4
20.3	8.4	20.6	6.3	3.7	6.5	5.4	2.4	15.5	5.4	2.3	-4.2
180.8	108.7	104.1	51.9	36.5	31.6	34.6	13.6	76.8	47.9	26.1	-18.7

1960s. The development of the bond market since World War II has had three distinct phases: (1) an emerging period, 1958–63; (2) the period of U.S. capital controls, 1963–74; and (3) a maturing period, after 1974.

Borrowing in the Eurobond market in 1987 reached $140 billion, up from $50 billion in 1983. The international bond market is sensitive to currency movements, and in recent years it has experienced substantial currency diversification. The dollar remains the most significant currency (about 90 percent of the Eurobond market in 1986). The use of other currencies, particularly deutsche marks (14 percent), the yen (14 percent), and sterling (10 percent), became widespread as investors attempted to diversify their portfolios. Eurobonds are also issued in ECUs (5 percent) and in the form of multiple-currency bonds, parallel issues, and composite units of bonds. See Table 4–11.

Table 4–11.
STRUCTURAL FEATURES OF THE INTERNATIONAL BOND MARKETS[a]
(billions of US dollars).

Items	1984	1985	1986	Year	1987 First Quarter	1987 Second Quarter	Third Quarter	Fourth Quarter	1988 First Quarter
Total issues	108.4	164.5	221.5	175.6	60.1	45.7	42.2	27.6	59.5
by type of issue:									
Fixed rate bonds	74.4	108.6	173.7	163.6	57.4	44.0	39.6	22.6	56.8
Floating rate notes	34.0	55.9	47.8	12.0	2.7	1.7	2.6	5.0	2.7
of which: equity-related[b]	*8.5*	*11.6*	*27.5*	*43.3*	*7.8*	*15.7*	*17.2*	*2.6*	*7.9*
by currency of issue:									
US dollar Euro	66.9	95.5	115.3	57.8	18.5	16.0	18.7	4.6	15.5
foreign	1.9	3.9	6.4	5.0	1.3	0.4	1.0	2.3	1.6
Yen Euro	1.2	6.9	18.2	23.1	8.5	8.6	0.9	5.1	4.9
foreign	4.7	5.4	4.4	1.6	0.6	0.0	0.7	0.3	0.9
Swiss franc	13.1	14.9	23.3	24.0	6.1	4.9	7.9	5.1	10.0
Deutsche mark	7.0	11.3	16.2	15.0	6.6	2.5	2.2	3.7	7.6
Sterling Euro	4.1	5.6	10.9	14.9	5.3	4.2	2.5	2.9	7.4
foreign	1.4	1.0	0.4	0.0	0.0	0.0	0.0	0.0	0.0
Australian dollar	0.3	3.2	3.4	8.7	3.1	3.3	2.2	0.1	1.6
ECU[c]	2.9	7.3	6.8	7.4	3.7	1.7	1.1	0.9	2.1
Other	4.9	9.5	16.2	18.1	6.4	4.1	5.0	2.6	7.9

Source: BIS, 58th Annual Report, June 1988, p. 126.
Note:
[a]Figures based on announcement dates.
[b]Convertible bonds and bonds with equity warrants.
[c]Excludes bonds issued in borrowers' national markets.

Originally the Eurobond market issued only straight bonds (that is, securities without rights of conversion into a borrower's common stock) but since 1968 has also issued convertible debentures (that is, fixed-interest securities convertible into the borrower's common stock on stipulated conditions). That option can be exercised between two dates fixed in the loan contract, at a fixed price. The difference between the price of ordinary shares at the time of the issue of the bonds and the rate at which they can be converted is the convertible premium. The attractiveness of convertible bonds is that there will be a rise in the price of common stock during the period of the convertible bond's life or an appreciation in the currency in which the common stock is quoted or both. Convertible bonds provide a hedge against considerable erosion of capital due to currency depreciation.

Convertible bonds with detachable warrants allow investors to purchase straight Eurodollar bonds with the option to purchase shares of the issuer's common stock. These options are called warrants. Almost all warrants may be detached from their bonds and traded freely in a secondary market, although they are not listed in Europe. When warrants are exercised (that is, converted into common stocks), outside capital is usually used to buy the shares. This is different from a convertible bond; in that case it is the principal amount of the security itself that is used to purchase shares.

Further growth of Eurobond issues depends on the market's capacity to absorb new issues and on the expansion of the secondary market, both of which give bonds a high liquidity and attract investors. Trading Eurobonds on the secondary market after floating an issue therefore is of utmost significance. It satisfies investors' desire for liquidity, which induces demand for bonds.

Eurobonds are listed on a number of stock exchanges, including the Luxembourg Bourse, which offers special fiscal incentives and other concessions to attract foreign issues. A listing of the bonds on the Luxembourg or London stock exchanges is usually applied for because many institutional investors are not allowed by law or internal regulations to invest in unlisted bonds. Inasmuch as dollar bonds are often payable in New York and are deposited there, they are also listed on the New York Stock Exchange.

The secondary market assumes the form of active dealings between financial houses on their own accounts, to or from each other and to or from their clients. Buying and selling is carried out by telephone and telex between banks and brokers, mostly outside stock exchanges. Because traders are no longer able to maintain active markets in all outstanding issues, lists are published to indicate those bonds in which they specialize as market markers.

The secondary market is made up of various types of investors, which may be classified into the following categories: (1) Central banks, government agencies, and international financial institutions; (2) investment funds, pension funds, and insurance companies; (3) bank trust departments; (4) bank portfolios; and (5) retail investors. The identity of most Eurobond investors is confidential and unknown because the securities are in bearer form and no records are kept of their ownership. The twenty banks that act as syndicate leaders on the market hold some 25 percent of the Eurobonds that have been issued. More than 50 percent of the outstanding bonds are held by private customers. Institutional investors (such as investment trusts, pension funds, multinational corporations, insurance companies, and monetary authorities) hold some 25 percent of the outstanding Eurobonds.

Eurobonds are priced on the basis of both fixed and floating interest rates. Issues with fixed interest rates and fixed maturities—straight bonds—represent the most important type. Short-term floating-interest-rate securities—floating-rate notes (FRNs)—are also available. Floating-rate notes are medium-term bonds (five to seven years) whose interest rate is reset at short-term intervals. They have been viewed as a substitute for both fixed-rate bonds and syndicated loans. Some straight issues carry guarantees either by a parent company for its foreign subsidiary if the latter acts as borrower in its own name or by governments for the issues of public agencies' borrowing.

The FRN's rate of interest is set at six months LIBOR, adjusted semiannually, plus a spread, usually between 0.25 percent and over 1.0 percent. These securities are particularly attractive during periods of rising interest rates, when the issues of straight bonds are subject to capital depreciation. Moreover, during periods of tight monetary conditions, this instrument provides an alternative to bank credit. The maturity of FRNs ranges from four to ten years, but maturities are concentrated in the range of five to seven years. The notes are typically callable after two or three years at par.

To protect investors against declining interest rates, an investor in FRNs normally receives a minimum rate below which the interest cannot fall. Floating-rate notes represent an increasing proportion of issuing on the Eurobond market. They are available in a number of currencies but at a higher cost than straight Eurobonds.

The price at which bonds are sold on issue is normally expressed as a percentage of the bond's face value, which is usually $1,000 in the Eurobond market. Par is the equivalent of face value; a sale price of $99\frac{1}{2}$ means that the bond is sold at a discount for $995; quotations above 100 represent a premium over face value. Repayment at maturity is usually at face value—that is, 100 percent of the principal amount. The annual payments of interest is the same each year and is expressed as a percentage of a bond's principal amount. For instance, a $1,000 bond with an 8 percent interest will pay an investor $80 per year. The interest payment is represented by a coupon, which must be clipped off each year and presented to an appointed paying agent for payment of interest.

The return, or yield to maturity, on a fixed-interest security is based on coupon price and its average remaining life. An 8 percent bond sold at par yields that return; it yields less than 8 percent if bought above par and more than 8 percent if bought below par. Current yield is calculated by dividing the interest payment, or coupon, by the security price. For instance, the current yield of an 8 percent coupon bond priced at $97\frac{1}{2}$ percent is 8.2 percent (8 percent $\div$ $97\frac{1}{2}$ percent). Yield to maturity consists of interest from the coupon and capital gain from the difference between the discount price at the time of purchase and the repayment price at maturity (almost always 100 percent). Using this calculation method at a price of $97\frac{1}{2}$ percent, an 8 percent seven-year bond yields approximately 8.50 percent, taking into account both the coupon and the $2\frac{1}{2}$ percent capital gain that will be realized in seven years and amortization over that same period.

Eurobonds are exempt from taxes and yield a higher return than domestic bonds with the same maturities and currency. The issue cost incurred by the borrower is 2 to $2\frac{1}{2}$ percent of the issue's principal amount and consists of management fee ($\frac{3}{8}$ to $\frac{1}{2}$ percent), underwriting commission ($\frac{3}{8}$ to $\frac{1}{2}$ percent), and placement fee or selling concession ($1\frac{1}{4}$ to $1\frac{1}{2}$ percent).

The main attraction of Eurobonds is their low cost. Because of differences in tax treatment or other regulations across countries or because of differences in investor preferences, borrowers frequently find that they can issue Eurobonds at rates lower than those available in their home markets.[4] The rate advantage of the Euromarkets over U.S. bond markets has often been substantial in recent years.

Eurobonds are placed by a lead bank manager and co-managers, which invite a great number of banks and brokers in a number of countries to participate in the placement of the issue either as under-writers or as members of the selling group. The underwriters undertake to provide a certain portion, ranging from 1.5 percent to 1 percent, of the issue's principal amount, depending whether they are major, submajor, or minor participants. The banks that act as underwriters receive the underwriting commission in addition to the selling concession, whereas the banks belonging to the management group (the lead manager and the co-managers) are also entitled to a management fee.

Euronotes

Euronotes are short-term unsecured corporate debt. Initially, most Euronotes were issued under a medium-term underwriting commitment by a bank or syndicate of banks, an arrangement that developed from syndicated bank loans.[5] More recently, notes have been issued without the backing of a syndicate of underwriting banks, known generally as Eurocommercial paper programs.

Since its beginnings in the early 1980s, the Euronote facility market was one of the most cost-effective, flexible, and rapidly growing sectors of the international capital markets. The flexibility and relatively low cost of Euronotes are among the factors that have contributed to the decline of syndicated lending and, more recently, to the slowdown in new issues of floating rate notes. In addition, these facilities have been used as substitutes for interbank lines and as back-ups for issuing commercial paper in the United States. The proliferation of Euronotes, which are only partly reflected in a bank's balance sheet, distorts international banking statistics.

Euronotes outstanding have grown from very small amounts at the end of 1987 to an estimated $85 billion, with most of the recent growth in nonunderwritten Eurocommercial paper. The boom is part of the securitization of international capital markets. At its present rate of growth the corporate Euronote market is rivaling the Eurobond market as a source of funds for international corporations.

As the market has developed, the investor base has expanded. In early 1986 as much as 50 to 75 percent of new notes in the Euromarket were being sold to nonbanks. The introduction of credit ratings and the possibility for investors to submit unsolicited bids have enhanced the attractiveness of this financing vehicle.

Euronote Characteristics

Back-up facilities are known under differing names, such as note-issuance facilities (NIFs), revolving underwriting facilities (RUFs), or multi-option funding facilities. The note-issuance facility consists of an arrangement whereby an underwriting syndicate consisting of banks commits itself for an annual fee for several years (generally three to five years but sometimes as long as ten years) to purchase from an international borrower notes of various maturities up to twelve months with a fixed spread (the cap rate) above a benchmark interest rate.[6] When the borrower activates the facility, notes are sold through bidding by tender or through negotiation to banks that then place the notes with investors. The cost to the borrower of such sales is usually below the cap rate. The underwriting banks are required to purchase only those notes that cannot be sold below the cap rate or to provide credit to the issuer for any unsold portion of the notes, although the underwriters may also be among the banks that acquire notes voluntarily. Notes are issued in bearer form and initially were for fixed maturities—typically one, three, or six months.

Although the bulk of the European notes are denominated in dollars and other major currencies, a notable feature is the growth of multi-component facilities that allow borrowers to draw funds in a variety of ways (such as short-term advances, bankers' acceptances, and swingline credits). The greatest attraction of a Euronote facility is that it dispenses with much of the rigidity of traditional borrowing vehicles by drawing on many of the best features of both the securities market and the syndicated loan market. With a Euronote facility an issuer can obtain funds tailored to its requirements.

An additional attraction for a borrower is the potential reduction in cost of medium-term credit as compared with a conventional credit or a floating-rate Eurobond. Originally NIFs were priced at spreads above

LIBOR. NIFS allow borrowers to raise funds at lowest cost with greatest flexibility. The cost savings to borrowers on NIFs as compared with Eurocredits range from about ten to around fifty basis points. The market for Euronotes of a particular issuer, or group of issuers, from the same country is thin, and therefore a modest increase in the supply of notes may drive the yield sharply, perhaps to levels above Eurocredit costs. Some borrowers who have arranged both types of facilities continue to obtain Eurocredits when NIFs have been cheaper for them.

The Euronotes themselves are fully negotiable and can be marketed at relatively low yields as compared with more traditional straight bank advances. The banks providing the back-up lines are prepared to accept lower facility fees against the risk of having to fund. Consequently Euronote facilities are suitable for a wide variety of uses, including both as a standby for the back-up of U.S. domestic commercial paper as well as for actual funding.

Underwriting banks have provided funds under NIFs in only the few instances where they have been required to or where they have voluntarily held Euronotes acquired at the time of issue. Euronotes acquired voluntarily by underwriting banks at time of issue are usually resold by them at a higher price in the market to nonbank and smaller bank investors.

Although most Euronotes are issued through a group of bidders called a tender panel, of which the underwriting banks are almost invariably members, two basic methods for distribution are used. The first type is analogous to the practice in the U.S. commercial paper market, where an investment bank acts as sole placing agent and a syndicate of commercial banks provides the back-up facility.[7] The second is analogous to an auction process in which, for each issue of notes, bids may be submitted by a number of institutions that form the tender panel. This panel is normally formed from the commercial banks that provide the back-up or underwriting syndicate as well as investment banks and other institutions interested in, and capable of, placing Euronote paper. Many variants and combinations of these two basic methods have been implemented, and further rapid development can be expected.

Several factors contributed to the development and growth of the NIFs market: (1) Borrowers have found it cheaper to fund themselves by issuing Euronotes; (2) bank deposits and CDs declined in popularity with secular investors, and alternative instruments, of which Euronotes are one, became more popular; and (3) banks have desired to slow the growth of their balance sheets, improve capital/asset ratios, and boost income fees derived from off-balance-sheet activities. The shift from Eurocredits to NIFs changed the role of large commercial banks from direct lending to primarily underwriting loans and to a lesser extent direct lending.

In 1987 the volume of new facilities arranged rose to $70 billion, and 143 by year end outstandings reached over $100 billion. Of the new NIFs arranged less than one-quarter had been drawn. The borrowers under NIFs include OECD countries and corporations therein. U.S. corporations have significantly increased NIFs use as back-up lines for domestic commercial paper issues. The share of corporate borrowers in new NIFs arranged expanded to 70 percent. More than 95 percent of the note-issuance facilities announced in 1987 were for borrowers from developed countries, by U.S. corporations in particular.[8]

Because the issuer in a committed facility relies on the mechanism for assured medium-term funding, the quality of the syndicate banks is of the highest importance. The particular risk for banks is that they have to fulfill their credit commitments or credit guarantees when the capital markets are less willing to provide funds. If this decreasing receptiveness is due to a deterioration in the creditworthiness of their customers, the banks are bound to be affected. Moreover, the refinancing capacity of the banks suffers if the receptiveness of the markets declines generally. The market for NIFs is affected by regulations. In April 1985 the Bank of England made NIFs subject to a 50 percent weighting in the computation of the risk/asset ratio. Similar regulations were introduced in several other countries, including France, Germany, Japan, and the United States.

Eurocommercial Paper

Eurocommercial Paper (ECP) is short-term debt in the form of Euronotes issued without the back-up of an underwriting commitment and sold on a best-efforts basis by banks that act as placement agents.[9] The ECP market is now well established: It allows major issuers to offer notes without any formal back-up commitment and is sufficiently liquid to provide funding at rates comparable to U.S. commercial paper.

A ECP program can be arranged through one or several placement agents for amounts as low as $10 million or in excess of $1 billion. In the case of some of the larger programs, paper is made available continuously, with bid and offer prices quoted daily for all maturities. The dealers provide liquidity to the market for their issuers' paper by agreeing to repurchase notes from investors before maturity, and some dealers make a secondary market for their customers' notes by actively quoting two-way prices for outstanding issues. In an effort to attract new investors, features previously found only in the U.S. commercial paper market have been added.

The operation of an ECP program is extremely simple and flexible and combines the best features of the traditional Euronote market and the U.S. commercial paper market:[10]

1 Placement in the Euromarket allows access to a vast pool of international liquidity provided by banks and other institutions.

144   2 Maturities can be conventional LIBOR periods, (one, two, three, or

six months) or other terms to suit individual requirements from
time to time.

3   Notes can be issued in either interest-bearing or discount form.
4   Pricing can be relative to LIBOR (or alternative-basis rates) or
absolute rate. Some of the larger, well-known corporate issuers
have been able to issue sizable amounts of Eurocommercial paper
at rates below LIBOR and equal to or lower than those available in
the U.S. commercial-paper market, particularly in longer maturities, where the U.S. market is very thin. Some of the programs
are global in that firms quote the same rates daily in both the U.S.
and offshore markets.
5   Bidding can be on a competitive basis, either inclusive or exclusive of
placement commissions.
6   Issuance can be at short notice down to same day.
7   The amount of each issue can be determined by the issuer.
8   There is no requirement for rating, registration, or other formalities.

ECP is a major development in the convergence of international
financial markets and offers new possibilities for funding management:

1   A ECP program can be established very quickly, with minimal
documentation and without disturbing bank relationships.
2   No underwriting fees are involved.
3   Arrangements can be varied to take advantage of market evolution.
4   The program can be used for occasional funding and regular access.
5   The introduction of ECP can provide a platform for future Euromarket financing such as committed Euronote facilities or
Eurobond issues.

The European market for commercial paper should be further
stimulated by the deregulation of markets for unsecured short-term
debt denominated in the major European countries. As a result, the
integration that occurred previously between the U.S. and European
market for long-term corporate debt is likely to spread to the short-term
markets as well.[11].

The unprecedented boom conditions in the international bond
markets have been stimulated by the following events:

1   The capital markets have been innovative and flexible.
2   Swaps have reduced the exposure of borrowers and lenders to the
markets for particular securities and currencies and have created
arbitrage opportunities made possible by regulatory barriers.
Consequently, interest-rate and exchange-rate features of a specific
issue have become less important.[12].
3   Deregulatory moves have been made especially by the United States,
which abolished the withholding tax on nonresident income from
U.S. securities. Furthermore, the growth of the securities markets
in 1985, 1986 and 1987 was closely related to regulatory changes

concerning both the permitted types of issue and the financial intermediaries authorized to arrange these issues. The most extensive deregulation took place in Japan, where more foreign borrowers were allowed to issue yen bonds in the Euromarket or in Japan.

4 Bank deposits have declined in attractiveness as a result of credit problems, which implies that some of the large sovereign borrowers could raise funds more cheaply in the capital markets than through the banks.

Foreign-Bond-Market Characteristics

Borrowing in the foreign bond reached $37 billion in 1987 and concentrated in the industrialized countries. The issuing of foreign bonds in a specific market is affected by market conditions, particularly interest and exchange rates. By type of bond, straight bonds accounted for the bulk of the issues, while convertible and warrant bonds were less than 10 percent. Foreign bonds have long maturities, usually extending to twenty years.

CONTROL OF THE EUROCURRENCY MARKET

The supervision of financial institutions and the regulation of markets face the problems associated with the international debt crisis and financial innovation. International banking has become more risky as a result of these two developments.

Since 1982 the problem of international indebtedness has posed serious difficulties for supervisory authorities in many countries[13]. The international debt crisis has required strengthening of banks' ability to sustain losses through increases in bank capital and in provisions against doubtful foreign loans. Moreover, recent innovations and technological changes in the banking industry have made supervision of banks more difficult. Financial innovations have resulted in the rapid growth of banks' off-balance-sheet activities, but prudential supervision of banks' new off-balance-sheet activities is still at an early stage of development.

Banking authorities recognize that their principle of supervision involves capital and capital adequacy and the practical application of the revised Basle Concordat, particularly concerning information flows. In practice, the adequacy of a bank's capital is measured in terms of the balance sheet and off-balance-sheet assets, both weighted in accordance with broad relative measures of perceived risk. Differences in national banking and supervisory policies create incentives for banking and other financial business to move from more regulated to less regulated centers, with a consequent increase in risk-taking that could, in the long run, harm both the efficiency and the stability of the financial system. Supervisors will therefore need to co-ordinate their activities internationally by attempting to achieve similar objectives within these different national frameworks.

The growing international interdependence of financial markets has led to increased international cooperation in the area of supervision. International cooperation has been conducted on multilateral and regional levels. However, the division of responsibilities of national supervisory authorities is not clear and is a source of disputed interpretation, thereby reducing the effectiveness of existing agreements and allowing some banks to escape supervision.

Because the Euromarket operates with a minimum of regulation, demand for its control has been made on many occasions since its emergence, particularly during periods of international monetary problems. The rapid growth in recent years of the Eurocurrency market and international lending has raised three main issues concerning (1) its effects on global macroeconomics conditions (such as inflation and balance of payments), (2) its effects on domestic monetary interdependence (such as the ability of national authorities to control domestic money supply and credit), and (3) its effects on prudential management of international banking activity, including foreign branches and subsidiaries.

Critics have charged that the Eurocurrency markets (1) created excessive expansion of world liquidity and international reserves, which in turn has caused inflation; (2) induced currency speculation and exchange-market instability; (3) reduced the balance-of-payments discipline or constraint on economic policies and induced inflation by making Eurocurrency credit available with limited conditionality (relatively easy credits enable countries to postpone the adoption of necessary adjustment policies, including appropriate anti-inflationary measures, with a consequent spillover of inflation); and (4) diminished the effectiveness of domestic monetary policies and contributed to excessive growth of the world money supply, thus worsening world inflation.

The role of the Eurobanks in lending to nonoil less developed countries have been a source of major concern. In view of the lack of control over the Eurocurrency market, the relatively higher country risk, and the problems of capital adequacy of the Eurobanks, the problems of bank stability in the event of a large-scale default by borrowers has become acute.

Calls for control of the Eurobanks' operations and regulation of their activities have resulted from the above concerns. Accordingly, proposals aimed at controlling the activities have been designed (1) to improve global macroeconomic conditions; (2) to enhance the effectiveness of domestic monetary policies; and (3) to improve the stability of the international financial system.

The rapid growth of the banks' international business has focused attention on a number of prudential problems, which include (1) the need for exercising effective control over banks' foreign subsidiaries, particularly where parent authorities do not supervise their banks on the basis of consolidated balance sheets and where supervisory arrangements in the countries in which the subsidiaries operate are inadequate; (2) the growth of banks' exposure vis-à-vis foreign countries, especially certain developing countries with substantial external indebtedness; (3) the banks' diminished profitability margins and the increase in the degree of maturity transformation; and (4) the weakened capital base of some banks.

The central banks of the Group of Ten countries and Switzerland Committee on Banking Regulations and Supervisory Practices was established in 1974. The Committee establishes broad principles that all supervisory systems can conform with in establishing their own arrangements. In addition, the Committee has searched for a way to improve international early warning systems for potential troubles in national banking systems that might have international repercussions.

To maintain the soundness of international banking and the world monetary systems, the governors of the BIS acted in three related areas: (1) lender-of-last resort reponsibilities; (2) information about market activities; and (3) excessive risk concentration and prudent bank-management practices of international banking activities. Last-resort-lending responsibilities are vital to prevent a banking panic in the event of a sudden withdrawal of deposits and a severe squeeze on liquidity. Default could have serious consequences if the national monetary authorities were not prepared to render aid and support. The central banks of eight European members of the BIS reached an agreement in July 1974 in Basle on lender of last resort for the Eurocurrency market in case of temporary liquidity problems. By the end of the year the United States, Japan, and thirty additional countries agreed to subscribe to the Basle accord.

The agreement is based on the broad principle of parental responsibility, according to which banks are responsible for their overseas branches. The central bank also has an indirect responsibility for such overseas operations and is to provide emergency facilities for parent banks in the event of a temporary liquidity crisis. Consortium banks, which have multinational bank participation, would be bailed out on a pro-rata basis by member parent banks. The latter would be backed by their own central banks.

The BIS agreement is unclear about who bears responsibility for losses or difficulties experienced by foreign subsidiaries of a bank. A subsidiary is legally an autonomous entity incorporated under the laws of the country in which it is located. The government of the parent company has no authority over foreign subsidiaries, and bank subsidiaries are often exempt from regulations by the host government as well. It is therefore unclear whose central bank is ultimately responsible to act as lender of last resort for bank subsidiaries.

There is also doubt as to the ability and willingness of central banks to provide lender-of-last-resort assistance on a coordinated basis. In fact, their differing interpretations of the Accord have led them to a dispute over their regulatory responsibilities.

The main dispute concerns the question of whether the host or home country bears the primary responsibility for supervision of the foreign branch, subsidiary, or agency. Some central banks believe that the primary supervisory responsibility for foreign branches or subsidiaries rests with the host country's authorities, whereas others maintain that responsibility depends on whether the foreign bank is a branch or subsidiary.

The Group of Ten Committee on Banking Regulations and Supervisory Practices has concluded that responsibility for supervising the liquidity of foreign branches must rest with the host supervisory authority but that a branch's liquidity cannot be judged wholly in isolation from that of its parent bank. Liquidity therefore is brought within the sphere of interest of the supervisory authority of the parent bank. Although the legal position of foreign subsidiaries and joint ventures is different from that of foreign branches, the parent authorities cannot be indifferent to the moral responsibilities that parent institutions have for ensuring that their offshoots do not default on their commitments. The division of supervisory responsibilities in relation to foreign banking establishments and the need for cooperation between host and parent supervisory authorities is further hampered by restrictions such as the prohibition on disclosing confidential information.

In ensuring solvency, the Committee concluded that host and home or parent supervisory authorities must share responsibility for supervision, with the emphasis varying according to the type of establishments concerned. For foreign subsidiaries and joint ventures, the primary responsibility must rest with the host authorities, but parent authorities need to assess their exposure based on their moral commitment to support their foreign offshoots.

The lender-of-last-resort agreement does not relieve the Eurobanks from the obligation to exercise prudence and restraint. Although the central banks have assumed ultimate responsibility for the Euromarkets, the market participants continue to carry primary responsibility for the functioning of the Euromarkets, obliging them to adhere to prudent banking practices.

Recently the Group of Ten and Switzerland adopted the following measures to improve the supervision of banks' international operations: (1) the use of consolidated balance sheets as the basis for supervising banks to determine prudent portfolio management criteria and excessive loan-risk concentration; (2) the supervision of banks' country-risk-assessment procedures to improve the quality of credit and reduce risk; and (3) the monitoring of the banks' maturity transformation and capital adequacy.

Banks in these countries are subject to close supervision by the BIS Committee on Banking Regulations and Supervisory Practices regarding the above issues. The Committee helps ensure bank solvency and liquidity by promoting cooperation among the supervisory and regulatory authorities. It has established guidelines concerning the division of responsibility between national authorities for the supervision of banks' foreign establishments to ensure that no foreign banking establishment escapes supervision.

The Bank for International Settlements Committee on Banking Regulation and Supervisory Practices issued in December 1987 "Proposals for International Convergence of Capital Measurement and Capital Standards". The proposed guidelines call for the establishment in the twelve member countries of uniform definition of bank capital, risk weights for various bank assets and off-balance-sheet exposure for the purpose of determining capital adequacy. The proposal calls for a common minimum capital level, expressed in terms of a certain percentage of risk-weighted assets and off-balance-sheet exposure. The committee proposed the complete adoption of the guidelines by the end of 1992.

The BIS proposal establishes a consistent approach for measuring and assessing capital adequacy for the banking industry. The banking supervisory authority in each country has the responsibility to adopt the proposed policy. The proposal will have significant implications for the global financial markets, particularly for bank debt and equity issuing activities, off-balance-sheet activities for example, currency options and currency swaps. (In January 1988, the Federal Reserve Board of Governors issued proposed guidelines relating to risk-based capital requirements for U.S. banking corporations for public comments.)

The Group of Ten and Switzerland have agreed to examine the development of international bank lending semi-annually on the basis of data collected by the BIS and to propose harmonized measures. A group of experts has been given the task of clarifying the technical details involved to establish a comprehensive reporting system of maturity transformation and exposure. This information will enable the central banks to assess the significance of the banks' international operations and will provide a framework for further cooperation. The European Community also provides a vehicle for international cooperation of banking supervision and is promoting coordination of practices and schemes for the exchange of information.

International lending is increasingly carried out through foreign subsidiaries (because of the various advantages of operating offshore) rather than through the parent company or home office. Bank-supervision regulations need to be enforced on the basis of consolidated balance sheets for banks. Proposed controls consider global management of international lending by banks on a coordinated basis. Accordingly, discussions have considered imposing direct controls in the form of capital deposits and loans ratios. One proposal calls for linking international lending to general ratios related to bank's own funds or capital adequacy on a consolidated basis.

Imposing formal reserve requirements is another possibility that Eurobanks may have to confront, although it is unlikely that those requirements will be implemented soon. To be effective they would have to apply in all Eurocenters and to all banks and even to nonbanking financial institutions.

Despite international agreement on international banking supervision, formal regulations of banking activities have not been established. Reaching agreement on the lender of last resort was significant. Controls will be effective only if they apply to all countries; otherwise they stand little chance of being either adopted or effective. In the absence of worldwide agreement, any government's attempts to impose direct controls on the market would result in Eurobanking business shifting either to a different jurisdiction or to a different group of Eurobanks.

The Eurocurrency market performs a significant and valuable function of intermediation in the international money and capital markets. Attempts to regulate it by imposing controls could have worldwide ramifications and adversely affect the flow of international credit and capital. Opponents of controls argue that the Eurocurrency market is already subject to sufficient national monetary authorities' influence in several ways: They affect domestic monetary conditions; they regulate and supervise banks headquartered and located in their respective countries; and they often regulate their residents' participation in the market through exchange and monetary controls. Additional controls are not felt necessary. In conclusion, the most likely developments in the Eurocurrency market in the near future are some agreement on capital adequacy and increased report requirements.

SUMMARY AND CONCLUSIONS

Unsettled international economic conditions—both cyclical and structural—create a difficult environment for the international financial market. Following two decades of rapid expansion, the world financial markets are now experiencing a consolidation process. The international money and capital markets have gone through a significant adjustment. New instruments have been created, and the role of financial intermediation has changed. The market has become more concerned with risk in the wake of the debt problems of 1982. Lending has consequently declined, while securitization has proliferated. Risk management through currency and interest swap has widened the scope of funding. The international markets have become more integrated with the domestic operations.

NOTES

1. Bank for International Settlements, *Fifty-Eighth Annual Report* (Basle: B15 1988.

2. Adopted from L. S. Goodman, "The Price of Syndicated Eurocurrency Credit," *FRBNY Quarterly Review*, 15(2) (1980): 39–49.

3. *Ibid*.

4. "Recent Developments in Corporate Finance," *Federal Reserve Bulletin* November 1986: 745–56.

5. *Ibid*.; OECD, *Financial Market Trends 35* (November 1986); B15, note 1 above.

6. Bank of America International Limited, *Euronote Facilities* (London: BAIL, July 1985).

7. *Ibid*.

8. OECD, note 5 above.

9. BAIL, note 6 above.

10. *Ibid*.

11. "Recent Developments," note 4 above.

12. Bank for International Settlements, *Fifty-fifth Annual Report* (Basle: B15, 1985).

13. Press Review, Bank for International Settlements Fourth International Conference of Banking Supervisors (October 10, 1986).

5 Financial Institutions in International Finance

ALEXANDER E. FLEMING

CHANGES in the international economic and financial environment during the 1970s and 1980s have brought with them marked changes in the ways in which international financial intermediation is conducted. There have been significant shifts in the roles played by private financial institutions (especially commercial banks and investment banks) on the one hand and official financial institutions (especially the IMF and World Bank) on the other. There have also been important shifts in the roles played by institutions within each category. This chapter examines some of the factors that have influenced the nature and scale of participation of the different types of institution in international finance.

INTERNATIONAL FINANCIAL INTERMEDIATION: AN OVERVIEW

The international financial system—encompassing institutional, governmental, and market arrangements for transactions between countries—performs on a global basis what national financial systems execute domestically. It provides a payments mechanism, offers facilities for borrowing funds and employing surpluses, creates different types of financial assets and liabilities, and intermediates between a variety of agents with portfolio preferences.

The demarcation between national and international financial systems has never been rigid because domestic institutions and markets have always to some extent performed international functions. Until the late 1960s, however, a reasonably coherent distinction could be made between the two systems. International financial intermediation and the financing of international payments imbalances were based mainly on governmental arrangements and official international organizations. Balance-of-payments financing was not, therefore, done predominantly through market mechanisms but rather through nonmarket operations.

The views expressed in this chapter are the personal views of the author and do not necessarily reflect the positions or policies of the World Bank.

153

Except for trade financing, most domestic financial institutions operated primarily in the domestic domain. But since the late 1960s the international and national financial systems have become more closely integrated. The formal distinctions between the intermediation mechanisms used by the two have become less obvious as national financial institutions have increasingly come to supply international financial intermediation services.

Over the 1970s, and in the context of a rise in both the absolute and relative size of international financial imbalances, the mechanisms of international financial intermediation changed markedly. A notable feature was the increasing role of international commercial banking and the greater importance of the private sectors. In terms of the provision of liquidity, the financing of the transfer of real resources and balance-of-payments financing, the private international commercial banking sector (measured in terms of onshore and offshore external lending of private banks) substantially increased its role both absolutely and relative to the official sector. This development was manifested in a substantial increase in the volume of external assets of commercial banks in major financial centers, a rise in the proportion of external assets and liabilities in commercial banks' total balance sheet positions, and a relative shift from trade financing to more direct balance-of-payments financing. Accompanying this was a substantial rise in the number of banks participating in international lending business and the emergence of new offshore financial centers. Earnings from international commercial banking business became increasingly significant over the decade, and the nationalities of banks participating on a significant scale in international lending also became much larger.

Among the official international institutions the role of the IMF changed significantly as it adapted its operations to the floating-exchange-rate environment and to the stagflationary pressures that were being felt in the world economy. During the 1970s the World Bank grew substantially as a lender to developing countries and as a borrower in international capital markets. The nature of its lending changed significantly during that decade also.

The 1980s, however, have seen a reversal of some of the trends among private institutions noted above. This reversal can be accounted for in part by the debt crisis, which discouraged commercial banks from lending, in particular to developing countries. At the same time a securitization of international markets has taken place that has given investment banks, as opposed to commercial banks, a larger role in international intermediation. The official international institutions themselves have also come to assume a large role as providers of funds and as catalysts for further private-sector fund flows to developing countries.

In sum, there has been a marked change in the pattern of institutional participation in international intermediation. The 1960s and early

1970s might be best described as a period of constrained intermediation. It was a period in which private intermediation was constrained internationally by the existence of exchange controls, and domestic intermediation was constrained by a rigid delineation of institutions by function and by a constricting set of monetary regulations that created an ossification of institutional structure and stifled competition. The balance of the decade of the 1970s up to about 1980 could be described as a competitive system. International banking business conducted in offshore centers was particularly competitive, but domestic intermediation also became much freer.

Since 1982 the system might be described as both highly competitive and coordinated. This is not a contradiction in terms for these two adjectives describe different segments of the system. The highly competitive segment involves private intermediation in and between the industrial countries for the most part. Fired by domestic financial market deregulation, by considerable innovation in domestic and international markets, and by great strides in computer technology applied to the financial sector, there has been a strong burst of competition between private institutions. The coordinated segment of the system relates solely to intermediation to the developing countries. The interruption of lending to developing countries caused by the debt crisis has required, in order to avoid the potentially harmful systemic effects of a default, a coordinated strategy involving commercial banks and the official institutions. It should be added, however, that the great bulk of global intermediation remains in the highly competitive sector.

PRIVATE INSTITUTIONS

A wide array of private financial institutions now participate in the sphere of international finance. Some institutions were established specifically to operate internationally (consortium banks, for instance), but the bulk are institutions that have started business in domestic financial markets and then subsequently sought new business in international markets. The main distinction that will be drawn here is between commercial banks and investment banks, although there are, of course, a host of other institutions that operate in international financial markets.

Commercial banks typically accept retail deposits or bid for deposits in the wholesale markets. Their assets are primarily loans of different types. Investment banks have a different function in that they typically arrange issues of securities for clients and function as advisors to them on a wide range of financial matters. In the United States, Japan, and some other countries, a sharp distinction has historically been drawn between these two types of institutions. In the United States the Glass-Steagall Act of 1933 separated the business of underwriting and selling securities from the taking of deposits subject to withdrawal on request. The Act followed the banking crisis of the early 1930s and was part of a considerable increase in United States regulation of the banking sector. It was passed in response to perceived abuses, including the insurance of bad loans and unsound securities, arising from the mixing of commercial and investment banking functions.

The participation of private institutions in international finance must be viewed in dynamic terms for the international financial markets have been subject to rapid change in recent years. Technological advances and innovations in financial instruments have provided an impetus to international financial market growth (see Chapter 2). As the markets have evolved, so have the nature and structures of the institutions that participate in them. The relationship is a simultaneous one, however, for the institutions are the market makers and the primary source of innovation.

The Internationalization Phase

During the 1970s strong forces encouraged institutional participation in the international markets. In the sphere of commercial bank lending the forces were so strong that they led to a major thrust toward the internationalization of lending.

In the immediate post–World War II period up to the end of the 1960s the movement of capital internationally was hampered by the existence of exchange controls that had been introduced to defend the parities of currencies in the fixed-parity system. The international financial system was dominated, as noted above, by the flow of official capital. Private markets provided relatively modest amounts of international financing. Most of it was either in the form of trade finance or domestic currency finance for companies that were extending their operations abroad.

A number of theories have been put forward to explain why this distinct process of internationalization in commercial banking took place in the 1970s. According to one theory, changes in the distribution of current surpluses and deficits around the world can have an important impact on the role of banks. That theory holds good, however, only if (1) the portfolio preferences of all lenders are not the same; (2) banks do not have the same perception of creditworthiness for all potential borrowers; and (3) there is operating friction in the interbank market that redistributes liquidity. This theory would suggest that a reorientation of global surpluses and deficits, such that the surpluses were held by wealth holders (like OPEC) with a high liquidity preference, would have a strong positive effect on commercial bank liquidity and lending.

The expansion of liquidity in the commercial banking markets coincided with a positive shift in the attitude of the banks toward international lending. After the first major increase in oil prices, when there was a need to recycle large amounts of funds, banks were lauded for the success with which they performed this function. Confidence in the banking system was maintained by central banks and deposit insurance agencies, which gradually increased their protection for depositors at the major banks. The behavior of regulators—or, more precisely, expectations of their behavior—gave comfort to depositors and helped attract money to commercial banks. This may have led banks, in turn, to take larger lending risks than would otherwise have been the case.

The preference of borrowing countries also encouraged the growth of commercial bank lending in the 1970s. Many borrowing countries were attracted by the fact that bank finance came with few conditions and by the large volumes and flexibility of instruments available at a time when alternative sources of finance were growing very slowly. Borrowers naturally favored the low or negative real interest rates charged by banks in preference to the conditionality attached to some official finance and the strict creditworthiness standards of bond markets.

In addition to the macroeconomic forces working to increase commercial bank lending in the 1970s, several factors specific to the behavior of commercial banks were pushing in the same direction. The first factor was increased efficiency. As in many other industries, international banking benefited from innovations that increased its efficiency. The growth of the Eurocurrency market was especially significant; because commercial banks operating there were free of reserve requirements, they were able simultaneously to offer higher interest rates to depositors and lower rates to borrowers than was possible on normal domestic banking business. The market was also efficient in that it could quickly mobilize very large loans.

A second factor was changes in the portfolio objectives and preferences of commercial banks. These banks radically changed their portfolio objectives in the 1970s, placing greater emphasis on balance-sheet growth than on the immediate rate of return on assets or other measures of profitability. International lending was a means of satisfying this aim when domestic loan demand was weak and when banking liquidity induced by easy monetary policy was high. Foreign lending also offered a means of diversifying portfolios, which was seen as a way of reducing risks because domestic lending often had an inferior loan-loss record. Banks saw the rapid growth achieved by many developing countries as an indication that the returns on lending to these countries would be high compared with the risks involved. Aside from the direct returns they expected on loans, commercial banks wanted to develop a wider and more profitable business relationship with international borrowers.

A third factor was innovation. Commercial banks proved adept at designing instruments—like the syndicated loan—that would match their portfolio requirements (for country-risk diversification and interest-risk minimization) with the requirements of borrowers (longer-

157

maturity, high-volume loans). This particular innovation enabled banks to make long-term loans on the basis of short-term deposits—a process of maturity transformation—without having to absorb the interest-rate risk themselves because lending rates were tied to a short-term rate (LIBOR). Other key innovations included the certificate of deposit (and variations on it), which allowed banks to offer a marketable and high-yielding asset to depositors while providing the banks themselves with flexibility in the management of their liabilities. The significance of this development for the subsequent growth of bank lending cannot be understated.

A fourth factor was the regulatory environment. In the industrial countries there was some easing of exchange controls that encouraged banks to lend abroad off their base of domestic deposits. But the persistence of regulatory barriers led to the growth of largely unregulated offshore banking centers where business flourished. All of these factors produced a strong momentum for international lending (see the tables in Chapter 4).

As noted above, the commercial banks were the primary institutions involved in international lending. The process of internationalization of lending did not take place at the same speed among different nationalities of commercial banks. In the 1960s and early to mid-1970s U.S. commercial banks—primarily the major money center banks—expanded their international lending and attained a dominant position in international finance. The international lending momentum continued through the 1970s with the entry of a number of European banks, particularly those from the United Kingdom, France, and West Germany. The Japanese banks also assumed an important role at certain phases in the 1970s—in 1970–73, 1978–79, and again more recently. The Japanese Ministry of Finance, however, closely controlled Japan's entry to international lending markets. New banking groups—such as the Arab banks—also joined in international lending toward the end of the 1970s. Overall the U.S. commercial banks have come to assume, as a share of total international lending, a declining share of the total. As Table 5–1 illustrates, banks from Japan have now become the largest nationality group of banks, accounting for over 30 percent of the total international assets of the Bank for International Settlements (BIS) reporting banks. The advance in the position of the Japanese banks since 1984 can be attributed to the fact that yen appreciation has increased the U.S. dollar equivalent value of the banks' yen capital, allowing the capital base to support a larger volume of foreign-currency lending. The fact that much of their lending is denominated in yen also leads to a higher measured U.S. dollar total for their lending. Deregulation in Japan (see below in this chapter), coupled with the export of large volumes of Japanese saving have meant that Japanese banks have been in an increasingly good position to increase their international business.

Table 5–1.

INTERNATIONAL ASSETS OF BIS REPORTING BANKS.

Nationality of Banks	September 1984		September 1986	
	$ bn	% share	$ bn	% share
France	194.5	8.7	264.5	8.2
West Germany	139.4	6.2	250.5	7.8
Japan	519.8	23.2	1,019.4	31.6
United Kingdom	178.7	8.0	213.1	6.6
United States	587.2	26.3	610.2	18.6
Others	616.3	27.6	880.2	27.2

Source: BIS.

As the commercial banks became increasingly active in the 1970s, many investment banks increased their business significantly. The world's bond markets—especially the Eurobond markets—grew at a relatively fast pace although slower overall than the international banking markets. Bond investors typically require very good credit ratings, and so the growth of the bond markets was to some extent limited by the availability of high-quality borrowers.

The momentum toward internationalization of commercial banking waned in the early 1980s. The onset of debt difficulties in a large number of developing countries led to a rash of reschedulings. Commercial banks sought, therefore, to decrease their international exposure, especially in developing countries. Bank regulators worldwide responded to the situation by seeking to monitor liquidity and solvency ratios more closely. The need to strengthen their capital ratios led to commercial banks placing greater emphasis on profitability; the growth of assets—an important engine behind internationalization—became less important. These changed attitudes to international lending on the part of commercial banks were reinforced by the emergence of profitable opportunities for lending within some industrial countries, particularly as economic growth revived. In addition, financial markets in a number of industrial countries began a process of deregulation (see below), so commercial banks faced greater competition from other financial institutions. They turned their attention increasingly toward consolidating their domestic position.

The Securitization Phase

If the 1970s were the decade of the internationalization of traditional bank lending, then the 1980s have been the decade of the internationalization of the securities markets. The securities markets include the markets for bonds and bond-like marketable instruments such as floating rate notes, and short-term securities like commercial paper and certificates of deposit. Securitization has led to a significant shift in the type of institutions operating in the international financial arena.

159

Investment banks that typically arranged bond issues for domestic customers began to do the same thing for an increasing number of international customers. Commercial banks in some instances drastically cut or closed down their syndicated loan departments and sought to make inroads into the business of the arranging of securities offerings. The rigid distinction between investment banks and commercial banks that had been enshrined in the Glass-Steagall Act in the United States was subject to significant pressures. Some U.S. commercial banks, for instance—like Bankers Trust—had in any case been involving themselves increasingly in securities business through their subsidiaries in financial centres such as London. Others, like Citibank, evolved into universal banks engaging in a wide range of business. Such distinctions had already been dropped in the United Kingdom, where commercial banks were permitted to involve themselves in most kinds of investment banking. In some other European centres this type of distinction had never been made.

But what forces have led to the securitization of international lending markets? Securitization is to some extent a reaction to the difficulties that emerged in international bank lending in the early 1980s. Many commercial banks wished to divest themselves of exposure to developing countries, and the securitization of lending was viewed as one way in which such risks could be more freely traded. There were, however, a number of other factors working to securitize international lending.

The economic fundamentals have been highly conducive to a growth in popularity of long-term—in many instances, fixed-rate—bond-market instruments. Of particular importance has been the reappearance of positive real interest rates and positively sloped yield curves that have enhanced the appeal of long-term bonds to investors. This has also made it more attractive for the market-makers to hold and trade inventories of such bonds. For many borrowers in international markets it has also been cheaper to borrow in the bond markets than from commercial banks.

Securitization has also been fostered by the maturing and increasing efficiency of the Eurobond markets. These markets, once segmented, have become broad and homogeneous, with standardized trading practices. Significant volumes of funds can now be raised through these markets at relatively short notice.

The internationalization of securities markets has not only been manifest in the Eurobond markets but also in national bond markets. Increasingly regulations with regard to market participation have been liberalized. Institutions, for instance, can now be involved in a much wider range of securities business internationally. The Japanese authorities, for instance, have recently permitted foreign institutions to manage Euroyen issues. In Germany, meanwhile, another recent liberalization measure has been that foreign-owned entities domiciled in Germany can now manage foreign deutsche mark bond issues. The

160

upshot is that investment banks have now become significant players in international finance. (The significant growth in the international bond markets since 1981 is clearly illustrated by the data in Chapter 4.)

The bond markets are, however, only one component of a fast-growing securities market. The other main component is the market for short-term notes. Notes consist of short-term Euronotes (underwritten by banks) and Eurocommercial paper (not underwritten). Banks have competed fiercely with one another to arrange such issues and to develop many new types of instruments. Significant growth has taken place in the Euronotes and Eurocommercial paper segments of the securities market also.

Globalization, Deregulation, and Innovation

The international markets are now intricately bound up with domestic financial markets. The term *global financial market place* has often been used to describe the present state of international financial integration. It is not surprising therefore that major developments in domestic financial markets—such as the deregulation that has taken place in many countries but especially in the United States, United Kingdom, and Japan—also can have major effects on the international markets. Accompanying these developments, and closely related to them, are strong forces of financial innovation that appear to have intensified over the past five years. Deregulation and innovation are rapidly changing the institutional landscape both in terms of operations and structures of existing institutions and in terms of the merging or conglomeration of groups of institutions.

The United Kingdom and Japan serve as noteworthy examples of the effect of deregulation. In the United Kingdom deregulation has taken many forms. It has involved removing barriers to competition between institutions. Increasingly, therefore, in their effort to secure new markets, institutions of different sorts have encroached on one another's territory. Commercial banks and building societies (the equivalent to savings and loan associations in the United States) have, for instance, begun to compete vigorously in certain spheres of business. London was also subject to a so-called Big Bang recently, which marked a major change in the way that the securities markets (equities and gilt-edged stocks) operated. Although other financial centers have had dual-capacity trading—dealers who trade on their own account and make prices as well as acting as agents for clients—the market in London has traditionally had single-capacity trading. The two functions were carried out separately by brokers and jobbers. Stock-brokers earned their income through fixed commissions. As part of the Big Bang dual capacity was established and fixed commissions were abolished. All of this has set off a spate of mergers and acquisitions among stockbrokers and jobbers. Moreover other banks and securities companies have been allowed (since March 1986) to own brokers and jobbers. The incentives for mergers have, for the brokers/jobbers, been the need for new infusions of capital so that they can compete more successfully. From the standpoint of the commercial banks or investment banks the mergers or acquisitions have permitted them to gain a foothold in new markets. For the commercial banks this has represented a way of expanding into the securities business. Table 5–2 shows the institutions that have acquired securities houses in the United Kingdom over the 1983–86 period. New conglomerates have therefore emerged that will compete not only within the confines of the United Kingdom but also internationally. Many of the institutions that have sought a foothold in the London market have come from overseas, especially the United States and Japan, and this is an important component of the globalization of the securities business.

A significant momentum has now developed toward financial deregulation in Japan. This will give financial institutions, both Japanese and foreign, a freer rein in the Japanese financial markets. Rather than one Big Bang, change in Japan has taken place through a large number of smaller deregulatory moves. The two main changes have come in the area of interest-rate deregulation and in the erosion of barriers between different types of domestic financial institution. Much of the need for deregulation in Japan has come from the need to finance a large government deficit; the development of a secondary market in government bonds has been encouraged. Deregulation has also been driven by the emergence of Japan as the largest supplier of capital to the world. The massive increase in the flow of funds between domestic and overseas markets has brought about significant changes in the structure and regulation of Japan's markets. To keep up with their corporate customers and to exploit the opportunities of large capital outflows Japanese firms have been striving to gain a presence in foreign markets. Although banks and securities firms in the Japanese markets still remain segregated (under Article 65 of the Securities and Exchange Law), they can compete vigorously with one another in international markets; the international business of Japanese banks has expanded rapidly in recent years (see Table 5–1). These developments have led to pressure from the

Table 5–2.
ACQUISITIONS OF SECURITIES HOUSES
IN THE UNITED KINGDOM, 1983–86.

	Brokers	Jobbers
By clearing bankers	5	2
By merchant banks	8	7
By foreign banks and securities houses	31	6
Other	13	1

Source: Euromoney April 1986, 107.

financial authorities in other centers to allow their financial institutions to gain a firmer foothold in the Japanese market. More competition in their home markets is likely to make Japanese financial institutions all the more keen to secure a significant presence in international markets.

The examples of the United Kingdom and Japan are typical of what is happening in other domestic markets. Forces have been set up that are leading to more intense competition, mergers, the breaking down of barriers between institutions, and a thrust into international business.

What has happened in London and Tokyo is but one element in an internationalization of equity markets that is rapidly leading toward global, twenty-four-hour trading in equity stock. Accompanying this development has been an internationalization of the portfolios of many of the large institutional investors in the industrial countries—the pension funds and insurance companies, for instance—encouraged in part by the dismantling of exchange controls.

The major innovations that have taken place in financial markets in recent years have implications for the structure and operation of institutions. Financial institutions must, for instance, be at the frontier of innovation if they are to succeed. This entails an ability to restructure their operations quite radically and at short notice. The evolution of certain hybrid instruments—that is, instruments like floating-rate notes or Euronotes that have features of both bank loans and securities—are also having the effect of blurring the distinction between the different types of institution that issue or deal in them.

Many of the other recent innovations—interest-rate swaps, currency swaps, and options of various types—give nonbank corporations as well as financial institutions the ability to fine tune the financial risks they carry. The risks associated with financial transactions can be decomposed (or unbundled) and then separately hedged. It is this sphere of financial business where other financial institutions have developed a specialist function. Insurance companies, for instance, have played a major role in fostering the growth of the financial guarantee markets. A financial guarantee can take many different forms, and in some cases they have been tailored to meet specific needs. An important form of financial guarantee is when an insurance company lends its high credit rating, for a fee, to a bond market issuer so that the latter can secure lower borrowing costs. But the concept also encapsulates a range of other financial business.

OFFICIAL INSTITUTIONS

The two main official international financial institutions—the International Monetary Fund and the World Bank—have been subject, over the last decade and a half, to many of the same forces that have shaped private institutions. Both institutions have grown significantly since the early 1970s. There are also been major changes in their operations and

163

structures. Various forces have brought about a closer relationship not only between the two but also with institutions in the private markets.

The International Monetary Fund

The last fifteen years have seen a significant change in the role of the IMF and in the way it functions. At the heart of its operations in the period after its inception up to the early 1970s was its overseeing of the par value exchange-rate system. This role was enshrined in the IMF's Articles of Agreement. Of less significance initially was its role as an intermediary, although it was called on, from time to time, to make significant volumes of resources available to some of its larger industrial country members.

The turbulence in the foreign-exchange markets in the early 1970s culminated in March 1973 with the breakdown of the system of par values. The situation had been brought to a head when the United States abandoned the official convertibility of the dollar into gold or other reserve assets in August 1971. As a result of this, all currencies floated. This provided a direct challenge to the IMF because its Articles of Agreement did not allow for its members to float their exchange rates. The IMF had no legal basis for approving the floating situation that had emerged. The subsequent increases in energy prices and the accompanying recessionary forces put considerable pressure on the economies of many IMF members, and it became clear that a transition back to the previous par value system would not take place. A provision that allowed members to choose their exchange arrangements were incorporated in changed Articles of Agreement.

The IMF's role as a policeman of exchange rates began to wane. The emphasis changed from the stability of the par values in the original Articles of Agreement to identifying the conditions conducive to stability in the system as a whole and the Fund's role in overseeing members' efforts in maintaining these conditions.

The other major development of the 1970s was the deep recession and stagflation of the 1974–75 period. Exchange rates became highly volatile, and many developing countries, meanwhile, accumulated large external indebtedness. In response to these changes the IMF undertook to reshape its functions and to redirect its activities.

In the second half of the 1970s lending to its members became the IMF's primary activity. Steps were taken to increase the IMF's lending activity and capacity, particularly in light of the major balance-of-payments imbalances confronted by many of its members. In 1974 a special temporary oil facility was created to be financed by borrowing from its members. An extended facility was introduced in 1974 to help developing countries, and in 1975 compensatory financing facility was liberalized. The IMF's capacity to lend was enhanced by two general reviews of members' quotas during the second half of the 1970s. With the growth of the international capital markets, however—particularly the major thrust toward international commercial bank lending—the IMF increasingly found that the leverage it had in modifying errant policies, especially in the industrial countries, began to decline. Many countries could borrow large volumes of funds from commercial banks without the conditionality attached to IMF funds.

The onset of the debt crisis in 1982 brought with it a new role for the IMF. Commercial banks were, as noted above, no longer willing to voluntarily lend new funds to developing countries that had encountered difficulties in servicing their debts.

After the first difficulties arose in Mexico in 1982, a number of Latin American countries, including Mexico and Brazil, came to the IMF for assistance. The IMF thus adopted a strategy of cooperation. This was a country-by-country approach, in collaboration with all the interested parties, comprising the two elements of adjustment and financing. The objective of Fund-supported adjustment programs was to achieve a viable balance of payments in the medium term and a more efficient use of scarce resources by introducing a number of incentives and measures to generate more domestic savings, more investment, and more exports.

The second element of the strategy was to facilitate financial flows. From the middle of 1982 to the end of 1984 the IMF lent some $22 billion in support of adjustment programs for sixty-six members, many of which had debt problems. In addition to its own financing, the IMF helped to arrange financing packages for debtor countries from governments, central banks, private commercial banks, the BIS, and the World Bank. This marked the beginnings of a catalytic role marked by a mobilization of funds from other lenders. A cornerstone of this new approach was the IMF's attempt to persuade the commercial banks to lend on the grounds that the adjustment policies being taken by debtor countries would depend on additional financial resources if they were to succeed. This coordinated strategy is examined further below.

In 1985 there was a subtle shift in the strategy to cope with the debts of developing countries. The Baker initiative of September 1985 recognized explicitly that the debt crisis was not a short-term one but rather one that needed a medium-term strategy. As part of this the emphasis was taken off short-term stabilization, the domain of the IMF, and placed onto medium-term adjustment, the domain of the World Bank.

The World Bank

The World Bank's primary function—like that of the other regional development banks—is the extension of financial and technical assistance for long-term development to developing countries. Both in terms of the volume of loans outstanding and in terms of the maturity of these loans the Bank has always performed a larger intermediary role than the IMF.[1]

The Bank has interrelated roles; it provides a resource transfer to developing countries by lending directly for high-priority projects and programs; it provides policy advice and technical assistance; and it helps to stimulate the flow of capital for development from other sources. These roles and the way that the Bank has sought to carry them out has changed over time. The World Bank has increased its lending to developing countries substantially, especially since 1970 (see Table 5–3).

Some distinct changes have taken place in the sectoral distribution of World Bank lending over time. During the 1950s the main thrust of World Bank lending was for the development of basic infrastructure; lending for power and transportation predominated. In the 1960s the Bank began to increase its lending for agriculture as food shortages became more acute and as the vital importance of agricultural growth to economic progress in developing countries was acknowledged. In the early 1960s, the Bank started lending for the development of education and, by the end of the decade, for population planning. In the 1970s, stronger emphasis was given to projects aimed at directly benefiting the poorest people in a society, particularly through projects for rural development, urban growth, health, and nutrition. The sharp increase in oil prices in the 1970s led to a growth in projects aimed at increasing energy production. Since 1980 a notable feature has been the growth in structural and sector-adjustment lending designed to help developing countries to adjust their economic structures to changes in the global economic environment.

In recent years the Bank has sought to respond particularly to the difficulties faced by many of the highly indebted middle-income developing countries. In the early phase of the debt crisis the primary emphasis in terms of official support was the IMF's role of helping develop programs of economic stabilization. The Bank's role, however, has grown as reflected in the Baker initiative of October 1985. Greater emphasis has been placed on longer-term programs of adjustment aimed at establishing a firmer basis for durable growth through structural change. The Bank has provided support for adjustment in three main ways: Helping prepare comprehensive medium-term adjustment

Table 5–3.
WORLD BANK LENDING TO DEVELOPING
COUNTRIES (billions of US dollars).

	1970	1980	1985	1986
Commitments	2.3	11.5	14.4	16.3
Disbursements	0.9	5.8	11.1	11.4

Note: Lending data relates to the Bank's fiscal year, which runs from June 1 to May 31.

programs for growth; expanding its own lending; and stimulating the flow of additional capital from other official and private lenders. It has also, importantly, increased its role as an advisor to developing countries on debt management policy.

The vast increase in the Bank's lending over the last decade and a half has meant that it has had to borrow a much larger volume of funds in the world's capital markets. Indeed the Bank has become the world's largest nonresident borrower in virtually all private capital markets. Like other borrowers, it is closely examined on an ongoing basis by investors. To maintain its high credit rating it follows a very prudent set of financial policies: Under its Articles of Agreement, its lending is not permitted to exceed its capital and reserves, for instance. The Bank has also become a market leader in many respects and has been responsible for pioneering the use of a number of market innovations. For example, in 1981 it was the first to arrange a currency swap when it exchanged dollar obligations with Swiss franc bonds issued by IBM, the computer manufacturer.

The Bank's links with private financial institutions is evident in three contexts. First, investment banks typically arrange for the launching and underwriting of the Bank's securities issues. Second, in the context of the institution's catalytic role the Bank has worked closely with commercial banks (see also the following section) in the context of cofinancing operations. The Bank has also begun to use its guarantee authority, to a limited extent, to guarantee elements (normally the later maturities) of credits made by commercial banks to developing countries. A third area in which the Bank will increasingly develop close links with private-sector institutions is in the context of the creation of the Multilateral Investment Guarantee Agency (MIGA). This agency has been designed to fill a gap in the market for political risk insurance for direct investment in developing countries. MIGA, through the re-insurance market, will forge close links with other political risk insurers when it becomes fully operational.

Coordination in International Finance

At the beginning of this chapter the period from 1982 onwards was characterized as in part coordinated. This term was applied to the segment of international financial activity involving financial intermediation to developing countries. The debt strategy adopted since 1982—discussed above—has involved greater cooperation with the IMF as well as with a number of other official institutions. Closer coordination among these institutions was enshrined in the strategy devised by U.S. Treasury Secretary Baker. Closer coordination has also taken place between the commercial banks that had lent extensively to the highly indebted developing countries and the official institutions. Much of the commercial bank lending to such countries is, of course, involuntary in nature. Coordination has therefore taken the form, in many instances, of providing additional resources in the context of restructuring a borrower's debt and supporting economic reform programs to stimulate growth.

WORLD BANK/IMF COOPERATION

Cooperation between the official institutions, particularly between the IMF and the World Bank, has intensified significantly in recent years. The need for closer collaboration resulted from the pressing resource needs of many developing countries, from the deep-rooted adjustment problems they faced, and from the need, therefore, for maximum efficiency in the deployment of funds and other resources in such countries. The essence of the cooperation between the two institutions is a consistent diagnosis of a member's problems through the close contact of their staffs. The different perspectives and specializations of the two institutions are viewed as complementary and reinforcing. The IMF has a particular expertise in the area of macroeconomics and the balance of payments, while the Bank's expertise lies in the areas of longer-term structural and development issues. Considerable efforts have been made by the two institutions to ensure consistency in their medium- to long-term projections.

Yet cooperation between the two institutions is not a new concept. During the latter half of the 1970s the lending activities of the Bank and the IMF brought the two institutions closer. The key role of structural and supply-oriented policies in the IMF's extended facility and the greater emphasis on these policies in its other facilities made it important for IMF staff to consult with Bank staff on the appropriateness of the policies proposed by member countries in support of using the IMF's resources. At the same time, the Bank required a program of policy actions that could be monitored as a condition for its structural-adjustment lending. It therefore became necessary to coordinate the country programs supported by the resources of the institutions to seek complementarity and avoid conflicting advice.

It was with the onset of the debt difficulties of some borrowers that cooperation, which had gradually deepened over the years, intensified considerably. To rekindle growth and reestablish balance-of-payments viability in developing countries it has been necessary to ensure an efficient use of productive resources in a setting of macroeconomic stability. It is this efficiency that collaboration is helping to achieve.

COORDINATION BETWEEN OFFICIAL AND PRIVATE INSTITUTIONS

The IMF and the World Bank play an important role in mobilizing official and commercial bank resources for member countries experiencing debt-servicing difficulties and in promoting efforts to restore balance-of-payments viability over the medium term. The two institutions work together to help member countries prepare policy reform programs and identify the financing required to make such programs viable. They then encourage official and private creditors to provide financing in support of the programs.

In providing such financing, commercial banks frequently associate the availability of their funds with satisfactory performance by the borrower under the program with the Bank and with the Fund. This form of cooperation between the various lending institutions has developed into a quite complex relationship. In the case of the relationship between the World Bank and the commercial banks the latter have required in some instances that the World Bank provide guarantees for a portion of a credit that has been extended.

The appropriate relationship between the commercial bank and the official institutions has been subject to considerable debate. The commercial banks have shown an increasing propensity to link their disbursements of lending to the implementation of IMF programs and structural reforms and projects supported by the World Bank. But in some instances, they have sought relationships that the official institutions would not have been able to accept. There has been concern when commercial banks have sought comfort through various forms of cross-conditionality.

In some instances commercial banks have attempted to make the absence of IMF involvement an event that would trigger default on a country's debt. Clearly it is not in the IMF's interest to jeopardize its relationship with a borrower through such devices. In the case of the relationships between the commercial banks and the World Bank constraints have arisen for similar reasons. In some instances, there has been pressure for direct cross-default mechanisms. With regard to the use of its guarantee authority, the Bank has wanted to use this sparingly. First, because a guarantee must be treated as a loan in the Bank's financial statements, the Bank has little incentive to provide guarantees unless the borrower clearly gains additional resources by so doing. Second, an overly tight relationship with commercial banks might jeopardize the Bank's standing in the world's capital markets. It is important, given that it is the largest nonresident capital market borrower, that the Bank maintain the highest credit rating it has traditionally held.

CONCLUSIONS

As well as helping shape the flow of international finance over the last decade and a half, the financial institutions themselves have been molded by the various forces working on the international system. An important distinction has emerged in recent years between intermediation involving industrial countries alone and that involving the flows of financial resources to the developing countries. In the former, financial institutions operate in a highly competitive and innovative environment. Securities business and its associated institutions have predominated in recent years. The question is whether the securities bias in the system will persist, particularly if inflation rekindles and interest rates rise sharply. The institutions operating in the increasingly integrated financial markets have been subject to strong forces that have changed their structure (through mergers and conglomeration) and altered the nature of their business (through innovation involving, for instance, new types of securities and financial product unbundling).

With regard to intermediation to developing countries there has been a distinct change in its pattern over recent years. The balance that had tilted toward commercial banks in the 1970s and away from the official institutions has tilted back toward the latter. Recently some banks have hastened this process by withdrawing from international lending, specifically by selling off existing loans or converting them, through a number of innovative schemes, into equity. Nonetheless the coordination between official and private institutions—which has, of necessity, evolved in recent years—seems likely to continue in the foreseeable future.

NOTES

1. The World Bank consists of the International Bank for Reconstruction and Development (IBRD), which lends primarily to the middle-income or more creditworthy borrowers; the International Development Association (IDA), which lends to the poorest countries; and the International Finance Corporation (IFC), which promotes the growth of the private sector in members countries.

REFERENCES

THE BANKER. Various editions.

BOCK, DAVID, AND CONSTANTINE MICALOPOULOS, 1986. "The Emerging Role of the Bank in Heavily Indebted Countries." *Finance and Development* (September).

DE VRIES, MARGARET GARRITSEN, 1986. *The IMF in a Changing World, 1984–85*. Washington, D.C: IMF.

EUROMONEY. Various editions.

FLEMING, ALEX, 1981. "Private Capital Flows to Developing Countries and Their Determination." World Bank Staff Working Paper. 484. Washington, D.C.: World Bank.

HINO, HIROYUKI, 1986. "IMF–World Bank Collaboration." *Finance and Development* (September): 10–14.

International Monetary Fund. 1986. *International Capital Markets: Developments and Prospects*. Washington, D.C.: IMF.

LLEWELLYN, DAVID, 1985. "International Financial Intermediation and the Role of the Banks in Balance of Payments Financing." Background paper for *World Development Report*. Washington, D.C.: World Bank.

WORLD BANK, 1974–86. *The World Bank Annual Report*. Washington, D.C.: World Bank.

—— 1985. *World Development Report*. Washington, D.C.: World Bank.

PART III

INTERNATIONAL
BUSINESS AND ITS
FINANCING

6 Multinationals and International Business

JOHN HEIN

EVERY August, *Fortune* magazine publishes a list of the fifty largest U.S. exporters. The list contains, not surprisingly, such industrial giants as General Motors, IBM, Du Pont, and Eastman Kodak. What perhaps is more surprising is that the top fifteen firms on the list account for almost 20 percent of total U.S. exports and almost 30 percent of exports of manufactures. The entire group of fifty companies provides 30 percent of total and 45 percent of manufactures exports.

These data prove, one might argue, that in the United States exporting remains the domain of a relatively small number of businesses. But the data also support the thesis that the large multinational corporation (MNC) does play an important role in world business. In fact, for two-thirds of the fifty companies on the *Fortune* list exports account for between 10 and 25 percent of total sales.

Exports are of course only one way in which large U.S. corporations have opened up the borders of the U.S. economy and have strengthened its links with the global marketplace. Over the past forty years or so, most of the world's large manufacturing firms—both in the United States and elsewhere—have been transformed from strictly national or domestic to multinational or international enterprises. By building up a network of foreign subsidiaries and affiliates, these corporations have greatly enlarged the scope of their production and distribution activities and hence have fostered the much talked-about interdependence of the various economies (Vernon 1986).

This development has been worldwide and recently has even included companies from developing nations. But the trend has been especially marked—and the available data have been most copious and most reliable—for corporations headquartered in the United States and for the U.S. affiliates of firms headquartered abroad. This chapter examines these MNCs—who they are, their size relative to national economies, why they go abroad, and finally their role in international business.

WHO THEY ARE

Business historians have described the 1960s and the 1970 as the "age of the multinationals," a time when large corporations "leaped across

175

national boundaries and seemed to challenge the power of governments to control them" (Janger 1980: v). Although this leap across national frontiers involved corporations based both in the United States and in other major industrial countries, little attention has been paid to the *relative* growth and standing of U.S. MNCs and their foreign counterparts.

Indeed, throughout the 1960s and the 1970s it was an all too familiar stereotype that the multinational corporation tended to be based in the United States. Much of this perception undoubtedly stemmed from Servan-Schreiber's famous *défi américain*, according to which it was "quite possible that the world's third greatest industrial power, just after the United States and Russia, will not be Europe, but American industry in Europe" (Servan-Schreiber 1983: 3). Correspondingly, the activities of U.S. MNCs tended to be identified both with a decline in U.S. economic power and with U.S. imperialism—to the extent that the term *multinational corporation* for quite some time was considered "a euphemism for the outward expansion of America's giant oligopolistic corporations" (Gilpin 1975: 15).

It is not surprising that MNCs used to be seen as typically U.S. creatures, since in many countries they were among the first to arrive and, outside Africa, often were the most visible. Moreover, U.S. firms were easier to study because data on their foreign activities were the most detailed and extensive available. Or as was noted in a somewhat facetious vein, "in part, *le défi américain* was the result of *les statistiques américains*" (Franko 1978: 97).

Over the past ten years, however, two distinct and important developments have taken place. One is the fairly rapid growth in foreign investment by firms from developing countries, often in other developing countries. Thus, Indian companies have established subsidiaries in Sri Lanka, Malaysia, and Kenya; Argentine firms have set up production facilities in Brazil, Chile, and Uruguay; and countries such as Indonesia find themselves hosting subsidiaries of companies headquartered in the Philippines, Korea, Taiwan, Singapore, and Hong Kong. Such investment offers developing countries looking for foreign technology or management skills "a politically and perhaps economically attractive alternative to the multinational enterprise" (Wells 1977: 133).

But easily the most significant phenomenon of the past ten years has been the much more rapid growth of MNCs based outside the United States relative to the growth of U.S.-based firms. This phenomenon can be examined in various ways. At the simplest level—that is, the absolute number of large corporations—non-U.S. firms have been in the majority since the late 1970s (Table 6–1). Whereas in 1963, U.S. MNCs accounted for two-thirds of the world's 100 largest companies and for three-fifths of the 500 largest, by 1985 their share had dropped to below one-half of each group. Moreover, when broken down by countries of origin, the list has been lengthening steadily and now includes compan-

Table 6-1.

THE WORLD'S 100 LARGEST INDUSTRIAL
CORPORATIONS, BY COUNTRY OF ORIGIN.

	1963	1971	1979	1985
United States	67	58	47	48
Germany	13	11	13	7
United Kingdom	7	7	7	5
France	4	5	11	5
Japan	3	8	7	12
Italy	2	3	3	3
Netherlands–United Kingdom	2	2	2	2
Netherlands	1	2	3	1
Switzerland	1	2	1	1
Canada	–	–	2	3
Australia	–	1	–	–
Belgium	–	–	1	1
Brazil	–	–	1	1
Mexico	–	–	1	1
United Kingdom–Italy	–	1	–	–
Venezuela	–	–	1	1
Austria	–	–	–	1
India	–	–	–	1
Indonesia	–	–	–	1
Korea	–	–	–	4
Kuwait	–	–	–	1
Sweden	–	–	–	1

Sources: J. Hein, *The World's Multinationals: A Global Challenge*, Information Bulletin No. 84. Conference Board, 1981; "The 500 Largest U.S. Industrial Corporations," *Fortune* April 28, 1986; and "The International 500," *Fortune* August 4, 1986.

ies from Mexico, India and South Korea. This reflects, in the cases of Mexico and India, the emergence of national oil companies into the top ranks.

The relative standing of the two groups emerges in greater detail from Tables 6–2 and 6–3. Table 6–2 gives the distribution of the world's 500 largest industrial corporations, broken down into U.S. and non-U.S.

Table 6-2.

THE WORLD'S 500 LARGEST INDUSTRIAL CORPORATIONS,
NUMBER OF COMPANIES BY SALES.

Sales ($ million)	1971		1979		1985	
	U.S.	Non-U.S.	U.S.	Non-U.S.	U.S.	Non-U.S.
Over $10,000	3	1	20	27	33	42
$5,000–$9,999	9	3	38	43	40	56
$3,000–$4,999	14	14	53	53	61	70
$1,000–$2,999	101	66	108	158	78	120
$800–$999	29	19				
$600–$799	51	48				
$400–$599	73	69				
Total	280	220	219	281	212	288

Sources: J., Hein, *The World's Multinationals: A Global Challenge*, Information Bulletin No. 84. Conference Board, 1981; "The 500 Largest U.S. Industrial Corporations," *Fortune* April 28, 1986; and "The International 500," *Fortune* August 4, 1986.

Table 6-3.

SALES OF 100 LARGEST U.S. AND 100 LARGEST NON-U.S. INDUSTRIAL
CORPORATIONS (billions of U.S. dollars).

	1971			1979			1985		
Company group	U.S.	Non-U.S.	Relative Size Ratio[a]	U.S.	Non-U.S.	Relative Size Ratio[a]	U.S.	Non-U.S.	Relative Size Ratio[a]
1–10	118.3	54.4	2.2	389.8	241.2	1.6	522.6	288.7	1.8
11–20	43.1	32.1	1.3	130.8	141.3	0.9	184.7	155.9	1.2
21–30	30.4	25.7	1.2	88.7	109.3	0.8	125.5	139.7	0.9
31–40	24.7	21.1	1.2	74.6	78.8	0.9	97.5	119.0	0.8
41–50	20.5	17.4	1.2	63.7	66.7	0.9	79.2	95.0	0.8
51–60	18.9	14.8	1.3	51.8	60.8	0.8	66.5	74.7	0.9
61–70	17.0	12.8	1.3	46.7	54.4	0.8	54.7	64.9	0.8
71–80	15.4	11.1	1.4	42.6	46.4	0.9	48.5	60.7	0.8
81–90	13.9	9.9	1.4	39.3	40.2	1.0	44.2	54.9	0.8
91–100	13.0	8.8	1.5	35.7	37.5	0.9	40.6	50.4	0.8

Note:
[a]Ratio of total sales of U.S. to non-U.S. corporations within a given grouping.

Sources: J., Hein, *The World's Multinationals: A Global Challenge*, Information Bulletin No. 84. Conference Board, 1981; "The 500 Largest U.S. Industrial Corporations," *Fortune* April 28, 1986; and "The International 500," *Fortune* August 4, 1986.

firms, by sales for 1971, 1979, and 1985. Although the United States accounts for only about two-fifths of the total output of the world's industrial countries, U.S. firms traditionally have been quite prominent among the corporations in the top sales categories. But this lead had disappeared by 1979, when it no longer held true even in the top (over $10 billion) bracket.

The phenomenon of relative size is examined from another angle in Table 6–3, which compares aggregate sales, by groups of ten companies, of the 100 largest U.S. and the 100 largest non-U.S. companies for the same three years. Two features of this table are worth noting. First, among the top twenty companies sales of U.S. MNCs are considerably larger than those of non-U.S. firms. Further down the line the relative size ratio declines, however, and from approximately the fiftieth largest corporation on it more or less stabilizes in all three years.

Second, within this general pattern the combined sales of the U.S. firms, relative to their foreign counterparts, have been declining in each category over the period covered. Thus, total sales for the ten largest U.S. firms were more than two times as large in 1971, but only slightly over one-and-a-half times as large in 1985. And by that year, U.S. sales in eight out of the nine remaining groups were smaller than non-U.S. sales.

Some students of multinationals have also compared the leading U.S. and non-U.S. companies in major industries (Hymer and Rowthorn 1970). Such comparisons are not very satisfactory because a given U.S. corporation faces the aggregate of its major foreign competitors in world markets—and not just the one that happens to occupy the equivalent place outside the United States. Moreover, in such an analysis the

178

results predictably vary from industry to industry. In chemicals, for instance, the largest U.S. firms are considerably smaller than their foreign counterparts, while in the automobile industry U.S. firms have a huge lead over their nearest foreign competitors.[1]

MULTINATIONALS AND NATIONAL ECONOMIES

The data presented in the previous section have made it amply clear that over the past twenty-five years or so non-U.S. multinationals, primarily from Western Europe and Japan, have greatly enhanced their position in the world economy at the expense of U.S.-based firms. In addition, competition from state-trading companies in developing countries, from state-trading activities in Socialist economies, and from nationally owned or closely controlled enterprises in major European countries all have brought about further fundamental changes in global trading and investment patterns (Aharoni 1980).

The temptation always arises to set these activities against the broader framework of world economic activity, although such a comparison is too facile and, in a sense, misleading. But even while cautioning against such a comparison, the United Nations has felt that "the general conclusion that many multinational corporations are bigger than a large number of entire national economies remains valid" (United Nations 1973: 13). A subsequent analysis found that in 1978 the world's top 100 economic units consisted of sixty-one countries and thirty-nine industrial corporations, twenty-one of which were based outside the United States (Hein 1980).

As that analysis stressed, ranking countries with companies obviously involves double-counting. The two do not fall into separate compartments since the output of a country's enterprises is a subset of that country's national product—and not additional to it. Moreover, gross national product merely tallies the value added by a country's producing units, while sales data reflect the cumulative cost of all components at successive stages of production. In addition, a company's receipts include sales at all levels, including sales of raw materials, intermediates, and finished products. A given end product may thus appear in the receipts of different companies and even more than once in the same company's receipts. Still, being fully aware of these and related qualifications, it is worth noting that in most of the major industrial countries the top ten corporations "account" for a larger role of total economic activity than in the United States (Table 6–4).

A perhaps more meaningful comparison is to estimate the importance of foreign-owned companies to the economies of the host countries. The data on investment proper tend to underestimate that importance, since foreign equity is only a fraction of the total assets and liabilities of such firms. Other sources of finance include borrowing from banks,

179

Table 6–4.

MULTINATIONALS AND ECONOMIC ACTIVITY, 1985.

	Sales of Top Ten Companies ($ billion)	Sales as percentage of GNP (percent)
Japan	159.4	12.0
United States	522.6	13.1
Canada	65.7	19.8
France	103.9	20.3
Germany	131.3	21.0
Italy	86.8	24.6
United Kingdom	127.9	28.1
Switzerland	37.1	38.2

Sources: "The 500 Largest U.S. Industrial Corporations," *Fortune* April 28, 1986; "The International 500," *Fortune* August 4, 1986; and International Monetary Fund, *International Financial Statistics* October 1986.

securities issues, and trade credit from unaffiliated suppliers. Comprehensive surveys of foreign-controlled firms in the United States and Germany made during the late 1970s showed the ratios of foreign equity to those firms' total assets or liabilities to have been 15 percent in the United States and 27 percent in Germany (Christelow 1982).

Another way of judging the role of foreign-owned MNCs in their host economies is their share of total sales. Such data can at best be only approximate. But it appears that in the late 1970s the share of foreign MNCs' sales in the manufacturing sector was less than 10 percent in the United States and Japan; around 20 percent in the major European countries; and between 30 and 60 percent in Argentina, Brazil, Canada, New Zealand, and South Africa.

WHY THEY GO ABROAD

Interest in the operations of multinationals, particularly their expansion abroad, quickened during the early and middle 1960s, when capital outflows from the United States increased sharply and, in turn, led to several types of restrictions, including controls on foreign direct investment. In the early 1970s, the U.S. Department of Commerce therefore published a series of studies designed "to develop better and more comprehensive information and analyses on the effects and trends of U.S. foreign investment as they relate to the U.S. and the world economies" (U.S. Department of Commerce 1972: 1).

A major finding of the Commerce Department project was that a significant relationship exists between foreign direct investment and foreign trade. In other words, a large share of total U.S. exports are directed to foreign affiliates of U.S. firms, mainly—but by no means exclusively—by their parent companies. Although the data are fairly impressive, one cannot assume that all of those exports are entirely dependent on the existence of the foreign affiliates. No doubt some of them would have been lost if the affiliates did not exist, but part of those exports might have taken place anyway, through different channels.

More specifically, direct investment abroad often takes the form of, or is associated with, the export of capital equipment needed by overseas production facilities. In addition, such investment may lead to a subsequent export of capital goods for replacement purposes. Foreign affiliates may purchase U.S.-made equipment because it is supplied directly by the parent company, but more often it is purchased from other U.S. suppliers for reasons of cost, quality, or familiarity.

Another large part of U.S. exports to foreign affiliates consists of raw materials or semimanufactured goods, such as parts and components, intended for further processing or assembly. Unlike capital equipment, such parts and components are mostly produced by the U.S. parents, who have direct interest in selling them to their affiliates. Such sales often are one of the factors considered in setting up production facilities abroad.

Exports of products for further processing tend to be highly concentrated. Nearly half of the total generally goes to automotive plants abroad, mainly in Canada, while the bulk of the remainder goes to affiliates in the machinery, chemicals, and rubber product sectors. Moreover, goods for further processing are more likely to be bought from parent companies by affiliates in areas where the United States has a long-established or dominant trading position, such as Latin America and Canada. There are also differences between industries, some requiring highly specialized parts and components available only from parents and others that use more standardized, and hence more widely available, goods.

U.S. exports to foreign affiliates of U.S. MNCs also include goods intended for resale, without further manufacturing. How necessary or effective are foreign affiliates as sales agents for U.S.-made products? There are various reasons why affiliates may sell more effectively than nonaffiliated distributors: They have a greater interest in promoting their parent companies' products; they may wish to fill out their own product lines with complementary products of their parents; and their sales facilities may make their parents more aware of opportunities in foreign markets.

The establishment of affiliates abroad also serves to stimulate U.S. exports in an indirect sense that is important, although difficult, to measure. The presence abroad of U.S. firms is likely to increase foreign interest in U.S. products in general, even though such demand may affect products quite unrelated to those handled by the affiliates themselves.

In examining the role of MNCs in world business, it is important to note that production abroad affects the parent country's exports as well as its imports. In other words, production abroad by U.S. affiliates often competes with or complements goods produced in the United States. However, importing some of the affiliates' output cannot be seen only as a detriment to the U.S. trade balance or to U.S. employment. For one thing, imports from mining and petroleum affiliates represent raw materials that either are not produced in the United States at all or can be produced only at much higher cost. Second, the rapid growth of U.S. imports in recent years has not come primarily from the foreign affiliates of U.S. firms, but from German, Japanese, and other foreign exporters that have successfully entered the U.S. market without any links to U.S. corporations.

These interrelationships still do not explain why companies go abroad. The discussion goes back quite a while, for just as the multinational firm itself it not new, neither is concern over its impact on U.S. employment and trade. Over fifty years ago, Frank Southard—who subsequently enjoyed a distinguished career at both the U.S. Treasury and the International Monetary Fund—examined the issues in a comprehensive study (1931). He found a number of factors that led U.S. companies to produce abroad, rather than export. These included—and the list has a familiar ring—high tariffs imposed after World War 1; high transportation costs for bulky or perishable products; product modification dictated by foreign tastes or preferences; patent laws requiring local production; and discrimination in government purchasing practices. Southard concluded (1931: 198–99):

> If the European market can be more profitably served from a European plant, it will be so served. To imply, however, that the American corporation is given a choice in the matter is scarcely accurate... The effect on American exports is not to be attributed so much to the actual migration of American industry as to the production and marketing conditions which made the migration necessary. The Detroit automobile workers or the Akron tire-makers may as well attempt to prevent the establishment of branch plants in California as to prevent their establishment in Europe. Many of the causal factors in the two situations are identical.

Some thirty-five years later, the argument had changed very little. U.S. MNCs participating in a survey by the Conference Board were almost unanimous that a "foreign presence" was "an important long- and short-term support for maintenance of exports at a high level" (Polk, Meister, and Veit 1966: 115).

At about the same time, the entire process of foreign investment and its implications for production and trade was being refined through the so-called product cycle theory (Vernon 1966). According to this theory, foreign markets for U.S. goods initially are small and local competition is undeveloped. As time passes, however, both foreign demand and foreign competition grow and the exporting firm establishes production facilities abroad to retain its market.

Thus, the theory explains the shift from exporting to foreign production over the life of a product: Once products have become more commonplace and both the product itself and its manufacturing process have been standardized, exporting becomes uneconomical and production abroad takes its place. This process—in which a product is first produced in the United States and then production begins abroad, with the U.S. share gradually declining—has of course been going on for at least a century. For example, firms such as Colt, Singer, and IT&T began production abroad during the nineteenth century in order to meet the competition of foreign producers.

One study in the Commerce Department project of the early 1970s specifically examined the motives underlying foreign investment by U.S. firms. The study was developed "primarily through discussions with business men responsible for the international operations of their companies" and thus provided an interpretation of "how they felt they could best operate and expand their operations" (U.S. Department of Commerce 1973: 2).

The five principal reasons for making investments abroad, according to the seventy-six companies participating in the survey, are shown in Table 6–5 in order of importance. Other reasons cited included lower wage cost and greater profit prospects abroad and the need to obtain local raw materials or components.

None of these studies and surveys, nor any other existing data, can show of course what effect the *absence* of foreign affiliates would have had on both U.S. exports and hence on U.S. employment. There simply is no way of proving whether the markets served by the foreign affiliates of U.S. MNCs could have been served by exporting, with a consequent increase in U.S. jobs.

But because a number of these studies have stressed that a primary reason for going abroad is the desire to protect foreign markets—and that without such investment those markets might have been lost—the answer probably is negative. The very high percentage of affiliate sales made in local markets tends to confirm this conclusion.

Table 6–5.
REASONS FOR FOREIGN INVESTMENT

	Mentioned by Number of Companies
Maintain or increase local market share	33
Unable to reach market from United States	25
To meet competition	20
To meet local content requirements	18
Faster sales growth abroad	15

FOREIGN MULTINATIONALS IN THE UNITED STATES

The reasons that U.S. MNCs have gone and continue to go abroad apply to non-U.S. MNCs as well. A student of European MNCs has noted that tariffs as well as other trade restrictions—such as exchange controls, quotas, and restrictions on patents—have been the primary influence on the decisions of European firms to establish manufacturing facilities in foreign markets (Franko 1974). But foreign direct investment in the United States, whether in the form of new plants or through acquisitions, presents some special characteristics that are unique and worth noting.

Foreign direct investment in the United States is not a new phenomenon. In the early days of the nation, British, Dutch, French, and German investments were largely responsible for erecting the infrastructure that stimulated the country's economic development. The expansion of the railroads, which began in the 1850s, likewise was made possible by foreign capital. In the second half of the nineteenth century, foreign investment moved directly into productive activities, such as mining, petroleum, milling, and textiles.

In the early part of the twentieth century much technology and many products that now are firmly associated in the public mind with "Made in the USA" were introduced by foreign investors. In a survey of the interwar period, the U.S. Department of Commerce noted that "foreign owners of trademarks, patents, and manufacturing processes have set up subsidiaries to manufacture such varying products as whisky, dessert powders, soap, and rayon yarn. Other important foreign investments have been in the industrial-chemical and machinery fields," and the department spoke of "205 foreign-controlled industrial enterprises in existence at the end of 1934" (U.S. Department of Commerce 1943: 105).

In a similar comment on the more recent "invasion" by foreign business interests, one author has observed that U.S. junk fund addicts could gorge on Libby fruit and vegetables, Keebler cookies, Stouffer cakes, Nestlé's chocolates, and Good Humor or Baskin-Robbins ice cream—all of which are products now owned by non-U.S. companies (Fry 1980).

Although foreign investment by non-U.S. companies is motivated by much the same factors that have already been described, the order of priorities and the importance attached to any one of them often differ. As a general proposition, it can be said that the multinational endeavors of non-U.S. corporations, both in the United States and elsewhere, reflect the simple desire to "grow big enough" in the world marketplace to compete both with U.S. firms and with each other. The original spread of U.S. MNCs did set in motion a far-reaching process of consolidation among smaller European firms, and the stronger and bigger firms that emerged from this process then were able to expand elsewhere in the world. Other factors that contributed to expansion abroad by non-U.S. companies were inflation and steeply rising wages at home, labor shortages that in some countries were compounded by restrictions on the use of foreign workers, and the desire to diversify their products as a hedge against domestic business uncertainties.

But there are further and perhaps more subtle differences. A European or Japanese company deciding to set up operations in the United States wishes, first of all, to obtain a slice of the world's largest, richest, and most competitive market. Secondly, such a company also wishes to learn from the experience of its U.S. affiliates in the fields of management, marketing, product planning, research, and so forth for the benefit of its home operations. The United States has, in fact, been described by some European executives as the world's most highly developed "common market." But in marked contrast to doing business in the European Community, a foreign firm operating in the United States does not have to cope with customs formalities, different languages, or workers from a number of foreign countries.

Foreign companies also have noted the advantages of exporting from the United States to third markets that could not be served as economically, if at all, by the parent. Thus, in some instances, a foreign company may have begun exporting for the first time to markets in Canada, Latin America, and the Far East from facilities in the United States. Another favorable factor often cited in connection with locating in the United States is the sheer size and breadth of the U.S. financial markets, which offer a wide variety of instruments and maturities to would-be borrowers.

Although they may be aware of all these advantages, foreign business executives at times have felt that the U.S. market might be too vast for small and medium-sized firms to compete in successfully. They eventually realize, however, that the United States actually consists of a series of markets within the larger national market. Foreign as well as domestic investors have discovered that, initially, they could produce or sell in one or more of the many local or regional markets and that they could then expand into other marketing areas as sales grew and experience was gained.

Foreign investors also discovered that small and medium-sized firms were far more typical of the U.S. business scene than the large U.S. corporations that had come to represent "U.S. industry" to them. From the foreign investors' point of view it was also important to discover that in the vast U.S. market large and small firms were not forced to compete with each other; rather, large firms often served as the principal market for the smaller firms' products.

In fact, operating managers of U.S. subsidiaries of European com-

185

panies with two to three years of experience behind them soon concluded that their parents' initial plans for the United States had been too modest, had been delayed too long, or had been programed to develop too slowly. They attributed this mostly to the intimidating size of the U.S. market—as seen from the other side of the Atlantic. As a senior officer of a French subsidiary remarked in the mid-1970s, "This company should have come into the U.S. market with greater strength far sooner than it did" (Conference Board 1974: 24).

One aspect rarely discussed in the vast literature on multinationals is that foreign companies often have gone beyond the basic practical considerations in deciding where to locate in the U.S. market. Many state development officials have noted that, once all the general financial, marketing, and operational comparisons have been drawn, final decisions may hinge on such factors as grass-roots "community acceptance" or the underlying quality of life offered by a particular locality or region. As the international division director for one state development agency remarked, "You eventually have to look at individual communities and the people in those communities and determine whether you like them and whether they are going to want you as a fellow resident and neighbor" (Conference Board 1974: 40).

MULTINATIONALS AND WORLD TRADE

It is clear that MNCs play an important role in international trade, but it is not easy to quantify that role. As a recent United Nations report noted, "Unfortunately, comprehensive data on the foreign trade of transnational corporations exist only for the United States" (United Nations 1985: 2). The United Kingdom publishes export data for both domestic and foreign-owned MNCs but not for their imports. Information for other countries, generally based on widely differing samples, is both sketchy and quite out of date. Very few developing countries attempt to collect trade data by type of ownership.

But even with these shortcomings, the available data do provide some idea of the magnitudes involved—especially since the United States, with relatively reliable data, accounts for the largest number of MNCs and at the same time plays host to the largest amount of foreign direct investment. For example, in 1970 manufactures exported by U.S. parents to their overseas affiliates accounted for over 20 percent of U.S. exports of manufactures. That same year, intrafirm trade within U.S. MNCs accounted for about 10 percent of world trade in manufactures.

In 1977, MNCs were responsible for 91 percent ($254 billion) of total U.S. foreign trade (Table 6–6). Of that total, $149 billion—or 53 percent of U.S. trade—represented transactions between unaffiliated parties ("arms-length") and $105 billion (or 39 percent) intrafirm trade. The latter is dominated by petroleum imports and by automotive trade under the U.S.-Canada Auto Pact. But even if those two flows are removed (from both intrafirm and total trade), intrafirm transactions still accounted for around 30 percent of all U.S. exports and imports.

The Commerce Department's latest benchmark survey of U.S. direct foreign investment, for 1982, shows little change in the share of *all* MNCs in total U.S. trade (94 percent). But it shows, not surprisingly, a marked increase in trade by foreign affiliates in the United States relative to that of U.S. MNCs since 1977 (Table 6–7).

In the United Kingdom, MNCs accounted for about 82 percent of total exports in 1981, with about 51 percent of exports originating with U.S.-based companies. Intrafirm exports were roughly 30 percent of total foreign sales. Estimates of the relative importance of MNC-related trade for other countries are based on studies using various company samples. According to one such study, the share of intrafirm trade in the 1977 exports of 329 parent MNCs was, on average, one-third (United Nations 1985: 4). The shares varied from 45 percent for the U.S. companies to less than 20 percent for Japanese firms. For European-based MNCs the share of such trade ranged between 30 to 35 percent. That same study also found that a large part of intrafirm transactions consisted of exchanges of parts and components and was highly concentrated in sectors characterized by newly evolving technologies.

A more recent survey by the Federal Reserve Bank of Boston has

Table 6–6.

U.S. FOREIGN TRADE ASSOCIATED WITH MNCs.

	Amount ($ billion)		Share (percent)	
	1977	1982	1977	1982
Total U.S. trade (exports plus imports)	278.7	456.1	100.0	100.0
MNC-associated trade	254.0	428.7	91.1	94.0
With unaffiliated parties	149.0	263.9	53.4	57.9
Intrafirm	105.0	164.8	37.7	36.1

Sources: "1977 Benchmark Survey of U.S. Direct Investment Abroad," *Survey of Current Business* April 1981; N. G. Howenstine, "U.S. Affiliates of Foreign Companies: Operations in 1982," *Survey of Current Business* December 1984; and B. L. Barker, "U.S. Merchandise Trade Associated with U.S. Multinational Companies," *Survey of Current Business* May 1986.

Table 6–7.

DISTRIBUTION OF MNC-ASSOCIATED TRADE.

	1977 ($254.0 billion = 100)	1982 ($428.7 billion = 100)
U.S. MNCs	74.3%	66.3%
U.S. affiliates of foreign MNCs	25.7	33.7

Sources: "1977 Benchmark Survey of U.S. Direct Investment Abroad," *Survey of Current Business* April 1981; N. G. Howenstine, "U.S. Affiliates of Foreign Companies: Operations in 1982," *Survey of Current Business* December 1984; and B. L. Barker, "U.S. Merchandise Trade Associated with U.S. Multinational Companies," *Survey of Current Business* May 1986.

reinforced these findings (Little 1986). Responses from fifty-seven New England MNCs (thirty-nine U.S. firms and eighteen foreign-owned affiliates) indicated that in 1983 over half of these companies' total foreign trade was "in-house." For the U.S. MNCs, intrafirm exports averaged 50 percent of their exports and intrafirm imports 58 percent. For the U.S. affiliates, 44 percent of exports and 70 percent of imports were with their foreign parents.

The survey results also revealed that the U.S. parents' trade with their two largest affiliates had grown much faster between 1979 and 1983 than their overall trade with the two countries where those affiliates were located. Total exports to the two most important affiliates rose by 35 percent over that period as against only 19 percent in overall exports to the host countries. Similarly, imports from major affiliates surged by 279 percent during 1979–83, as against 56 percent for all imports from the host countries. The survey notes, however, that many of the affiliates concerned were established since 1979 and their trade thus expanded from relatively low levels.

Given this reliance on intracompany trade, U.S. multinationals have little interest in protectionist legislation. To the extent that these companies rely on imports from their own affiliates they are much less likely to join the cry for import relief. There may in fact be a growing disparity between what the Boston Fed survey calls the "haves" and the "have-nots" among U.S. firms. Those with affiliates abroad will clamor for increased access to foreign markets, while those without foreign affiliates will be petitioning for additional import barriers. As more of U.S. industry migrates abroad, therefore, the demand for erecting specific U.S. trade barriers may become less persuasive, while pressures for dismantling foreign trade restrictions will intensify.

A special word should be said about the role of MNCs in the expansion of exports from developing countries. These firms have a thorough knowledge of the markets of their home countries, and their affiliates can rely on the parents' research and development activities, their advertising and marketing skills, and their financial clout. Although it has not been proven conclusively that affiliates in developing countries are more export-oriented than domestic firms, the evidence that such may be the case is strong.

Various studies, based largely on data from the 1970s, have shown that the share of foreign-owned firms in the exports of manufactures were over one-third for both Mexico and Korea. An analysis of 318 Brazilian firms, accounting for nearly two-thirds of manufactured exports, found that MNCs accounted for over half of those firms' shipments abroad. And in Singapore, according to a mid-1970s census, foreign affiliates provided 91 percent of total exports of manufactures (United Nations 1985: 10).

These transactions, it might be added, have been boosted by new forms of association between MNCs and the host countries. These include joint ventures with domestic firms in which MNCs have minority participation; the rapid growth of international subcontracting; the establishment of export-processing zones; and the presence of the large Japanese trading companies. This is not to say that MNCs have been the main engine in export-oriented industrialization in the developing world. The MNCs have generally tended to establish their operations in countries with upper- or middle-income levels that already had a small industrial base, could offer a skilled and disciplined labor force, and where the policy environment was favorable to export growth in general.

NOTE

1. The data on U.S. and foreign multinationals used in this chapter are taken from *Fortune* magazine's annual listings of the 500 largest U.S. and non-U.S. industrial firms, respectively. The *Fortune* rankings are based on sales, and all tables in this chapter reflect that basis. One may debate how best to measure business size, but sales can be considered a fairly appropriate index.

   In comparing sales data for U.S. and foreign firms one runs into the difficulties of both different accounting and reporting practices and currency conversion. In Europe, for instance, some companies include subsidiary sales only in proportion to their holdings, thus making it almost impossible to arrive at exact comparisons between sales data for U.S. and non-U.S. firms. Moreover, reporting periods—that is, the companies' fiscal years—often differ widely.

   The data are further distorted by changes in relative currency values. Thus, in a year in which the dollar declines sharply against other major currencies—as it did in 1985—sales data for companies from those countries increase more in dollars than in local currencies, and the companies appear to have "grown" faster than they actually did. In dollar terms, companies from the same country may even switch rankings between two given years merely because of exchange-rate shifts in the interim.

REFERENCES

AHARONI, Y. 1980. "The State-Owned Enterprise as a Competitor in International Markets." *Columbia Journal of World Business* 15 (1) (Spring): 14–21.

CHRISTELOW, D. 1982. "International Direct Investment in World Market Economies: Changing Country Roles and Changing Policies." Federal Reserve Bank of New York, Research Paper No. 8208. Mimeo.

CONFERENCE BOARD. 1974. *Foreign Investment in the United States: Policy, Problems and Obstacles.* New York: The Conference Board, Report No. 625.

FRANKO, L. G. 1974. "The Origins of Multinational Manufacturing by Continental European Firms." *Business History Review* 48 (3) (Autumn): 300–12.

189

————. 1978. "Multinationals: The End of U.S. Dominance." *Harvard Business Review* 56 (6) (November-December): 93–101.

FRY, E. H. 1980. *Financial Invasion of the U.S.A.* New York: McGraw-Hill.

GILPIN, R. 1975 *U.S. Power and the Multinational Corporation: The Political Economy of Foreign Direct Investment* New York: Basic Books.

HEIN, J. 1980. "The Top 100 Economies." *Across the Board* 17 (5) (May): 8–11.

————. 1981. *The World's Multinationals: A Global Challenge*. New York: The Conference Board, Information Bulletin No. 84.

HYMER, S. and ROWTHORN, R. 1970. "Multinational Corporations and International Oligopoly: The Non-American Challenge." In *The International Corporation*, edited by C. P. KINDLEBERGER, pp. 57–91. Cambridge, Mass.: MIT. Press.

JANGER, A. R. 1980. *Organization of International Joint Ventures*. New York: The Conference Board, Report No. 787.

LITTLE, J. S. 1986. "Intra-Firm Trade and U.S. Protectionism: Thoughts Based on a Small Sample." Federal Reserve Bank of Boston. *New England Economic Review* (January-February): 42–51.

POLK, J., I. W. MEISTER, and L. A. VEIT, 1966. *U.S. Production Abroad and the Balance of Payments: A Survey of Corporate Investment Experience*. New York: National Industrial Conference Board.

SERVAN-SCHREIBER, J. J. 1968. *The American Challenge*. New York: Atheneum.

SOUTHARD, F. A. 1931. *American Industry in Europe*. Boston: Houghton Mifflin.

UNITED NATIONS. 1973. *Multinational Corporations in World Development*. ST/ECA/190. New York: United Nations.

————. Center on Transnational Corporations. 1985. *Transnational Corporations and International Trade: Selected Issues*. ST/CTC/54. New York: United Nations.

UNITED STATES DEPARTMENT OF COMMERCE. 1943.*The United States in the World Economy*. Economic Series No. 23. Washington, D.C.: U.S. Government Printing Office.

————. 1972. *The Multinational Corporation*. Studies on U.S. Foreign Investment. Volume 1. Washington, D.C.: U.S. Government Printing Office.

————. 1973. *The Multinational Corporation*. Studies on U.S. Foreign Investment. Volume 2. Washington, D.C.: U.S. Government Printing Office.

VERNON, R. 1966. "International Investment and International Trade in the Product Life Cycle." *Quarterly Journal of Economics* 80 (2) (May): 190–207.

————. 1986. "Multinationals Are Mushrooming." *Challenge* 29 (2) (May-June): 41–47.

WELLS, L. T. 1977. "The Internationalization of Firms from Developing Countries." In *Multinationals from Small Countries*, edited by T. AGNON and C. P. KINDLEBERGER, pp. 133–56. Cambridge, Mass.: MIT Press.

International Trade and Its Financing

JOSEPH A. ARNETT

TRADE PATTERNS

IN 1986 U.S. exports reached $220 billion and imports were $365 billion, accounting for some 12 and 20 percent of the world's exports and imports, respectively. Yet trade constitutes a relatively small proportion of the U.S. GNP, between 7 to 10 percent, compared with much higher proportions for Western Europe and Japan. Manufactured goods account for the bulk of our trade, approximately 75 to 85 percent, while the balance consists of raw materials. U.S. main trading partners are Canada, a market for 20 and 25 percent of our exports and imports, followed by Japan, 12 and 22 percent, and Western Europe, 24 and 27 percent (see Table 7–1).

U.S. multinational corporations (MNCs) account for over 77 percent of U.S. exports and for over 42 percent of imports, but a relatively small

Table 7–1.
U.S. DIRECTION AND GROWTH OF TRADE (percentage).

	Exports		Imports	
	Share	Growth Per Annum	Share	Growth Per Annum
Total	100.0	2.0	100.0	7.0
Industrial countries	63.2	6.0	64.6	9.7
Canada	20.9	−4.1	17.7	−1.1
Japan	12.4	18.8	22.1	18.1
Australia, New Zealand, and South Africa	3.5	2.9	1.2	3.7
EEC	24.5	8.5	20.5	11.0
Other Europe	3.6	−9.2	1.0	2.1
Developing countries	33.5	−4.0	29.7	−0.3
OPEC	4.8	−13.2	5.1	−8.5
Non-OPEC LDCs	28.7	−22.0	24.6	1.5
Africa	1.3	−17.0	2.8	−12.0
Asia	11.0	−4.2	12.3	9.3
Middle East	4.8	−15.4	2.3	29.6
Latin America	14.3	0.2	11.4	10.2
Soviet Bloc	0.7	−44.3	0.2	26.8

Source: Calculated by Harvey A. Poniachek, from IMF, Direction of Trade Statistics, Yearbook 1987, IMF, Washington D.C., April 1987.

Table 7–2.

U.S. FOREIGN TRADE PATTERNS BY TRANSACTING PARTY
(percentage of distribution).

	Exports		Imports	
	% of U.S.	*% of MNCs*	*% of U.S.*	*% of MNCs*
U.S. total	100		100	
U.S. MNCs	79	100	38	100
Shipped to/by affiliates	33	42	17	45
Intracompany	28	35	13	35
Shipped to/by nonaffiliates	46	58	21	55
Foreign MNCs	15[a]		40[a]	
Non-MNCs related	6[a]		12[a]	

Source: Calculated by Harvey A. Poniachek, from Obie G. Whichard, "U.S. Multinational Companies; Operations in 1986," *Survey of Current Business* (June 1988).
Note:
[a] = own estimates.

number of companies, about 250 to 300, control the bulk of it. Furthermore, approximately 35 to 45 percent of the trade is intracompany, and in some sectors the proportion is much higher (see Table 7–2).

Over 50 to 65 percent of intracompany trade is composed of petroleum and transportation equipment. Some 40 percent of U.S. intracompany trade is conducted through Canada, of which some 60 percent is in transportation equipment. The EEC accounts for 25 percent of U.S. intracompany exports, primarily of chemicals and machinery, while MNCs' imports are somewhat smaller and particularly concentrated in petroleum. Japan, Asia, and the Pacific account for relatively small fractions of the intratrade flows. U.S. trade flows are distributed primarily to the industrial countries (60 percent) and to a lesser extent to the LDCs (40 percent).

TRADE FINANCE

International trade finance means different things to different people. For the importer it may mean the ability to obtain goods from far-off lands and sell them to willing consumers. For the exporter it may mean expanding marketplaces for goods that are hitting the saturation point in U.S. markets. For the banker it may mean facilitating and financing imports and exports for fee income.

U.S. companies, to a great extent, do not possess the trade finance expertise equivalent to their foreign trading partners that have been at it a few centuries longer than they. Some U.S. companies are more careful selling to Topeka, Kansas, than to Rio de Janeiro. This is understandable because the details of trade finance—details necessary to ensure profit margins—require study and practice. This chapter discusses issues and methods concerning trade financing. The subject is addressed throughout most of the chapter in terms of how to do it and it examines the ground rules and sometimes treacherous waters of international trade finance.

The details of trade finance do not apply equally to or share the same perspective for all parties. The concerns of importers differ from those of exporters. Too often customers do not know how a bank regards the financing of international trade, nor do customers always understand where to tap into a large international bank to find the right banker to fit their needs.

Companies dealing internationally must acquire a clear understanding and appreciation of the basics of both the finance function as well as the sales function. Fundamental misunderstandings by the sales force when contracts are being negotiated probably do more to contribute to later problems than any other error.

METHODS OF PAYMENT

When an importer and exporter begin negotiations, one of their primary objectives should be to determine in what form payment will be made: (1) prepayment, (2) open account, (3) documentary collections, or (4) letter of credit. The chosen method often depends on factors such as industry practices or whether it is a buyers' or sellers' market. Other factors such as previous experience, as well as the economic and political situations in the countries, should also be taken into account.

Prepayment

Payment for the goods in advance is preferred by the exporter. Risk is nonexistent, and cash-flow implications are apparent. Equally apparent, however, is the risk to the importer. Goods may never be shipped or may arrive in an unsuitable condition. Because prepayment gives the exporter great protection and the importer virtually none, prepayment is seldom used in international trade.

Open Account

The risk tables are turned in favor of the importer with the open account payment method. The exporter must ship the merchandise, trusting that the importer will make payment. This method is not generally recommended, unless a great deal of trust exists between the two involved parties. Even if trust is not a question, political considerations like foreign-exchange controls could prevent an exporter from agreeing to this method of payment.

Documentary Collections

This payment method is not unlike open account from a risk standpoint to the exporter. With documentary collections the exporter still

193

looks to the buyer's commitment to pay and remains exposed to the effects of foreign-exchange controls. Shipping documents and payment instructions travel through bank channels, and payment, if made, also arrives through bank channels. However, if the importer does not pay, the exporter has no recourse except within the judicial system of the importer's country.

There are two kinds of documentary collections: Documents against payment (DP) and documents against acceptance (DA). With DP the importer must pay the sight draft in order to obtain documents. With DA the importer must only accept the usance or time draft in order to obtain documents. This time draft accepted by the importer is called a trade acceptance or, in accounting language, an account payable.

Letters of Credit

A letter of credit (LC) is a trilateral agreement among the importer, exporter, and issuing bank. The bank promises to pay on correct presentation of documents specified in the LC. Both parties are protected: The exporter is assured that if documents are presented in order payment will be effected; the importer is assured that until documents are presented in order the bank will not pay. When issuing a letter of credit a bank deals only in documents. Quality of the underlying merchandise is of no concern to the bank, nor are other contractual obligations that may have been entered into outside the LC.

As with collections, there are two basic types of commercial letters of credit: Sight and usance (time). With a sight letter of credit, assuming that all documents are in order, payment is immediate. With a usance letter of credit, payment may be effected up to six months later, or the usance draft may be discounted by the accepting bank. This accepted time draft is known as a banker's acceptance and is only one way that acceptance financing occurs. Both types of banker's acceptance financing represent inventory financing by the bank for the importer. In either case, the primary undertaking to pay the exporter is the bank's.

BILL OF LADING

One of the most important documents involved in moving merchandise is the bill of lading because it acts not only as a receipt for the goods but also as a contract for delivery. There are two basic kinds of bills of lading, order and straight. Order bills of lading can be considered negotiable title documents and typically are issued in full sets of three originals and four duplicates. Any one of the originals gives the bearer title to the merchandise in question. Ocean bills of lading are normally of this type. Title protection for the exporter under a letter of credit is accomplished because of the nature of this document. Order bills of lading do not accompany the shipment but rather are sent through banking channels with other documents to be presented when drawing on a letter of credit. If the bank determines that discrepancies exist between the documents and the terms and conditions of the letter of credit, and the importer will not approve them, the exporter still maintains title control to the merchandise. The bank will not release the bills of lading to the importer unless all documents are in order and it can pay the exporter, or unless the importer approves any existing documentary discrepancies in relation to the terms and conditions of the letter of credit.

Straight bills of lading, on the other hand, are not negotiable documents of title but must be consigned to a specific party. Air, truck, and rail bills of lading are typically of this type. Therefore, when an exporter loads goods on an airline, the name of the consignee will be requested by the airline. If the consignee is the importer, then the exporter has effectively lost title control to the merchandise. All the consignee has to do to obtain the merchandise is to present identification to the airline. If a letter of credit is being used as the payment mechanism, and the exporter presents documents correctly to the issuing bank, payment will be made by the bank. However, if documents are presented with discrepancies and the importer will not approve them, the exporter has essentially made an open account shipment.

CHARACTERISTICS OF PAYMENT METHODS

For practical purposes it is important to examine payment methods from the perspectives of both importer and exporter. Each payment method has advantages as well as disadvantages. Importers and exporters would do well to review each while developing their internal policies. The following comparison is provided to assist companies in accomplishing that objective.

For the Importer

PREPAYMENT:
    Advantages: No bank fees; cash in advance should command a discount.
    Disadvantages: Adverse cash flow; no control of quality or quantity of merchandise; no control of shipping; no control of time of shipment.
OPEN ACCOUNT:
    Advantages: Flexible; cash is not utilized until merchandise arrives; terms may be available; quality and quantity controlled; no bank fees.
    Disadvantages: Timing of shipment is not assured; may restrict sources of supply.

195

DOCUMENTARY COLLECTIONS:

Advantages: Payment usually is not made until goods have arrived; fees lower than LC; terms may be negotiated.

Disadvantages: Timing of shipment not controlled; shipment may arrive before documents through bank channels.

LETTERS OF CREDIT:

Advantages: Payment is not required until documents presented correctly; terms may be available through usance LCs; more assurance of timely shipment; control of various requirements through documents required in LC.

Disadvantages: Bank line of credit required; bank fees.

In each of these payment mechanisms the subject of foreign exchange should also be considered. The importer may find it necessary to accept a quote in a foreign currency. Whether to maintain an open position or to hedge the need to buy a currency in the future with a foreign-exchange contract is one that must be decided for each individual transaction.

For the Exporter

PREPAYMENT:

Advantages: Payment is guaranteed; cash flow.

Disadvantages: Restriction of sales.

OPEN ACCOUNT:

Advantages: Sales increase; a premium may be negotiated.

Disadvantages: Buyer's promise to pay; cash flow; control of merchandise.

DOCUMENTARY COLLECTIONS:

Advantages: Bank channels established for payment; sales may increase vis-à-vis letters of credit.

Disadvantages: No guarantee of payment; buyer's promise to pay, not bank's.

LETTERS OF CREDIT:

Advantages: Substitutes bank's promise to pay for buyer's promise; bank promises payment if documents are in order.

Disadvantages: A complex transaction; bank fees; documentation cumbersome; staff time.

Some feel that the U.S. exporter is particularly vulnerable in international trade. Because counterparts in other countries have been exporting much longer, the U.S. exporter should seek assistance in formulating an export policy based on an analysis of the risks undertaken when exporting.

Risks of exporting can be broken down as follows:

1 COMMERCIAL RISK: The buyer does not pay for reasons of insolvency, or delay.

2 POLITICAL RISK: The buyer is unable to pay due to foreign-exchange restrictions precluding the exchange of local currency into U.S. dollars.

3 TITLE TO GOODS: The buyer obtains title to the exporter's merchandise before payment.

These risks can be paired with the payment mechanisms and viewed from the standpoint of which risks are covered or exposed (see Table 7–3). Once viewed from this perspective, only the exporter can decide if the risk warrants the payment mechanism or if an exception should be made to the company's normal export payment policy. Table 7–4 shows assessed methods of trade finance around the world.

Table 7–3.
PAYMENT METHODS AND RISK.

	Commercial Risk	*Political Risk*	*Title*
Open account	Not covered	Not covered	Not covered
Documentary collections	Not covered	Not covered	Ocean shipments: D/P covered D/A not covered Air/truck/rail shipments consigned to buyer: Not covered
Letters of credit	Buyer covered Bank covered if confirmed Bank not covered if advised	Covered if confirmed Not covered if advised	Ocean shipments, air/truck/rail shipments consigned to buyer, not covered

Table 7–4.
METHODS OF TRADE FINANCE.

	US Finance	Global Finance
LCs and banker's acceptances	30%	30%
Open account	30	30
Direct financing	40	40

Source: Estimates by Harvey A. Poniachek May 1985.
Note: LCs and Banker's Acceptances include documentary collections. Open account financing includes prepayments.

LETTERS OF CREDIT

Importers and exporters can best understand through practical experience in the complexities of letters of credit their own as well as the bank's obligations in an LC transaction. Some of the specialized topics often discussed in relation to letters of credit are briefly discussed below.

*International Chamber of Commerce Publication 400, Uniform Customs
and Practices for Documentary Credits (1983 Revision)*

These are the rules to which most letters of credit adhere. They establish
guidelines as to what each party in the letter-of-credit transaction is
responsible for, as well as criteria for correct document presentation.
Because these rules can be very specific and even a small deviation from
them could prevent the payment of the letter of credit, it is important
that all parties become familiar with the rules. Full understanding of
these rules and their ramifications by the importer's custom's broker or
by the exporter's freight forwarder is also in order. Copies of these
regulations can be obtained from the international department of any
bank or from the International Chamber of Commerce directly, at ICC
Publications Corporation, 801 Second Avenue, Suite 1204, New York,
New York 10017.

International Chamber of Commerce Publication 350, INCOTERMS

Included in this ICC publication are acronyms known as shipping
terms, the most familiar being FOB and CIF. Shipping terms are often
one of the most misunderstood areas within a letter of credit. Ignoring
them can spell disaster for a company, for shipping terms not only
specify what both the importer and exporter are responsible for
(insurance, freight, costs, risks) as well as who will pay, but they also
drive the documentation logic of the letter of credit. Letter-of-credit
departments understand these terms and will expect their customers to
be familiar with them. Copies of the INCOTERMS can be obtained
from the international department of a bank or by writing to the ICC
Publications Corporation listed above.

Letter-of-Credit Terminology

Understanding international terminology makes it easier to deal with
letters of credit. Importers and exporters do best when they speak the
same language as that spoken by the bank. The following are some
common terms found in a letter-of-credit transaction.

ACCOUNT PARTY: Typically the importer/buyer; sometimes known as
the accountee.
BENEFICIARY: The seller or shipper.
ISSUING BANK: The bank that opens the letter of credit.
ADVISING BANK: The bank in the exporter's country that gives the
LC to the exporter; also has a specific risk connotation—in
accepting an advised LC the exporter is looking at the commercial
risk of the issuing bank and the political risk of the country in
which the issuing bank is located.
CONFIRMING BANK: Procedurally like an advised LC, but the
beneficiary benefits from the presumably greater commercial

strength of the confirming bank and the reduced political risk of the country in which the confirming bank is located. The issuing bank must be the party to ask another bank to confirm its letter of credit. When a bank confirms a letter of credit, it essentially extends credit to the issuing bank; if the issuing bank is unable to pay for commercial or political reasons, the confirming bank will.

NEGOTIATING BANK: The bank at which documents are presented to be checked against the terms and conditions of the letter of credit; a bank may play more than one role in a letter of credit—for example, a negotiating bank may also be the issuing bank, or the advising or confirming bank.

PAYING BANK: The bank on which the draft is drawn; if the letter of credit has been issued in the currency of the importer, then the paying bank will usually be the issuing bank; if the LC has been issued in a currency other than that of the importer, then the paying bank usually will be the advising or confirming bank.

Transferable Letter of Credit

This type of letter of credit is typically used when an importer does not apply for a letter of credit, either because he does not want to use an already existing bank line of credit or because the bank is unwilling to extend further credit. The importer then turns to the ultimate buyer, requesting that the buyer open a transferable letter of credit in favor of the importer (first beneficiary). The importer then transfers all or part of this letter of credit to a second beneficiary, usually the ultimate supplier. Thus, the supplier (second beneficiary) ships, either to the importer or to the ultimate buyer, presents documents under the transferred letter of credit, and obtains payment. The importer (first beneficiary) then substitutes drafts and invoices and draws the remaining portion of the letter of credit.

In order for a letter of credit to be transferable, it must state that it is transferable. Asking for a transferable letter of credit may give the ultimate buyer previously unknown information. The ultimate buyer will now know that the beneficiary is a middleman. Further, the middleman may not be able to open a letter of credit on his own and is unable to obtain open account terms from the supplier.

Transferable letters of credit also must call for identical documentation except for the buyer's name, seller's name, amount and unit prices, latest shipment date, and latest expiration date. All other terms and conditions must be the same. This is often difficult to accomplish, particularly when the middleman wants to conceal information about the supplier from the ultimate buyer. They work the best when all parties involved are aware of the transaction and are tied together contractually.

Assignment of Proceeds

The proceeds of any letter of credit may be assigned to a third party. However, in order to receive any payment, the third party must release the merchandise to the actual beneficiary of the letter of credit, hoping that documents will be presented correctly so that there will be proceeds. If the beneficiary of the actual LC is unable to obtain payment through the letter of credit, then there will be no proceeds, and the supplier may no longer be able to locate the original merchandise. Assignment of proceeds usually works only in situations where there is a great deal of trust between the supplier and the middleman.

Back-to-Back Letters of Credit

One structure found in this type of situation involves one letter of credit issued in favor of an importer, which the importer wishes to use to obtain another letter of credit. The intent is that the incoming letter of credit supports or "backs" the insurance to the other. Parties often approach banks with requests for this type of letter-of-credit structure. However, these parties frequently do not have the credit strength to issue a letter of credit on their own. Many banks will not handle this type of letter-of-credit structure but prefer to issue a letter of credit based on the financial strength of the importer, rather than on a letter of credit received in the importer's favor. The issuing bank will be concerned that documents will be correctly presented under their letter of credit but not under the incoming letter of credit in the importer's favor. Some banks will treat an incoming letter of credit as a glorified purchase order. They take this view because in order to receive payment under the letter of credit, the importer must ship the merchandise and present documents correctly. If anything goes wrong, the issuing bank may find itself in the position of having to pay out per letter of credit and unable to be reimbursed by the incoming or backing letter of credit.

Standby Letters of Credit

This type of letter of credit is used in situations where the issuer must indemnify another party to ensure that a contractual obligation has taken place. The ICC400 rules that apply to commercial LCs also apply to standby LCs; however, their uses are quite different. Usually, the intent of a commercial LC is that it will be drawn on and of a standby LC is that it will *not* be drawn on. Standbys are commonly used in such situations where performance or bid bonds are called for. They are also used to support the issuance of commercial paper and to support certain lending situations.

It should be noted that standby LCs are quite easy to draw on. Documents normally required to draw are a sight draft and a beneficiary's statement that the contractual obligation has not been fulfilled. Banks will not put themselves in the place of making a subjective judgment relative to the beneficiary's statement. Words such as "*authorized* signature" or such phrases or words that would put the issuing bank in that position are typically not allowed.

BANKER'S ACCEPTANCE FINANCING

Banker's acceptance financing has historically been the least costly source of financing second only to commercial paper borrowing. It is simply another source of pricing or funding a loan, identical, from a credit standpoint, to any other short-term borrowing. It has many applications: Short-term inventory financing for importers (included in this category are direct borrowings funded by a banker's acceptance as well as banker's acceptances created under usance LCs); accounts receivable financing for exporters; storage of readily marketable commodities; and domestic shipment. The Federal Reserve Regulations, not logic, govern banker's acceptance financing. Although many situations qualify, generally speaking, banker's acceptances finance either the flow of trade of the storage of goods. Financing working capital is the main area prohibited by Federal Reserve regulations. Banker's acceptances pricing is low for two major reasons: (1) The U.S. government does not charge reserves to the commercial bank creating the acceptance, and (2) funds come from investors rather than from a bank's loanable funds.

To create a banker's acceptance to finance the shipment or storage of goods, the borrower presents a usance (time) draft drawn on the bank. The bank accepts the draft, thereby creating a banker's acceptance. The accepting bank will then normally discount this draft and sell it in the marketplace to an investor interested in short-term paper. The funds received by the bank from the investor are used to provide funds to the borrower. At the maturity of the acceptance, the borrower repays the loan and the investor receives the face amount of the acceptance that had been purchased. Both sides of the transaction are handled on a discounted basis, with the borrower receiving a discounted amount from the investor (usually through the accepting bank's investment division), who has paid a discounted amount to purchase the acceptance. At maturity of the acceptance the investor receives the full face amount of the acceptance from the borrower repaying the face amount.

Procedurally, banker's acceptance financing differs from usual borrowings. The commercial banker, or the trade finance specialist, will be in a position to explain the various situations under which banker's acceptance financing may occur.

Banker's acceptance financing, however, is not without its risks. Rates are quoted on a fixed basis for the tenor of the acceptance. If other short-term financing rates fall during the tenor of the acceptance, the borrower loses the opportunity to take advantage of the falling rates because the acceptance may not be prepaid. Also the tenor of the acceptance must be closely linked to the tenor of the underlying shipment or storage transactions that it finances. However, many borrowers are able to satisfactorily manage their cash flow, funding their general financial needs with a mix of acceptances (to the extent they qualify under the Fed rules) and other sources.

FOREIGN EXCHANGE

Foreign exchange is possibly the most interesting and complex of the topics concerning the issue of trade finance. From a financing perspective, foreign exchange may enhance a company's competitiveness, or may enable a company to safely participate in a transaction that would otherwise be considered too risky. The need for a foreign exchange line of credit arises when an importer is required to accept a price denominated in a foreign currency, or an exporter is required to quote a price denominated in a foreign currency for its products. Both have concerns regarding the exchange rate and the dollar equivalent, when the transaction is materialized.

Forward foreign-exchange contracts may be entered into to lock in the rate at which currencies will be exchanged at the future date, commonly up to one year in major convertible currencies. Lines of credit are available from banks that allow such contracts. However, a bank will view foreign-exchange contracts as an extension of credit, the approval of which, as with any credit extension, depends on the company's financial strength. A banker will usually consider two risks—contract risk and settlement risk—and both contract and settlement limits will be established within foreign-exchange lines of credit. Contract limits typically mean the cumulative dollar amount that the customer may have outstanding in forward contracts at any given time. Settlement limits typically mean the largest dollar amount that the customer may have maturing, or settling, on any one day. Settlement risk exists because the bank must send payment instructions delivering the foreign currency in question before they are assured that the dollars involved have been collected. Therefore, 100 percent of the settlement limit is typically considered unsecured exposure, to be included and considered in overall credit extension to the company in question.

If an importer or exporter is able to price or obtain prices denominated in their home currency, then the need for foreign-exchange coverage *per se* does not exist. Examples, however, can be found where U.S. companies, although getting or giving prices in their home currencies, find themselves with foreign-exchange risk due to contractual negotiations. For example, a U.S. importer purchasing on an open account basis having been quoted a price in U.S. dollars may not be concerned with foreign-exchange exposure. However, care should be taken to ensure that the underlying contract does not contain a clause that states that the dollar price quoted is firm only if the U.S. exchange rate vis-à-vis the seller's currency remains within certain limits. The contract may further state that should the foreign-exchange rates move outside those limits, the importer will absorb the change. An importer may be willing to accept such a clause in the contract or may be unaware that it is there.

EXPORT FINANCE

Export finance is a complex and specialized area of international finance; the intention here is only to give a general introduction to this type of financing. Details can be obtained from a bank's export financing specialist or from Eximbank or FCIA directly.

In general, the term *export finance* refers to the use of a country's public and private export-incentive agencies, usually in concert with a commercial bank, to structure loans that will enable a manufacturer to participate in bidding on contracts being offered by foreign buyers. These buyers shop throughout the world markets for both the best products and the best financing packages. Most major industrialized countries have such export-finance agencies. The major agencies performing this function in the United States are the Export Import Bank of the United States (Eximbank) and the Foreign Credit Insurance Association (FCIA).

The following examples discuss a domestic finance transaction compared to an export finance transaction. A domestic transaction might involve a Californian manufacturer of tractors that has received an invitation to bid on an order from a Florida buyer for a large number of tractors. However, in order for the manufacturer to submit a bid, a financing package must be provided because the buyer needs to arrange three-year financing. The manufacturer brings the proposal to its banker. The banker may be able to arrange for a loan that essentially purchases the projected three-year note with or without recourse to the manufacturer, or the banker may decide to finance the Florida buyer directly. Either way, the objective of the transaction has been accomplished: The tractors have been sold because financing was arranged. Some bankers say this sounds like financing an auto dealership, and the analogy is quite close.

If the tractor is moved from Florida to, say, Brazil, the financing structure would be the same, but the risk is quite different. Instead of U.S. political risk, the banker would be confronted with Brazilian political risk, and instead of the commercial risk of a U.S. buyer, there is the commercial risk of a Brazilian buyer. Neither the manufacturer nor the banker may be willing to take on this foreign commercial and political risk without some sort of risk coverage. This is where the U.S. export agencies step in. As can be seen, coverages are not complete but constitute a risk sharing with the commercial bank structuring the financing.

The following are the risks as defined by Eximbank/FCIA:

POLITICAL RISK: Covers war, expropriation, and currency inconvertibility.

COMMERCIAL RISK: Covers buyer insolvency and protracted default (a buyer in protracted default is still in business but paying other sellers, not you).

BUSINESS RISK: Concerns warranties and disputes and is *not* covered by either Eximbank or FCIA. Because of this risk, banks may be unwilling to extend financing without recourse to the exporter and may require the exporter to accept recourse for losses not covered.

Short-term coverages are available, normally through FCIA, covering export sales of consumer goods and spare parts for up to 180 days. Other private short-term export receivables coverages may also be available. Both Eximbank and FCIA offer medium-term programs for export sales of capital equipment for up to five years. Long-term coverage for large infrastructure projects such as chemical plants is available from both Eximbank and other U.S. export-financing agencies.

Both Eximbank and FCIA offer commercial and political risk-sharing programs that may make the Brazilian tractor transaction described above acceptable to the financing bank from a risk point of view. Generally, under its commercial bank guarantee program, Eximbank covers 90 percent of the commercial risk and 100 percent of the political risk. FCIA has two coverages to choose from: 90 percent of the commercial risk and 100 percent of the political risk or 95 percent of both. These coverages are subject to change as these agencies update their programs. As has been said, these programs tend to be complex in their requirements, documentation, and structuring time frames. Dealing with a bank that has export finance specialists is key in the successful completion of such transactions.

Other U.S. agencies that offer their own foreign-exchange or programs that are complementary to Eximbank include the following:

PEFCO: The Private Export Funding Corporation offers loans to public and private borrowers located outside the United States who require medium- and long-term financing for purchase of U.S. goods and services. It is privately owned by fifty-four commercial banks.

OPIC: The Overseas Private Investment Corporation insures and finances eligible U.S. private investments in developing countries.

CCC: The Commodity Credit Corporation is a U.S. Department of Agriculture program that offers credit terms of up to three years for the purchase of U.S. agricultural projects.

U.S. importers may be able to participate in the export-finance programs made available by other nations. Mexico is a good example. The FOMEX (Fondo para el Fomento de las Exportaciones de Productos Manufacturados) financing program exists to promote the export of Mexico's manufactured products through special financing arrangements. Inventory financing for importers of these goods can be made available, at very attractive rates, by U.S. banks participating in the FOMEX program. Again, contact should be made with a commercial bank having expertise in this field.

COUNTERTRADE

An expanding area of international finance is countertrade. An increasing number of countries are in financial difficulties, and in order to finance their purchases, they are encouraging reciprocal trade, particularly for government contracts.

Usually involving large dollar amounts, countertrade transactions involve countries that will import only if another country purchases its products. A bank may be able to arrange the counter purchase of products by a company other than the one that wants to sell to the country. The buyer in the country receives the wanted product; the exporter/seller makes the sale and receives hard currency or sometimes a different product (oil is sometimes an acceptable alternative) in payment. This payment does not come from the buyer located in the country in question but rather from another company that the bank has arranged to purchase the product. This is a very specialized area of international finance and requires the substantial expertise usually available from the international division of a large commercial bank.

FOREIGN SALES CORPORATIONS

For U.S. companies that export, a substantial tax savings may be accomplished by establishing a Foreign Sales Corporation, commonly known as a FSC. Unlike the former Domestic International Sales Corporation (DISC), the FSC offers a partial tax exemption, not just tax deferral, if certain requirements are met. Under the Deficit Reduction Act that went into effect on January 1985, FSCs qualify for tax exemption on substantial portions of their export profits. Also, no U.S. corporate income tax is imposed on dividends from the exempt income distributed by the FSC to its corporate stockholders. Establishing a FSC requires tax and legal advice, but an international bank may be able to handle the details required by law in establishing it.

DOWN TO THE CASH CYCLE

A company does not need financing when it finds itself at either end of the cycle: Cash, inventory, accounts receivable, cash. All that is left to finance is inventory and accounts receivable.

An importer needs financing for the transit time of the inventory, for the inventory period itself, which may consist of a manufacturing phase, for transit time to ship the finished goods to the buyers, and for an accounts receivable period. These financing needs may be handled by the seller, by a bank, or by a combination of both.

A seller may offer open-account or documentary-collection terms to an importer, allowing the importer to delay payment until the goods are sold and the receivable is collected. This may be the importer's preferred method of financing, depending on how much is built into the price by the seller as compensation for handling the transaction. If this method is not feasible, then a bank may step in and issue a sight LC to finance the transit time of the merchandise or a usance LC to finance not only the transit time of the merchandise but also the inventory period and perhaps also the accounts receivable period. Exactly the same financing, from a bank's credit perspective, might occur by the bank opening a sight LC on behalf of the importer, then refinancing that sight drawing for a mutually agreed on period of time for either the inventory period, the accounts receivable period, or both. The funding of this refinancing of the sight LC could take the form of a banker's acceptance, a Eurodollar advance, a reference-rate-related advance, or the like. Whatever form it takes or name is used, the financing is still of the plain old cash cycle.

An exporter is on the opposite end of the cash cycle and may require financing to manufacture products as well as to finance his foreign accounts receivables. Advance payment in full or in part would satisfy the exporter. If this financing by the buyer is unavailable or unrealistic, then bank financing may be requested.

Finally, the manufacturing period can be treated by the banker in two basic ways: (1) Consider that the goods are destined for export and may be covered by an export contract or even by a letter of credit in the manufacturer's favor; or (2) finance the exporter as a pure manufacturing concern based purely on cash flow. The approach a bank takes depends on its credit policies and on its view of the support offered by an export contract or export LC.

Some banks that may only be willing to finance the manufacturing process based on its cash flow may, however, be willing to finance the foreign receivable when supported by some form of export receivable insurance like Foreign Credit Insurance Association (FCIA). Many banks are unwilling to finance foreign receivables without such support because they are unable to obtain perfected security interests in foreign receivables as they are able to do on domestic receivables. Such support as FCIA may be considered as taking the place of such security interests.

FUNDING

Once the loan is approved, funding of financing for both importer and exporter may be by means such as reference-rate related, Eurodollars, or banker's acceptances. Minimum drawdowns may apply depending on bank policy.

Funding is also available in other currencies, mainly drawn from offshore or Eurocurrency markets. A bank may require hedging of loans funded in this manner. A bank will be concerned about a borrower's ability to pay back a loan funded in a currency other than its home currency should the currencies fluctuate adversely between the time the loan is drawn down and the time payments are due. Forward foreign-exchange contracts are available in major convertible currencies, matched to loan amortization schedules, which will erase foreign-exchange exposure and lock in total borrowing costs. A bank may consider making unhedged loans denominated in foreign currencies if a borrower has receivables or income-earning assets denominated in the same currency as the loan sufficient to cover loan principal and interest payments.

To many banks, trade finance is not a stand-alone area of financing. It is treated, from a credit standpoint, as any other type of balance sheet lending. Borrowers are either financially strong enough to command unsecured credit, or they may be required to support their borrowings with some form of collateral. Whether these borrowings are used to finance international trade, domestic trade, or the manufacturing process, the same credit criteria of prudent lending may be applied.

DEALING WITH THE BANK

Trade finance services at commercial banks are commonly provided through either one, or a combination, of the following delivery systems: (1) Account officers, (2) specialists, and (3) specially designated entities. Tiered calling is a concept popular among bankers who strive for ongoing relationships with their customers. An account officer will ensure that every level, or tier, of the customer's business is covered by the appropriate specialist from the bank. Customers who seek such commitments should expect their bankers to provide them with the key contacts within each bank department so that optimal service can be obtained. This is particularly true when dealing with the international division of the bank. A company's vice president of finance or treasurer will probably find the account officer or account manager to be their best contacts. However, trade finance expertise can differ widely among

207

account officers. Some banks have trade-finance specialists who work with account officers to insure that the bank fulfills the global needs of the customer. But often the customer's perception of the service being provided by a bank is determined as much by the specialists within the bank as by the account officer. Nowhere is this truer than in a letter-of-credit department.

Bank LC departments tend to be populated by people from around the world who have developed expertise in the mysterious world of letters of credit. Learning and understanding the organization and functioning of this department, as well as its people, is the key to successful linkage between a customer and its bank. The vice president of finance or treasurer may not totally appreciate this fact, but the export manager or head of importing certainly does.

An LC department may be separated into import and export or into issuing and negotiation. If the former structure prevails, all import LCs or export LCs are then issued and negotiated with that particular section. If the latter organization occurs, import LCs are issued, and export LCs are advised or confirmed in the issuing section, while the negotiating side handles both documents being presented under both import as well as export LCs. Proponents for each structure exist, but for the customer the division matters little. What does matter is knowing who does what to whom. LC departments are staffed by native English speakers as well as those for whom English is a second language. It sometimes happens that people who are totally understandable in person can become unintelligible over the phone: In interpersonal communication, two senses are at work, sight as well as sound; take sight away, and the ear cannot always fill in the gaps. The key here is to meet the bank personnel with whom you will be working. Banks provide essentially the same products and services: All other things being equal, it is the connections that develop between people that can either cement or destroy a business relationship.

NEW TECHNOLOGY

Microtechnology advances have found their way into international banks. This technology, when applied to letters of credit, has created startling new products. The letters-of-credit issuing process can be streamlined to a point that companies that issue a large volume of import letters of credit cannot imagine how they ever got along without the products.

Companies can use personal computers, usually requiring a hard disk, to complete entire letter-of-credit applications and amendments and to electronically transmit them to the bank's letter-of-credit department. Some of these microproducts can use hard disks to store samples that are instantly retrievable when new letters of credit are needed. Versions also exist which handle export letters of credit. The most impressive products contain history files on their hard disks that track every aspect of the LC transaction, from issuing to negotiation, and also allow the user to perform complex management information functions. These products should be examined by any company that issues a large volume of letters of credit.

CONCLUSION

This overview of financing international trade has introduced a complex subject that is not easily mastered. Fortunately, many experts in the field are available: The banker; the freight forwarder, the customs broker, insurance agencies, shipping companies, and so forth. Consult with them. If you try to do it all yourself, you may find yourself swimming alone in the treacherous waters of international trade.

8

Foreign Direct Investment

DAVID GOLD

FOREIGN investment by multinational corporations (MNCs) is an important element of the world economy. The world's stock of foreign direct investment (FDI) was measured at almost $600 billion as of the end of 1984.[1] Subsequent growth probably pushed that figure to about $750 billion by the end of 1987. The United States is by far the largest country of origin for FDI, followed by the United Kingdom, Germany, the Netherlands, and Japan (see Table 8–1).

Table 8–1.
DISTRIBUTION OF THE WORLD STOCK OF
FOREIGN DIRECT INVESTMENT, BY
COUNTRY OF ORIGIN (percentage).

Country	1960	1973	1984
United States	47.1%	48.0%	40.0%
United Kingdom	18.3	13.0	13.3
Germany	1.2	5.6	7.8
Netherlands	10.3	7.5	7.1
Japan	0.7	4.9	6.4
France	6.1	4.2	5.4
Canada	3.7	3.7	5.3
Switzerland	3.4	3.4	4.3
All developing countries	1.0	2.9	3.1
Total billions of dollars	$67.7	$211.1	$595.7

Source: U.S. Department of Commerce, International Trade Administration, "Direct Investment Update: Trends in International Direct Investment" December 1986.

DEFINITION, ACTIVITIES, AND GEOGRAPHIC LOCATION

The United States defines FDI as occurring when a foreign citizen or firm owns a minimum of 10 percent of the equity of a domestic enterprise. If the ownership stake is less than 10 percent, the investment is defined as portfolio investment. The figure of 10 percent has been adopted as a rule of thumb of the U.S. Department of Commerce; 211

there is obviously no hard-and-fast line between an active investment, where a foreign owner exerts significant or total control over the management of a domestic firm, and a passive investment, where the owner has little or no involvement with management. In some cases, with even less than 10 percent ownership of an affiliate, a corporation can exert effective control over its operations, particularly when it supplies a key input (such as technology). In other cases, companies with substantially larger equity stakes may have little control and may treat their investment much in the manner of a portfolio investment.

The annual flow of FDI is currently about $50 billion per year, higher than during the recession years of the early 1980s but about the same as the late 1970s. The vast bulk of foreign investment originates in developed countries and flows to other developed countries. The United States remains a large home, or source, country for FDI but in the 1980s also has emerged as the dominant host country for investment originating in Europe and Japan. At the same time, Japan has become an important home country, as foreign investment from Japan has been flowing in increasing amounts to the United States and Canada, to Western Europe, and to Latin America, in addition to its more traditional destination in the developing nations of Asia (see Table 8–2).

About one-third of the FDI undertaken by United States-based MNCs is in manufacturing industries, including chemicals, motor vehicles, machinery, electrical appliances and equipment, and basic metals. Another 30 percent is in finance, mostly insurance, and some 15 percent is in petroleum ventures, largely refining and extraction. The remainder of U.S. FDI is in trade; services such as consulting, hotels, and health services; and activities such as construction, communications, and public utilities. FDI in the United States by foreign MNCs is also in manufacturing (25 percent), with the other large categories being trade (20 percent), finance (20 percent), petroleum and mining (13 percent), and real estate (8 percent).[2]

Table 8–2.
OUTFLOW OF FOREIGN DIRECT INVESTMENT
FROM JAPAN (millions of US dollars).

Host Region	1975	1980	1985
North America	$905	$1,603	$5,495
Western Europe	210	577	1,930
Other Western Hemisphere	371	582	2,616
Asia	1,124	1,195	1,469
Other	547	730	708
Total	$3,280	$4,695	$12,218

Source: "Recent Developments Related to Transnational Corporations and International Economic Relations," Report of the United Nations Secretary-General (E/C.10/1987/2) January 30, 1987.

The vast bulk of MNCs are headquartered in the developed economies, especially in the United States, Western Europe, and Japan.
There are some MNCs in the developing countries, especially in the
newly industrializing countries of East Asia and Latin America. Very
little foreign investment originates in developing countries, and only a
fraction of that involves activity in the developed economies. Some
Third World MNCs are state-owned, as in the petroleum sector. There
are also a few multinational enterprises from Socialist countries, but
their international investment activity is far too small to have a
noticeable impact.

MACROECONOMIC INFLUENCES

All investment decisions occur within a context dominated by macroeconomic conditions, policies of host and home country governments,
and political conditions within host countries. In making its foreign
investment decisions, a firm needs to understand what these conditions
are at present and formulate judgments as to their course over the
expected life of the investment.

The most important macroeconomic variable is economic growth.
High levels of worldwide growth, both current and expected, are a
strong indication of market opportunities. The slowdown of foreign
investment in the 1980s can be attributed to the stagflation of the 1970s
and the sharp recession of the early 1980s. Similarly, differential growth,
where some countries and regions grow more rapidly than others, can
also help explain why the location of foreign investment shifts. This also
occurred in the 1980s, when foreign investment flows became increasingly concentrated in developed economies at the expense of developing economies. Especially since the intensification of the Third World
debt crisis, starting in 1982, growth rates in many developing countries
largely collapsed as more and more debtor countries adopted austerity
policies. In addition, more optimistic growth prospects in the United
States, especially since the end of the recession in 1982, have contributed to a significant shift in foreign investment flows within the
United States. After years of being the country with the largest outflows
of foreign investment, it has become the largest recipient of investment.

Growth is also important because higher rates of economic growth are
usually associated with an increase in the profitability of corporations.
MNCs frequently use retained earnings of affiliates to finance their
overseas expansion, especially in cases where exchange restrictions or
exchange-rate fluctuations may make it difficult or costly to move funds
across borders. Even where funds can move relatively freely internationally, retained earnings are an important means of financing new
investment. Thus, both because economic growth expands markets and
increases profit flows, foreign investment tends to follow income
growth and adopt a pro-cyclical character (see Table 8–3).

213

Table 8–3.

FOREIGN DIRECT INVESTMENT FLOWS IN THE
1980s (billions of special drawing rights).

	1981	1982	1983	1984	1985
Inflows:					
United States	21.6	12.6	11.2	24.7	17.7
Western Europe	14.4	13.5	15.3	10.6	14.3
All developed countries	36.0	27.2	31.3	38.7	33.5
Developing countries	12.2	13.3	10.6	12.0	12.8
Total inflows	48.2	40.5	41.9	50.7	46.3
Outflows:					
United States	8.1	2.2	2.5	7.6	15.1
Western Europe	24.3	17.8	20.3	23.6	22.1
Japan	4.2	4.1	3.4	5.8	6.3
All developed countries	42.8	21.1	31.7	42.7	49.8
Developing countries	0.2	0.9	0.9	0.5	0.9
Total outflows	43.0	22.1	32.6	43.2	50.7

Source: "Recent Developments Related to Transnational Corporations and
International Economic Relations," Report of the United Nations Secretary-
General (E/C.10/1987/2) January 30, 1987.
Note: Inflows and outflows will not balance due to data errors and differences
in sources of original data.

Changes in financial variables and innovations in the international
financial system can have an impact on international portfolio investment. High interest rates would not, however, be a factor in explaining
the increase of direct investment into the United States. As discussed
above, economic growth is probably the most important determinant
of such flows. The increasing securitization of financial markets allows
MNCs greater access to a wider variety of financing instruments than in
the past. One prominent example is the growing popularity of below-
investment-grade securities, commonly labeled as "junk bonds," in the
United States.

Exchange rates may affect foreign investment flows, although the
impacts may not always be straightforward. The decline in the international value of the dollar in the 1970s made U.S. assets cheaper for
holders of foreign currency and led to a wave of foreign investments,
including both acquisition of existing assets and construction of new
facilities. In the 1980s, however, the high dollar did not deter foreign
investment into the United States. Apparently, future growth prospects, as well as depressed prices for equities on U.S. stock exchanges,
provided prospects for future gains that were sufficiently optimistic to
offset possible losses from a falling dollar.

Since 1973 currencies have fluctuated continuously, and companies
doing business across borders have been forced to guard against losses
stemming from currency fluctuations. Several MNCs have established
production facilities in both Europe and the United States with the
explicit objective of allowing them to shift between exports and
domestic production depending on which is more profitable as

exchange rates fluctuate. By early 1987 several Japanese MNCs had begun exporting from their U.S. affiliates in response to the falling dollar. Honda was considering exporting cars built at its U.S. factory back to Japan.[3]

Domestic macroeconomic conditions are also important determinants of foreign investment. Both Japan and Germany have experienced an increased outflow of foreign investment in the 1980s. In both countries, high domestic savings rates and a shift in fiscal policy toward balanced budgets have generated a surplus of savings over investment. This situation has led Japanese and German financial institutions to increase their portfolio investment abroad and has contributed to the growing tendency for Japanese and German MNCs to engage in foreign direct investment.

FOREIGN INVESTMENT DECISIONS BY MNCs

The volume of foreign investment is determined primarily by three sets of considerations. One is the broad strategies and specific decisions of MNCs. The MNC is defined as a firm with ownership of significant production facilities in at least two countries. Decisions by MNCs to establish, or expand, facilities in countries other than their home country form the basis of the growth of foreign investment.

A second set of factors is broad economic variables, such as interest rates, exchange rates, growth of world trade, or growth of demand in specific countries or regions. The essentially microeconomic decisions of MNCs occur within a context established by these key macroeconomic variables. The third set of factors is government policies, especially policies on tariffs, taxes, local content, profit remittances, currency exchange, and other factors affecting the ability of corporations to conduct business across borders.

MNCS invest abroad to achieve a variety of objectives. In some cases, the basic objective is to obtain a supply of raw materials that are necessary for a firm's production process. Other instances of foreign investment involve firms seeking low-cost environments to produce products for export back to the home market and to sizable markets in other countries. In such examples of export-related investment, the size of the host-country market is far less important than production and transport costs to target markets. A third objective of foreign investment is as a means of penetrating markets in large and/or rapidly growing economies.

At first glance, it would appear that a few economic variables would be sufficient to explain the foreign investment that is undertaken in pursuit of these objectives. A U.S. aluminium producer and an Italian oil refiner do not have domestic sources of supply of bauxite and petroleum. Low unit labor costs will attract a clothing manufacturer or a producer of consumer electronics to a country to produce for export.

215

In fact, a growing number of developing countries, particularly in South East Asia and Latin America, have sought to attract this kind of FDI by setting up export-processing zones. Firms located in these zones benefit from a variety of incentives, including duty-free imports of raw materials and components to be used in exported output, tax concessions, and low rentals or utility charges.

In reality, the factors affecting a foreign investment decision are complex, and the range of choices facing firms is quite wide. An Italian oil refiner, for example, can engage in oil exploration by itself or through a joint venture with other multinational oil firms, or it can purchase its supplies of crude oil via long-term contracts with a producing nation or on the international spot market. A European consumer goods company can expand into the U.S. market by building new production facilities, by purchasing an existing company or division of a company, both of which are acts of direct investment, or by exporting directly or via a contractual arrangement with a U.S. firm. Each course of action has benefits and risks, and a firm will need to evaluate these in deciding on its individual course of action.

In a number of instances, it has been observed that firms selling similar products have adopted different strategies toward foreign markets. For example, until recently, Japanese automobile producers had entered foreign markets primarily via exports, while U.S. manufacturers relied more heavily on direct investment. One reason for this difference is that U.S. firms tended to compete more via marketing skills, while Japanese firms, with more flexible manufacturing techniques, had driven unit costs low enough that they could absorb transportation expenses and still offer a price-competitive, attractive product. Recently, with rising protectionism increasing the costs of exporting and with the appreciation of the yen cutting into their price advantage, Japanese manufacturers of motor vehicles and electronics goods have been constructing production facilities in North America and inside the European Economic Community.

An MNC's choices, then, may depend not just on quantifiable market variables but on the particular strengths and weaknesses that the firm possesses relative to its competitors. These strengths, for example, could emerge from an organizational structure that is particularly well suited to remote decision making and therefore adaptable to a far-flung network of branch plants. Another firm may have a strength that is more difficult to transmit across borders and may feel itself to be at a disadvantage when competing against local producers.

The competitive advantages held by an MNC are frequently called ownership advantages. An MNC also needs to consider the relative costs of entering a foreign market by exporting or through direct investment. The benefits of the latter, called locational advantages, can include savings on transportation costs, the ability to avoid high tariffs and other import barriers, better knowledge of local markets, and possibly lower costs of labor and other inputs relative to producing at home. All firms, however—including other MNCs and actual or potential local competitors—have access to these local advantages. The key to explaining why a firm engages in foreign investment rather than remain an exporter lies in the interaction of local and ownership advantages.[4]

FORMS AND STRATEGIES OF INVESTMENT

Foreign investment has usually taken the form of building new facilities and establishing a new affiliate, or obtaining existing assets by purchasing entire firms or divisions of a firm. The former, called greenfield investment, allows an MNC to establish its own production system with the most up-to-date equipment. Japanese MNCs, as they have expanded their direct investments in the 1980s, have constructed new factories in the United States and in England. In both countries, Japanese MNCs have tended to locate in labor-surplus areas away from their domestic competitors and have succeeded in obtaining substantial incentives from local governments.

Purchasing existing assets can save time, a key consideration for an MNC that is seeking to overcome a lead held by competitors already active in the target market. In addition, such a purchase can give an MNC a known brand name and a market network in addition to production facilities. This has apparently been an important motive for a number of European consumer goods firms, such as Electrolux (Sweden) and Nestlé (Switzerland), that have recently purchased U.S. corporations.

In recent years there appears to have been an intensification of competition among MNCs in many key product areas. The slowing down of worldwide economic growth in the 1970s was one factor, as many firms had committed themselves to a level of productive capacity that was obviously excessive. The emergence of MNCs from Japan, and to a lesser extent from newly industrializing developing countries such as South Korea, has also been an important factor, because these firms have frequently become the lowest-cost producers in their market segment. In addition, the maturation of a number of key postwar technological developments—such as electronic miniaturization, computers, and biotechnology—has helped create new products and new production methods at a rapid rate.

This new environment has raised the costs and the risks for many firms seeking to do business outside of their home countries. New technologies have raised the costs of new investments in many industries and have speeded up the life cycle of many products, such as video cassette recorders and portable tape players. These developments mean not only that firms are forced to spend more to develop and produce new products but that the potential payback period is shorter, as competitors quickly produce similar or superior products.

217

MNCs are responding to the new competition in a variety of ways. Firms would traditionally exploit profit opportunities domestically and then expand abroad first via exports to test foreign markets for product acceptance before engaging in foreign investment. Today, however, new products are frequently designed to be sold, and produced, in many markets simultaneously. Expanding the initial market potential is one way of compensating for higher costs and shorter payback periods.

Another strategy emerging from the present period of heightened competition is the tendency for firms in similar or related industries to cooperate in certain aspects of their activities while continuing to compete in others. There has been a marked increase in international joint ventures both between firms in the same industry and between firms in previously unrelated industries. A joint venture is when two or more firms combine in a specific project or establish a separate entity through a sharing of equity. One prominent example of an international joint venture is New United Motors, a 50–50 joint venture between Toyota and General Motors producing small cars for the U.S. market. General Motors entered this joint venture to gain direct experience with Toyota's production methods, while Toyota wanted access to GM's dealer network and marketing experience. Ford–Mazda and Chrysler–Mitsubishi are other examples of United States–Japan joint ventures in automobiles. These firms, of course. continue to compete among themselves with models produced outside of their respective joint ventures.

Telecommunications, semiconductors, and computers, with the rapid introduction of costly new technologies, have also experienced an increase in cross-border joint ventures, with such ventures often cutting across industry and product lines, also. For example, AT&T, seeking to enter computers and be a force in office automation, and Olivetti, seeking larger sales in the United States, have joined in a personal computer venture aimed primarily at the U.S. market.

In addition to joint ventures, MNCs have other means of cooperation. One is original equipment manufacturing (OEM), whereby one firm manufactures a product that is marketed under the trademark of a second firm. OEM allows the manufacturer to enter a large market, while the marketing firm gains access to an efficient manufacturing process. Licensing agreements are also becoming more popular, where one firm is granted a license by a second firm to produce, and frequently market, a product. Such cooperative arrangements are not considered as foreign direct investment, *per se*, because they do not involve equity transactions.

THE REGULATORY ENVIRONMENT

Policy actions by host country governments are another major factor affecting foreign-investment decisions. Governments have adopted various forms of barriers to protect domestic industries from import competition, including tariffs, quotas on the quantity of goods that can be imported, and local content regulations stipulating a minimum percentage of the weight or value of a good that must be produced domestically. For many MNCs, the most effective way to avoid these protectionist barriers is to engage in FDI and become a local producer.

The existence of protectionist barriers and the fear of higher ones is behind some of the shifts in FDI flows observed in the 1980s. Increased investment in the United States is partly due to rising protectionist sentiment as the U.S. trade balance deteriorated. Similarly, foreign investment in Europe is a means of getting behind the Common Market's trade barriers. This is especially the case in low-wage countries like Spain, a recent entrant into the EEC. The increase in FDI from Japan can be partly attributed to the desire of Japanese exporters to retain their markets in the United States and Western Europe and to do so by establishing production inside protectionist walls. Having invested because of fears of protectionism, a number of Japanese MNCs are finding that their productivity and profitability in the United States and in England are much better than expected, and this will likely encourage further FDI by Japanese firms.

Other forms of government policy are designed to directly impact on FDI. Many governments in both developed and developing countries use various forms of incentives to attract investment by MNCs. These incentives can include tax holidays, subsidized finance, accelerated depreciation, subsidized leasing, restrictions on import competition, and so forth. The use of such incentives by countries seeking new investment has probably increased in recent years. LDCs have seen the flow of new capital drop essentially to zero following the surfacing of the debt crisis in 1982, and many of these countries have intensified their efforts to attract new FDI. Developed countries have also sought new foreign investment to offset stagnationist tendencies.

It is not clear how effective these incentives are, however, in attracting new investment. For example, MNCs have located large, new factories in the north of England, and in Kentucky, Tennessee, Pennsylvania, and Ohio in the United States—largely due to low wages, low land prices, and ready access to nationwide transportation networks, conditions that are beyond the ability of a locality to create. In the case of many LDCs, political stability is another factor that is important to MNCs but is usually beyond the ability of a government to insure. Available evidence suggests that while incentives may influence location choice when other conditions are roughly equivalent, incentives generally do not have a significant effect on foreign-investment decisions by MNCs.[5]

Other types of government policies can also affect foreign-investment decisions. Governments can insist on performance requirements that MNCs must meet. For example, an MNC can be required to produce a minimum proportion of its output for export or to include a minimum proportion of locally produced material in its final product. Restrictions on foreign workers, especially at the managerial or skilled technical level, have been employed to encourage MNCs to hire and train local talent. There are also numerous examples of restrictions on remittance of profits and dividends or restrictions on foreign-exchange conversion that effectively force the MNC to reinvest profits locally.

Many of these restrictions have been imposed in an attempt by governments to protect their economies from perceived negative effects of MNCs. The existence of both restrictions and incentives, at times within the same country, reflects an ambivalence within many LDCs toward foreign investment.

Policy issues are likely to remain important for some time. Many governments are seeking to attract greater international investment by MNCs in order to obtain scarce capital and technologies. This has been the stance of a number of debtor developing countries that have seen a drain on their capital resources because of debt-service payments and capital flight. At the same time, there is continued pressure to restrict the activities of MNCs in a number of areas. One of these is environmental, especially since the chemical accident at Bhopal, India, in 1984. Another area is where countries seek to preserve a key economic sector for domestic investment. Some countries, for example, are restricting foreign investment in data services, in the hope of allowing their nationals to gain a significant presence.

Many of these issues are currently being discussed in various international bodies, including the United Nations and the General Agreement on Tariffs and Trade (GATT). The current GATT negotiations, for example, will discuss the issue of whether the rules governing trade in commodities can be extended to services, an activity where international investment is growing in importance. The outcome of such discussion will have an important influence on future investment flows.

FUNDING SOURCES AND CONCLUSIONS

The recent growth of foreign investment into the United States has occurred largely through the acquisition of existing assets. More than 80 percent of new investments in the 1984 to 1986 period were for acquisitions, while less than 20 percent involved the establishment of new enterprises. This growth in acquisitions reflects not only the general attraction of the United States for foreign investors, but the increased participation of foreign MNCs in the United States merger wave. [6]

With economic growth rates in the United States, Europe, and Japan recovering from the recession of the early 1980s, retained earnings of MNCs and their affiliates have grown and have provided a source of funds for the expansion of FDI. Retained earnings are strongly cyclical, however, and MNCs use a number of other sources of funds. Bank loans, both in home countries and in host countries, are an important source of funds for MNCs. The recent expansion of FDI from Japan has been aided by close ties between Japanese MNCs and Japanese financial institutions.

MNCs also raise funds by issuing notes or bonds on international securities markets. Such securitized lending has become increasingly important in recent years, as the proportion of bank loans in international finance has dropped. In some cases, MNCs have helped finance a foreign acquisition by reselling some of the acquired company's assets.

Governments are also possible sources of financing. State and local governments in the United States have found subsidized finance for MNCs in some instances or provided tax breaks that serve to increase a MNC's cash flow over time. Government-aided financial arrangements are often available in developing countries, especially since 1982. The debt crisis has led large international lenders to cut their new lending to developing country markets essentially to zero. One recent government program in Chile, Mexico, and other Third World debtor countries encourages holders of debt to swap their loans for equity investments, which reduces the country's external debt while giving the foreign investor an asset with profit-earning potential.

The growth of foreign investment in recent years has been stimulated by economic growth and changes in the competitive environment facing MNCs and has been aided by government policies and financial innovations. The continued expansion of FDI will depend on how successfully MNCs, governments, and the financial sector interact to maintain the necessary environment.

NOTES

1. U.S. Department of Commerce, International Trade Administration, "Direct Investment Update: Trends in International Direct Investment," (Washington, D.C.: U.S. Government Printing Office, 1986).
2. Based on data for 1983 and 1984. See Michael A. Shea, "U.S. Affiliates of Foreign Companies: Operations in 1984," *Survey of Current Business* (October 1986); pp 31–45; R. David Belli, "U.S. Multinational Companies: Operations in 1983," *Survey of Current Business* (January 1986), pp 23–35.
3. See, e.g., Bernard Wysocki Jr., "Battling a High Yen, Many Japanese Firms Shift Work Overseas," *The Wall Street Journal* (February 27, 1987); Douglas R. Sease, "Japanese Firms Export U.S.-Made Goods," *The Wall Street Journal* (March 3, 1987).
4. Recent work on the theory of the MNC emphasizes the advantages that a firm possesses when it uses FDI internalize a large number of transactions, as opposed to greater reliance on the market when it exports. See, e.g., Richard E. Caves, *Multinational Enterprise and Economic Analysis* (Cambridge: Cambridge University Press, 1982).

5. See the recent discussion published by the United Nations Centre on Transnational Corporations, Stephen E. Guisinger, "Investment Incentives and Performance Requirements: They Matter," *The CTC Reporter* 20 (Autumn 1985), pp 38, 40, 42; Trevor Farrell, "Incentives and Foreign Investment Decisions: An Opposing View," *ibid.*, pp 39, 41, 42; Louis T. Wells, "Investment Incentives: An Unnecessary Debate," *The CTC Reporter* 22 (Autumn 1986), pp 58–60.

6. Ellen M. Herr "U.S. Business Enterprises Acquired or Established by Foreign Direct Investors in 1986," *Survey of Current Business* (May 1987), pp 27–35.

9 The Balance of Payments and Its Financing

JOSEPH G. KVASNICKA

THE BALANCE of payments exerts significant influence on the environment of the multinational corporation. It affects key financial and economic variables, such as the exchange rate, currency controls, country risk, availability of capital and funding sources, interest rates, and investment feasibility. These variables, in turn, affect MNCs worldwide. In addition to discussing the conceptual framework of the balance of payments, this chapter examines its accounting, financing, and interaction with the national and international sectors.

CONCEPTUAL FRAMEWORK OF THE U.S. BALANCE-OF-PAYMENTS STATISTICS

The U.S. balance-of-payment statistics measure the value of transactions between U.S. residents and the rest of the world over a period of time, typically a year. The term *U.S. residents* includes individuals who are U.S. citizens, corporations that are incorporated in the United States, and various units of the local, state, and federal governments.

Conceptually, transactions recorded in the U.S. balance of payments are divided into two broad categories: Current transactions, which are "real" transactions in goods, services, and transfer payments (such as pensions), and capital transactions, which are typically financial transactions involving loans, investments, funds transfers, and government reserve transactions.

To facilitate further analysis, these broad categories are divided into more detailed subcategories. The official U.S. balance-of-payments statistics published by the U.S. Department of Commerce in the March, June, September, and December issues of the *Survey of Current Business* contain literally hundreds of such subcategories (see Table 9–1).

In this exposition of the basic principles of the balance-of-payments accounting, we shall present a simplified picture, using only the following main categories as they are used in the official balance-of-payments statements:

223

Table 9-1.

U.S. INTERNATIONAL TRANSACTIONS (millions of U.S. dollars).

Line	(Credits +; debits −)[a]	1985	1985 II	III	IV
			Not seasonally adjusted		
1	Exports of goods and services[b]	358,498	90,984	87,561	92,37
2	Merchandise, adjusted, excluding military[c]	214,424	55,472	50,185	53,42
3	Transfers under U.S. military agency sales contracts	9,001	2,209	2,195	1,89
4	Travel	11,663	3,003	3,186	2,46
5	Passenger fares	2,989	841	833	66
6	Other transportation	13,972	3,399	3,526	3,67
7	Royalties and license fees from affiliated foreigners[d]	4,123	906	886	1,47
8	Royalties and license fees from unaffiliated foreigners	1,700	422	428	43
9	Other private services from affiliated foreigners	2,526	621	599	69
10	Other private services from unaffiliated foreigners	7,235	1,804	1,795	1,84
11	U.S. government miscellaneous services	874	230	273	15
	Receipts of income on U.S. assets abroad:				
12	Direct investment	34,320	8,238	9,723	12,07
13	Other private receipts	50,180	12,700	12,256	12,21
14	U.S. government receipts	5,491	1,139	1,677	1,38
15	Transfers of goods and services under U.S. military grant programs, net	64	12	15	2
16	Imports of goods and services	−461,191	−117,971	−115,946	−119,38
17	Merchandise, adjusted, excluding military[c]	−338,863	−85,824	−83,830	−90,39
18	Direct defense expenditures	−11,918	−2,938	−2,814	−3,22
19	Travel	−16,502	−4,512	−5,536	−3,45
20	Passenger fares	−7,322	−2,440	−1,932	−1,45
21	Other transportation	−15,928	−3,994	−4,123	−4,24
22	Royalties and license fees to affiliated foreigners[d]	−467	−97	−119	−12
23	Royalties and license fees to unaffiliated foreigners	−380	−94	−95	−9
24	Other private services to affiliated foreigners	694	131	196	27
25	Other private services to unaffiliated foreigners	−3,965	−971	−984	−1,00
26	U.S. government miscellaneous services	−1,737	−429	−468	−40
	Payments of income on foreign assets in the United States:				
27	Direct investment	−8,068	−2,691	−2,144	−75
28	Other private payments	−35,429	−8,841	−8,727	−9,12
29	U.S. government payments	−21,306	−5,272	−5,369	−5,36
30	U.S. military grants of goods and services, net	−64	−12	−15	−2
31	Unilateral transfers (excluding military grants of goods and services), net	−14,983	−3,375	−3,891	−4,50
32	U.S. government grants (excluding military grants of goods and services), net	−11,196	−2,577	−3,087	−3,30
33	U.S. government pensions and other transfers	−2,171	−424	−466	−78
34	Private remittances and other transfers	−1,616	−374	−337	−41
35	U.S. assets abroad, net (increase/capital outflow (−))	−32,436	−3,022	−5,734	−21,68
36	U.S. official reserve assets, net[c]	−3,858	−356	−121	−3,14
37	Gold				
38	Special drawing rights	−897	−180	−264	−18
39	Reserve position in the International Monetary Fund	908	72	388	16
40	Foreign currencies	−3,869	−248	−245	−3,12
41	U.S. government assets, other than official reserve assets, net	−2,824	−1,003	−437	−45
42	U.S. credits and other long-term assets	−7,579	−2,495	−1,727	−1,56
43	Repayments on U.S. credits and other long-term assets[f]	4,644	1,230	1,270	1,21
44	U.S. foreign currency holdings and U.S. short-term assets, net	111	262	20	−10
45	U.S. private assets, net	−25,754	−1,664	−5,176	−18,07
46	Direct investment	−18,752	−4,495	−6,004	−8,59
47	Foreign securities	−7,977	−2,325	−1,664	−1,41
48	U.S. claims on unaffiliated foreigners reported by U.S. nonbanking concerns	1,665	1,706	−1,517	41
49	U.S. claims reported by U.S. banks, not included elsewhere	−691	3,450	4,009	−8,48
50	Foreign assets in the United States, net (increase/capital inflow (+))	127,106	25,358	35,665	51,83
51	Foreign official assets in the United States, net	−1,324	8,486	2,577	−1,32

| | Not seasonally adjusted | | | Seasonally adjusted | | | | | |
| | 1986 | | | 1985 | | | 1986 | | |
	I	II	III	II	III	IV	I	II	III
	90,891	93,861	89,821	89,350	90,234	90,873	91,593	92,060	92,531
	53,525	56,737	52,926	58,875	52,498	52,727	53,661	55,149	55,318
	2,022	2,342	2,346	2,209	2,195	1,898	2,022	2,342	2,346
	3,085	3,228	3,686	2,874	2,840	2,918	3,125	3,096	3,266
	712	918	1,002	758	694	772	836	831	843
	3,447	3,547	3,785	3,383	3,451	3,668	3,547	3,529	3,703
	894	1,191	1,244	932	953	1,298	969	1,210	1,320
	478	488	492	422	428	434	478	488	492
	619	775	702	627	630	627	645	783	738
	1,918	1,902	1,096	1,804	1,795	1,840	1,918	1,902	1,906
	165	107	134	213	248	182	176	94	117
	10,510	9,832	8,668	8,285	10,647	10,938	10,693	9,747	9,579
	11,934	11,501	10,914	12,700	12,256	12,214	11,934	11,501	10,914
	1,582	1,293	2,017	1,268	1,599	1,357	1,589	1,388	1,989
	22	12	15	12	15	28	22	12	15
	118,995	−125,251	−125,987	−115,309	−114,688	−120,324	−122,608	−122,394	−124,634
	−88,084	−92,671	−92,591	−84,242	−84,173	−90,079	−90,120	−90,818	−92,987
	−3,088	−3,037	−2,970	−2,938	−2,814	−3,220	−3,088	−3,037	−2,970
	−3,303	−4,755	−5,954	−4,136	−4,138	−4,194	−4,479	−4,361	−4,398
	−1,511	−1,997	−1,647	−1,860	−1,847	−1,882	−1,757	−1,515	−1,575
	−3,834	−4,091	−4,352	−3,883	−4,031	−4,313	−3,973	−3,975	−4,254
	−145	−149	−173	−97	−119	−124	−145	−149	−173
	−111	−110	−109	−94	−95	−97	−111	−110	−109
	290	326	275	131	196	279	290	326	275
	−1,064	−1,067	−1,058	−971	−984	−1,009	−1,064	−1,067	−1,058
	−446	−390	−436	−415	−443	−431	−462	−377	−412
	−2,391	−2,164	−1,847	−2,691	−2,144	−759	−2,391	−2,164	−1,847
	−9,600	−9,587	−9,429	−8,841	−8,727	−9,126	−9,600	−9,587	−9,429
	−5,708	−5,560	−5,697	−5,272	−5,369	−5,369	−5,708	−5,560	−5,697
	−22	−12	−15	−12	−15	−28	−22	−12	−15
	−2,916	−4,068	−4,040	−3,458	−4,001	−4,244	−3,023	−4,079	−4,177
	−2,069	−3,245	−3,388	−2,577	−3,087	−3,307	−2,069	−3,245	−3,388
	−464	−529	−432	−530	−538	−554	−559	−563	−530
	−384	−294	−220	−351	−376	−383	−395	−271	−259
	−14,700	−26,010	−29,149	−2,793	−5,867	−23,266	−12,898	−25,550	−29,082
	−115	16	280	−356	−121	−3,148	−115	16	280
	−274	−104	163	−180	−264	−189	−274	−104	163
	344	366	508	72	388	168	344	366	508
	−185	−246	−391	−248	−245	−3,126	−185	−246	−391
	−380	−146	−1,371	−1,055	−422	−540	−250	−209	−1,346
	−1,808	−1,636	−3,930	−2,495	−1,727	−1,564	−1,808	−1,636	−3,930
	1,411	1,446	1,682	1,178	1,285	1,126	1,542	1,383	1,708
	16	44	876	262	20	−102	16	44	876
	−14,204	−25,881	−28,058	−1,382	−5,324	−19,579	−12,533	−25,357	−28,016
	−11,562	−8,610	−7,714	−4,213	−6,152	−10,101	−9,891	−8,086	−7,672
	−6,133	−1,664	163	−2,325	−1,664	−1,411	−6,133	−1,664	163
	−2,842	−1,220	n.a.	1,706	−1,517	418	−2,842	−1,220	n.a.
	6,333	−14,387	−20,507	3,450	4,009	−8,485	6,333	−14,387	−20,507
	36,620	47,526	69,133	25,358	35,665	51,837	36,620	47,526	69,133
	2,469	14,704	15,839	8,486	2,577	−1,322	2,469	14,704	15,839

continued

Table 9-1. continued.

Line	(Credits +; debits -)[a]	1985	Not seasonally adjusted 1985		
			II	III	IV
52	U.S. government securities	-841	8,821	-35	-2,14
53	U.S. Treasury securities[g]	-546	8,685	-81	-1,97
54	Other[h]	-295	136	46	-17
55	Other U.S. government liabilities[i]	483	606	58	26
56	U.S. liabilities reported by U.S. banks, not included elsewhere	522	-107	2,932	72
57	Other foreign official assets[j]	-1,488	-834	-378	-16
58	Other foreign assets in the United States, net	128,430	16,872	33,088	53,15
59	Direct investment	17,856	5,757	6,111	2,38
60	U.S. Treasury securities	20,500	5,123	7,484	5,67
61	U.S. securities other than U.S. Treasury securities	50,859	7,223	11,628	22,44
62	U.S. liabilities to unaffiliated foreigners reported by U.S. nonbanking concerns	-1,172	-1,837	589	2,23
63	U.S. liabilities reported by U.S. banks, not included elsewhere	40,387	606	7,276	20,42
64	Allocations of special drawing rights				
65	Statistical discrepancy (sum of above items with sign reversed).	23,006	8,026	2,344	1,35
65a	Of which seasonal adjustment discrepancy				
	Memoranda:				
66	Balance on merchandise trade (lines 2 and 17)	-124,439	-30,352	-33,645	-36,97
67	Balance on goods and services (lines 1 and 16)[k]	-102,694	-26,988	-28,384	-27,00
68	Balance on goods, services, and remittances (lines 67, 33, and 34)	-106,481	-27,785	-29,188	-28,20
69	Balance on current account (lines 67 and 31)[k]	-117,677	-30,362	-32,275	-31,51
	Transactions in U.S. official reserve assets and in foreign official assets in the United States:				
70	Increase (-) in U.S. official reserve assets, net (line 36)	-3,858	-356	-121	-3,14
71	Increase (+) in foreign official assets in the United States (line 51 less line 55)	-1,807	7,880	2,519	-1,58

Source: U.S. Department of Commerce, Bureau of Economic Analysis, "U.S. International Transactions, Third Quarter 1986, *Survey of Current Business* December 1986.

Notes:
[a]Credits, +: exports of goods and services; unilateral transfers to United States; capital inflows (increase in foreign assets (U.S. liabilities) or decrease in U.S. assets); decrease in U.S. official reserve assets; increase in foreign official assets in the United States.
    Debits, -: imports of goods and services, unilateral transfers to foreigners; capital outflows (decrease in foreign assets (U.S. liabilities or increase in U.S. assets); increase in U.S. official reserve assets; decrease in foreign official assets in the United States.
[b]Excludes transfers of goods and services under U.S. military grant programs (see line 15).
[c]Excludes exports of goods under U.S. military agency sales contracts identified in Census export documents, excludes imports of goods under direct defense expenditures identified in Census import documents, and reflects various other adjustments (for valuation coverage and timing) of Census statistics to balance of payments basis.
[d]Beginning in 1982, line 7 and line 22 are redefined to include only net receipts and payments for the use or sale of intangible property rights, including patents, industrial processes, trademarks, copyrights, franchises, designs, know-how, formulas, technique and manufacturing and technical services, charges for use of tangible property, film and television tape rentals, and all other charge and fees are shown in line 9 and line 24. Data on the redefined basis are not separately available prior to 1982.
[e]For all areas, amounts outstanding December 31, 1986, were as follows in millions of dollars: line 36, 48,086; line 37, 11,08[...] line 38, 8,295; line 39, 11,922; line 40, 16,785.

1 *Merchandise trade*: This category records transactions between U.S. and foreign residents (including individuals, corporations, and the governments) involving shipments of goods that are sold, given away, or otherwise transferred to and from the United States.

2 *Services*: This category records the value of services provided by U.S. residents to foreigners and foreigners to U.S. residents. These include transportation services rendered by U.S.- and foreign-operated land, ocean, and air carriers, and services provided to foreigners traveling within the United States and to U.S. residents

| Not seasonally adjusted | | | Seasonally adjusted | | | | | |
| 1986 | | | 1985 | | | 1986 | | |
I	II	III	II	III	IV	I	II	III
3,079	13,894	11,986	8,821	−35	−2,147	3,079	13,894	11,986
3,256	14,538	12,262	8,685	−81	−1,976	3,256	14,538	12,262
−177	−644	−276	136	46	−171	−177	−644	−276
288	679	954	606	58	263	288	679	954
−1,261	662	3,201	−107	2,932	722	−1,261	662	3,201
363	−531	−302	−834	−378	−160	363	−531	−302
34,151	32,822	53,294	16,872	33,088	53,158	34,151	32,822	53,294
1,422	4,088	3,432	5,757	6,111	2,382	1,422	4,088	3,432
7,666	3,807	597	5,123	7,484	5,676	7,666	3,807	597
18,686	23,018	17,078	7,223	11,628	22,441	18,686	23,018	17,078
−2,057	−1,644	n.a.	−1,837	589	2,232	−2,057	−1,644	n.a.
8,434	3,553	32,187	606	7,276	20,427	8,434	3,553	32,187
9,100	13,942	222	6,852	−1,343	5,125	10,316	12,437	−3,771
		−1,174		−3,687	3,771	1,216	−1,505	−3,993
34,559	−35,934	−39,665	−30,367	−31,675	−37,352	−36,459	−35,669	−37,669
28,104	−31,390	−36,166	−25,959	−24,454	−29,451	−31,015	−30,334	−32,103
28,951	−32,213	−36,818	−26,840	−25,368	−30,388	−31,969	−31,168	−32,892
31,020	−35,458	−40,206	−29,417	−28,455	−33,695	−34,038	−34,413	−36,280
−115	16	280	−356	−121	−3,148	−115	16	280
2,181	14,025	14,885	7,880	2,519	−1,585	2,181	14,025	14,885

Includes sales of foreign obligations to foreigners.
Consists of bills, certificates, marketable bonds and notes, and nonmarketable convertible and nonconvertible bonds and notes.
Consists of U.S. Treasury and Export-Import Bank obligations, not included elsewhere, and of debt securities of U.S. government porations and agencies.
Includes, primarily, U.S. government liabilities associated with military agency sales contracts and other transactions arranged with through foreign official agencies.
Consists of investments in U.S. corporate stocks and in debt securities of private corporations and State and local governments.
Conceptually, the sum of lines 69 and 64 is equal to "net foreign investment" in the national income and product accounts (PA's). However, the foreign transactions account in the NIPA's (a) includes adjustments to the international transactions accounts the treatment of gold, (b) excludes capital gains and losses of foreign affiliates of U.S. parent companies from the NIPA measure income receipts from direct investment abroad, and from the corresponding income payments, (c) includes an adjustment for the erent geographical treatment of transactions with U.S. territories and Puerto Rico, and (d) includes an adjustment for services nished without payment by financial intermediaries, except life insurance carriers and private noninsured pension plans. In addition, NIPA purposes, U.S. government interest payments to foreigners are excluded from "net exports of goods and services" but luded with transfers in "net foreign investment." A reconciliation table of the international accounts and the NIPA foreign nsactions account appears in the "Reconciliation and other Special Tables" section in this issue of *the Survey of Current Business*.

traveling abroad. In addition, the account records the value of services derived from the use of intangible property such as trademarks, patents, and copyrights. Finally, and perhaps most important, the account records payments for services rendered by "capital"—that is, interest and dividends payments made and received by U.S. residents.

3 *Unilateral transfers*: This account records transactions where no *quid pro quo* has been rendered in the current period. This includes government grants, foreign aid, Social Security payments to

227

former U.S. residents who live abroad and to whom the government sends the checks, and private gifts or goods and services.

4 *Capital account*: This account records financial transactions between private U.S. and foreign residents. Some transactions differentiate between short-term and long-term. The short-term transactions are those where the maturity of the underlying instrument is less that one year; the long-term transactions are those where the maturity is more than one year. The long-term financial transactions are, in turn, divided into portfolio investments, and direct investments. Portfolio investments are those transactions where the acquisition of a financial claim does not convey control over the underlying asset—as, for example, a purchase of a bond. Direct investment transactions are those where the ownership title is conveyed. An example of such a transaction would be the acquisition of a factory abroad by a U.S. resident. The acquisition of common stock is treated either as a direct investment or as a portfolio investment, depending on the implied control over the underlying asset. If the acquisition of a share brings the holding to 10 percent of the total voting stock outstanding, such an acquisition is treated as a direct investment; otherwise, an acquisition of a share is treated as a portfolio investment.

In addition to private capital transactions, the capital account typically contains a separate category that records official government transactions. These include acquisition by foreigners of U.S. government securities, as well as changes in the U.S. government's holding of foreign currencies and other reserve assets.

THE ACCOUNTING FRAMEWORK OF THE U.S. BALANCE-OF-PAYMENTS STATISTICS

The basic accounting framework used for recording of the country's international transactions is the same as is commonly used for the recording of business transactions in general: So-called double-entry bookkeeping. In that system, the dollar amount of each transaction is entered twice in the record-keeping books. The logic of this procedure is not as farfetched as it may seem initially. Even though we may think of a purchase of an item such as a computer as a single act, there are actually two distinct steps involved in the transaction: One is the acquisition of the computer that occurs when the seller delivers to us the package containing the product. The other occurs when we surrender to the seller a payment in currency, check, some form of IOU (such as credit card), or some form of payment in kind (as, for example, a trade-in). The double-entry bookkeeping captures these two counterpart transactions and records them in separate categories called debits and credits.

Which part of the transaction is debit and which is credit has been a source for much confusion in balance-of-payments accounting. The roots of that confusion probably lie in the popular notion that credits are good or favorable developments, while debits are bad or unfavorable developments.

To avoid this popular confusion, it is useful to think of the recording process in the following way: In the double-entry bookkeeping each transaction appears *twice*, both as a credit and as a debit. Obviously, there is both a "good" part to a transaction and a "bad" part. The good part is when we are handed the package containing the computer; the bad part is when we hand over the payment. Conceptually, therefore, the two sides cancel each other, and we are left with a transaction that is, in accounting sense, devoid of any ethical connotation, either good or bad. How do we determine which part of the transaction is entered as a debit and which as a credit? The following rule might help:

Debit is the part of a transaction that results in a U.S. resident making a payment to or incurring a debt with a foreigner, but that *in itself* increases our "wealth" or "well-being" or *in itself* reduces our liabilities to foreigners.

Credit is the part of a transaction that results in a foreigner's making a payment to or incurring a debt with a U.S. resident, but that *in itself* reduces our "wealth" or "well-being" or *in itself* increases our liabilities.

These guidelines will, hopefully, become clear from the specific examples that follow.

RECORDING U.S. INTERNATIONAL TRANSACTIONS

This section discusses how typical international transactions fit into the framework of the balance-of-payments accounts. The following examples of various balance-of-payments transactions use the so-called T-accounts where, by convention, the left side is reserved for debit transactions and the right side for credit transactions.

Imports

A U.S. importer receives a shipment of French wine worth $1,000 that he purchased from a French exporter on credit, with payment due in ninety days.

Merchandise Trade		Short-Term Capital	
Debit	Credit	Debit	Credit
(1a)			(1b)
$1,000			$1,000

229

EXPLANATION

The landing of the shipment constitutes a commercial interaction by one of the U.S. residents with residents of a foreign country, and as such, it must be entered into the country's balance-of-payments accounts. The first question we must ask in determining whether the transaction is a debit or a credit is, what did the transaction do to our collective wealth? Because that shipment of wine landed at the port side, our collective well-being and wealth was increased: We now have a shipment of wine that we did not have before. The first part of the Transaction is therefore entered as a debit in the Merchandise Trade account on the left side of the T-account, as transaction (1a).

There is another part to the transaction—namely the issuance of an IOU that the importer gave to the exporter before he could claim the shipment. The importer, a U.S. resident, now owes $1,000 to a foreigner. The act of contracting that debt in effect increased our collective liabilities to foreigners, and as such it must be recorded as a credit in the country's capital accounts. Given its maturity, the transaction would be recorded in the Short-Term Capital account as transaction (1b).

TECHNICAL NOTE NO. 1.

Transaction (1a) is an example of transactions entered in the official U.S. balance-of-payments statistical presentation published in March, June, September, and December issues of the *Survey of Current Business* (Table 9-1, Line 17, Merchandise Imports, Adjusted, Excluding Military). This account measures all movable goods that are sold, given away, or otherwise transferred from foreign to U.S. ownership. Excluded are (1) goods purchased abroad by U.S. military agencies, whether used abroad or physically imported into the United States directly by such agencies, and (2) goods purchased and used abroad by U.S. nonmilitary agencies.

The basic data are Census Bureau trade statistics. Since 1974 imports in the Census Bureau statistics are, in general, valued f.a.s. (free alongside ship) foreign port of export and reflect selling price, f.o.b. (free on board) interior point of shipment (or cost if not sold), plus packaging costs, inland freight, and insurance to foreign port of export. Adjustments to the Census Bureau statistics are made for timing, coverage, and valuation in order to bring them more into conformity with concepts used in the international accounts. Timing adjustments are made to correct Census Bureau statistics for transactions that occur in periods other than the periods in which they are reported. Covered adjustments are made for Virgin Islands imports from foreign countries, electrical energy imports from Canada, purchases of foreign vessels, U.S. imports from the Panama Canal Zone, and repairs in foreign ports to U.S. vessels. Valuation adjustments are made for reconciliations of U.S.-Canadian trade statistics.

Transaction (1b) is an example of transactions entered in Table 9-1, Line 62, U.S. Liabilities to Unaffiliated Foreigners Reported by Non-banking Concerns. This account measures changes in liabilities to unaffiliated foreigners. Included are direct borrowings from foreign banks by U.S. companies; accounts, notes, bills, and drafts payable to foreigners; and advance payments by foreigners for future delivery of U.S. goods and services. Estimates are based on reports collected by the Federal Reserve System for the Treasury Department. Adjustments to the Treasury Department data are made to account for proceeds of foreign short-term loans obtained by U.S. parent companies through their Netherlands Antilles finance subsidiaries. These adjustments are based on reports to the Bureau of Economic Analysis (BEA).

Export

A U.S. exporter sells a machine worth $2,000 to a French importer. The machine is shipped on a U.S. ship, and the importer agrees to pay for the transportation, which costs $20. The French importer pays for the machine and the transportation costs in cash by drawing on a checking account he maintains with a U.S. bank.

Merchandise Trade		Services		Short-Term Capital	
Debit	Credit	Debit	Credit	Debit	Credit
	(2a) $2,000		(2b) $20	(2c) $2,020	

EXPLANATION

In the first part of the transaction, the U.S. residents are actually parting with two things of value: The machine worth $2,000 and the services of the U.S. shipping line worth $20. The former will be recorded as a credit in the Merchandise Trade account (transaction 2a); the latter will be recorded as a credit in the Services account (as transaction 2b).

The financial part of the transaction needs a somewhat more detailed explanation. The U.S. dollar has been an important world currency used for settlement of transactions around the world. The holding of dollar deposits on which the holders can write checks, or use them to make electronic transfers of funds, has been widespread. The holding of such deposits is not recorded in the balance-of-payments accounts because the balance-of-payments statement captures only flow transactions. What is recorded, however, are changes in these accounts, as these accounts are used to make payments to U.S. residents. That has been the case in the above transaction: A foreign resident has used his U.S. account to make a payment to two U.S. entities—the exporter and the shipper. Drawing on that account transfers the ownership of the balances to U.S. residents and in effect reduces our collective liabilities to foreigners. A transaction that reduces our liabilities to foreigners is treated as a debit transaction. Thus, the payments by the French importer to U.S. residents will be recorded as a debit entry (2c) in the Short-Term Capital account.

TECHNICAL NOTE NO.2.

Transaction (2a) is an example of transactions typically entered in the official U.S. balance-of-payments Table 9–1, Line 2, Merchandise Exports, Adjusted,

231

Excluding Military. This account measures all movable goods that are sold, given away, or otherwise transferred from U.S. to foreign ownership. Excluded are (1) transfers of goods under U.S. military agency sales contracts, whether physically exported from the United States or sold from U.S. installations abroad; (2) transfers of goods by U.S. nonmilitary agencies from U.S. installations abroad; and (3) transfers of goods under U.S. military grant programs.

The basic data are Census Bureau trade statistics. Exports in the Census Bureau statistics are, in general, valued f.a.s. (free alongside ship) U.S. port of export and reflect selling price, f.o.b. (free on board) interior point of shipment (or cost if not sold), plus packaging costs, inland freight, and insurance to place of export. These statistics record the physical movement of goods out of the United States, rather than change of ownership, and differ in other aspects from the definition of merchandise exports stated above. Adjustments to the Census Bureau statistics are also made for timing, coverage, and valuation in order to bring them more into conformity with concepts used in the international accounts. Timing adjustments are made to Census Bureau statistics for transfers that occur in periods other than the periods in which they are reported. Coverage adjustments are made for Virgin Islands exports to foreign countries, gift parcel post exports, electrical energy exports to Canada and Mexico, sales of vessels, U.S. exports to the Panama Canal Zone, and exports of exposed motion picture film for rental rather than sale. Valuation adjustments are made for U.S. inland freight to the Canadian border and for reconciliations of U.S.-Canadian trade statistics.

Transaction (2b) is an example of transactions typically entered in Table 9–1, Line 6, Other Transportation. This account measures (1) freight revenues of U.S.-operated ocean, air, and other carriers (including rail, pipeline, and Great Lakes shipping) for the international transportation of U.S. exports; (2) freight revenues of U.S.-operated carriers for the transportation of foreign freight between foreign points; (3) port expenditure receipts, representing payments for goods and services purchased in the United States by foreign-operated carriers; and (4) receipts of U.S. owners from foreign operators for the charter of vessels and rental of freight cars and containers.

Ocean freight revenues are estimated by multiplying average freight rates by the corresponding data on tonnage shipped by U.S.-operated carriers. Ocean port expenditure receipts are estimated by multiplying average port expenditures per ton by the corresponding data on tonnage shipped by foreign-operated carriers. Average freight rates and port expenditures are derived from information reported to BEA by shipping companies. Tonnage data are derived from Census Bureau trade statistics. For the other components of this account, estimates are based on reports to BEA by transportation companies and information provided by U.S. government agencies and foreign governments.

Transaction (2c) is an example of transactions entered in Table 9–1, Line 63, U.S. Liabilities Reported by U.S. Banks Not Reported Elsewhere. This account measures changes in liabilities to private foreigners and international financial institutions reported by U.S. banks for their own accounts and for the custody accounts of their customers. Included are demand, time, and savings deposits; time certificates of deposit; liabilities to affiliated foreign banks; and other liabilities. Estimates are based on reports collected by the Federal Reserve System for the Treasury Department.

Services

A U.S. resident flies to Jamaica on Air Jamaica for a week's vacation. She prepays for her transportation and hotel by charging the $800 cost on her Visa account and pays for food and other miscellaneous expenses of $200 in cash by converting U.S. dollars into Jamaican dollars at a bank in Jamaica after her arrival there.

Services		Short-Term Capital	
Debit	Credit	Debit	Credit
(3a) $1,000		(3b) $800	
		(3c) $200	

EXPLANATION

The traveler's total expenditures of $1,000 will be treated as payments for services. The actual balance-of-payments statement would differentiate between transportation services of $800, and tourist expenditures of $200 within the Services subcategories accounts. In our simplified framework, we shall simply lump both transactions in the Services account. Because the transaction "enriches" us collectively as a nation by making it possible for the traveler to absorb some sun on behalf of all of us, it must be treated as a debit transaction.

The financial side of the transaction again needs some more detailed explanation. When the transportation and hotel expenses are charged on the Visa account, the bank will credit the checking account that Air Jamaica maintains with it. This will result in an increase in that bank's liabilities to foreigners, and as such the transaction will be entered as a credit in the Short-Term Capital account. The other $200 that the traveler spent in Jamaica could be treated conceptually as an increase of claims of foreigners in the United States; the Jamaican bank now holds $200 in U.S. currency, and that currency represents a claim on U.S. resources. More realistically, what would happen is most like this: The Jamaican bank would not want to hold U.S. currency in idle balances in its vaults because such holdings are costly in terms of forgone interest that could be earned if they were invested in some interest-bearing assets. The bank would therefore ship the currency to a bank in the United States with which it maintains a correspondent relationship and an account. Once the currency is received by the bank in the United States, the bank will credit the account of the Jamaican bank—that is, it will increase the amount of liabilities that the bank has toward the Jamaican bank. Such an increase in liabilities will of course be then recorded as a credit entry in the Short-Term Capital account.

TECHNICAL NOTE NO. 3.

Transaction (3a) is an example of a transaction typically entered in the official U.S. balance-of-payments statistics, Table 9–1, Line 20, Passenger Fares, and

Line 4, Travel. The Travel account measures expenditures in the United States by foreign travelers (excluding foreign government personnel and their dependents and other foreign citizens residing in the United States) for lodging, food, transportation within the United States, entertainment, personal purchases, gifts, and other outlays associated with travel in the United States. Transocean passenger fares are excluded; however, fares received by U.S. carriers from Canadian and Mexican travelers visiting the United States are included.

Travel receipts from each major world area are estimated by multiplying average expenditures per traveler for a particular area by the corresponding number of travelers from that area; area totals are then summed to arrive at total travel receipts. Average expenditures per traveler by area are derived from BEA surveys of foreign travelers. Numbers of foreign travelers by area are derived from data provided by the Immigration and Naturalization Service.

The Passenger Fares account measures passenger fares paid to foreign ocean and air carriers by U.S. residents traveling between the United States and foreign countries. Excluded are passenger fares paid to Canadian and Mexican carriers by U.S. travelers visiting Canada and Mexico.

Passenger fare payments to each major world area are estimated by multiplying average round-trip fare per traveler for a particular area by the corresponding number of U.S. travelers to that area; area totals are then summed to arrive at total travel payments. Average round-trip fares per passenger by area are derived from BEA surveys of U.S. travelers. Numbers of U.S. travelers by area are derived from data provided by the Immigration and Naturalization Service. Adjustments for interairline transfers are made on the basis of official reports of U.S. international air carriers.

Transactions (3b) and (3c) are typical of transactions entered in Table 9–1, Line 63, Other Transportation, as discussed in Technical Note No. 2.

Investment Transaction

A U.S. corporation decides to build a plant in Spain at a cost of $10,000. The construction is to be financed by issuance of thirty-year bonds to investors in Spain. The plant is equipped with $2,000 worth of machinery shipped from the company's home plant in Chicago.

Merchandise Trade		Direct Investment		Portfolio Investment	
Debit	Credit	Debit	Credit	Debit	Credit
	(4c) $2,000	(4a) $12,000			(4b) $10,000

EXPLANATION

The total value of the plant once completed is $12,000. The plant is fully owned by the U.S. corporation and is thus under full control of a U.S. resident. Its "maturity" is clearly more than one year. As such, the first part of the transaction has all the characteristics of Direct Investment. It is therefore entered as a debit in the Direct Investment account as transaction (4a).

There are several parts to the second part of the transaction. First, by issuing bonds in its name in Spain, the U.S. company contracts a long-term liability. Because the liability does not convey ownership title to either its home plant or to its subsidiary to the holders of the bond, the transaction must be treated as portfolio investment by foreigners; and because it represents an increase in long-term liabilities to foreigners by a U.S. resident, it must be entered as a credit in the Portfolio Investment account of $10,000 as transaction (4b). The shipment of machines to equip the plant reduces the collective wealth because the machinery is no longer a part of the domestic plant. As such it is a credit entry in the Merchandise Trade account as transaction (4c).

TECHNICAL NOTES NO. 4.

Transaction (4a) is an example of transactions typically entered in Table 9–1, Line 46, Direct Investment. This account measures equity and intercompany account transactions between U.S. direct investors and their foreign affiliates. U.S. direct investors are U.S. residents who own or control 10 percent or more of the voting securities of an incorporated foreign business enterprise or an equivalent interest in an unincorporated foreign business enterprise. Also included are transactions of U.S. residents with unaffiliated foreign residents that result in the acquisition of at least a 10 percent ownership interest in previously unaffiliated foreign business enterprises, in the acquisition of additional ownership interests in existing foreign affiliates or in total or partial sales of ownership interests. Equity and intercompany account transactions include net changes in capital stock (voting and nonvoting) and capital contributions, in intercompany accounts with incorporated foreign affiliates and in U.S. direct investors' net equity in unincorporated foreign affiliates. Estimates are based on reports to BEA by major U.S. direct investors. To these data are added verified transactions of nonreporters.

Transaction (4b) is an example of transactions typically entered in Table 9–1, Line 61, U.S. Securities Other Than U.S. Treasury Securities. This account measures net purchases of U.S. equity and debt securities by private foreigners and international financial institutions. These securities have no contractual maturities or maturities of more than one year. Included are U.S. corporate new issues of debt securities in foreign markets trading in outstanding stocks and bonds issued by U.S. corporations and state and local governments, and trading in nonguaranteed U.S. government agency securities.

Estimates are based on data collected by the Federal Reserve System for the Treasury Department. Adjustments to the Treasury Department data are made for securities newly issued by Netherlands Antilles finance subsidiaries to the extent that proceeds are transferred to U.S. parent companies; these adjustments are based on reports to BEA. Estimates of major types of transactions are made by BEA based on market information.

Transaction (4c) is an example of transactions typically entered in Table 9–1, Line 2, as discussed in Technical Note No. 2 above.

Reinvestment and Repatriation of Foreign Earnings

The subsidiary of the U.S. company operating in Spain earns $1,000 in profits; $500 is reinvested in expanding the facility in Spain, and $500 is repatriated to the parent company. The transfer is effected by a transfer of funds to the parent's account at a Spanish bank.

Services		Direct Investment		Short-Term Capital	
Debit	Credit	Debit	Credit	Debit	Credit
	(5a) $1,000	(5b) $500		(5c) $500	

EXPLANATION

The earnings abroad represent, conceptually, the payments by foreigners for services rendered by the U.S. capital; it was the U.S. investment in the factory that produced the goods that were sold to realize profits. The first part of the transaction will therefore be entered as a credit in the Services account (5a). The reinvestment of profits increases the value of the direct investment that the U.S. company holds abroad; it is therefore entered as a debit entry in the Direct Investment account (5b). The deposit of the $500 in the accounts of the parent maintained at a Spanish bank leads to an increase in the claims held by U.S. residents on foreigners; the transaction is therefore treated as a debit entry in Short-Term Capital account (5c).

TECHNICAL NOTE NO. 5.

Transaction (5a) is an example of transactions typically entered in Table 9–1, Line 12, Receipts of Income on U.S. Assets Abroad: Direct Investment. This account measures receipts of U.S. direct investors from their foreign affiliates of (1) interest (net of interest payments by U.S. direct investors to their foreign affiliates and net of withholding taxes); (2) dividends (net of withholding taxes); and (3) earnings of unincorporated foreign affiliates (net of foreign income taxes). Receipts are reported as accrued. When funds are not actually transferred in the reporting period; offsetting entries are made in line 49. Estimates are based on reports to BEA by major U.S. direct investors.

Transaction (5b) is an example of transactions typically entered in Table 9–1, Line 46, as discussed in Technical Note No. 4 above.

Transaction (5c) is an example of transactions typically entered in Table 9–1, Line 48, as discussed in Technical Note No. 3.

Gifts

A recent immigrant to the United States decides to send a gift to his parents in the United Kingdom. For $50 he purchases from a U.S. bank a bank draft denominated in pounds sterling and mails it to his parents in London.

Unilateral Transfers		Short-Term Capital	
Debit	Credit	Debit	Credit
(6a) $50			(6b) $50

The sending of a gift is an example of a unilateral transaction where U.S. residents receive nothing of material value in return for an asset they have given up. The well-being of one of the members of society is increased by the good feeling derived from knowing that he has made his parents happy, however, and we know that an increase in the well-being of one of the members of the society adds to the well-being of the whole country. It is this reasoning that provides a rationale for entering the first part of the transaction on the debit side of the Unilateral Transfers account (6a).

To understand the rationale for the entries of the second part of the transaction, we must again recall how international banking transactions are settled. The U.S. bank where the immigrant purchased the draft maintains correspondent balances with a U.K. bank. The draft that the bank sold to the immigrant is actually a form of a check drawn on those balances. As the recipient of the draft cashes the draft at the bank on which it has been drawn, the British bank reduces the amount of balances that the U.S. bank has available in that account. From the viewpoint of the U.S. bank, its claims on foreigners—its foreign assets—have been reduced. As such, therefore, the transaction is entered as a credit in the Short-Term Capital account (6b).

TECHNICAL NOTE NO. 6.

Transaction (6a) is an example of transactions typically entered in Table 9–1, Line 34, Unilateral Transfers, Private Remittances and Other Transfers. This account measures net private unilateral transfers of goods, services, cash, and other financial claims between U.S. private residents and foreign residents. Receipts include postal money orders received by U.S. private residents, German government pension and indemnification payments, Canadian government pension payments to eligible persons residing in the United States, and immigrants' transfers. Payments include cash and goods distributed abroad by U.S. religious, charitable, educational, scientific, and other nonprofit organizations; personal remittances by U.S. private residents through banks, communications companies, and the U.S. Postal Service; parcel post shipments; and emigrants' transfers. Estimates are based on reports to BEA by U.S. banks, nonprofit organizations, U.S. and foreign government agencies, and publications of foreign governments.

Transaction (6b) is an example of transactions typically entered in Table 9–1, Line 49, U.S. Private Assets, Net, U.S. Claims Reported by U.S. Banks Not Included Elsewhere. This account-measures changes in claims on foreigners reported by U.S. banks for their own accounts and for the custody accounts of their customers. Included are loans, collections outstanding, acceptances, deposits abroad, claims on affiliated foreign banks, foreign government obligations, and foreign commercial and finance paper. Estimates are based on reports collected by the Federal Reserve System for the Treasury Department.

Government Transactions I

Germany's central bank intervenes in the foreign-exchange markets to prevent a decline in the value of the dollar relative to the deutsche mark (or, to look at it from Germany's side, a rise in the value of the deutsche mark relative to the dollar) by purchasing the excess supply of dollars in the foreign exchange markets that is causing the weakness of the dollar. The amount purchased is $1,000.

Official Transactions		Short-Term Capital	
Debit	Credit	Debit	Credit
	(6b) $1,000	(6a) $1,000	

EXPLANATION

Assume that the dollars are purchased from a commercial holder who typically maintains them on deposit with a commercial bank in the United States. If the seller is a foreign entity—for example, a German exporter who just sold some goods to a U.S. importer and has been paid in dollars that were deposited in his account at a U.S. bank—the first part of the transaction would involve a reduction in short-term liabilities to private foreigners—that is, a debit entry in the Short-Term Capital account (6a). The other part—namely, the acquisition of dollar balances by the German central bank—represents an increase in our liabilities to foreign official institutions, and as such the transaction would be recorded as a credit in the Official Transactions account as transaction (6b).

TECHNICAL NOTE NO. 7.

Transaction (7a) is an example of transaction typically entered in Table 9–1, Line 63, Other Foreign Assets in the United States, U.S. Liabilities Reported by U.S. Banks, Not Included Elsewhere. This category has been discussed in Technical Note No. 2.

Transaction (7b) is an example of transactions typically entered in Table 9–1, Line 56, Foreign Official Assets in the United States, Net, U.S. Liabilities Reported by Banks, Not Included Elsewhere. This account measures changes in liabilities to foreign official agencies reported by U.S. banks for their own accounts and for the custody accounts of their customers. Included in these liabilities are demand and time deposits, time certificates of deposit, and other short- and long-term liabilities. Estimates are based on reports collected by the Federal Reserve System for the Treasury Department.

Official Transaction II

The value of the U.S. dollar continues to drop, and the U.S. Treasury decides to moderate the decline by intervention in the foreign-exchange markets by selling of foreign currencies against the dollar. To obtain the currencies needed for the intervention, the Treasury sells $100 worth of gold in the London gold market to obtain pounds sterling, uses its holding of special drawing rights (SDRs) to obtain $200 worth of deutsche marks, and uses its IMF reserve position to obtain $300 worth of Japanese yen. These currencies are then sold in the market for dollars, and the dollars so obtained are added to the balances held in the Treasury's Exchange Stabilization Fund.

Official Transactions		Short-Term Capital	
Debit	Credit	Debit	Credit
(8d) $600	(8a) $100	(8f) $600	
	(8b) $200		
	(8c) $300		
	(8e) $600		

EXPLANATION

In our simplified framework, all transactions would be entered in the aggregate Official Transactions account. (For details of actual entries see Technical Note No. 8, below.) The reduction in the country's official reserve assets is recorded as credit entries (8a, 8b, and 8c); this is offset by a debit entry of $600, indicating the acquisition of foreign currencies to be used in the intervention (8d). The second set of entries (8e and 8f) indicate the actual intervention. As for foreign currencies are sold for dollars held by foreign residents as deposits in U.S. banks, credit entry (8e) is made, indicating a reduction in U.S. official assets. This is offset by a debit entry in the Short-Term Capital account, indicating a reduction in liabilities to private foreigners who sold their dollars to the U.S. Treasury for the foreign currencies (8f).

TECHNICAL NOTE NO. 8.

Transaction (8a) is an example of transactions typically entered in Table 9–1, Line 37, U.S. Official Reserve Assets; Gold. This account measures transfers of monetary gold between U.S. government agencies (including the Exchange Stabilization Fund) and foreign governments or international monetary institutions. Transactions with foreign governments are generally valued at the official par value of the U.S. dollar. Transactions with the International Monetary Fund are valued at the U.S. dollar equivalent of the established price of gold in terms of special drawing rights. Estimates are based on reports to BEA from the Treasury Department.

Transaction (8b) is an example of transactions entered in Table 9–1, Line 38, Special Drawing Rights. This account measures changes in U.S. holdings of special drawing rights (SDRs) in the special drawing account at the International Monetary Fund. It reflects allocations to the United States, other U.S. acquisitions, and U.S. uses of SDRs. Excluded are changes in the value of U.S. SDR holdings resulting from changes in the U.S. dollar value of the SDR. Beginning in July 1974, the value of the SDR is based on a weighted average of exchange rates for the currencies of selected member countries; before that date, it was linked to the U.S. official price of gold. Estimates are based on reports to BEA from the Treasury Department.

Transaction (8c) is an example of transactions typically entered in Table 9–1, Line 39, Reserve Position in the International Monetary Fund. This account measures changes in the U.S. reserve position in the International Monetary Fund (IMF). The reserve position is equal to the sum of the U.S. quota in the IMF and net U.S. lending to the IMF, minus the IMF holdings of U.S. dollars. The reserve position represents the amount of foreign exchange the United States can automatically draw from the IMF. Excluded are changes in the value of the U.S. reserve position resulting from changes in the U.S. dollar value of special drawing rights. Estimates are based on reports to BEA from the Treasury Department.

Transaction (8e) is an example of transactions typically entered in Table 9–1, Line 40, Foreign Currencies. This account measures net changes in the Treasury Department and Federal Reserve System holdings of foreign currencies identified as international reserves. These holdings include currencies acquired under reciprocal currency (swap) arrangements with foreign monetary authorities. Estimates are based on reports to BEA from the Treasury Department.

Transaction (8f) is an example of transactions typically entered in Table 9–1, Line 63, discussed in Technical Note No. 2.

MEASURING THE BALANCE

By convention, each debit entry is viewed as having a negative sign (−) attached; each credit entry is treated as having a positive sign (+). Using this convention, we can now calculate whether the country in our hypothetical example has been running a deficit or a surplus in its balance of payments. Or can we?

Superficial reasoning would suggest that when debits exceed credits—that is, when the sum total of the entries with negative and positive signs has a negative sign—the balance-of-payments statement would show that a country is running a deficit; a positive sign would indicate a surplus. However, a somewhat more thoughtful look at the statistical statement as we have developed it so far immediately reveals the basic accounting truth: In a double-entry bookkeeping system, the debits must always equal credits, by definition. If they do not, you had better fire the accountant!

TECHNICAL NOTE NO. 9.

Ideally, the balance-of-payments statement should be a complete record of international transactions in goods, services, and capital and of the payments and transfers related to them. Actually, however, data on the two sides of a single transaction usually come from different sources and may be inaccurate or incomplete. The fact that the source data covering the international transactions of the United States are incomplete reflects in part the freedom that U.S. residents have in undertaking international transactions.

If a transaction is omitted entirely from the balance of payments, so that there is no entry on either side, the two sides will still balance. If, on the other hand, a sale of goods or services is recorded but the related payment is not, or if the payment is recorded but the underlying sale of goods or services is not, the two sides of the balance of payments will not be equal. Similarly, if the goods, services, or capital transfers are entered at a value different from that of the corresponding payment, the two sides will not balance.

The item Net Errors and Omissions is the statistical discrepancy between total recorded entries under receipts and total recorded entries under payments (including official settlements). It is entered as either net receipts or net payments on errors and omissions to fulfill the accounting principle that the sum of receipts and payments must balance. In Table 9–1, this correction is entered on Line 65, as Statistical Discrepancy.

This points to a very important principle in balance of payments accounting: The balance-of-payments deficit or surplus is not an accounting concept. It is an analytical concept. In order to arrive at a deficit or surplus, an analyst must determine which particular accounts will give the analytical information being sought. The selection of these accounts, and their segregation from the rest of the statistical material, provides the basis for the calculation of a "balance."

The decision as to which categories of the balance-of-payments statement shall be segregated for purposes of calculating the deficit depends on the purposes to which the calculation is to be put. The four most commonly used balances, and the analytical reasoning behind them, are discussed below.

HISTORICAL NOTE.

From World War II until 1976 the U.S. government used two concepts as the measures of the country's balance-of-payments deficit or surplus: The liquidity balance, and the official reserve transaction balance. Both measures were developed to gage the country's capacity to fulfill its commitment to maintain the convertibility of the U.S. dollar into gold at a fixed price, an arrangement that was the linchpin of the postwar international monetary system. The official reserve transactions balance measured, essentially, the changes in the country's gold supply and the changes in foreign claims on that gold held in the hands of the foreign official institutions to whom the privilege of converting dollars into gold on demand was officially extended.

The liquidity balance was a sort of an early-warning measure that measured the accumulation of liquid dollars in the hands of all foreigners (including private holders) plus changes in the U.S. government's holding of gold and of other reserve assets. The theory behind this measure was that although private foreigners could not convert dollars held by them at the U.S. treasury, they could quickly sell these liquid dollars in the foreign-exchange markets for foreign currencies. Such sales would necessitate foreign central bank intervention to maintain the value of their currencies fixed as per the international agreement that marked the functioning of the system and would directly lead to increases in the holding of dollars by the official institutions—holdings that were directly convertible into gold.

Trade Balance

The trade balance is the most commonly used measure of the country's balance-of-payments performance. Its analytical purpose is to measure the flows of physical goods to and from the United States. It is derived by segregating from the overall balance of payments the trade account entries. In our example, the trade balance is calculated by adding the debits and credits in the Merchandise Trade account.

Merchandise Trade

Debit	Credit
(1a) $1,000	(2a) $2,000
	(4c) $2,000

Trade Surplus: $3,000

TECHNICAL NOTE NO. 10.

In the official U.S. balance-of-payments statistical presentation, the trade balance is shown in Table 9–1, Line 66, as Balance on Merchandise Trade. Further considerable details on U.S. imports and exports by area and by commodities involved are regularly provided in Table 3, U.S. Merchandise Trade, published as part of the U.S. official statistical presentation.

The Merchandise Trade balance as reported in the official U.S. balance of payments statistics *differs* from data reported by the U.S. government as the monthly trade balance typically released a few weeks after the end of the month for which the data is reported. These early released figures are the U.S. Customs data, with imports reported on the c.i.f. basis—that is, cost of goods, insurance, freight, and other charges incurred in bringing the merchandise from the country of exportation to the first port of arrival in the United States. These data are then reported to the U.S. Census Bureau and subsequently released as the Census Trade data. These data are adjusted to exclude merchandise exported and imports under U.S. military agencies sales and other minor adjustments. So adjusted, the figures then become the U.S. merchandise trade, balance-of-payments basis, as reported in Table 9–1 of the official U.S. statistics.

Balance on Goods and Services

This balance is calculated by entering all debits (with negative sign) and credits (with positive sign) from the Merchandise Trade account and the Services account.

Analytical Interpretation

The balance on goods and services is analytically the most important balance in the country's balance-of-payments accounting. Its importance derives from the fact that the balance-of-payments transactions used to calculate this balance are the same as those that are included in the all-important measure of the country's overall economic perfor-

Balance on Goods and Services

Debit	Credit
(1a) – 1,000	(2a) + 2,000
(3a) – 1,000	(4c) + 2,000
	(2b) + 20
	(5a) + 1,000
– $2,000	+ $5,020

Goods and services surplus: $3,020

mance, the country's gross national product (GNP), which measures the value of all goods and services produced in a country over a given period.

In a closed economy (that is, one that is closed to all interaction with foreign countries) the goods and services produced are either accumulated as additional inventories, added to the capital stock, or consumed by the residents. In an open economy some of the goods and services that are produced are not consumed by the residents and are exported. At the same time, some of the consumption and additions to the capital stock are not produced in the country but are imported from abroad. The balance on goods and services thus dovetails conceptually with the National Income accounts. It is entered in these accounts (after some minor adjustments) as the Net Exports. We shall return to this important consideration in the final section of this article where the interaction between the country's balance of payments and the national economy will be discussed in much greater detail.

Balance on Current Account

This balance is computed by segregating from the overall balance of payments the debits and credits entered in the Merchandise Trade, Services, and Unilateral Transfers accounts.

Balance on current account

Debit	Credit
(1a) – 1,000	(2a) + 2,000
(3a) – 1,000	(4c) + 2,000
(6a) – 50	(2b) + 20
	(5a) + 1,000
– $2,050	+ $5,020

Current account surplus: $2,970

243

Analytical Interpretation

The current account balance is the most widely used measure of the balance-of-payments performance internationally. Its usefulness lies in the fact that it separates the overall balance of payments into two broad categories: Current transactions and capital transactions. We already know that an overall balance of statement that records *all* international transactions undertaken by the residents of a country is always in balance because debits must equal credits by definition of the accounting procedures used for the compilation of this statistical statement. Once certain debit and credit entries are segregated from the overall statement to calculate a balance, it must be necessarily true that the sum total of the remaining debit and credit entries must exactly equal to the sum total of the debits and credits segregated for purposes of calculating the balance with the sign reversed. When we segregated the debits and credits of all the current transactions in the balance-of-payments statement in our simplified example, we calculated the current account surplus to be $2970. When we add up all the remaining debit and credit entries (with appropriate signs attached) in all the remaining accounts, we get a total equal to − $2970. This residual is the net sum total of all capital transactions undertaken by U.S. residents, including individuals, corporations, and government, with the rest of the world. The negative sign indicates that there was a net *outflow* of capital from the United States over that period in the amount equal to the current account surplus.

In general, therefore, a surplus in any country's current account indicates that that country has been a capital exporter. Conversely, a deficit in the current account balance indicates that the country has been importing capital—that is, it has been a net international borrower.

For these reasons, the current account balance derived in the official U.S. balance-of-payments statistics is used in the National Income and Product accounts (the GNP accounts) as the net foreign investment account. This, too, will be discussed in more detail in the final section of this chapter.

Basic Balance

This balance measures the country's current transactions, plus its transactions in long-term capital, both private and official. (Transactions recorded in our Official Transactions examples are excluded because they are basically of short-term nature; however, government grants and long-term loans would be included in this balance.)

Basic Balance

Debit	Credit
(1a) – 1,000	(2a) + 2,000
(3a) – 1,000	(4c) + 2,000
(6a) – 50	(2b) + 20
(4a) – 12,000	(5a) + 1,000
(5b) – 500	(4b) + 10,000
	(6b) + 50
– $14,550	+ $15,070

Basic balance surplus: $520

Analytical Interpretation

The analytical advantage of the basic balance is that it separates autonomous international transactions from those transactions that are essentially designed to finance these transactions—that is, transfers of short-term capital. The autonomous transactions take place in response to broad economic forces impacting on the economy—for example, importers responding to favorable price abroad or investors responding to favorable investment climate in a country. On the other hand, short-term capital transactions, as we have seen in our examples above, are typically undertaken merely to finance these basic transactions.

In this sense, the basic balance provides a quick overview of the country's economy. For example, an analyst observing a deficit in a country's trade balance may conclude that the country is heading for a period of internal adjustments that will be needed to eliminate the deficit. However, if the deficit in the trade account is offset by a surplus in the long-term capital account—that is, by spontaneous inflow of long-term foreign investment—then the overall picture of the country is substantially different. The basic balance provides that picture at a glance.

There are, however, some pitfalls to using the basic balance for this purpose. The main problem lies in the fact that it is at times difficult to separate conceptually long-term capital flows from short-term financing transactions. This is particularly true of countries such as the United States whose broad capital markets are used worldwide for short-term investment purposes. Take, for example, a situation where a foreign investor wants to invest funds for a very short period. Under normal circumstances, a short-term money market instrument such as a thirty-day Treasury bill, or a bank CD, would provide a suitable investment medium. However, if the investor firmly believes that the interest rates on long-term investment instruments such as thirty-years government bonds will decline in the next thirty days, the investor

245

stands to realize a capital gain on this short-term investment in addition to the interest that would be earned over the period, if he invests in such instruments. Because the compilers of the country's balance-of-payments statistics have no way of knowing the investors's motives, his purchase of long-term bonds would be recorded by them in the long-term government account and, as such, would appear in the country's basic balance. This would then present the analyst with a misleading picture.

For these reasons, the basic balance is seldom used for measurement of the balance-of-payments performance of more advanced industrial countries whose capital markets typically serve this investment function. The balance is, however, frequently used as a measure of balance-of-payments performance of developing countries where long-term capital inflows are more readily identifiable as such.

THE U.S. BALANCE OF PAYMENTS AND THE NATIONAL ECONOMY

International transactions are so closely integrated into our daily lives that we hardly perceive them as such. We rarely notice that the shirt we are wearing was made in Taiwan or that the money we borrow to buy a new refrigerator came from the savings of a Japanese resident. In the aggregate, however, these transactions have an important effect on the national economy. The primary purpose of the balance-of-payments statistics is to segregate and highlight these international transactions and thereby permit an evaluation of that impact.

To formalize the relationships between U.S. international transactions and the national economy, we will use a simple framework based on the most comprehensive measure of the country's economic activities, its gross national product (GNP). In a closed economy—that is, an economy with no interaction with economies abroad—the GNP measures the value of all goods and services produced in the country over a period of time. For analytical purposes, we can divide this output into various categories and express it as:

$$Y = C + I + G \qquad (9.1)$$

where

Y = GNP
C = production of consumer goods and services
I = production of investment goods and services
G = government-produced goods and services

Once the economy is opened to foreign trade, the total amount of goods and services produced domestically and available for domestic consumption is supplemented by imports. At the same time, a portion of the domestic production is exported. Recognizing this, we can rearrange equation (9.1) by writing

$$Y = C + I + G + (X - M) \qquad (9.2)$$

The term $(X - M)$ is the by now familiar net exports term that was derived in calculating the country's balance on goods and services in the previous section. Because the goods and services account balance differs from the current account balance merely by the absence of the unilateral transfers, we can think of the $(X - M)$ term in our simplified framework as being also the current account balance in an economy where no such transfers occur.

Equation (9.2) brings into focus the relationship between the foreign sector and the rest of the economy. For example, it shows that when the country's current account is in balance—that is, when $(X - M) = 0$, the foreign sector has a neutral impact on the country's GNP. The emergence of a deficit—that is, the $(X - M)$ term becoming negative—will, all other things being equal, lead to a reduction in the country's GNP as measured by Y, while an emergence of a surplus will be generally expansionary for the economy.

This simple analytical framework may also be used to shed some light on the relationship between the country's balance of payments and its international wealth position. To do this, we can rearrange equation (9.2) as follows:

$$(X - M) = Y - (C + G + I) \qquad (9.3)$$

Equation (9.3) shows that as long as the country's foreign account is in the equilibrium position—that is, neither deficit or surplus—with $(X - M) = 0$, the country is simply using its own GNP. However, when the term $(X - M)$ becomes positive—that is when the country develops a surplus in its Current account—the $Y - (C + G + I)$ term must also become positive in the same amount. That means that the country uses domestically less than it produces—that is, Y is larger than $(C + G + I)$—leaving a "surplus" that is invested abroad. On the other hand, when a country runs a deficit, the usage of resources exceeds the country's GNP and this is financed by foreign capital inflows.

This follows from the relationship between the country's current account and its capital account discussed in some detail in the previous section: A country's current account deficit is necessarily matched (because to the structure of the balance-of-payments accounts) by an increase in claims on the country by foreigners, both short-term and long-term—that is, by net foreign investment inflows into the country. Conversely, a surplus—$(X - M) > 0$—is necessarily matched by capital outflow from the country of the same magnitude. These relationships explain the process that led to the emergence of the United States as a major international debtor in the mid-1980s.

In most years during the postwar period, the United States ran a surplus in its current account. This resulted in an ever-increasing net foreign investment position, which reached a peak of some $150 billion in 1982. In 1982 the country's current account turned sharply negative, and as the deficit continued, so did accumulation of foreign claims on the United States. By 1985 the net foreign investment position of the United States was dissipated, and the country became a net international debtor.

Finally, our simple model can help us to focus on the connection between the government's budget deficit and the country's balance-of-payments deficit. To do so, we need to expand somewhat our basic relationship that we developed in equation (9.2) above. That equation gave us a particular perspective on the country's GNP—namely, a view from the production side. We can also look at the country's GNP from the expenditures side to see how the national income is distributed among various uses. In general, there are three basic end-uses of income generated in producing the GNP: Consumption, saving, and taxes. We can formally express this by writing

$$U = C + S + T \tag{9.4}$$

where

C = consumption expenditures
S = saving
T = taxes

Because Y is the same in both the equation (9.2) and equation (9.4), we can write

$$C + I + G + (X - M) = C + S + T \tag{9.5}$$

Using some basic algebraic rules, we can rearrange equation (9.5) as follows:

$$(S - I) + (T - G) = (X - M) \tag{9.6}$$

This expression brings to light some interesting relationships. It shows that a surplus in the foreign sector of the economy $((X - M) > 0)$ must be matched either by a surplus in the government budget $((G - T) > 0)$ or, if that is in balance, by an excess in domestic saving over domestic investment $((S - I) > 0)$. Applying these principles to the U.S. economy as it existed in 1979, we can rewrite equation (9.6) by "plugging in" real numbers (in billion of dollars) and write

$$(\$ - 9.0) + (\$ + 11.5) = (\$ + 2.5) \tag{9.6a}$$

In 1979 the U.S. economy generated $445.8 billion gross savings, while gross investment amounted to $454.4 billion. This left a shortfall of private saving needed to finance private investment of $9.0 billion. However, with total federal, state, and local government receipts running at $779.8 billion, and expenditures at $768.3 billion, the public sector was generating a surplus of $11.5 billion. This surplus more than offset the shortfall in the private sector of the U.S. economy and made it possible for the United States to be a net exporter of capital in that year.

By 1986, the situation had changed dramatically. Plugging in the preliminary figures for 1986 we have

$$(-\$6.0) + (-\$143.1) = (\$-149.1) \qquad (9.6b)$$

The large government deficit, and the shortage of domestic saving needed to finance domestic investment, were being financed by inflows of foreign capital, which were the counterpart of the current account deficit experienced that year. Equations (9.6), (9.6a), and (9.6b) are actually identities that do not tell us anything about the *causal* relationship between the variables. But they nevertheless raise some intriguing questions about the relationships between the country's balance-of-payments deficit, the large government deficit, and the insufficiency of domestic savings experienced in the United States over that period. These are just a few of the many perspectives of the U.S. economy one can gain from a better understanding of the country's balance-of-payments statistics.

Part IV

INTERNATIONAL
CORPORATE
FINANCIAL
MANAGEMENT

10 Financing of Foreign Operations by MNCs

LAWRENCE M. KRACKOV

FUNDING a foreign subsidiary operation of a multinational corporation can be done through a variety of sources and financial instruments. The choice among the various alternatives is determined by availability, cost, risk, and the parent company's capital structure considerations. The subsidiary funding must, however, accommodate all of the host country's legal and financial requirements. This chapter examines the general principles of funding a foreign subsidiary or affiliate with debt versus equity; reviews the sources of funds, both internal and external, and examines the implications of the multinational corporation's overall financial strategies. It concludes by reviewing some empirical evidence on the financial structure of overseas subsidiaries and U.S. corporations.

GENERAL PRINCIPLES OF FUNDING WITH DEBT VERSUS EQUITY

Capital Structure Framework

The type of funding, whether debt or equity, and the sources of funds, whether internal or external, are determined by the capital structure framework of the entity and a host of other considerations.[1] The corporation's capital structure determines the optimum composition of debt and equity that minimizes costs and risk and that must be maintained for the consolidated corporation. A foreign subsidiary's capital structure may also conform to the parent company's overall capital structure, but it is commonly modified because of specific conditions in the markets and specific corporate financial strategies.

Within the context of the capital structure, the foreign subsidiary financing decision is influenced by four considerations or goals:

1 *Flexibility:* To ensure ease of future financing decisions and cash utilization;
2 *Management psychology*: To motivate the local subsidiary management to control the balance-sheet investments and compete aggressively against competitors in the local marketplace;

253

3 *Bank relations*: To satisfy local banking practices and thereby achieve adequate lines of credit and banking services, especially where there is no worldwide relationship between the bank and/or its parent and the multinational corporate parent;

4 *Government politics*: To satisfy the minimum equity investment requirements for both legal and political purposes.

The above goals are shaped by the multinational parent corporation's commitment to stand behind local subsidiary debt and fund the local subsidiary operating requirements when needed. The former is easy to demonstrate with comfort letters, and even guarantee letters, given to local banks by the parent company. Most companies are quite willing to provide such letters since they would not desire to walk away in any case from creditors who have relied on the parent company and with whom they had participated in arranging credit.

A parent company can use its track record to show that it stands behind its subsidiaries in the given foreign country, or in other foreign countries, by ensuring their adequate funding. Also, if a subsidiary's business is obviously valuable, then it may be easier for the parent to demonstrate commitment. For losing operations with little equity funding, however, commitment can become quite an issue. Moreover, proving that a parent company is committed can remain a problem in terms of relations with the local governments and unions, even if the banks and creditors can be satisfied or legally safeguarded as to their creditor risks.

Several alternative policies can be used by multinational firms to finance their foreign subsidiaries, of which at least four are worth outlining:

1 *Autonomous approach*: Setting debt and equity levels for each subsidiary that will yield acceptable debt/capital, earnings-coverage, and fixed-charge-coverage ratios, compared with other companies in the given country and especially with local competitors in the same industry;

2 *Minimum-equity level*: Financing all foreign capital funding requirements first with local foreign debt and then with intercompany debt, except for the minimum amount of equity that is designated by law, tax considerations, or local banks;

3 *Operating/strategic decision classification*: Financing all long-term asset requirements with equity and all net working capital requirements with debt;

4 *ROE target*: Setting ROE targets for each local foreign operation equal to the corporate target after covering interest expense, adjusted for local risk levels.

The examples in Table 10–1 will help clarify the above issues.

For an efficient corporate financial policy, the minimum equity

Table 10–1.

SUBSIDIARY CAPITAL STRUCTURES UNDER DIFFERENT CORPORATE PHILOSOPHIES.

Capital Structures	Debt	Equity	Debt/Capital Ratio[a] (percentage)
Autonomous			
Debt = 40% × $75	$30	$45	40%
Minimum equity			
Equity = 20% × $100	55	20	73
Operating decision			
Equity = $50	25	50	33
ROE target			
ROE = ($10 – $1.65) ÷ $42	33	42	44

[a]Capital = Total assets less interest-free liabilities.
Note: Assumptions:
Local/competitor debt/capital ratios = 40%;
Legal minimum equity level = 20% total assets;
Total assets = $100, with $50 fixed and $50 current;
Trade payables = $25;
Profit before interest after taxes = $10;
Post-tax interest = 5%;
ROE target = 20%.

approach might be most appropriate for the sake of repatriation flexibility. When excess cash is available after local operating needs have been met, funds can immediately be used to reduce the consolidated corporate capital by repaying the debt. Even if no dividend-remittance capacity exists, debt can usually be repaid, especially to local banks. The reduced debt means reduced overall capital, and the savings will be at the full cost of capital, not merely the lower cost of debt. This nearly always exceeds local interest income on investments of the excess cash.

Two of the other three approaches could also have significant, worthwhile benefits (although some still prefer the maximum flexibility afforded by maintaining minimum equity levels). The autonomous approach gives local management the same return-on-investment and interest-cost perspectives for pricing and other decisions as their competitors and local peer groups. The operating/strategic classification encourages local management to emphasize the part of the balance sheet they can and should control, and it removes their concern for the equity-funded remaining portion. The ROE target, however, is more of a rationalization to show local managers that they can still attain adequate profitability in terms of returns on equity, despite a given debt level. If an adequate ROE cannot be obtained because debt or equity is too high (but it is usually the latter that is the problem, as long as the return on capital exceeds the interest rate), this might be too much of a disincentive for local managers.

Local Liquidity Considerations

In establishing a new subsidiary, or in deciding on any equity investment by the parent company, the level of interest-free equity to be

255

contributed, compared with the interest-bearing debt-financing to be sought, is automatically determined once the capital structure is designated. Even if excess funds are already available in the subsidiary, after they are generated from operations, the amount of internal funds used should still be a function of the retained-earnings level that exists compared with the retained-earnings level required to maintain the desired capital structure. Additional accumulated earnings should not be retained but should be remitted.

Some subsidiaries have the ability to generate cash without retained earnings. Low capital intensity or significant balance-sheet reserves can allow cash to accumulate at levels disproportionately high relative to the retained earnings level. This then may be used as a reason for setting a lower percentage of equity in the capital structure target itself.

Implications for Working Capital Management

Another decision that is influenced by the capital structure philosophy is the local working capital management. To the extent that equity allows cash to build up more easily, this raises the minimum level required to run the business, contrary to the goal of tight balance-sheet control. The local management will not see any cost for the working capital funded by equity. For receivable and inventory financing they will also see either no cost, or at most the lost interest on bank deposits, which could be much less than the borrowing cost for funds. Again, a minimum equity level, or at least a limit on equity equal to the noncurrent assets level, would prevent this type of problem. Of course, local management should treat the cost of working capital as the cost of capital, which is much higher than interest costs and applies to all funds whether borrowed or not.

Although this analysis of the capital structure and its implications is fairly straightforward, local financial management, especially in foreign countries, may not agree with it. For example, we know that the real cost of funds retained by subsidiaries is the cost of capital and that a mere interest charge on local financial statements is really very generous. Often local managers argue that they cannot afford to borrow money for their working capital needs because they cannot cover the interest expense. In such cases, they would certainly invest the money because covering about three times the interest expense—on a foreign-exchange-adjusted-dollar basis—is required for an adequate return. That is why a rationalization or political compromise may be necessary to sell any capital-control program to local management.

One such sales approach is the debt level that still allows an overall ROE target to be met, and others may be needed to sell any of the other three approaches we discussed to local management. Remember, many local managers feel that the best capital structure is always to use 100 percent interest-free equity funding.

The minimum-equity approach in setting target capital structures for foreign subsidiaries is mainly aimed at the maximum flexibility to prevent a buildup of excess cash abroad. The rationale, of course, is to limit situations where 8 percent returns are earned on consolidated capital investments, rather than a 25 to 30 percent required returned, because the money cannot be brought home and removed from the capital structure or reinvested in the business. One company, for example, basically zeroes out all cash and equivalents in the United States, but averages approximately $100 million in foreign balances of cash and equivalents because of this problem. Without exerting significant effort on repatriation programs, however, the problem of low-return excess foreign cash could become much worse.

Arbitrage is another area of potential increases in capital that is heightened by the international aspects of a business. Different capital markets and different currencies provide many opportunities to earn higher interest in one place than interest is charged in another place, even on a dollar-equivalent basis.

For example, there was recently a more pervasive and more surprising situation in Germany where U.S. corporations could borrow money more cheaply than the rate paid on German government securities. Some U.S. corporations, therefore, borrowed money in Germany and reinvested the funds in the higher-yielding government securities. It appeared initially that the accountants would allow both the "riskless" asset and the debt to be netted and reflected at zero on the balance sheet, thereby leaving the interest-rate spread as additional income without any additional capital investment. When this was true, that was a good deal. Now, however, it appears that the accountants will force the increase in capital to be reflected on the balance sheet, and even a fifty-basis-point interest-rate spread represents a poor marginal return— that is 8½ percent versus the 25 to 30 percent required return.

Similarly, there are many countries where foreign subsidiaries cannot borrow without matching deposits at a bank in the United States or some similar stable environment. Nevertheless, the additional tied-up capital must be taken into account and charged the 25 to 30 percent cost of capital, not the 8 percent interest rate.

In other words, matched funding is really another form of a parallel loan. The purpose is to fund your cash-poor subsidiary, rather than remove cash from your cash-rich subsidiary, but the results are the same. In both cases, the additional asset on the corporate balance sheet prevents the parent corporation from efficiently achieving its goal.

INTERNAL FUNDING

Types of Internal Funding

We have concentrated on the level of internal funding, versus external   257

Table 10–2.

SOURCES OF INTERNAL AND EXTERNAL
FUNDS.

	Type
Internal Sources	
Foreign subsidiary	Depreciation
	Other non-cash charges
	Retained earnings
Corporate family	
Parent	Equity
	Loans
	Trade credit
	Borrowing with parent guarantee
Sister companies	Trade credit
External Sources	
Parent company home country	Debt market
	Equity market
Foreign affiliates' host country	Official credit
	Debt market
	Equity market
	Joint venture
Third country	Eurocurrency market
	Eurobond market
	Debt market
	Equity market

funding, and a few of the major types that affect corporate strategies, but perhaps a more complete list of all internal sources of funds should at least be considered. The first, and most obvious, group is at the subsidiary operation itself, which is a function of its own profitability, capital intensity, and the parent corporation's repatriation policy. The second group is the funding from other parts of the corporation, both the parent and affiliates, and is usually a direct alternative to external financing discussed later in this chapter. A summary overview of the individual sources within each group is outlined in Table 10–2.

Hybrid Equity Funding via Intercompany Loans and Trade Credit from the Parent

There is a hybrid form of funding that is partially equity from the parent and partially debt. Intercompany loans from the parent company or an affiliate place the same business-risk exposure on the parent as an equity contribution. Intercompany loan payments may be more easily remittable in the future than dividends, so the risk of blocked funds is somewhat reduced. Such loans therefore are an excellent adjunct to a minimum-equity capital structure in countries where debt funds are readily available on reasonable terms. There may also be a transfer of foreign-exchange gains and losses from the special equity section of the balance sheet to the income statement. Nevertheless, intercompany loans should be viewed as a form of equity contribution from the parent company or the affiliates.

The equity nature of intercompany loans to foreign subsidiaries may best be demonstrated by the accounting treatment. For a consolidated subsidiary, the loan payable to the parent or another consolidated subsidiary and the loan receivable from the parent or another consolidated subsidiary are eliminated on consolidation. Cash has moved within the corporation without affecting either the consolidated debt or equity accounts. This is exactly the same as an equity investment by the parent or another consolidated subsidiary.

Subsidiary		Parent	
Cash + 100	Loan payable + 100	Cash − 100	
		Loan receivable + 100	

Consolidated	
Cash 0	Loan payable 0
Loan receivable 0	

Loans to an unconsolidated subsidiary or affiliate, however, possess more qualities of debt. The loans will remain on both the consolidated balance sheet and the separate balance sheet of the subsidiary. The foreign-exchange exposure and the remittance capability are even more likely to be treated as debt. Nevertheless, the investment risk is still borne by the overall organization, as opposed to the transfer of a portion of the risk to outside creditors. The latter, however, is often not possible with any debt in light of parental guarantees, comfort letters, and plain ethics in dealing with outside creditors.

In addition to the ease of remittance, intercompany loans may be used to satisfy some of the other capital-structure goals. Local management incentives, for example, will be to control working capital to save interest expense, whether or not the loan is internal.

There may also be tax reasons to use intercompany loans. Under U.S. tax laws, for example, corporate interest is allocated to foreign subsidiaries before foreign income and foreign tax credits are calculated. Parental borrowing and intercompany loans may reduce excess foreign tax credits that can raise the total tax on repatriated income above U.S. tax rates.

Intercompany lending can be used with the same effects without formal loan procedures. Trade credit, for example, given to a foreign subsidiary by the parent on goods or services can be extended to provide financing. If interest is then charged on past-due payables, all of the elements of a loan can be created routinely in the normal course of business, as needed.

Concentration bank accounts or bank pools are also a form of intercompany loans for this purpose. When a cash-rich subsidiary and one cash-poor subsidiary have a combined banking relationship, the overdrafts or bank loans taken out by the latter can automatically be used to offset the cash deposits of the former. Although the individual operating units think they have cash deposits and loans, respectively, the overall corporate account in a given country will reflect only the net position.

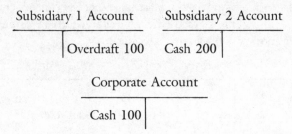

Subsidiary 1 Account   Subsidiary 2 Account

Overdraft 100   Cash 200

Corporate Account

Cash 100

Future Internal Funding and Dividend Levels

For future investment decisions, the level of retained earnings that should be maintained for future internal funding needs will be a function of the dividend/fee accrual/remittance policy. Once the investment requirements and capital structure are determined, the level of dividends is merely a residual factor from the other decisions. This approach is similar for a foreign subsidiary and its parent corporation. The following five-step system for setting foreign dividend levels may help clarify matters: [3]

1 *Calculate effective equity level* by adding capital stock, retained earnings, and interest-free intercompany liabilities.
2 *Define normal equity level* based on the target capital structure.
3 *Calculate excess or deficiency of equity* by subtracting the normal equity in step 2 from the company's effective equity in step 1.
4 *Designate dividends to be paid or equity deficiency to be eliminated*, with the latter requiring either an equity infusion versus a dividend *or* merely a deferral of a dividend until an excess position is attained. In cases where there is a lack of legal dividend capacity, the external dividend declared should be limited to that capacity for the legal entity and paid to the parent company or any other affiliate which is the immediate parent of the subsidiary. Any further excess equity in step 3 should become an internal dividend to be designated as corporate division funds on special internal financial statements to be prepared locally and/or by the parent.
5 *Finance both internal and external dividends*, using excess cash first and then any interest-bearing intercompany loans considered desirable, per the discussion below. External borrowings, such as bank overdrafts and loans, are perfectly acceptable and should be used next, at least to the extent the normal equity level in step 2 is maintained after the cash proceeds from the additional debt are used to pay the dividends.

Sources of Debt

Bank financing may be the most common source of debt used to finance foreign operations. It can take the form of overdrafts, lines of credit, and loans with specific principal amounts and specific maturity dates.

In the absence of local commercial paper markets in most countries, bank debt may represent the easiest method of matching funding maturities with the assets being funded, at least for short-term working capital needs. Lines of credit can be arranged to be drawn down only as borrowing needs arise, even on a seasonal basis.

Other multinational corporations can also provide loan funds. In fact, during credit crunches where funds are scarce, this is often an excellent source of debt. Also, in countries where multinational corporations have blocked funds, they are often interested in lending them to fellow multinational corporations whom they trust and with whom they can tailor a loan agreement for mutual benefits and safety.

When foreign credit is really scarce, matched funding may became a requirement. In such cases, the parent corporation deposits funds with the bank, the multinational corporation or an affiliate in the United States or some other country with hard currency, political safety, and freely available foreign exchange. Unfortunately, the real funding source

Table 10–3.
INFLOWS/OUTFLOWS.

Year	0	1	2	3	4	5
Purchase:						
Purchase price (including sales tax)	$1,411					
Service, property tax, and depreciation		$389	$341	$293	$244	$195
Gain on sale						(126)
Income and capital gains taxes[a]	(31)	(195)	(170)	(147)	(122)	(67)
Net costs	$1,380	$195	$170	$147	$122	$ 4
Noncash items[b]	–	337	288	242	193	289
Net *cash* cost	$1,380	($142)	($118)	($ 95)	($ 71)	($285)
Lease:						
Rent and property/ sales taxes		$398	$398	$398	$398	$398
Income taxes[a]		(199)	(199)	(199)	(199)	(199)
Net cash cost		$199	$199	$199	$199	$199
Calculations:						
Net cash flows of lease vs. purchase	($1,380)	$341	$317	$294	$270	$484

NPV @ 8% Pretax or 4% post-tax = $131
IRR = 7% post-tax or 4% pre-tax

Notes:
[a]No investment tax credit.
[b]Depreciation and book value on disposition.

on a consolidated basis is the parent company, in terms of both the risk retained and the capital tied up.

Local capital markets may also be a source of debt funds for foreign subsidiaries. This is not true in many countries and not true for most subsidiaries. Large subsidiaries with their own name recognition may be capable of obtaining their own funds, and this may be preferable to having the parent company access capital markets and make intracompany loans to the subsidiaries. The risk is borne by the local subsidiary, and the debt is automatically denominated in the local currency of the subsidiary, so no forward contract is necessary to cover the foreign-exchange exposure. If the subsidiary bears responsibility for both foreign-exchange losses and interest expense, intracompany loans funded by the parent's capital markets combined with forward contracts can simulate local capital market funding. For the sake of further clarification, Table 10–2 outlines all of the major sources of external funding for foreign subsidiaries.

Business-Related and Asset-Related Borrowing

Project financing and real estate mortgages are two similar forms of local financing that often are made readily available to subsidiaries by local banks and other local lenders. The local collateral adds safety for the lender and thus yields respectable credit terms, even for a subsidiary with less of its own credit rating. This type of financing should also automatically match maturities of the asset and the liability. On the short-term side, receivables factoring by local banks or other credit organizations can give a local subsidiary similar benefits based on the collateral and matched maturities.

Leasing of fixed assets, both real estate and equipment, can also provide similar benefits, for both initial financing and sale/leaseback alternatives. If enough of the economic risk is transferred, so that the subsidiary need not buy the asset at the end when economic value remains, then an off-balance-sheet accounting treatment may be possible. This would reduce the total capital investment and debt reflected on the balance sheet, although the "operating lease" would still be cited in the notes to the financial statements. As in the United States, the interest-rate premium usually required must be weighed against the beneficial accounting treatment. The interest rate itself should be calculated as shown in Table 10–3 (at 7 percent post-tax and 14 percent pre-tax) and then compared with the cost of other debt financing (shown in Table 10–3 at only 4 percent post-tax and 8 percent pre-tax).

Foreign leasing is sometimes tax driven. Both general tax benefits in some countries and specific investment incentives in other countries are discussed later in this chapter.

Trade financing is another form of financing directly tied to specific assets, such as inventory being exported or imported. The general subject is discussed in Chapter 7 of this book, however, and the government-subsidy aspects are discussed below.

Government Subsidies

All countries, including the United States, give favorable treatment to some type of transactions in the form of tax benefits and low-interest-rate financing. The former should be treated as future cash inflows in the same manner as any tax shield, which will increase the return on the investment. The latter can be accounted for in two ways.

The first method of incorporating favorable financing into the calculations is to use the lower interest rate on a dollar-equivalent basis to modify the debt component of the weighted-average cost of capital that serves as the basis for the hurdle rate against which a project's return must be measured. The second method first calculates the present value of the benefit using the company's normal dollar-equivalent interest rate as the discount rate and then subtracts this value from the total investment outlay in the overall cash-flow calculations:

Loan amount = $10 million
Loan life = 10 years
Normal interest rate = 10 percent
Subsidized interest rate = 4 percent
Tax rate = 50 percent
Present value of subsidized interest-rate benefit
  = Present value at 5 percent post-tax of 10-year annuity of $300m/year post-tax
  = $2.3 million

The most obvious types of government subsidies that are available for foreign subsidiaries therefore take the form of low tax rates, tax credits, or low interest rates for projects desired by the government or investments supporting imports and exports needed for government programs on the trade balance. These will usually fall into the area of trade financing or project financing.

Leasing can provide more indirect tax benefits. In the United Kingdom for example, there were incentives for local British film production given in the form of lower taxes. A British bank could then buy U.S. films meeting the minimum required level of British filming and actors and pass the benefits on to U.S. filmmakers.

In Japan the high local tax rates and lenient amortization deduction privileges allowed assets such as films to be sold to Japanese investors, who could obtain all of the tax benefits, even though most of the economic risk remained with the multinational company through a leaseback-type of arrangement. This type of subsidy, however, is really more indirect and unintentional, whereas the U.K. subsidy was part of a government program to increase local film production.

Choice of Currency

The foreign-exchange-adjusted interest rates in most countries are approximately equal to the U.S. interest rates. Although in less developed countries and in some special situations dollar-equivalent interest rates can be higher, risk is usually higher accordingly. Apart from some arbitrage opportunities, therefore, borrowing in one currency versus another will not save risk-adjusted interest costs. (Please note that some economists feel that Brazil and Argentina have recently presented such arbitrage situations where real interest rates were high as a result of supply/demand imbalances.) The parent company, however, can borrow in the United States and make intercompany loans to the subsidiary. This makes sense in either of two cases: When the parent feels that local risk is not as great as the market fears; or more likely, when the parent is already committed anyway, so local borrowing could not transfer risk. Then a local-loan interest-rate premium may be unwarranted.

Borrowing in local currency, however, does have many other advantages. For most subsidiaries, the loan creates no foreign-exchange transaction exposure that would need to be covered in the forward market. Also, the interest rate that the capital markets are charging for local operations are obvious, whereas borrowing in other currencies splits the interest cost into two pieces—interest and forward contract premium/discount. Some foreign subsidiaries are not even responsible for foreign-exchange costs, so the management-control incentive might be lost completely. For others, the separation of the two costs provides a scapegoat—that is, the subsidiary management feels that it can cover its low-interest expense with operating profits, but this uncontrollable foreign-exchange problem is distorting its bottom line. In reality, the interest rate is distorted, but this distortion may never be recognized.

In hyperinflationary countries and others where exchange translation of all the net monetary assets causes additional losses, on the income statement and/or the balance sheet, these exposures may be an additional concern. For hyperinflationary countries, such exposures cannot be covered with forward contracts. Thus, in order to shorten the net monetary position of the subsidiary in local currency, local-currency-denominated debt can serve as a simulated hedge. Instead of paying a high premium on forward contracts to cover the exposure, you pay a high interest rate on the debt in order to reduce net foreign-exchange losses.

Transfer Risk

Perhaps the greatest benefit of choosing local borrowing versus parent-company funding via equity contributions or intercompany loans is the transfer of risk. The most significant type of risk to be considered for this purpose is blocked funds. Intercompany loan repayments and interest are more easily remittable than dividends, but they still can become blocked or restricted at many points in time in many countries. Local debt, therefore, has the benefit of an obvious use for local cash as it builds up but cannot be remitted. Very rarely would local debt repayments be restricted by a government, even for a multinational corporation's subsidiary.

If a parental guarantee, comfort letter, or ethical obligation is involved, then the transfer of credit risk is limited. Vis-à-vis blocked funds, however, the parental obligation to pay may be met by the subsidiary repaying debt locally. If a nonlocal creditor, such as a U.S.-based multinational corporation, is involved, then the obligation may be to make payment in the United States, and then blocked funds risk would be a problem. Most local debt, however, even with parental obligation supporting the credit, can be satisfied by local payment.

Political risk and the possibility of expropriation are a greater problem. Any parental obligation to pay a creditor, even locally, may or may not be triggered by the expropriation of the local subsidiary assets. Of course, there is at least a chance of avoiding total expropriation, so the more local a liability is, the more risk will be transferred to the creditor or at least away from the parent.

EFFECTS ON AND OF A PARENT COMPANY'S WORLDWIDE FINANCIAL STRATEGIES

Internal and External Funding Levels

If the corporation's consolidated debt/capital position is highly leveraged, then the parent company may be more reluctant to borrow funds to make equity contributions or intercompany loans to its foreign subsidiaries. Although local debt will also usually add to the consolidated debt levels, the overall capitalization ratio may not be that important for local borrowing of subsidiaries with strong balance sheets. By the same token, if the parent company has excess cash, an equity contribution or intercompany loan makes the most sense for funding foreign subsidiaries to remove this excess cash.

For the most part, the choice among external sources of funds is independent of the financing of specific foreign subsidiaries. Neither a parent corporation's preference for the capital markets versus private placements and bank financing, nor its preference for continuous refinancing via commercial paper versus fixing debt costs via long-term bonds, should affect the decision on when to use internal funding versus local foreign-credit financing in most cases. One exception is where the parent company has inadequate debt capacity. Another exception is in the unusual situation where there is a great availability of a specific type of financing in only one local foreign market.

Many types of subsidiaries' foreign financing could be more readily available to foreign subsidiaries. If this is the case, such debt financing should be considered on behalf of the overall corporate financing needs, even when the local subsidiary has excess cash, if that cash can be repatriated. The overall corporation's cost of capital will be lowered. Some specific financing terms or structures may be available only in a given local foreign market. If access is limited to a local legal entity or a local operation, the foreign subsidiary could be the only vehicle for obtaining the benefits. In most cases, however, either the parent company can access the market as well, or the subsidiary will not be able to access the market at all.

Generally, the exceptions in this area can be approached in a two-step decision process. First, determine how the foreign subsidiary operation should be financed. Second, determine any foreign subsidiary available for overall financing plans. The latter may cause a different financing source for the former, but it is really a separate decision.

Choice of Currency

Generally, a corporation should seek the lowest all-in dollar-equivalent interest cost for corporate-level financing. The most common foreign-currency debt opportunities that can yield such benefits are linked with a favorable-rate currency swap. For such cases, there is usually no link between the corporate financing plans and foreign-subsidiary needs. Again, if a specific source of foreign-currency debt were available only for a local entity, then this would present an exception.

In terms of foreign-currency exposures of foreign subsidiaries, the use of external local-currency debt provides the benefits of not creating translation exposure and even reducing net-asset translation exposure. Once external financing is chosen for a foreign subsidiary, therefore, local currency debt is usually the best. In the uncommon situation where the overall corporate position on a given currency would be worsened by local-currency-denominated debt, however, another currency could be better and would avoid possibly expensive long-term forward contracts or currency swaps.

The most common relationship between overall corporate and foreign subsidiary needs is the designated-hedge strategy under the accounting rules of FASB 52. If the subsidiary net assets in its local currency are positive, foreign-currency debt can be issued or more easily obtained through a currency swap, to be designated as a hedge of these net assets. If the currency is one in which the interest rates are low, then overall corporate interest expense can be reduced. The expected offset is a foreign-currency loss on the debt, but it is hung up on the balance sheet, in the special equity section, and bypasses the income statement. It works like this:

U.S. dollar interest rate = 10 percent
Local currency interest rate = 5 percent
Foreign-exchange forward contract annual discount of 4.76 percent*
  Applied to 100 percent principal = 4.76 percent
  Applied to 5 percent LCY interest = 0.24 percent

*$ discount = (Interest – Rate differential) – (100 percent + LCY
          interest
     = (10 percent – 5 percent) – 105 percent
     = 4.76 percent

The foreign subsidiary debt would not usually be affected by this strategy because the parent corporation usually has access to Euro-foreign-currency markets. If not, however, the local subsidiary entity might be used to borrow more and lend the money to the parent. The asset position of course, is tied to the subsidiary. For this strategy, it represents an opportunity to aid overall corporate needs, as opposed to a need to be fulfilled by the parent company.

SUMMARY OF EMPIRICAL DATA

The balance-sheet data from the U.S. Department of Commerce, shown in Table 10–4 suggest that foreign affiliates have a significantly different composition of assets but only a moderately different structure of liabilities. Although the asset structure is affected by the varying type and nature of the operations, its composition is determined to a great extent by the overall corporation's capital structure, at least for many

Table 10–4.
BALANCE SHEET STRUCTURE (Percentage Distribution).

	Majority Owned Affiliate	U.S. Corporations
Assets:		
Current	48.7%	38.2%
Inventories	11.1	16.5
Noncurrent	51.3	61.8
Total assets	100.0	100.0
Liabilities:	59.2	52.1
Current	33.1	25.4
Noncurrent	26.1	26.7
Long-term debt	15.9	17.4
Owners' equity	40.8	49.7
Total liabilities and equity	100.0	100.0

Source: U.S. Department of Commerce, Bureau of Economic Analysis, *U.S. Direct Investment Abroad, Preliminary 1984 Estimates* (October 1986); U.S. Department of Commerce, Bureau of Census, *Quarterly Financial Report for Manufacturing, Mining, and Trade Corporations, Fourth Quarter* 1985.
  Note: Data for the U.S. corporations includes manufacturing companies with assets of $25 million. These companies are proxies for U.S. parent corporations.

corporations. Nevertheless, the capitalization of foreign affiliates and parent corporations is somewhat different; and this is probably mostly accounted for by intercompany transactions and the parental guarantees of the affiliates. As expected, therefore, foreign affiliates are less capitalized with equity than their parent companies.

NOTES

1. Lawrence M. Krackov and Surendra Kaushik, *Financial Management: A Practical Approach to Avoiding Financial Bloopers* (New York Institute of Finance, 1988), ch. 22.
2. See for instance, David K. Eiteman and Arthur I. Stonehill, *Multinational Business Finance*, 3rd edition (Reading, Mass.: Addison-Wesley, 1982), p. 472.
3. Krackov and Kaushik, note 1 above.

11 Foreign-Currency Exposure and Hedging Policies

HARVEY A. PONIACHEK

BECAUSE multinational corporations (MNCs) are deeply involved in international business, they are especially vulnerable to foreign-exchange-rate volatility. The average MNC exports and imports; has outstanding short- and long-term foreign-currency loans, assets, and liabilities; and operates numerous subsidiaries and affiliates abroad. Since the adoption of the floating exchange-rate system in the early 1970s, this sensitivity to currency-rate volatility has increased, and preoccupation with foreign-exchange exposure management has proliferated.

This chapter discusses foreign-exchange exposure and management of an MNC or a corporation that conducts a substantial amount of international business. Currency exposure, or risk, is defined in terms of transaction, translation, and economic exposure. These concepts are universal and generally applicable to all corporations, not necessarily to those subject to U.S. accounting standards. These exposures could alter a firm's equity position, profitability, cash flow, and market value. MNCs and corporations with substantial international business seek to measure their foreign-exchange exposure and manage it in order to minimize the adverse implications of currency-rate fluctuations. This chapter describes the various types of currency exposure, their accounting requirements, and the strategies and policies of exposure management, particularly for translation and transaction exposure. An appendix describes foreign-exchange exposure management practices at CBS, Inc.

TYPES OF FOREIGN-EXCHANGE EXPOSURE

Translation Exposure

Translation exposure, or accounting exposure, arises when an MNC prepares its consolidated financial reports in its home currency or the reporting currency. To prepare these reports it is necessary to translate into the home currency the financial statements of foreign subsidiaries

269

and affiliates that are denominated in foreign exchange. For instance, in preparing the financial statements of a U.S. MNC in dollars and in conformity with U.S. accounting principles it is required to translate the financial data of the foreign subsidiaries and affiliates into dollars. Translation exposure measures potential changes in a corporation's consolidated financial reports that result from volatility in the exchange rates. The value of foreign-currency denominated accounts is modified by currency-rate changes when translated into or remeasured in, for instance, dollars.

The definition and measurement of translation exposure depend on the accounting rules used, which are established by the parent firm's government, by an accounting association, or by the firm itself. In the United States the Financial Accounting Standards Board (FASB) has established uniform accounting standards for the measurement and reporting of currency gains and losses that occur in the process of translation in preparing consolidated financial statements.

There are three basic conventions for translation of foreign-currency accounts into the reporting currency for consolidation:

1 The current-rate method;
2 The monetary/nonmonetary method, which is referred to as the
      temporal method in the United States; and
3 The current/noncurrent method.

Hybrid translation methods based on these approaches have also been used.

Translation exposure is defined by the difference between certain exposed assets and liabilities, or the net exposed assets. It measures the change in the value of the net exposed assets resulting from fluctuations in the exchange rates in which the accounts of the subsidiaries and affiliates are denominated.

In December 1981 the FASB issued "Statement of Financial Accounting Standards No. 52 (FAS 52), Foreign Currency Translation."[1] This standard suspended "Financial Accounting Standards No. 8 (FAS 8), Accounting for the Translation of Foreign Currency Transaction and Foreign Currency Financial Statements," which was in effect from January 1976 to December 1982. FAS 52 is based on the current-rate method, while FAS 8 is based on the monetary/nonmonetary method, or the temporal approach.

FAS 52 presents standards for currency translation that are designed to meet the following objectives:

1 Provide information that is generally compatible with the expected
      economic effects of an exchange-rate change on the company's
      cash flows and equity;
2 Reflect in consolidated statements the financial results and rel-
      ationships as measured in the currency in which each entity
      conducts its business;

3 Measure individual financial statements not as if their operation has been conducted in the same economic environment of the reporting currency, as was the case under FAS 8, unless the foreign operation is merely an extension of the parent firm.[2]

According to the current-rate method, on which FAS 52 is based, the translation of an affiliate's financial statements into the reporting currency, or the currency in which the consolidated financial reports are denominated, follows the following procedures:

1 All assets and liabilities are translated at the current rate of exchange, which is in effect on the balance-sheet date;
2 Income statement items are translated at either the actual exchange rate on the dates of these items or at a weighted average exchange rate for the period;
3 Existing equity accounts are translated at historical rates;
4 Gains and losses caused by translation adjustments are not included in the net income but are disposed of in a separate equity account entitled Cumulative Translation Adjustment or Equity Adjustment from Foreign-Currency Translation.

Under the monetary/nonmonetary method or the temporal method in the United States on which FAS 8 is based, the following translation convention is applied:

1 Assets (cash, marketable securities, and account receivables) and monetary liabilities (current liabilities and long-term debt) are translated at the current exchange rate, while all other assets and liabilities are translated at the historical rates;
2 Income statement items are translated at the average exchange rates for the period, except certain items that are directly associated with the nonmonetary assets and liabilities, such as depreciation and cost of goods sold, which are translated at historical rates;
3 Income gains or losses are recorded in the income statement.

Functional Currency

FAS 52 differentiates between a functional and reporting currency. A functional currency is defined as the currency of the primary economic environment in which a foreign subsidiary or affiliate operates and in which it generates cash flows. The reporting currency is the currency in which the parent firm prepares its consolidated financial statements, normally the home country currency.[3]

Once a foreign entity's functional currency is determined, it should be applied consistently. However, significant changes in economic conditions might indicate that the functional currency has changed. The functional currency will not always be the currency of the country in which the foreign subsidiary or affiliate is located or the currency in which the records are maintained. For instance, when the entity is merely an extension of the parent company, its functional currency would be the currency of the parent company.

The functional currency (or currencies) of a foreign entity is basically a matter of fact. In some complex cases, however, a company will not be able to clearly identify a single functional currency. In a complex situation the determination of the functional currency depends on

Table 11–1.

TRANSLATION OF THE BALANCE SHEET OF ABC COMPANY, WEST GERMANY (thousands of deutsche marks).

| | | Current Rate Method | | | | Temporal Method | | | |
| | | Before Devaluation | | After Devaluation | | Before Devaluation | | After Devaluation | |
	DM	DM/$	$	DM/$	$	DM/$	$	DM/$	$
Cash	8,000	2.0000	4,000	2.5000	3,200	2.0000	4,000	2.5000	3,200
Account receivables	16,000	2.0000	8,000	2.5000	6,400	2.0000	8,000	2.5000	6,400
Inventory	12,000	2.0000	6,000	2.5000	4,800	2.0000	6,000	2.0000	6,000
Net fixed assets	24,000	2.0000	12,000	2.5000	9,600	1.8000	13,333	1.8000	13,333
Total	60,000	2.0000	30,000	2.5000	24,000		31,333		28.933
Account payable	12,000	2.0000	6,000	2.5000	4,800	2.0000	6,000	2.5000	4,800
Short-term debt	16,000	2.0000	8,000	2.5000	6,400	2.0000	8,000	2.5000	6,400
Long-term debt	20,000	2.0000	10,000	2.5000	8,000	2.0000	10,000	2.5000	8,000
Capital	12,000	1.8000	6,667	1.8000	6,667	1.8000	6,667	1.8000	6,667
Translation adjust			−667		−1,867		667		3,067
Total	60,000		30,000		24,000		31,333		28,933

How to Measure Net Exposed Assets?

| | Translation Method | | Translation Method | |
| | Current | Temporal | Current | Temporal |
		$		DM
Assets:				
Cash	4,000	4,000	8,000	8,000
Account receivables	8,000	8,000	16,000	16,000
Inventory	6,000		12,000	
Net fixed assets	12,000		24,000	
	30,000	12,000	60,000	24,000
Liabilities:				
Account payable	6,000	6,000	12,000	12,000
Short-term debt	8,000	8,000	16,000	16,000
Long-term debt	10,000	10,000	20,000	20,000
	−24,000	−24,000	−48,000	−48,000
Net exposed assets	6,000	−12,000	12,000	−24,000
Devaluation				
$(2-2.5) \div 2.5 \times 100 =$	20%	20%		
Translation loss				
Net exposed assets × devaluation	−1,200	2,400		
Dollar value at DM/$ 2.0000			6,000	−12,000
Dollar value at DM/$ 2.5000			4,800	−9,600
Translation loss/gain			−1,200	2,400

Source: Harvey A. Poniachek (1987).

management assessment on the basis of cash flows, sales prices, markets, expenses, financing, intercompany transactions, and arrangements.

In highly inflationary economies, in which the cumulative inflation is approximately 100 percent or more over three years, the reporting currency is the functional currency. Under these circumstances, the temporal method of FAS 8 is used for translation. For instance, the functional currency of a German subsidiary of a U.S. MNC that operates in Germany would be the deutsche mark. If the subsidiary has transactions in other currencies, those first must be translated into the deutsche mark, the functional currency, with any gain or loss included in the subsidiary's net. Then its financial statements would be translated into U.S. dollars according to FAS 52.

If the functional currency of a U.S. subsidiary in Germany is the dollar, the same as the reporting currency, no translation is needed. However, the remeasurement of the accounts in deutsche marks into the U.S. dollar is done according to FAS 8.

Table 11–1 shows the balance sheet of a foreign subsidiary denominated in deutsche marks, its functional currency, and then translated into the reporting currency of its parent currency, the dollar, according to FAS 52 and FAS 8. As shown, balance-sheet exposure and currency gains/losses depend on the accounting method used. It should be noticed that the two approaches produce different results in magnitude and direction.

Transaction Exposure

Transaction exposure arises when commitments in foreign currency are subject on settlement to exchange-rate gains and losses due to changes in the currency rates. A change in exchange rates between the functional or reporting currency and the currency in which a transaction is denominated increases or decreases the expected amount of the functional or reporting currency cash flow on settlement of the transaction. The increase or decrease in expected cash flow is defined as a foreign-currency-transaction gain or loss and is included in the net income for the period in which the exchange-rate changed. The exceptions to the requirement for including of transaction gain and loss in the income statement pertain to certain intercompany transactions—transactions that are designed as economic hedges of net investment, and foreign-currency commitments.

The following transactions give rise to currency exposure:

1 Purchasing or selling on credit goods and services whose prices are stated in foreign currencies (recorded as account receivables and account payables);
2 Borrowing or depositing funds denominated in foreign currencies (reflected in foreign debt and credit);
3 Transacting a forward-exchange contract;

4 Exchange gains or losses arising from long-term intercompany transactions (considered translation adjustment); those arising from short-term intercompany business are reported as current income;
5 Various transactions denominated in foreign exchange.

As suggested above, transaction exposure can be a variety of foreign-currency-denominated assets (export receivables or bank deposits), liabilities (account payables or loans), revenue (expected future sales), or expenses (expected purchase of goods), or income (dividends). FAS 52 requires that a foreign-currency transaction be booked at the exchange rate prevailing at the transaction date and be revalued at each subsequent reporting date until it is settled.

In determining the company's exposure several observations are necessary:

1 Cash balances do not contribute to exposure because their value is presently known;
2 Intercompany transactions do not cancel out, and commitments and liabilities of affiliates to their parents or other affiliated companies in the parent's reporting currency constitute part of the affiliate's transaction exposure;
3 Exposure is cumulative, and the total transaction exposure by currency of the parent company and its subsidiaries and affiliates must be aggregated;
4 For each affiliate, unfilled customers' orders are netted against future purchase commitments in each currency.

Internal Management Reports

Treasury managers have developed several internal currency exposure reports from the information used to prepare consolidated financial statements. The typical reports are

1 Translation exposure report,
2 Transaction exposure report, and
3 Cash flow reports by currency and entity and for the entire corporation.

A translation exposure report is derived by determining the net exposed assets as shown in Table 11–1 above.

Transaction exposure can be defined by the balance sheet, by the cash flow, or on an ad hoc basis as shown in Table 11–2. Starting balance-sheet exposure relates to certain foreign-currency-denominated assets and liabilities appearing on the balance sheet of the parent and its foreign subsidiaries at any given time. To overcome the static nature of this report, a monthly or quarterly cash-flow schedule by currency and entity, and an aggregated corporate report by currency are produced. The cash-flow report is superior to the balance-sheet report because it

Table 11–2.
CORPORATE TRANSACTION EXPOSURE.

Definition	*Advantages/Disadvantages*
Balance-sheet approach; protect balance-sheet exposure but ignore cash flows.	Efficient if the balance sheet is not subject to major frequent changes.
Cash-flow approach; concentrate on cash flows and disregard balance sheet completely.	Appropriate for companies that do most of their business under firm commitments or contractual arrangements.
Ad hoc approach; hedge transactions with fixed maturities and develop an overall policy on the basis of the balance sheet.	Some hedging might not be consistent with the overall position of the company; exposure arising from individual transactions can be partially offset or even completely neutralized.

Source: Harvey A. Poniachek (1987).

includes existing commitments and anticipated cash-flow items, and it permits better timing of exposure policies. Finally, the ad hoc definition based on the balance sheet and the cash-flow is easy to derive. To determine the company's worldwide cash-flow report several observations are necessary:

1 Transaction exposure is measured by the parent and each of its foreign subsidiaries and affiliates as well as by currency. An entity cannot have an exposure in its functional currency.
2 Intercompany transactions do not cancel out, and commitments and liabilities of subsidiaries and affiliates to their parent companies or to their affiliates in the parent's reporting currency constitute part of the subsidiary's transaction exposure.
3 Exposure is cumulative, and the total transaction exposure of the parent company and its subsidiaries and affiliates must be aggregated.
4 For each affiliate, unfilled customers' orders are netted out against future purchase commitments in each currency.
5 Outstanding commitments in forward-exchange-rate transactions are included in assessing the company's exposure.

The foreign-currency cash-flow reports are prepared monthly and/or quarterly by the parent company and its major subsidiaries and affiliates by currency and per period. See Table 11–3. The reports show the supply and demand for specific currencies at different periods.

Economic Exposure

Economic exposure is caused by a change in the inflation rate or the exchange rate that modifies the cash flow of the corporation—for instance, a deterioration in export receipts due to appreciation of the home currency, or a decline in the value of foreign income caused by an appreciation of the foreign currency. Economic exposure measures the

275

Table 11–3.

ABC COMPANY AND ITS AFFILIATES EXPOSURE REPORT
December 31, 19XX Dollar Equivalent, 000.

U.S. parent	$	DM	FF	SF
Account receivables		7,000	2,800	4,200
Account payables		5,250	1,750	2,800
Short-term bank loans		3,500	1,750	1,750
Long-term bank loans		5,250	1,400	2,100
Forward exchange contracts		1,750	700	1,050
Unfilled customers' orders net of purchase commitments		1,400	1,050	700
Total		24,150	9,450	12,600
ABC subsidiary, W.G.				
Account receivables	1,000		1,000	2,000
Account payables	500		750	1,250
Short-term bank loans	300		500	1,000
Long-term bank loans	250		1,000	1,000
Forward exchange contracts	100		200	300
Unfilled customers' orders net of purchase commitments	100		150	250
Total	1,300		3,600	5,800

ABC COMPANY AND ITS AFFILIATES CASH FLOW BY CURRENCY December 31, 19XX Dollar Equivalent, 000.

	1st Q	2nd Q	3rd Q	4th Q
$				
Receipts	7,000	7,000	7,000	7,000
Disbursements	6,000	6,000	6,000	6,000
Net $ receipts	1,000	1,000	1,000	1,000
DM				
Receipts	3,500	3,500	3,500	3,500
Disbursements	3,250	3,250	3,250	3,250
Net $ receipts	250	250	250	250
FF				
Receipts	950	950	950	950
Disbursements	625	625	625	625
Net $ receipts	325	325	325	325
SF				
Receipts	950	950	950	950
Disbursements	2,500	2,500	2,500	2,500
Net $ receipts	-950	-950	-950	-950

Source: Harvey A. Poniachek (1987).

potential impact of unexpected exchange rate changes on the cash flow generated by subsidiaries and affiliates and the entire corporation.

The net present value of the firm's expected cash flows will increase or decrease with changes in the foreign-exchange rates. The exact outcome depends on the distribution of sales between domestic and international markets, the elasticity of demand in each market, the cost structure of the overseas entities, price competition, and the ability to adjust the output mix in response to currency-rate changes. The existence of purchasing-power parity conditions (that is, overvaluation or undervaluation of the domestic currency vis-à-vis other currencies or a basket of foreign currencies) is also significant in determining the effect of currency changes on the corporation.

Economic exposure is more important for the long-term conditions of a company. Planning for economic exposure rests with senior management because it involves finance, marketing, and production, which require close coordination.

EXPOSURE MANAGEMENT AND POLICY

General Policy

MNCs differ in their foreign-currency-exposure management objectives and strategies, although they usually seek to protect profits from the adverse effect of unexpected exchange-rate volatility. Corporations commonly formulate specific objectives and employ various hedging techniques. Hedging policies differ significantly and depend whether the exposure is translation, transaction, or economic.

FAS 52, as opposed to FAS 8, relieved MNCs from their excessive preoccupation with translation exposure management because the consequences of currency fluctuations on the balance sheet do not affect the income statement. An increasing emphasis, however, has been placed on management of transaction and economic exposure.

A successful currency-exposure management program should include the following ingredients:

1 Determine the type of exposure to be monitored and managed (Table 11–2 suggests three alternatives).
2 Formulate general corporate objectives, and specify acceptable cost and risk levels.
3 Assign responsibilities for the various type of exposure.
4 Specify an exposure-management/hedging policy in terms of various hedging methods.
5 Develop a management information system to monitor and control hedging activities.

When should a corporation engage in currency management? There are several alternatives with different advantages and disadvantages associated with each:

When to hedge?	Advantages/disadvantages
Always	Easy to implement but could be too costly.
Usually	Easy to implement, allows flexibility, and is cost effective, but is subject to discretion.
Sometimes	Allows too much discretion to managers who implement corporate policy; could be too risky.
Never	Too risky.

277

Exposure management can be active or passive. Should management follow an active policy? Those advocating it believe that international money and currency markets are inefficient, and those opposing an active strategy assume that the markets are generally efficient. Managers and practitioners usually side with the inefficient interpretation and maintain that a firm can protect itself against unexpected currency changes and reduce the variability of earnings. In addition, management's general risk-aversion attitude also influences whether an active or passive strategy is pursued.

Managing economic exposure is very difficult because exchange-rate fluctuations affect the cash flows over an extended period of time. An internationally well-diversified MNC may follow a passive currency-exposure policy because the diversity of its cash flows reduces the volatility of the overall net cash flows. However, MNCs with insufficient diversification should follow a more active exposure policy by adjusting activities abroad.

Table 11–4.
HEDGING INSTRUMENTS.

Instrument	Characteristics
Forward	Good for fixed dates; cost implicit in price.
Currency futures	Availability is limited to the major currencies for fixed maturies through organized exchanges. Transactions involve commisions and margins, and generate cash flows.
Financial market hedging	Good for fixed dates; cost reflected in interest-rate differentials and forward discount and premium. The hedging results are the same as under the forward-market hedge if interest parity conditions are maintained.
Currency options	Suitable for uncertain time tables; settlement is not necessary but involves an immediate expense.
Currency and credit swaps	Feasible primarily for large companies with good access to financial markets.
Leading and lagging of invoicing	Good particularly for intercompany transactions; could compromise the corporations's credit standing if applied on a widespread basis outside the company. Often prohibited by the authorities.
Working capital management	Effective but subject to operational constraints and ratio requirements; could involve considerable business restructuring with undesirable results.
Currency selection of invoices	Subject to market condition and conventions.
Exposure netting	Highly effective in reducing currency exposure but requires a well-organized network of communications and execution.
Transfer pricing	Might be feasible for intercompany international transactions but is prohibited by tax authorities and international tariff and trade regulations.

Source: Harvey A. Poniachek (1987).

Hedging Instruments

Hedging refers to a wide range of transactions and activities that offset or counterbalance, entirely or partially, the risk of loss from a change in the foreign-exchange rates. MNCs practice, in varying degrees, some or all of the hedging activities listed in Table 11–4.

Hedging Translation Exposure

A balance-sheet hedge, or adjustment of working capital, is most appropriate for managing translation exposure. For instance, if the company has a net exposed position as shown in Table 11–1, it could reduce its assets or liabilities and thereby reduce its net exposed assets. The feasibility of this policy depends on regulatory requirements in the host market and operational conditions.

Forward-currency contracts and money market hedges can also be used but involve some speculative risk. For instance in the case shown in Table 11–1 there is a translation loss of $1.2 million. Given the currency market rates specified in Table 11–5, the company can hedge through a forward currency market by selling DM forward and purchasing DM on the spot in the future. Here is a brief cost and benefit assessment of this hedge:

$$\text{Forward contract size} = \frac{\text{Potential translation loss in dollars}}{\text{Forward rate} - \text{Future spot}}$$

$$= \frac{\$1.2 \text{ million}}{0.5128 - 0.4000} = \text{DM } 10.6 \text{ million}$$

Sell DM 10.6 million forward:

Receipt at maturity	$10.6 \times 0.5128 =$	$18.2
Purchase DM on the spot market	$10.6 \times 0.4000 =$	$14.2
Profit		$1.2

The forward-market hedge is speculative because the future spot rate could change and produce different results entirely.

A money-market hedge involves borrowing deutsche marks, exchanging the funds into dollars, placing them on deposit, and at maturity exchanging enough dollars to purchase DM to cover the principal and interest cost. The calculation for how large should the loan be is as follows:

L DM loan
10 percent German interest rate
20 percent U.S. interest rate
3 months

$$((L/2.000) \times (1.20) \times 3/12) \times 2.5000 - (L \times 1.20 \times (3/12))$$
$$= \text{DM } 8 \text{ million}$$

Table 11–5.

FORWARD MARKET HEDGING (millions of deutsche marks).

Obligations in Deutsche Marks	Receipts in Deutsche Marks
Wait till maturity and purchase DM on the spot at a cost of $400,000.	Wait till maturity and obtain $400,000.
Purchase DM forward at a cost of $512,820.	Sell DM forward and obtain $512,820
Profit results if future spot is DM/$ 2.500.	The forward market transaction is the most appropriate for the company because the currency depreciates.
If DM/$ appreciates beyond DM/$ 2.000, the company could suffer losses.	The company will lose if the exchange rate of the DM drops below the current spot or forward rate.

[a]The deutsche mark per dollar exchange rates are as follows:

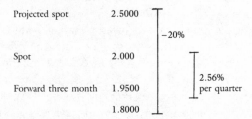

Projected spot	2.5000	
		−20%
Spot	2.000	
Forward three month	1.9500	2.56% per quarter
	1.8000	

Solving this equation for L suggests that the size of the DM loan required is DM 106.6 million. If interest parity conditions exist, there is no difference between the forward-market hedge and the money-market operation. However, the money-market hedge inflates the companies' liabilities and their final outcome depends on the future spot rate.

Swapping dollar debt into local currency debt would eliminate the rate advantage of borrowing uncovered dollars but provide the necessary protection. Currency options could provide a hedge for an MNC at a high cost of premiums and commissions. Leads and lags of payments can also be used but involve primarily intercompany business.

Hedging Transaction Exposure

Transaction exposure includes, among others, foreign-currency-denominated loans, export and import activities, and remittances of dividends. Any policy to offset foreign-exchange liabilities through the forward or money market could involve a substantial increase in the cost of doing international business and offset entirely the cost advantage in incurring them. An MNC's international activities involve the creation of translation and transaction exposure.

Transaction exposure can be offset by hedging in the forward-currency market, the money market, and the options market as described in the section on translation exposure hedging. For instance, if the parent company expects DM receipts or payments from or to its German subsidiary, Table 11–5 shows the cost and benefit of hedging through the forward currency market, based on the financial data listed therein.

Managing Economic Exposure

The primary goal of economic exposure management is to protect corporate profit from the negative impact of exchange-rate fluctuation. Diversification reduces the variability of the overall cash flow, while hedging otherwise might not be adequate. MNCs need to consider the implications of how currency-rate changes affect various aspects of their long-term international activities.

ORGANIZATION

Hedging of foreign exchange should be centralized and handled by an assistant international treasurer in cooperation with a foreign-exchange managing committee and the financial managers of the primary subsidiaries. A centralized approach can take a consolidated view in managing translation and transaction exposure. It allows management to net out and match exposures on a global basis.

Evidence shows that currency exposure policymaking may be outlined by headquarters, while detailed planning and implementation are carried out by subsidiaries and affiliates. However, in highly centralized corporations, all these functions are carried out at headquarters. The attitude has, however, swung back and forth during the last decade on the subject of the centralization of currency-exposure management in the MNC. In recent years, a more flexible approach has emerged, with cash flow being managed at the individual subsidiary or affiliate and the translation hedging done in a centralized fashion at headquarters.

The assistant international treasurer should oversee or keep in close contact with the manager of the corporate international netting system. Most foreign subsidiaries and affiliates communicate their exposure data on a monthly basis through telex, mail, or electronic mail. Major banks offer reporting and communication networks to their clients at reasonable cost. The ideal planning horizon should be three to six months, with the shorter period preferred. Currency management requires periodic currency forecasting, a centralized surveillance function to monitor transactions, a high degree of sensitivity through the purchasing, billing, and planning departments of each subsidiary to pricing and exchange rates, and a plan to protect profit and investment.

SUMMARY: RISK AND HEDGING

The question of how much to hedge and at what cost depends primarily on risk and cost considerations and on the currency outlook. The more risk averse the company, the higher the cost it is willing to incur to cover its exposure. A corporation cannot fully hedge simultaneously the three types of currency exposure. In a sense, offsetting both transaction and translation exposure is virtually impossible. Companies usually seek a positive balance between cost and benefits.

The level of risk is defined in terms of anticipated currency losses, which, in turn, depend on the exposed currency outlook and the net exposed position. The cost proxy of protection is reflected by the forward premium/discount, by the cost of engaging in various capital market transactions, the balance-sheet adjustment, and real economic activities to offset the exposure.

Policies vary among companies, depending on their preference for risk and cost. Some companies leave most of their exposure unhedged, while others hedge their exposure to a great degree, or fully. Most companies elect to minimize currency losses by the least expensive plan. The cost of protection could be excessive if full protection is sought.

The extent of hedging depends on the currency outlook, the probability attached to the different projections, and the related cost of protecting the position. Once a currency outlook is prepared and the firm assesses its exposure, the problem of exposure management could be reduced to an insurance problem. That is, should a firm self-insure against the risk of unexpected currency rate changes or lay them off to the financial market?

The insurance approach involves setting exposure limits for different currencies in order to reduce periodic losses due to currency volatility. The maximum ceiling on unhedged positions on a currency by currency basis can be specified by setting a higher percentage for those currencies that have been historically more stable or by gauging the degree of risk the firm can tolerate by purchasing insurance. This approach suggests that partial hedging of currencies that are subject to substantial volatility is warranted, rather than complete hedging. Minimizing the probable exchange losses and the cost of protection might require a partial hedge position, however.

Can a corporation formulate an effective hedging strategy? It depends on the extent and frequency of the firm's exposure. For an MNC that has a continuous flow of income and expenses in several currencies, ongoing forward-currency hedging might be too costly and of little benefit. This company might be better off to remain unexposed, unless it has a high degree of risk aversion. In addition, if the forward rate might be an unbiased predictor of future spot rates, there is no long-term advantage in forward-currency hedging. A similar outcome is expected by hedging in the money market if international interest-rate parity is maintained.

NOTES

1. Financial Accounting Standards Board, "Statement of Financial Accounting

Standards No. 52, Foreign Currency Translation" (Stamford, Conn.: FASB, 1981).

2. Hortense Goodman and Leonard Lorensen, "Illustration of Foreign Currency Translation, A Survey of the Application of FASB Statement No. 52" (New York: American Institute of Certified Public Accountants (AICPA), 1982).
3. Peat, Marwick and Mitchell, "Statement of Financial Accounting Standards No. 52, Foreign Currency Translation: An Executive Summary and a Detailed Review of the Standards" (New York: PMM, 1981).

CBS Inc.'s Foreign-Exchange Exposure Management Practices

LAWRENCE M. KRACKOV

THIS appendix demonstrates how CBS Inc. has combined several contrasting elements into a coherent foreign-exchange exposure management program. CBS takes a highly risk-averse approach to the management of foreign-exchange exposures, but one that is also very active and involves more than $1 billion in foreign-exchange contracts annually. The program is highly centralized, but it involves the netting and hedging of all exposures at numerous decentralized subsidiaries. Generally, the CBS approach aims to neutralize any negative effects of foreign-exchange-rate changes on the income statement by hedging transaction exposure and selected economic exposure.

Foreign-Exchange Exposures to be Covered

Foreign-exchange exposure is identified and evaluated with respect to the potential risk for the income statement. The high-risk profits that directly affect the foreign-exchange line of the income statement are always hedged in the forward market, if they can easily be covered with forward contracts. The low-risk profit exposure, or the one that is difficult to cover, may not be hedged.

The following types of exposure are most significant for CBS and could have an economic impact but no direct accounting effects (so the foreign-exchange gains and losses are not booked on the foreign-exchange line of the income statement):

Planned dividends scheduled for specific time periods merely affect expected income levels and not the consolidated income statement, prior to declaration. This is true even if they are specifically designated in the company's formal foreign dividend budget that is an input to the domestic cash-flow budget of cash available for corporate-level, worldwide spending programs. Thus, such planned dividends are not hedged.

Subsidiary earnings in local currencies present an exposure for the consolidated reported earnings, so they may be hedged. CBS encourages local price increases whenever possible to compensate for devaluation that merely reflects local inflationary pressures. However, if an operating division, which manages several subsidiary operations, feels that it cannot pass on the negative effects of local devaluation by raising local prices to maintain dollar-equivalent income levels, then forward contracts are purchased by the Corporate Treasury Department to cover each month's budgeted earnings.

Purchase commitments in the form of future invoices for imported inventory of raw materials and supplies, or for imported equipment, may be hedged. Hedging is done by the Corporate Treasury Department whenever the operating division feels that it cannot pass on local currency devaluation with selling price increases.

On the other hand, the following transactions exposures—with both economic effects and direct effects on the foreign-exchange line of the income statement—are always hedged as soon as a notice of their booking is received by the Corporate Treasury Department:

Receivables in a foreign currency, including bank deposits and accrued interest;

Payables in a foreign currency, including bank loans and accrued interest.

Conversely, translation of the net exposed assets of the local subsidiary balance sheets does not usually affect the foreign-exchange line of the income statement but does affect the special equity section of the consolidated balance sheet. All such exposures, therefore, are not hedged with forward currency contracts. For hyperinflationary countries, however, translation of the net monetary assets gives rise to gains and losses on the foreign-exchange line of the income statement. Thus, such exposures could be hedged, if approval of the chief financial officer were obtained and if efficient forward markets could be found for such currencies. The latter has not been true recently for currencies such as the Brazilian cruzado, Mexican peso, and Argentine australe.

Organization Responsibility

Under the approach outlined above, the Corporate Treasury Department bears the responsibility for all the direct accounting impacts of fluctuation in foreign-exchange rates. Treasury covers all on-balance-sheet transaction exposures, such as foreign-currency-denominated receivables and payables, that affect the foreign-exchange line of the income statement.

The operating divisions bear the responsibility to protect local dollar earnings from any indirect effects of such fluctuations, through pricing policy or requests for hedges. These indirect effects can either be on the local currency profit margins or the dollar-equivalent levels of local-currency earnings. It is clear, therefore, that the foreign-exchange exposure data base and trading must become totally centralized, despite the diversity and decentralization of the operations.

Centralized Netting and Hedging of Exposure

As can be inferred from the above discussion, the largest amounts of foreign exposures designated to be hedged with forward contracts at CBS are the on-balance-sheet transaction exposures—namely, payables and receivables of all types. Such payable and receivable amounts in each nonlocal (nonfunctional) currency are reported into the Corporate Treasury Department. They are then consolidated in the corporate computer model to yield worldwide net exposures in each of the major currencies, similar to the following simplified summary shown in Table 11–A1. Then the net exposure, shown at approximately $40 million in the table, is offset with many forward contracts totaling approximately the same amount.

The corporate computer model allows hedging cross-currency exposures (that is, a guilder payable on CBS Germany's books) as well as individual foreign-currency exposures (that is, a French franc receivable on CBS corporate books in the United States). The long or short position of each exposure in the nonlocal currency is input, and the model calculates the local-currency offset. Then, the net amounts in each currency are calculated and bought or sold forward against the dollar to offset their net short and long positions. The simplified output form presented in Table 11–A2 shows the forward contracts that are required by net short exposures of $75 in French francs. If a forward

Table 11–A1.
NET EXPOSURES AND HEDGES (thousands of US dollars).

	CBS Net Exposure by Division			Corporate Hedges	Net Total
	A	B	C		
Sterling	$(1,339)	$3,440	$4,156	$(6,257)	$0
Deutsche marks	3,467	0	2,163	(5,630)	0
French francs	(193)	0	4,984	(4,791)	0
Italian lire	4,088	0	0	(4,088)	0
Spanish pesetas	825	(449)	(7)	(369)	0
Japanese yen	3,198	(1,322)	0	(1,876)	0
Australian dollars	4,625	1,666	401	(6,692)	0
Canadian dollars	6,631	1,234	0	(7,865)	0
Other	3,046	0	(135)	(2,911)	0
Total	$24,348	$4,569	$11,562	$(40,479)	$0

Table 11–A2.
FOREIGN CURRENCY EXPOSURES, (Dutch
Guilders and French Francs).

| | Nonlocal Currency Exposure | | | Local Currency Exposure |
	$	DG	FF	
Dutch guilders	25	0	150	(100)
French francs	50	100	0	(600)
Total exposures	75	100	150	
Total offsets	0	(100)	(600)	
Net exposures	75	0	(450)	

Dutch guilders/$ = 2 : 1.
French francs/$ = 6 : 1.

Table 11–A3.
FORWARD CONTRACT EXPOSURES,
(US Dollars and French Francs).

| | Nonlocal Currency Exposure | | Local Currency Exposure |
	US dollars	French francs	
US dollars	0	450	(75)
Total exposure	0	450	
Total offsets	(75)	0	
Net exposures	(75)	450	

Table 11–A4.
NET COVERED EXPOSURES.

| | Nonlocal Currency Exposure | | | Local Currency Exposure |
	US dollars	Dutch guilders	French francs	
US dollars	0	0	450	(75)
Dutch guilders	25	0	150	(100)
French francs	50	100	0	(600)
Total exposures	75	100	600	
Total offsets	(75)	(100)	(600)	
Net exposures	0	0	0	

contract is then taken out by CBS to purchase FF450, the net effect
would be entered as in Table 11–A3. When the hedges and exposures
are then consolidated, the net exposure will be totally eliminated, as
shown in Table 11–A4.

At CBS, the goal is to change the hedge contracts constantly, as
reported exposures change, to keep the net level as close to zero as
possible. The net foreign-exchange gains and losses are monitored to
see if they are close to zero, or if we have a problem in our exposure
reports. If errors are found, then the exposure report is corrected.

Corporate Attitude toward Speculation

CBS has a negative attitude toward speculation in foreign exchange. It

287

defines speculation broadly, as the taking of any action based on any viewpoint with respect to foreign-exchange-rate fluctuations in the future. The consistent application of an antispeculative philosophy and policies therefore prohibits the utilization of the following hedging practices commonly used by antispeculative companies and often cited by the foreign-exchange trade press:

Selective hedging, where exposures are hedged only when the currency-rate forecasts call for losses greater than that implied by forward market rates;

Partial hedging of a percentage of exposed long or short positions, based on the currency-rate forecasts and the probabilities of losses greater than that implied by forward market rates;

Selective removal of hedges, where exposures still remain, but the currency-rate forecasts call for losses greater than that implied by forward market rates.

Currency Debt Swaps

Although speculation on exchange-rate forecasts is not allowed, and translation exposures are not hedged under the CBS approach, currency debt swaps designated as hedges of net assets are used to reduce reported interest expense and increase reported earnings without income-statement risk. Merely swapping U.S. dollar-denominated debt for lower-interest-rate foreign-currency debt saves no interest under the CBS policy because covering the principal and interest obligations with forward contracts is required to offset the on-balance-sheet transaction exposures thus created. Then, the premium cost on the contracts approximately offsets the entire nominal interest savings. See the 11½ percent Eurodollar rate and the 11½ percent forward-contract-covered rate in Figure 11–A1.

If the debt swap is made into a currency where there are net assets supporting the operations in that currency's home country, however, then the principal of the debt can become a designated hedge of these net assets. In such cases, any foreign-exchange gains and losses on that principal will be shown only in the special equity section of the balance sheet and by-pass the income statement. This accounting convention recognizes that economically the changes in the value of the liability will be offset by the changes in the value of the underlying assets. The forward contracts need only cover the interest obligations in the foreign currency. See the 2 percent savings from the Eurodollar rate or the 9½ percent net-asset-covered rate in Figure 11–A1.

The currency debt swap shown in Figure 11–A2 may help to highlight all the elements of the structure more clearly. The high 14½ percent dollar interest payments and $60 million of principal (at maturity) are paid to CBS. The company in turn pays the bank only 8½ percent in foreign-currency interest and a principal amount to be determined at

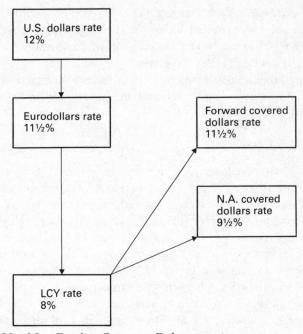

Figure 11–A1. Foreign-Currency Debt.

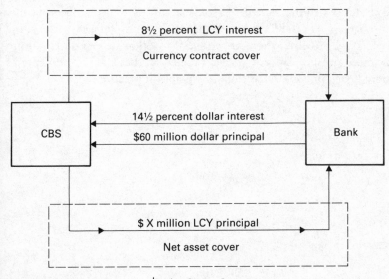

Figure 11–A2. Currency/Debt Swap Structure.

the new exchange rate at maturity. The 8½ percent foreign-currency interest payments are covered with forward contracts represented by the box at the top; but the principal exposure is covered without premium costs by the net asset hedge, represented by the box at the bottom of the figure. Other similar net-income-improvement strategies, which do not require speculating on foreign-exchange-rate trends, have also been utilized by CBS.

Conclusions

CBS Inc. foreign-exchange exposure management has contributed to a reduction in losses on the foreign-exchange line of the income statement of more than 50 percent, or $10 million per year. Also, the hedging program itself has attained a 95 percent efficiency in eliminating potential unexpected gains and losses. The less than $1 million in net losses for currencies and operations included in the forward-contract hedging program can now be solely attributed to premiums paid for low-interest currencies when the forward contracts are taken out. Moreover, these contracts allow more monetary assets to be held in high-interest currencies; and the assets earn additional interest income that nearly perfectly offsets the premium and discount costs.

On the pro-active side, twelve currency swaps and one foreign-currency debt issue have been used in the last three years, with the principal amounts exceeding $300 million. It is estimated that cumulatively—over the lives of the thirteen transactions that vary from a few months to ten years—more than $20 million of interest-expense savings have been generated by these designated hedges.

Unfortunately, there are no comparable figures for other MNCs with which to compare with the above results, but the CBS approach can be contrasted with that described by several treasury staff members in other companies. The CBS foreign-exchange program appears to be more centralized, to cover more of the specific worldwide exposures, and to be more antispeculative. CBS feels, therefore, that it has implemented a pure hedge philosophy as fully as possible in practice.

290

12 International Cash Management and Positioning of Funds

DAVID SPISELMAN

MANY of the functions and operations of domestic and international cash managers are similar. However, cash managers in multinational companies must cope with a multitude of currencies, countries, cultures, languages, and practices. These differences affect the financial staff structure, banking relationships, movement and positioning of funds, and risk and tax considerations. These factors make the job of international cash managers more complex than that of their domestic counterparts.

The corporation's demand for cash balances is determined by transaction, precautionary, and speculative motives. Cash balances, including marketable securities, are held for transaction and precautionary purposes, in anticipation of daily disbursements and as protection against unanticipated payments. The cash manager seeks to reduce cash balances and attain maximum cash availability, employing funds not needed for operations by either investing to earn interest income or repaying borrowings to decrease interest expense.

The corporation's management of receipts and disbursements affects its daily cash position. The general approach is to collect receivables as fast as possible and delay outgoing payables, while maintaining the company's credit standing and relationships with suppliers and customers.

Most corporations use sophisticated techniques to speed up collections and tightly control disbursements. The methods designed to maximize available cash include concentration accounts, lock boxes, and multilateral netting.

Local personnel will be responsible for the bulk of the tasks performed by the foreign affiliate. These people will either be natives who might have some difficulty understanding the linguistic and cultural nuances of the personnel in headquarters to whom they report or come from headquarters and have some difficulty with the norms of the host country.

291

This chapter addresses the principles of international cash management. It discusses management of receipts and disbursements, investments and borrowing, scheduling and forecasting of available cash, and positioning of funds. The chapter concludes with a treatment of technological issues.

FOREIGN CURRENCY AND BANKING RELATIONSHIPS

The key difference between international and domestic cash management is the added dimensions of foreign-currency transaction, translation, and tax, which entail risk and may require hedging. Although the added dimension of multiple currencies complicates matters, many of the solutions have been modified and applied to domestic cash management practices. Assume a multinational corporation based in the United Kingdom, whose revenue is generated primarily through customers in the United Kingdom who pay in pounds sterling. Assume also that the predominant currency of disbursements is the U.S. dollar. If the dollar is weak against the pound sterling, unhedged transactions will result in unexpected gains. Conversely, unexpected losses occur when the dollar strengthens against the pound sterling. These gains and losses have little to do with operations. If the cash flows are grossly mismatched, the corporation can find that its primary business has become that of foreign-exchange speculation.

International banking services are generally similar to those available domestically, but the number of banks in most countries is fewer than in the United States. The services are often driven more by regulatory requirement than by competitive offering and may be uninspiring and antiquated in form and function. The cash manager of a multinational corporation faces vast differences in the information available from each entity abroad.

A significant issue in international financial management is choosing banking service providers. Some services may be provided by the corporate treasury staff, and some by multinational, international, or local banks. Local banks provide the corporate treasurer with some advantages. They may have better access to local currency and a superior branch network. Legislation is likely to favor them over their nonlocal peers, and they may be members of the local clearing house while other banks may have to clear checks through them. However, the local bank is not without its shortcomings. It may have no understanding of international cash management. Finally, the local bank may have little or limited capability in international telecommunications, leaving its corporate clients with traditional correspondent banking as the means of transferring money across country borders.

The international bank can offer the corporation a global multibank multicurrency balance report, while the local bank performs most of the local banking business, including local clearing of checks. Although multinational banks may face formidable competition from their local peers, they have major advantages as well. Their worldwide branch networks are connected through sophisticated international communications systems, offering sophisticated cash management products, services, and systems that maintain internal consistency. However, they are frequently subjected to discriminatory legislation, which restricts their effectiveness.

MANAGING RECEIPTS AND DISBURSEMENTS

Accounts receivables are generated through sales to affiliates and independent foreign buyers. The location, currency, and amount of intercompany receivables is a policy issue in global resource allocation. Two techniques that are useful for this function are reinvoicing centers and leading.

The institutional setting influences receipt and disbursement flows. The differences in services and products offered to treasurers imply a greater importance for forecasting and scheduling of cash receipts anticipated and pending disbursements. The Financial Sales Corporation (FSC), which has replaced its predecessor, the DISC, is a sophisticated form of reinvoicing through a netting center among subsidiaries of a multinational corporation (MNC). This turns the treasury of the MNC into a "bank," where the MNC treasury "loans" money to divisions and subsidiaries that have cash shortfalls, and "invests" money of cash-rich subsidiaries.

International collection methods differ markedly from domestic methods, due in part to different traditions, methods, and cross-border currency flows. In the very worst case, the payor has mailed a check drawn on an overseas bank to the corporation, with the mail typically taking between four and twelve days. Another day or two is expended with the envelope reaching the correct department within the corporation. Again, in a day or two the check reaches the lead bank of the corporation, which routes it to the bank's collection department. The collection department then mails the check to the paying bank on which the check was written, using another four to twelve days in the mail. In effect, between ten and twenty-eight days are spent in float prior to beginning the collection process, which itself can take a month.

The postal systems outside the United States are relatively slow in mail delivery, with the prize going to Italy. In one mail float study, mail traveling between two points in Rome was measured as moving at about 600 feet per day. Surprisingly, the "post banks" that exist outside the United States do an acceptable job of moving money between individuals and corporations, through "giros," to pay for goods and services. In the United Kingdom, for example, the majority of working

293

people prefer to use the post bank's giro to make payments rather than use checks drawn on a bank.

The method of speeding collections most similar to the U.S. practice is through the lock box. Letters of credit are often used to accommodate international transactions. Where checks denominated in foreign currency have been used as the method of payment in a cross-border transaction, an international collections service, provided by a bank, is used to obtain the funds for the supplier.

The lock box was created many years ago in the United States, and until recently there was no comparable equivalent outside North America. Its purpose is to eliminate the time span between receipt of the remittance by a corporation and its deposit into their bank. The arrangement is usually on a regional basis. The main advantage of a lock box system is that checks are deposited at banks sooner and become collected balances sooner than if they are processed by the corporation prior to deposit. Some banks in Europe and Asia have established lock boxes in those places. The effect is to decrease collection float by substituting domestic mail time for international mail time and by eliminating the corporation's internal processing float. The net impact is to speed international collections by as much as six to twenty-two days.

Conceptually, the lock box is identical to its domestic model, except that checks mailed to the lock box may cross country borders or be drawn on a currency requiring the lock box bank to use international collections to obtain available funds. The lock box bank obtains the right to access a post office box to which the corporation directs incoming mailed payments accompanied by invoice. The bank may process the invoices and checks in any way acceptable to both parties, with high-volume low-dollar-amount mass processing referred to as "retail lock box" processing. Customized processing is provided to accommodate special invoices or other special handling, referred to as "wholesale lock box" processing, at a higher fee per item. Checks are deposited promptly into an account at the lock box bank, and invoices are shipped to the corporation, sometimes in a magnetic media to be processed by the corporation's accounts receivable system.

Some corporations take special care to ensure that all mailed check payments are directed to a local lock box, thereby also almost guaranteeing that the check will be in the currency accepted within the particular country. This intercept point typically reduces the mail time to a total of one to two days and almost always eliminates international collection float. Domestic clearing items are typically credited to the corporation's account within one to three additional days, and this float is not reducible except through substituting an electronic payment.

The oldest and most commonly used methods of financing international trade are the letter of credit and the documentary collection. The documentary collection is the most common form of international transaction, with no guarantees made by any of the banks involved about the payment.

The giro system for payments is a common substitute for checking accounts in many countries. The giro is an accepted and established method used by individuals to render payments for goods and services. The service works as a form of postal money order, and many of the individuals issuing this form of payment do it in preference to checks drawn on banks. Because the service is sponsored by the country's government, individuals who do not trust banks are assumed to be the primary customers.

Positioning of Funds

Multinational corporations are centralizing cash management on a global basis. Cash management requires a location perspective that includes the currency in which funds are held and the country where holdings are placed. In an MNC, political, tax, foreign-exchange, and liquidity factors restrict the movement of funds. These constraints create the environment for special consideration of the international funds positioning function. Various techniques exist to move funds internationally.

A parallel loan provides the corporate financial manager with a method of reducing the risk. For example, a U.S. corporation and a Colombian corporation might each be interested in establishing a factory in the other's home country. Using parallel loans, each corporation borrows an equivalent amount from the other, in the location and currency of the country where the facility is to be built. The U.S. corporation will repay its loan to the Colombian corporation in amounts that, at the day the deal is undertaken, equal those that the Colombian corporation repays to the U.S. corporation. Except for the hedging that either firm might initiate to limit exposure to changes in the relative value of the repayments in its obligation to its partner, each party has virtually no default risk; it has title to the other's asset and possession of the facility in the other's country. If either were to default, or if their countries were to go to war and sequester each other's foreign assets, each corporation could simply exchange title with the other. If foreign-currency controls were to be put in place, it would simply have some impact on the timing of the simultaneous equal repayments that each party is obligated to make to the other. Parallel loans are not an acceptable procedure everywhere. Often either an international bank or a pair of local banks in each of the countries involved will act as intermediary.

There are some rather sophisticated methods of electronically moving funds around the world, but the speed is often reduced by government regulation, trade, and currency controls. Money positioning issues concern the location and currency of funds. The corporate financial manager seeks to eliminate foreign-exchange rate and country risk that arise through timing differences in the relative values of foreign-currency payments, between the time that goods are sold and payments are collected. Over the years, methods have been developed by corporate financial managers to hedge, control, and monitor these risks. Recent surveys indicate that minimizing the risk and cost of foreign-currency exchange remain one of the top two objectives for international financial managers.

The Clearing House Interbank Payment System (CHIPS) is one of many "net settlement" electronic funds clearing systems that exist. CHIPS is a subscribed system whose members are most of the major domestic and international banks in New York City. Information about all cash transfers that were executed between member institutions are stored during the day, and at the end of the day the transfers and their settlements actually occur, through the member accounts at the Federal Reserve Bank. Most international U.S. dollar transfers clear through CHIPS.

The Society for Worldwide Interbank Financial Telecommunications (SWIFT) is a subscriber international communications system with more than 1,000 members. The system routes cable messages between member banks, in a prescribed format. Cash transfers initiated through SWIFT are settled either through CHIPS or through the correspondent banking system, which consists of book entry transfers. SWIFT also carries information on bank balances of corporate account holders for balance reporting purposes and detailed information connected to financial transactions.

The oldest concept in correspondent banking is the notion of two banks in different countries, each having money on deposit in accounts with each other. Each bank refers to its account with the other bank as the "nostro" and the other bank's account with it as the "vostro" account. Most international wire transfers and many interbank transfers not using wires involve debiting or crediting balances at these correspondent accounts. The process involves book entry correspondent transfers. Where a payment is made between two banks that have no correspondent relationship, the procedure usually involves routing the transfer through a third bank that has correspondent relationships with both of the principal banks.

Back-to-back loans are substitutes for intracompany international funds transfers and foreign-exchange transactions, where the need for cash in the receiving country is for a short duration and there would soon be a reverse set of transactions to return the funds to the originating party. For example, a German subsidiary of a U.S. corporation might need cash for thirty days while it awaits a payment from a local customer. A back-to-back loan could be initiated by the U.S. parent corporation, through a deposit by the parent into a U.S. branch or subsidiary of a German bank, which then agrees to hold the cash as collateral for a loan in Germany to the U.S. corporation's German subsidiary. The corporation pays the interest-rate differential approximating what it could earn if it invested the U.S. dollar deposit while the German subsidiary borrowed deutche marks abroad. The banking system typically absorbs the risk of foreign-exchange fluctuations.

Investments and Borrowings

Conceptually, international and domestic portfolio management are similar. However, the need to deal with multiple currrencies complicates the activity. The objective remains to ensure safety of principal while placing the correct amount of funds at the correct place at the proper time in the right currency. Cash excesses or shortfalls in an unneeded currency remain the most serious problem. Although the financial manager may choose to move money from one country to another, often it is cheaper to invest in the country with the excess cash and use the investment principal as collateral for a corresponding loan in the cash deficient country. Borrowing arrangements are similar to those of the U.S. marketplace, but investments have a few additional outlets.

The major added forms of investment typically used by international corporate financial managers are Eurodollar time deposits, banker's acceptances (BAs), and Eurodollar certificates of deposit (CDs). These forms of investment have been in existence for many years and have well-established markets.

The sweep account is a concentration account where the funds constituting the compensating balance are referred to as the "peg" amount and where all excess funds are automatically invested overnight in a convenient form. Such accounts are now becoming available in the United States but have long been a fixture in international finance.

INTERNATIONAL SCHEDULING OF FUNDS AND FORECASTING

Scheduling means, "You know what you've got, but you don't know exactly when." Forecasting means, "You don't know when you are going to have it, but you can accurately guess how much it's going to be." Forecasting and scheduling of cash receipts and disbursements are more difficult in a multiple currency environment. Something more sophisticated than a microcomputer worksheet or spreadsheet program is required. The use of a sophisticated time-series analysis system can greatly assist the treasury staff in avoiding the type of errors that computer worksheets often generate.

The cash-schedule worksheet should display cash available and cash needed by currency within bank and city. The cash forecast procedure

297

should draw on this cash schedule, and on historical data of payments received and payments made during the past years, to account for trends, business cycles, seasonality, and day-of-month and day-of-week effects. Information should include currency type billed and currency of payment, date of invoice, date of funds' clearing (into or out of a corporate bank account), and customer or supplier demographic information, including geographic location and size.

The international cash schedule of incoming and outgoing payments has two major complications beyond the domestic version. First and foremost, multiple currencies and their value relative to each other must be considered to facilitate development of an operational or tactical plan to move or borrow/invest funds. Second, due to the international collections process, there are much longer time spans to consider, making the scheduling process more difficult to perform by a human.

In the simplest example, a corporation with offices in the United States and the United Kingdom has two currencies and international collections extending about six times further into the future than domestic payments. The longer collections time is a result of complications in the international collections process that involves multiple banks in different countries. In creating and using a cash schedule, these complications make an unclear dividing line between operational and tactical decisionmaking for the funds-positioning process. Rather than limiting operational considerations to the current day, week, or month, and letting tactical decisions run from there through the current quarter or year, the financial manager must also include international cash flows whose operational impact may remain unclear for additional months. There is often an additional requirement to hedge these international cash flows into the corporation's reporting currency, and this implies an additional process for the individual responsible for preparing the cash schedule.

The process of preparing an international cash schedule is simple. There are two major steps—data collection and entry, and information analysis. First, the financial manager must obtain from the banks and other corporations with which they deal the payments collected and those in the process of being collected into the corporate checking account, by currency and location. Second, a list of all maturing investments and borrowings must be obtained by currency and location. Next, a list of the invoices issued to other corporations must be obtained, since these represent incoming payments.

Data collected must be entered into a worksheet, where the column headings are the dates starting with today in the first numerical column. The row headings are the currency, within which the subrow heading is the type of cash flow. The most minor row heading is the location of the account into which the funds will flow in or out. Each bank/investment/ledger account number is listed along with its account type, and the cash flow amounts are posted into the columns by day into the future. In Table 12–1, a question mark implies a numerical result calculated by a worksheet formula, and a dash implies data entered after a decision made by the financial manager.

The second step, information analysis, involves determining where money is needed and deciding how to obtain it there, in the correct

Table 12–1.
INTERNATIONAL CASH SCHEDULING WORKSHEET.

US$/London	12/12	12/13	12/14	12/15	12/16
Balances:					
Checking:					
Bank 1					
12345678	83,658	?	?	?	?
23456789	38,579	?	?	?	?
34567890	3,288	?	?	?	?
Investments:					
Broker 1					
987654321	39,746	?	?	?	?
Borrowings:					
Bank 2					
87654321	⟨8,474⟩	?	?	?	?
Net cash balance	165,271	?	?	?	?
Bank transactions:					
Clearings in:					
Deposits:					
Bank 1					
12345678	546	0	893	?	?
23456789	0	7,689	14,820	?	?
34567890	3,467	15,832	9,768	?	?
EFT:					
Bank 1					
12345678	10,000	—	—	—	—
23456789	0	—	—	—	—
34567890	0	—	—	—	—
Clearings out:					
Checks:					
Bank 1					
12345678	0	0	⟨1,163⟩	?	?
23456789	⟨25,564⟩	⟨7,654⟩	0	?	?
34567890	⟨5,378⟩	⟨948⟩	⟨4,587⟩	?	?
EFT:					
Bank 1					
12345678	0	—	—	—	—
23456789	0	—	—	—	—
34567890	⟨10,000⟩	—	—	—	—
Credit uses:					
Investments made:					
Broker 1					
987654321	⟨3,564⟩	—	—	—	—
Repayment due:					
Bank 2					
87654321	⟨324⟩	0	⟨8,006⟩	?	?
Credit sources:					
Investments maturing:					
Broker 1					
987654321	5,678	8,604	7,693	?	?
Borrowings made:					
Bank 2					
87654321	57,567	—	—	—	—
Total available cash	187,688	211,201	230,614	?	?

Source: David Spiselman

currency. Some factors cannot easily be included in a simple worksheet. The fees associated with electronic funds transfers, investments, and borrowings and the implied opportunity cost of float are not present in this example but could be placed in a more sophisticated model. However, the decision to move funds across a border and then move them back to the original account versus the alternative of arranging a back-to-back loan would require a more careful analysis than what could be accomplished by using this model. Financial managers typically perform this function using "what if" analysis where the numbers are determined through trial and error. A slight improvement is to place calculations in the worksheet that iterate toward an optimal solution without human intervention.

After preparing the schedule, it is merged with a forecast, which accounts for projected cash flows between the operational period's end and the strategic period's start. The forecast is therefore a tactical procedure. This process is easier by far than what follows it: Transaction execution to implement decisions made.

Methods of Cash Forecasting

Traditional cash-forecasting methodologies are procedures designed to predict net cash within an acceptable error rate over some predetermined time period. Those methods presented below are a hybrid of traditional and new techniques, designed to improve the accuracy of cash forecasting and other high-variance items.

The concept of a distribution forecast assumes that some predictable pattern of funds clearings follows certain events that can be grouped into classes. The classic example is payroll check encashment and clearings, which tend to follow an almost immutable pattern: Payroll checks issued on day 1 will clear out of the employer's account over a period of just a few days, with a similarly fixed percentage spread over the days in a near-identical pattern with each issuance of a payroll. For example, measured in total dollars, a $1 million payroll for a small factory in the Mid West might typically see $400,000 clear out of the account on day 1, $300,000 clear out on day 2, $200,000 clear out on day 3, and the remainder on day 4. Monitoring the actual amounts and adjusting the forecasts is very simple to do.

Autoregressive integrated moving average (ARIMA) methods account for the month-to-month variations across years and the year-to-year variations across months for any variable influenced by trend, cycle, or seasonality factors. If these factors are present, they are likely to be recognized by the people who deal with the affected variable, and the benefit of forecasting is a quantification of the factor. In general, the following methodology can be applied to a forecasting problem, with the forecaster determining the value of weights and factors within the algorithm:

$$Sn = \frac{\{(Sw \times ((X[n-1]) \times Sfn)) + (Tw \times ((X[n-12]) \times (Tfn)))\}}{\{(Sw + Tw)\}}$$

where

Sw and Tw = the relative weighting factors of seasonality and trend;

$X[n-i]$ = the actual observation for the period occurring i months ago;

Sfn = the seasonality factor, computed as a weighted running percentage change from month to month within a year, in the formula

$$Sfn = 1. + E\frac{\{(X[n-i]) - (X[n-(1+i)])\}}{\{(X[n-(1+i)])\}}/\{i/12\}$$

$i = 12, 24, ..., 60$

and

Tfn = the trend factor, computed as a weighted running percentage change within a month from year to year in the formula

$$Tfn = 1. + E\frac{\{(X[n-i]) - (X[n-(12+i)])\}}{\{(X[n-(12+i)])\}}/\{i/12\}$$

$i = 12, 24, ..., 48$

with the condition that the weights, ($\{i/12\}$), for the trend and seasonality factors may be altered to emphasize more recent observations.

Although this methodology is adaptable to most situations, it is a small piece of the forecasting procedure specifically designed for the financial working of short-term corporate finance. Optimizing the weights can be done by hand but it is possible to automate the optimization and dramatically diminish the human labor requirements of the procedure. The remainder of the procedure follows below.

To obtain reliable forecasts, information about the corporation's pending payables and anticipated receivables is an absolute requirement. Obtaining this information is easiest when the accounting systems and treasury systems are integrated. This means that the systems can share data. From an integrated approach an improved understanding of the financial workings of the business itself can also be gained: All of the financial flows through the corporation and their timings, in support of all business activities.

Information can be derived from integrating subledger systems with the treasury management systems. If there is a normal yield curve, forecasts that combine accounting and bank information can enable the financial manager to gain more interest income or lower interest expense from investing or borrowing over a longer term. Forecasting capabilities can also provide you with an advanced warning of the net changes in cash.

Information within the treasury work station reflects payments that have cleared and payments that have just been deposited. It does not tell you much of value about the future. Forecasting using only that information is like steering a car with the rear-view mirror. The other half of the picture is derived from accounting information that can be found on the mainframe computer. The original forecasting systems that used only the bank data were not always accurate. Those forecasting systems that originally ran on the mainframes did not work much better because they too were working with only half the data, but they did use a lot of computer resources and did not necessarily make friends with the systems manager. Now things have finally changed, through the possibility of systems integration.

The bank systems almost always supply good summary information that is adequate for cash scheduling. The scheduling problem is relatively easy. The financial manager can do that on the kind of worksheet that is often provided on the bank's treasury work station. The banks usually refer to the scheduling problem as the forecasting module. It is not. This is compounded by the cash basis of treasury information, which is not compatible with the accrual basis of accounting, creating a soluble but challenging data integration problem.

For the purposes of forecasting, let us examine information from the accounting systems, not the general ledgers but the subledgers. Three types of information are of interest:

1 Some checks are received each day after the bulk mailing invoice date. You know from where the checks were received and when they were mailed from examining the postmarks on the envelopes and determining the clearing patterns. All this can be done using information from an automated accounts receivable system if within the system demographic information is maintained about the parties with which you do business.

2 With accounts payable the pattern of clearings into expense posting accounts occurs on a very regular basis and this can be forecasted with more accuracy than the receivables. The receivables problem amounts to a curve-fitting problem. Payables are more of a scheduling problem.

3 The payroll system is the easiest to prepare a cash schedule for because almost always very regular set patterns appear for the funds that clear out. This information is obtainable through the bank systems.

The next logical step, after resolving where to find the data, is to develop a forecasting technology that works within your own environment. There are many good methodologies available, each of which has a special use. For example, linear regression is good for long-term trends. Trends go on for the term of a strategic plan—a very long time. Multiple regression can determine the cycle within the trend. Box Jenkins is very good for forecasts of seasonality. Finally, Professors Stone and Wood came up with a day-of-month and day-of-week forecasting system called a payment cycle forecasting system that works very well for disbursements. Used in a vacuum, each of these methodologies has its own type of errors, which are rather perverse because they do not reflect each of the other methodology's strengths. For example, a Stone and Wood model used alone would not reflect seasonality, cycle, or trend. It is possible to use all four of these methodologies to forecast all four of these kinds of factors simultaneously. If you examine a curve for disbursements on a given week, it is possible to difference out, or "layer down," that curve. Remove the trend, remove the cycle, remove the seasonality, and take out the day of month and day of week; each of those factors sits on top of the one below it. Through this procedure of sequential decomposition you can create a more accurate forecast. The general procedure is to successively model and subtract out each of those factors: day of month, day of week, seasonality, business cycle, and trend. Model each factor, separately, and always difference the residual series so that the more global forecast generates a baseline flowing under the more local series under observation.

The first step is to model the trend line, a baseline underlying the series. Cut that out and flatten the series down; just subtract it out. Then try to extract the cycle. Take that out and it will flatten the series again. Repeat this procedure until you can get to the most local series, which is day of week. Continually subtract out the series above it. The information on a mainframe can be downloaded to a micro. There are no effective mainframe packages currently available to perform this function right now. Adequate micro packages are available now, and more are coming.

Remember to examine the errors that your forecast generates. If they have a pattern, you can improve the results of the forecast; include a forecast of the pattern for the errors. When just a random series remains, the job is finished.

Trend is a linear component and relatively easy to implement. The cycle is slightly more difficult. Whatever it is that causes your budget to change and run a pattern over a period of years—say, three to five years—would comprise the cycle component of the forecast. These factors could be pulled out by multiple regression or a harmonic filtering type of forecast. The cycle factor is information that can be derived by analyzing the numbers stored in the accounting system, which looks back into the past over a long period of time, to create a formula that you can apply to the numbers that are in the computer now.

The day-of-the-month factors include rent, electric, and telephone. Usually just a couple of days after payments are mailed, the money will

303

clear out of the account. Assume about five days for the money to clear out of the account.

Day-of-week factors are exemplified by payroll: If it is a biweekly payroll, the nonpayroll week probably will be a lot flatter for the day-of-week curve. A payment-cycle forecast will work fine because when you use the "day off" methodologies you deal with a scheduling problem, not a forecasting problem.

The next step is to combine these mini-forecasts together, by adding them. Because we originally "differenced" each factor from the aggregate series through subtraction, this step reconstitutes the forecasted series.

A computer can do this better than a human being. Most technologies suggest that we forecast aggregates, and this works adequately when there is a relatively simple forecast to be performed manually; the idea of creating a baseline is statistically unacceptable when we are taught to see zero as the median point of the forecast. Making zero the baseline point of the forecast actually works better in a computerized procedure.

The information should be downloaded in a summary form that retains the essential characteristics of the things you want to forecast. For example, when you pay suppliers or vendors, you want to know what the clearing pattern approach is for them. Are they in the same country and region? Will the check clear out in one day? Do they use the same bank? Will it clear out that night? The objective is to retain the demographic characteristics that relate to the item being forecasted.

A few additional helpful points are in order. Do not attempt to forecast a specific point value for money: You want to forecast with a range. There is an old Polish proverb: "Big target makes sharpshooter." If you aim from far away at a distant point, you are likely to miss; that is why they give ranges on the weather forecast.

The interval is derived by computing the standard deviation of the variable to be forecast and then matching the standard deviation to how much accuracy you need. If you want 66 percent probability of being correct, bracket your estimate plus or minus one standard deviation. If you want 95 percent accuracy of being right, bracket by two standard deviations; 98 percent is a three standard deviation bracket. If your forecasts consistently fall beyond your acceptable interval, that is a signal that the technique you are using does not work.

Categorize the receipt or disbursement according to float characteristics for mail time, processing time, and clearing time. Group vendors, customers, or employees (depending whether you are forecasting payables, receivables, or payroll, respectively) into these categories. You will be left with many small forecasting problems, each with a small potential error, instead of a large aggregated multiplicative error. These small errors will be more easy to identify, control, and correct.

Break down the components into "certain" and "uncertain" components. Certain components are to be scheduled; you just need to know when, but you know how much and you can schedule the cash inflow or outflow for a particular day. The forecasted components are those where you do not know exactly how much and when but can statistically make a good guess. The forecasted and scheduled components should be handled separately, otherwise it might make the inevitable forecasting errors very difficult to reconcile and adjust later on.

Finally, expect your error rate to increase as the forecast moves further away from the present time. You should generate your forecast every day, or at least often enough to compensate for disintegration of forecasting accuracy as the forecast moves further out into the time horizon.

What can be achieved through forecasting is the major benefit for the financial manager: The benefit of planning. Through planning you can move from cash management reactiveness to working capital management proactiveness.

Reinvoicing and Netting

Reinvoicing is designed to manage intercompany receivables in an environment where the corporate treasury function is not highly centralized. The reinvoicing center can be placed abroad so that the function bypasses foreign-exchange fees, risks, and delays deemed to have the highest level of expense. The procedure is otherwise very similar to netting. In effect, all exposure is concentrated at the reinvoicing center, with title to the goods passing to and from the netting center while the physical goods travel directly between the subsidiaries as they did before instituting the reinvoicing procedure.

The quantitative benefits to netting include reduction in the frequency of misdirected and duplicate payments, and a reduction in the total head count for the global corporate treasury function. Also, centralization of the exposure management function reduces the risk of continuing unhedged foreign-exchange losses. The qualitative advantages include consolidated record keeping and management reporting, improved tax planning, and less risk from accidentally unhedged foreign-exchange positions.

The things to consider prior to deciding whether to establish a reinvoicing center are issues related to cost, international regulation, and systems capability. These centers are expensive to maintain. Some countries, usually those with weak currencies, either restrict or regulate the center's operations, and some countries prohibit the existence of this practice. Other countries, such as the Netherlands and Panama, are considered to be excellent tax environments for locating a reinvoicing center. Both treasury expertise and foreign-exchange skills are required for the proper operation of a reinvoicing center, and excellent account-

305

ing systems and treasury systems are required for effective operations. These systems should be integrated to maximize performance.

Netting of payments is useful where a large number of separate foreign-exchange transactions occur between affiliates. Netting reduces the foreign-exchange settlement costs of what would otherwise be a large number of crossing spot transactions. Multilateral netting systems are usually maintained in a single currency of measurement.

To envision the operations of a netting operation, assume a multinational corporation that has four international subsidiaries: New York (NY), Brussels (B), London (L), and Amsterdam (A). Each buys and sells goods and services to each of the other subsidiaries. Without an international netting network to minimize the intracompany payments necessary to settle current outstanding intracompany invoices, the international payments look as depicted in Figure 12–1. For the sake of convenience, all currency amounts are expressed in U.S. dollar amounts. In a bilateral netting configuration the number of transactions and total dollars to be moved would be reduced as shown in Figure 12–2.

In a multilateral netting configuration using a clearing center, the number of transactions and dollars to be moved could be reduced even further, as shown in Figure 12–3. The total costs saved through using a multilateral netting arrangement will vary greatly from one corporation to another but often are quite large. The additional control achieved through using a single office for the management of intercompany payments provides a major qualitative benefit.

International Finance Companies

The international finance company can factor or buy the receivables of an international corporation, using its local presence to collect the

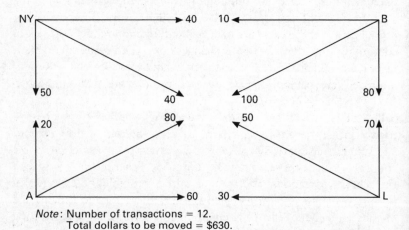

Note: Number of transactions = 12.
Total dollars to be moved = $630.

306 **Figure 12–1.** Intercompany Payments Flows without Netting.

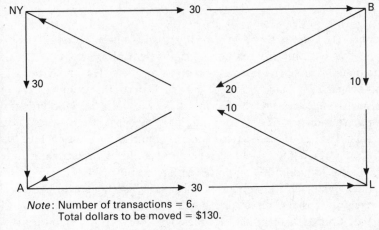

Note: Number of transactions = 6.
Total dollars to be moved = $130.

Figure 12-2. Bilateral Netting.

checks and deposit them within the country where the payor is located. This practice is identical to its domestic counterpart. Where the finance company is a subsidiary of the international corporation, the finance company is (similar to) a FSC or DISC.

Leading and Lagging

These two procedures are used to hedge against potential swings in the rates of foreign exchange among intracompany payments. If the future rate of exchange is expected to decrease the value of the receipt at corporate headquarters, then the payment may be precipitated and made before it is due. This is leading the payment. Lagging the payment is the reverse—delaying the payment to benefit from an exchange rate that is growing stronger for the payor's currency.

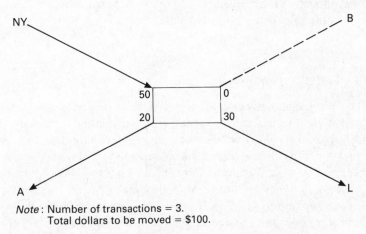

Note: Number of transactions = 3.
Total dollars to be moved = $100.

Figure 12-3. Multilateral Netting.

Pooling

Pooling is a process that aggregates the available balances of a corporation that has multiple accounts at the same bank. For example, if a corporation has twelve checking accounts for its twelve wholly owned subsidiaries at the same branch of a bank, the accounts could have their balances pooled to greatly decrease the probability of an overdraft. Those subsidiaries having cash surpluses subsidize those with cash deficits. This service is available in some countries of Western Europe but not in the United States. It is permitted in Belgium, Germany, and the United Kingdom and permitted with restriction in the Netherlands, Italy, and France. Although it is permissible in Spain and Switzerland, it is rarely used there. Other places where it is possible to use pooling include Canada, Argentina, Hong Kong, Korea, Australia, and New Zealand.

Pooling greatly facilitates control over cash within a country by using a single bank. The pooling bank becomes the concentration bank within that country. Because cash shortfalls in some subsidiaries may be partially or even totally offset by cash excesses in other subsidiaries, interest expense can be greatly reduced. Intercountry pooling is difficult or impossible except through the use of a finance company. However, an international bank might provide some arrangement to permit cash shortfalls in one country to be offset by excesses in another, using book entries. Of course, some accommodation would have to be made for the changing foreign-exchange rates for the countries involved. The limiting factors are the requirement to deal with a single branch of the bank within that country, the inevitable reduction in the local financial manager's autonomy, and the additional governmental regulation or influence that often follows those using the practice. Central money posts are usually maintained in major money centers such as London, New York, and Hong Kong and in tax haven countries such as Luxembourg and the Bahamas. Use of a centralized depository system implies use of as many banks as are desired.

TECHNOLOGY

The technological advances of recent years have altered the state of international financial management, in terms of methods, practices, and bank relationships, as corporations have begun to recognize the value and competitive importance of automated support. Treasury management systems—whether supplied by a bank or built by the corporation's systems staff, whether interfacing with banks only or also with the corporate accounting systems—have become commonplace in the typical treasury operation. Systems do not replace people; they make them more productive. The cost includes building or buying the system, training the people to use it, and enhancing it when changes in the business require automated support.

Treasury Management Systems

Perhaps the most illustrative difference between domestic and international roles for a cash manager is the difference in requirements for an automated treasury management system. Systems typically available for domestic use are functionally complete but are operationally difficult or even impossible for anyone to use, but the problems are exacerbated for international users. Domestic systems provide functions that include banking relations, portfolio management, cashbook accounting, cash scheduling, and forecasting. Operations include data collection, data analysis, and transaction execution. Work for a single user location is usually sequenced so that operations are critical, while locations containing more staff are typically functionally organized. Because the multinational corporation tends to have its cash management staff distributed across the globe, each location tends to operate alone for that city, country, and region. To be easy to use, the system should be operationally organized rather than functionally organized. The advantage is that while collecting information about investments and borrowings, receipts collected and payments disbursed, and funds transfers executed the previous day, the local cash manager need not bounce up and across the menu of functional activities. For example, to determine if there is a cash excess or shortfall, the cash manager must examine balances from the bank accounts, available and unused short-term credit lines, and portfolio accounts for investments. Although these are different functional areas, the activity that unites them is that of "data collection." The optimal system would be organized with a cross-index to access an operation through a function, or a function from an operation, by being command-driven instead of, or as well as, menu-driven.

International cash management requires some activities that are not widely available through treasury management software built and vended in the United States. International reinvoicing and netting are available from few software vendors, and foreign-exchange activities are rarely found in these systems. The decision support activities that might assist the cash manager in hedging or controlling risk are missing from U.S. designs. However, European-designed systems have some of these features.

Anyone considering the acquisition of a treasury management system for international use should consider the issue of data security before deciding on a course of action. This is not wholly a soluble problem. Authentication and encryption merely keep someone from another location from pretending to be at your location. Security must also be provided within the corporate office.

Another concern is that the technology will change at a dizzying pace, with hardware and software that seems adequate on the date of purchase appearing to be frustrating and limiting within months, in comparison with what is becoming available. While time to obsolescence is longer for the more robust mainframe systems, which can be custom built by the corporation's systems staff, the latter must be trained to understand the treasury business functions, and management must learn how to communicate effectively with them. This is not a trivial task, and quantums more money will be spent on custom-building a system than in buying a packaged system that almost fits. The more one has to rely on a system that does not perform as described by the systems staff, the more one might wish that one-fifth the money was spent on buying a package. However, the more one has to deal with software that does not even begin to work in the way that the treasury function works, the more one might wish that the money had been available to custom-build a system.

Bank Services

Many of the large U.S. money center banks provide worldwide balance reporting and transaction execution facilities through their global telecommunications networks. These networks are available around the clock to execute payment transactions. Even some of the traditionally manual processes, such as issuance of a letter of credit, can be executed using a bank-provided software package within the corporation's microcomputer linked to the bank's computer through a local telephone connection. Services provided by non-U.S. banks are sometimes less expensive and sometimes more sophisticated but are typically nonstandard from one country to the next. It might help the corporate builder of a multinational financial management system to determine if the local methodology can be integrated with global methodologies supplied by international banks. If it is worthwhile to have a worldwide report of balances and transactions, the country-specific technologies should be avoided.

Systems Integration

Integration across corporate systems is the other unresolved issue of major importance. Information from banks and brokers must be integrated within the treasury management system to yield a full picture of available monetary balances. This information must be added to the pending payables and receivables from the accounting systems, yielding a cash schedule for planning and hedging purposes. The information flow is bidirectional: The accounting systems can make use of information that is the residue of treasury-initiated transactions, such as funds transfers and the fees from banking transactions. A system that can automatically feed this information to the posting pool of the accounting system for manual review on a CRT screen prior to their acceptance would reduce their work efforts in dealing with the international treasury function.

CONCLUSIONS

International cash management remains a mixture of antiquated and traditional practices combined with leading-edge technologies. Those responsible for making sense of the corporation's international financial transactions are themselves dispersed across the face of the earth and are unlikely to share customs. English is probably the common language and dollars are the most common currency of translation.

Some practices are hundreds or even thousands of years old. However, most fascinating may be that even the oldest practices are now being automated, and many practices that for years were associated only with international finance are now emerging in altered form as new domestic methods of hedging risk. The practice of international cash management and positioning of funds is likely to continue providing domestic practitioners with new ideas.

REFERENCES

BOKOS, WILLIAM J., AND ANNE P. CLINKARD, "Multilateral Netting," *Journal of Cash Management* (June/July 1983): 36.

GILLESPIE, RICHARD, "Workstation Technology Dominates Conference," *Pension and Investment Age* (November 12, 1984): 25.

KOENIG, PETER, "How Competition Is Sharpening Cash Management," *Institutional Investor* (June 1982): 227.

MANNING, GEORGE, AND DAVID SPISELMAN, "How to Manage the Shrinking Float," *Boardroom Reports* (May 18, 1981): 9.

MARSHALL, R. G. CLARE, "Managing Short-Term Multicurrency Portfolios," *Journal of Cash Management* (November/December 1984): 64.

PARKINSON, KENNETH L., "Dealing with the Problems of International Cash Management," *Journal of Cash Management* (February/March 1983): 16.

SANGER, DAVID E., "Multinationals Worry as Countries Regulate Data Crossing Borders," *Wall Street Journal* (August 26, 1981): 1.

SOKOL, MARSHALL, AND DAVID SPISELMAN, "Automation—A Brief Overview," *Corporate Accounting* (Winter 1985): 92.

SOKOL, MARSHALL, AND DAVID SPISELMAN, "Integrating Cash Management and Accounting Systems: Measuring the Stakes," *Corporate Accounting* (Fall 1984): 74.

SPISELMAN, DAVID, "The Role of Automation in Cash Management," in *Current Asset Management*, edited by J. KALLBERG AND K. PARKINSON (New York: John Wiley, 1984).

13 MNC Taxation

RICHARD M. HAMMER AND CHARLES T. CRAWFORD

THIS chapter is an overview of a very complex subject. It is intended to alert the business executive who is not a tax specialist to the basic tax problems in MNC operations and to planning opportunities. Action should not be taken without professional advice.

Basis of Taxation

Most of the major industrial countries tax the worldwide income of resident corporations. The United States taxes the worldwide income of corporations *incorporated* in the United States, under a principle that recognizes only place of incorporation as determinative of corporate residence. A number of countries, most notably the United Kingdom and many Commonwealth countries, tax the worldwide income of resident corporations determined without regard to place of incorporation. In these countries, corporate residence generally is the place where a company's "mind and management" are located.[1] A few countries, including Canada, tax the worldwide income of companies if they are *either* incorporated or resident locally.

A few countries do not tax the foreign business income of locally resident or incorporated companies. This territorial system of taxation is followed to varying degrees by France, Switzerland, and Hong Kong.

Foreign Tax Credit

The United States, and the other countries that tax their resident corporations on worldwide income, mitigate double taxation by way of a credit against home country taxes for income taxes paid to foreign governments (that is, a full offset dollar-for-dollar for foreign taxes against home-country taxes). In the case of the United States (and several other countries offering the foreign tax credit), such credit includes an indirect credit on receipt of dividends from foreign subsidiaries with respect to foreign corporate income taxes paid by the subsidiaries on the earnings out of which such dividends are paid. In some cases, this indirect credit is extended downward through tiers of foreign corporations (three in the case of the United States.).

313

The foreign tax credit generally is limited to the home country tax on foreign source income. Some countries apply this limitation on the overall basis—that is, for measuring the limitation, the taxes paid to all foreign countries are aggregated and compared to (that is, limited to) the home country tax attributable to all foreign source income. Some countries use a "per country" limitation method, under which a limitation is calculated separately for each foreign country's tax—that is, the credit for tax paid to each foreign country is limited to the *home country* tax on income arising from sources in that foreign country. The per country approach is much more restrictive because it does not allow for averaging foreign income taxes to maximize utilization of credits. Under the overall approach, the taxes paid high- and low-rate countries are averaged. Another approach is the "per item" approach used by the United Kingdom, under which the limitation is calculated, within each country, for each item of income (such as dividends and interest) arising in that country. The United States uses a form of overall approach, but under the 1986 Act, by segregating income into ten different classifications of income for computing the limitation, the United States severely limits the averaging of high- and low-taxed income.[2]

A major obstacle in attempting to maximize a U.S. MNC's foreign tax credit is the requirement to allocate against its foreign source income an appropriate portion of U.S.-incurred expenses. Generally, the over-riding tax planning goal of a U.S. MNC is full utilization of its foreign tax credits.

Deferral of Tax on Foreign Subsidiaries

Corporations generally are not taxed on the income of their foreign subsidiaries until the income is remitted to the parent. This is known as "deferral." A growing number of countries tax certain earnings of tax haven affiliates.[3] The United States led the way in this area with the enactment of its original Subpart F legislation in 1962, which taxes U.S. parent companies on the passive income and certain related party income of "controlled foreign corporations."

Taxation of Shareholders

The dividends that U.S. MNCs pay to their individual shareholders (out of after-tax income) are *fully* taxed again in the hands of the shareholders. This is known as the "classical" system. A growing number of industrial countries have integrated corporate/shareholder taxation by providing individual shareholders, on the receipt of dividends, full (or partial) credits for income taxes paid by the corporation (that is the "imputation" system).[4]

Income Tax Treaties

All the industrial countries and some of the developing countries have wide-ranging bilateral tax treaty networks.[5] Their treaty partners include each other and a growing number of developing countries. Tax treaties (1) minimize double taxation of the same (cross-border) income, (2) spell out in detail how and when residents of one country will be taxed by another country (such as the degree of presence necessary for business profits to be taxed), and (3) generally provide for lower withholding rates on dividends, interest, and royalties than the statutory rates. For example, the U.S. statutory withholding rate on these items is 30 percent, but U.S. treaty policy (as reflected in a U.S. model treaty) aims for a 15 percent rate for dividends (5 percent where the payer is at least 10 percent owned by the payee) and zero for interest and royalties. Most countries tax foreign residents on income from "doing business" within their borders. Tax treaties provide that business profits are not to be taxed unless the foreigner has a local "permanent establishment," a term that treaties define in detail. Treaty policies as to withholding and what constitutes a "permanent establishment" strongly reflect a country's status as a capital importer or exporter (for example, developing countries favor high withholding rates and a low threshold of presence and/or business activity to establish a "permanent establishment").

Intercompany Transfer Pricing

Proper transfer pricing between commonly owned corporations is a major enforcement issue for revenue departments around the world. Tax laws uniformly provide that transactions between related parties can be adjusted to reflect arm's-length considerations or prices. The United States has very detailed regulations prescribing how arm's-length interest rates and prices of goods and services, *inter alia*, are to be determined.[6] These regulations are generally more detailed than those of other countries, and they are a major source behind the transfer pricing legislation adopted by Japan in 1986. The OECD has studied transfer pricing at length and has issued several noteworthy reports.

Tax Incentives

Many countries provide tax incentives to encourage (1) investment in the country by foreigners and (2) exports by domestic producers. Developing countries often give substantial "tax holidays" to foreign companies that establish job-producing activities. Developed countries often give tax inducement to foreign MNCs to establish "clean" activities like area headquarters offices and research and development centers.[7]

The United States has no investment incentives at the federal level, but foreign (and U.S.) MNCs have bargained for (and received) sizable local property tax and state income tax concessions when establishing new manufacturing facilities in a particular state. The FSC (Foreign Sales

Corporation) is the latest U.S. export incentive vehicle.[8] Use of an FSC can reduce the income tax on export sales by U.S. manufacturers and producers as much as 15 percent.

Unitary Taxation

Concern about the ability to properly monitor transfer pricing is the reason given by a number of U.S. states for taxing MNCs by the "unitary" method. This method taxes an *MNC group* on a portion of its worldwide income rather than on the actual profit derived from activities in the state.[9] California, the most important state to use the worldwide unitary approach, and most other unitary states have recently adopted "water's-edge" limitations under pressure from the federal government and non-U.S. MNCs.[10]

Transfer of Assets out of the Jurisdiction

Although industrial countries provide for, in varying degrees, (1) tax-free corporate reorganizations, (2) tax-free contributions to the capital of subsidiaries, and (3) tax-free liquidations of subsidiaries, these provisions are generally restricted when they involve the transfer of appreciated assets out of the taxing jurisdiction. The United States leads the way in these restrictions, which have been substantially tightened the past few years.[11]

Planning for International Expansion

A primary goal of an MNC based in a country that taxes its worldwide income is to avoid international double taxation. This requires judicious use of tax treaties together with a proper structuring of income flows. The latter could include, in appropriate circumstances, repatriating funds as deductible interest and royalties (rather than as nondeductible dividends) to the maximum extent possible. This is particularly important for U.S. MNCs because of the recent decline of the U.S. corporate rate (to 34 percent in 1988), which will make it lower than the rates in most foreign countries. A second goal is to accumulate and utilize low-taxed foreign profits offshore as long as possible, without subjecting them to home country taxation. A third goal, recognizing that overseas operations may contract some day, is to ensure that the expansion structure provides for (1) minimizing taxes if operations are sold at a gain and (2) utilizing losses if unsuccessful ventures are sold at a loss or closed down.

PRINCIPLES OF U.S. MNC TAXATION

Consolidated Income Tax Returns

U.S. tax law permits U.S. parent companies and their "80 percent or more" owned (and controlled) U.S. subsidiaries to file consolidated income tax returns (corporation *A* owns 80 percent of corporation *B* which owns 90 percent of corporation *C*; *A*, *B*, and *C* can file a consolidated return). [12] Some corporations are eligible to be included in a consolidated filing, such as foreign-incorporated companies, except that Mexican and Canadian corporations, which were established and maintained solely to comply with the local laws for holding property, [13] are eligible for inclusion in a consolidated filing.

In a consolidated filing, the group is treated, in effect, as a single taxpayer. Consolidated filing thus postpones recognition of income on intercompany sales until the goods in question are sold outside the group and allows the losses of unprofitable affiliates to offset the earnings of profitable affiliates.

Consolidated filing is elective but once elected must be continued. There is virtually no disadvantage to consolidated filing, and eligible groups invariably do so. This includes groups of U.S. corporations owned by foreign MNCs.

A growing number of countries either permit consolidated filing or allow the transfer of losses among commonly controlled corporations. [14] The latter is referred to as "group relief."

Foreign Tax Credit

U.S. taxpayers may claim foreign tax credit for (1) foreign "income" taxes[15] and (2) foreign taxes imposed "in lieu of" foreign income taxes. [16] The latter are liberally construed and include many taxes levied on gross income, although they do not include excise taxes, sales taxes, or VAT (that is, transactional taxes). The most significant restriction relates to income taxes incident to oil production, aimed at the OPEC countries where the state generally owns all natural resources. Because income taxes and usage royalties both enure to the Crown, there is the possibility that these countries will classify an excessive portion of their oil revenue as "income tax" to accommodate the foreign oil companies (which would rather pay creditable income taxes than deductible royalties). Thus, U.S. tax law imposes restrictions to prevent this distortion. [17] Foreign tax credits that exceed the foreign tax credit limitation can first be carried back to the preceding two taxable years and, if unused, then carried forward to the five succeeding taxable years. [18]

On a year-to-year basis, U.S. taxpayers can elect to claim foreign taxes as a credit *or* a deduction. Because a credit generally is so much more valuable than a deduction, taxpayers elect to deduct income taxes only when they believe that a large part of the excess credits cannot be used within the two year carry-back and carryover period. For example, if a U.S. MNC has a taxable loss, it obtains no immediate benefit from claiming foreign income taxes as either a credit or a deduction, but the

317

fifteen year carryover of net operating losses makes it more likely that claiming foreign income tax in a loss year as a deduction will produce some benefit.

Deemed-Paid Foreign Income Taxes

The United States (and most industrial countries) provides for corporate taxpayers to claim credit for foreign income taxes paid by foreign subsidiaries. These are called "indirect" or "deemed-paid" credits. In the United States corporations are entitled to credit for the foreign income taxes attributable to dividends that they receive from foreign corporations in which they have at least a 10 percent ownership.[19] For dividends paid out of a foreign subsidiary's pre-1987 earnings, the deemed-paid taxes equal (1) the subsidiary's income taxes *for the year* multiplied by the ratio of (2) the amount of the dividend to (3) the subsidiary's "earnings and profits" (E&P) *for the year*. Thus, the lower the E&P, the higher the deemed-paid income taxes. This was a year-by-year determination. The Tax Reform Act of 1986 changed the deemed-paid rules requiring the accounting for both E&P and taxes in multiyear (rather than single-year) pools. (The deemed credit calculation was also impacted in the wake of the changes to the foreign tax limitation—particularly the creation of more separate limitation income categories.

E&P is the equivalent of "earned surplus" as computed under U.S. accounting rules but specifically applying accounting methods, inventory methods, and depreciation methods prescribed by U.S. tax law.[20] There are a number of accounting elections a U.S. parent can make with respect to a foreign subsidiary to lower a foreign subsidiary's E&P, such as accelerated depreciation. In addition to increasing deemed-paid taxes, reducing E&P through elections could mean that less gain will be taxed as ordinary income (rather than long-term capital gain) when subsidiaries are sold or liquidated. (It should be noted that the distinction between ordinary income and capital gain ended on January 1, 1988, when the corporate rate for all income became 34 percent.)

Dividends are required to be grossed-up to include in income the deemed-paid foreign taxes.[21] This is tantamount to including in income the amount of the pre-tax income of the subsidiary dedicated to the payment of the deemed-paid. For example:

Earnings before income tax of foreign corporation for 1987	$ 1,000
Foreign income tax at 30 percent	300
Earnings and profits (E&P) for 1987	$ 700
Dividend paid to U.S. parent company	350
Less foreign withholding tax, at 10 percent	35
Net dividend received in the United States	$ 315

Foreign creditable taxes:

Direct credit for withholding tax	35

Deemed-paid credit for subsidiary's tax

$$\frac{350 \text{ (Dividend)}}{700 \text{ (E\&P)}} \times 300 \text{ (Foreign tax)} = \qquad \underline{150}$$

Total creditable taxes	$ 185
Included in parent's U.S. income:	
Net dividend received	315
Foreign withholding tax	35
Foreign deemed-paid tax	150
	$ 500
U.S. tax at 40 percent (1987 rate)	200
Less foreign tax credit	185
U.S. tax payable	$ 15

On these facts, the reduced U.S. rate effective for 1988 generates excess foreign tax credits, as follows:

U.S. tax at 34 percent	$ 170
Less foreign income tax credit	185
U.S. tax payable	-0-
Excess foreign tax credit	$ 15

This illustrates that reduced home country tax rates do not necessarily translate into reduced taxes on foreign income unless foreign income taxes also can be reduced.

Foreign Tax Credit Limitation

The purpose of the foreign tax credit is to prevent international double taxation—that is, taxation of the same income by the United States and a foreign country. The purpose of the foreign tax credit limitation is to keep foreign taxes from being taken as a credit against the U.S. tax on U.S. source income.

To accomplish the latter goal, the foreign tax credit is limited to total U.S. income tax (pre–foreign-tax credit) multiplied by the ratio of foreign source U.S. taxable income to total U.S. taxable income (i.e., the U.S. tax attributable to foreign source income). For many years, taxpayers could choose whether to compute this limitation on a per-country basis or on a worldwide (or overall) basis. In the worldwide computation, all foreign income taxes were aggregated, so that higher-than-U.S.-rate taxes could be averaged against low-rate foreign taxes. In the per country limitation, the credit for foreign taxes incurred in a given country was limited to total U.S. income tax (again precredit) multiplied by the ratio of U.S. taxable income arising from sources in

319

that country to total U.S. taxable income.[22] The per country limitation often gave the best result if the MNC had losses in some countries and profits in others.

In 1976 the overall method was made mandatory through the repeal of the per country limitation. Prior to 1976 (beginning in 1963), the concept of separate income categories, now referred to as baskets, was introduced on a minor scale. Oil income, certain interest income, and DISC income, and the foreign income taxes attributable to each, were assigned to such separate baskets, and the foreign tax credit limitation was to be computed separately for each basket. This was another anti-averaging device. For example, the foreign taxes on interest income could be limited to the total U.S. income tax (pre-credit) multiplied by the ratio of foreign source taxable interest to total taxable income. Oil generally is highly taxed in the source countries, often at a rate far higher than the U.S. rate. Thus, isolating oil tax and oil income often produces sizable excess credits. On the other hand, interest income often bears little or no foreign income tax. Isolating this lightly taxed foreign source income excludes it from the numerator of the overall basket calculation, thus lowering the limitation (that is, allowable tax credit) for the overall basket.

Foreign Tax Credit Limitation—1986 Tax Reform

The Tax Reform Act of 1986 lowers the corporate tax rate to 40 percent in 1987 (from 46 percent) and to 34 percent in 1988 and (supposedly) thereafter. It also broadens the tax base by, among other things, eliminating the investment credit, extending depreciation periods, imposing a much more burdensome alternative minimum tax, and tightening (and complicating) the foreign tax credit limitation. The U.S. income tax paid by corporations as a whole is expected to increase by about 20 percent.

The TRA of 1986 theoretically retains the "overall" limitation concept, but (1) further fragments it into baskets (now up to ten), (2) imposes "look-thru" rules to characterize income received from "controlled foreign corporations" (CFCs are, in general, majority-owned subsidiaries), and (3) imposes a "per company" limitation on "deemed-paid" foreign income taxes paid by non-CFCs (that is, foreign companies between 10 percent and 50 percent U.S. owned). The latter change makes non-CFC status prohibitively expensive in high-tax countries and means that there will be fewer *incorporated* joint ventures between U.S. corporations and foreign interests, where the U.S. party has 50 percent or less of the equity. Such joint venture forms have been a popular way for U.S. MNCs to do business abroad for many years.

Ten "Baskets" of Income

The ten "baskets" of income are discussed below.

1 *Passive income*: Generally, interest, dividends, rents and royalties. Rents and royalties are active ("overall" limitation) income if connected with a trade or business of the recipient. Under the "high-tax kickout" rule, passive income taxed at more than the U.S. corporate rate of 34 percent is also assigned to the "overall" basket. The 34 percent effective rate is computed after allocating U.S.-incurred expenses (such as stewardship in the case of dividends, R&D in the case of royalties, and interest expense in the case of any class of income). The "look-thru" rules (see below) can also result in a recharacterization of passive income to overall income.

2 *Financial services income:* Income from banking, insurance, and financing, including fund management, fiduciary services, and credit card services. If an entity is predominantly in the financial services business, its passive income also will be included in this basket.

3 *Shipping income*: Generally foreign base company shipping income and certain income from space or ocean activities, as defined under Subpart F.

4 *High withholding tax interest:* Interest subject to a gross withholding tax of 5 percent or more. When received by a non-CFC (a 10 percent to 50 percent owned foreign corporation), the excess is not treated as a foreign income tax for deemed-paid tax purposes to a U.S. corporation receiving dividends from that non-CFC. Interest earned in certain export activities is exempt from this provision.

5 *Dividends from each noncontrolled foreign corporation:* There is a separate limitation for dividends from each non-CFC (as mentioned above this is a per-*entity* limitation).

6 *DISC/former DISC income*: Income from this export incentive vehicle, which, in general, was replaced by the FSC on January 1, 1985.

7 *FSC/former FSC:* Dividends received from a "foreign sales corporation" (the United States' current export incentive vehicle).

8 *Foreign trade income dividends*: The nonexempt portion of an FSC's income that is currently taxable to it.

9 *Foreign oil and gas extraction income.*

10 *Other income*: The remaining (now residual) "overall" limitation.

"Look-thru" Rules

Under the TRA of 1986, the characterization, for assigning among the various baskets, of remittances by CFCs is determined by "looking-thru" (the spelling in the statute) to the CFCs' underlying income. Accordingly, remittances from a CFC to a related U.S. person in the form of dividends, interest, rents, or royalties, or Subpart F inclusions

321

(deemed remittances) will be recharacterized by looking at the underlying pool of earnings from which paid. The look-thru rules do not apply to remittances from non-CFCs.

CFCs will maintain multiyear (perpetual) post-1986 pools for each category of separate limitation income (which also will be used to compute the deemed-paid credit discussed above). Interest payments of a CFC are deemed to be paid first from the passive pool. All other remittances are deemed to come proportionately from each pool. If the post-1986 pools are used up, later remittances are deemed made out of pre-1987 accumulated earnings (on a year-by-year basis).

Under the look-thru rules, if all of a CFC's income is operating income, all of its payments to its U.S. parent will be deemed operating income (that is, will fall in the "overall" basket), whether the payments are dividends, interest, rents, or royalties. Thus, high-taxed dividends (deemed-paid taxes plus withholding taxes) can be averaged with low (or no-) taxed interest and royalties. In addition, there is a *de minimis* rule. If a CFC's Subpart F income is less than the lesser of (1) 5 percent of its gross income or (2) $1 million, its passive income will flow through as "overall" basket income. This is also the new Subpart F *de minimis* exception.

Foreign Losses

Foreign source losses in any "basket" will proportionately reduce the foreign source income in other "baskets" before reducing U.S. source income. To the extent that an overall foreign loss offsets U.S. source income, subsequent foreign source income will be reclassified as U.S. source.

Deemed-Paid Taxes under the TRA of 1986

Under the TRA of 1986, a dividend (or Subpart F inclusion) carries with it a pro-rata share of the accumulated foreign taxes based on the foreign corporation's multiyear (perpetual) pool of accumulated E&P.[23] Another 1986 act change was the elimination of a rule that dividends paid during the first sixty days of a foreign subsidiary's fiscal year were deemed to be paid out of the E&P of the preceding year or years. These changes mean that U.S. MNCs no longer can benefit from a long standing tax planning device known as "dividend skipping" with respect to subsidiaries in split-rate countries like Germany. Deemed-paid taxes will now be reflected at the average rate of tax paid during the pooling period (that is, for all years after 1986) rather than as before, for years for which the taxes were incurred.

Source of Income

322   Much of the tax planning of U.S. MNCs is to generate foreign-source

income or to convert domestic to foreign income, so as to increase the numerator of the foreign tax credit limitation fraction and to do so without increasing foreign tax burdens. As a general rule, income from foreign branch operations is foreign source, as is dividend income, interest income, and royalty income paid by foreign subsidiaries. Income from the sale of products purchased in the United States and sold outside the United States is entirely foreign source income. Income from products manufactured by the taxpayer in the United States and sold outside the United States is allocated by a regulatory formula that generally produces a 50/50 split of the net product sales between U.S. source and foreign source. A sale is deemed to take place where the rights, title and interests of the seller pass to the buyer.[24]

However, the TRA of 1986, with its ten income "baskets," has eliminated much planning potential by isolating in a separate basket the kind of low-taxed income that most easily can be shifted. As discussed, many items of highly taxed investment income (interest, portfolio dividends, etc) will now fall into the "passive" basket and thus can no longer be averaged with the usually higher taxed business income from branch or subsidiary operations. Moreover, to prevent highly taxed passive income from being averaged with low-taxed passive income, passive income taxed at a rate higher than the U.S. corporate rate is "kicked over" into the "overall" basket. The foreign tax rate is determined after reducing passive income to reflect allocations and apportionments of deductions (see discussion below).

Allocation of Deductions against Foreign Source Gross Income

To compute foreign source taxable income, deductions (such as interest, R&D, and home office "stewardship" expenses) must be allocated and apportioned between foreign source gross income and U.S. source gross income.[25] There are different rules for different classes of deductions, and some of them are extremely complex.[26] The same rules (except those for interest expense) apply, in reverse, to foreigners doing business in the United States and thus are used to determine the head office expenses that foreigners can deduct in computing the taxable income of their U.S. branch operations.

An item of home office expense will be allocated to an activity to the extent it can be identified with and related to it, under the so-called factual relationship test. For example, all the expense of the "international department" normally would be allocated against foreign source income. For expenses that cannot be identified, such as, perhaps, the salary of the president, chief financial officer, and other top management officers, the regulations provide that any reasonable overhead allocation method will be acceptable. Deductions that are not related to any item of gross income (such as charitable contributions) are allocated on the basis of the ratio of consolidated foreign source gross income to total consolidated gross income (the Revenue Act of 1986 mandated that these allocations and apportionments be done on a consolidated [i.e. group] basis rather than an entity by entity basis). Interest expense, and research and developmental expenditures follow special rules which are discussed below.

Allocation of R&D Expense

The research and development expense allocation rules have changed several times since the relevant allocation regulations were adopted in 1977. The regulations break R&D expenses into thirty-two product categories. Within each category, if 50 percent or more of the R&D expense is incurred in one geographic area (such as the United States), then 30 percent of the total R&D expense is allocated to that area. The remaining R&D is allocated within each product category on the basis of sales of the relevant product—foreign sales to total sales, with sales by licensees of patents and know-how included on a look-thru basis. The allocation also can be made on the basis of gross income, which is subject to limitations and which must be applied to the entire R&D expense (not on a product category basis). The 50 percent geographic threshold for a 30 percent front-end allocation of R&D expense to U.S. source income was an incentive for MNCs to continue their R&D in the United States.

In 1981 Congress gave additional incentive by overriding the regulations described above and providing that, for two years, all U.S.-incurred R&D would be allocated to U.S. source income. Subsequent legislation continued this suspension of the regulations until 1986. The 1986 Act provided that, for taxable years beginning after August 1, 1986, and before August 2, 1987, 50 percent of U.S.-incurred R&D (after special allocations) will be apportioned to U.S. source income. The remaining 50 percent is apportioned, at the taxpayer's option, to U.S. and foreign source income on the basis of either (1) sales (as described above) or (2) gross income.[27] This special treatment has not been extended by Congress, so the original regulations (described above) take renewed effect for taxable years beginning on or after August 2, 1987. There are, however, proposals presently before Congress to provide a permanent override to these regulations as a continued incentive for U.S. multinationals to continue their major R&D facilities and activities in the U.S.

Interest Expense Allocation—The "Fungibility" Approach

Interest expense for all U.S. taxpayers, except foreign corporations doing business in the United States, is apportioned between foreign source and U.S. source income on the ratio of the tax book value (or fair market value) of foreign assets (assets producing, or capable of producing, foreign income) to total assets.[28] The TRA of 1986

overrode regulations that allowed taxpayers to allocate interest on the
basis of gross income (subject to limitations). The 1986 Act also
provides that the tax book basis of shares of subsidiary corporations
must include increases or decreases in E&P of foreign subsidiaries
(and unconsolidated U.S. subsidiaries) since such subsidiaries were
acquired.[29]

This asset approach is based on the premise that money is fungible,
and interest expense is thus attributable to all activities on the basis of
capital utilized, regardless of the purpose for incurring specific debt.
Interest can be allocated to specific assets only when stringent tracing
requirements are met, including that the debt be nonrecourse.

Tax Haven (Subpart F) Rules

MNCs use tax haven subsidiaries to serve, among other things, as (1)
sales and service companies to accumulate profits at low tax rates, (2)
holding companies to take advantage of low tax rates and/or treaty
networks, (3) international finance subsidiaries, and (4) captive insurance companies. The ideal tax haven has low taxes, an extensive treaty
network, good banking facilities, communications and transport, no
currency controls, and political stability.

A growing number of the major industrial countries have anti-tax
haven laws.[30] The U.S. Subpart F legislation was the first (enacted in
1962 effective for 1963), and it has been more or less the model for
other countries in structuring their own tax haven legislation. Subpart F
applies to U.S. shareholders who own 10 percent or more (voting
stock) of "controlled foreign corporations" (CFCs). A CFC is a foreign
corporation more than 50 percent owned (value *or* voting control) by
10 percent or more U.S. shareholders. Thus, a foreign corporation
owned 9 percent by each of eleven U.S. shareholders would not be a
CFC. The TRA of 1986 added the value test for determining control;
previously only voting control was considered.[31] Ten percent or more
U.S. shareholders are taxed currently on the following income of
CFCs:[32]

1 Foreign personal holding company income, which consists of passive
   income such as dividends, interest, royalties, capital gains, and
   income from certain personal service contracts. This category
   includes dividends, interest, and capital gains derived in the active
   conduct of a banking business and an insurance business;[33]
2 Sales income from property, either bought from or sold to a related
   person, that is both (a) manufactured and (b) sold for use outside
   the seller's country of incorporation;
3 Income from services rendered outside the renderer's country of
   incorporation for or on behalf of (broadly defined) a related
   person;

4 Certain oil related refining income and shipping income.[34]

These four categories are "foreign base company income" and are subject to a 5 percent to 70 percent rule. Under this rule, if the total base company income of a CFC is less than 5 percent of its gross income (*and* less than $1 million), the CFC is treated as having no "foreign base company income" for that year; if the total should exceed 70 percent of the CFC's gross income, then all of its gross income is treated as "foreign base company income." Prior to the TRA of 1986, the *de minimis* threshold was 10 percent of gross income, without any dollar limitation.

The following also are Subpart F income, but without regard to the 5 percent/$1 million *de minimis* exception:[35]

1 Income of offshore insurance subsidiaries, including virtually all income of captive insurance companies and many mutual insurance companies:
2 Amounts of income deemed invested in U.S. property at the end of a CFC's taxable year. This includes loans for more than a year to related U.S. companies (and guarantees of such loans);
3 International boycott income (aimed at MNCs that participate in boycotts of Israel, but not limited to such boycotts);
4 Amounts of income earned by a CFC equal to any foreign illegal payments (bribes) made by it.

Transfer Pricing

All countries reserve the right to adjust the taxable income of a corporation within their jurisdiction with regard to transactions with related parties involving sales of goods, services, or the use of money,[36] where such transactions are not conducted at arm's length. The incentive for manipulation is great, for example, when an MNC group can save taxes by having a member of the group in a high-tax country sell at an unrealistically low price to a related corporation in a low-tax country (or buy from such a company at an unrealistically high price). If, through a pricing manipulation, too little tax was paid to the high-rate country, it follows that too much tax was paid to the low-tax country. Despite the tax-rate differential, if the high-tax country makes a pricing adjustment, there will be double taxation unless the low-tax rate country allows a "correlative adjustment" (that is, permits a refund claim based on the revised transfer price). Today, few MNCs artificially shift income through pricing manipulation, but there is always room for honest disagreement between a taxpayer and the revenue authorities, or between two taxing authorities whose interests in cross-border related party transactions are opposed, on a proper arm's-length price. Most tax treaties provide that representatives of the two countries involved in a transfer pricing dispute ("competent authorities") will try to negotiate to avoid double taxation after one country has made a transfer pricing adjustment on a cross-border transaction. [37] But there are no guarantees and the process is, at best, slow and expensive. In the absence of a tax treaty, such a correlative adjustment is not possible.

U.S. Transfer Pricing Rules

The regulations under Section 482 of the U.S. tax law provide, with regard to intercompany sales of goods, that arm's length pricing of property must be determined under one of several prescribed (by regulation) methods, to apply in the order listed (despite prioritization, a major issue often is which method applies):

1 The "comparable uncontrolled price" (CUP) method applies if there are identical or nearly identical sales to unrelated parties (by the taxpayer or by someone else). To the extent sales are not identical, numerical adjustments can be made to account for the differences. There often is controversy over whether or not the differences are so substantial that they can even be quantified in a meaningful way under the circumstances. If not, another method must be used.
2 The "resale" price (R–) method, the second method in the prioritization, applies where goods are sold to a related party who then resells them to unrelated parties with no (or minimal) further processing or value added. The arm's-length price is the selling price to the unrelated party minus a reasonable (third party) markup for the related seller's services.
3 Under the "cost plus" (C+) method, the arm's-length price is computed by adding an appropriate gross profit (again a third party markup) to the cost of producing (or acquiring) the item sold.
4 If none of the three methods provides a reasonable result, another method, an appropriate taxpayer constructed method, considering all the facts and circumstances, may be used. This is a true alternative to the first three methods.

It should be noted that all three methods are, in actuality, variations of a single method—the "comparable uncontrolled transaction" (CUT) method, whereby a third-party standard is the touchstone, a third-party price for CUP compared to a third-party gross margin (mark up) for R– and C+.

The Section 482 regulations also provide rules for pricing between affiliates of services, the use of tangible and intangible property (rent and royalty), and the use of money (interest). The regulations provide safe-haven interest-rate ranges (for U.S. dollar obligations only) that are changed from time to time to reflect changing market conditions.

327

Transfer Pricing Changes—TRA of 1986

The TRA of 1986 provides that intangibles transferred both into and out of the United States to related parties, by either sale or license, must be priced so as to reflect future income potential of the intangibles.[38] This means that the IRS can adjust transfer prices to reflect income earned by the transferee even though the price was concededly fair under the rules provided in the regulations under the facts available at the time of the transfer (the traditional determination of an arm's-length price has not looked beyond date-of-transfer facts). It is hoped that this provision will be used by the IRS only in unusual circumstances so as not to completely destroy the application of the arm's-length methodology to intercompany intangible property transactions, a standard that is strictly adhered to by the rest of the world. Other nations (both taxpayers and revenue authorities) are concerned over this new legislation.

The TRA of 1986 also provides that importers buying from related suppliers cannot use a transfer price for U.S. income tax purposes that is higher than the dutiable value they claim for U.S. customs purposes.[39] This would appear to be the first attempt to relate transfer pricing to customs valuation.

Income Tax Treaties

The principal purpose of income tax treaties is to eliminate, to the extent possible, double taxation. One of the key elements in accomplishing this goal is the reduction of withholding tax rates on cross-border flows of dividends, interest, rents, and royalties. For example, the U.S. statutory withholding tax rate is 30 percent on dividends, interest (bank deposit interest and some portfolio interest is tax free), rents, and royalties. The U.S. Model Treaty (that is, the expression of the U.S. negotiating position) provides 15 percent withholding on portfolio dividends, 5 percent withholding on direct investment dividends (that is, dividends from affiliated corporations 10 percent or more owned), and exemption for interest and royalties. The U.S. treaties with other industrial countries generally reflect these rates. The OECD Model Treaty also suggests 5 percent and 15 percent dividend withholding rates (although the direct investment threshold in this model is 25 percent ownership), exemption for royalties, and a 10 percent rate on interest. Industrial countries with more inbound than outbound direct investment, like Australia and Canada, attempt to negotiate higher treaty rates (for example, the U.S.–Australia treaty withholding rates for interest and royalty are 10 percent).

Developing countries have not given income tax treaties as much emphasis as the developed countries because direct investment tends to be a one-way inbound street. Today, however, more developing countries are establishing a treaty network; however, they tend to insist on higher withholding rates (for example, the U.S. treaty with Morocco provides for a 15 percent withholding rate on interest flows and on all dividends, portfolio or direct).

Treaty shopping

"Treaty shopping" is an old phenomenon which has received great attention in recent years as an abuse that needs to be dealt with (particularly by the United States). Treaty shopping involves nationals of one country investing in a target country through an intermediary country that has a favorable tax treaty with the target country. For example, Netherlands Antilles corporations have been widely used by nationals of countries that do not have income tax treaties with the United States, to invest in the United States. U.S. MNCs also have used Netherlands Antilles corporations to issue portfolio debt abroad (to avoid withholding tax on the interest payments). Treaty shopping into the U.S. has been greatly curtailed by the December 31, 1987 termination of the Netherlands Antilles treaty by the United States[39A] (except that pre-June 1984 Eurobond issues have been "grandfathered").[39B]

It now is formal U.S. treaty policy to have its tax treaties contain anti-treaty shopping provisions.[40] These provisions provide that certain treaty benefits are denied to corporations that are not substantially owned by residents of the treaty country (together with U.S. citizens or residents) or whose income is used substantially to meet liabilities owed to residents of third countries (such as for interest and royalties). The IRS also ruled, in 1984 but to be applied permanently on a prospective basis, that the Netherlands Antilles treaty no longer could be relied on by third-country residents to lend to their U.S. subsidiary corporations[41] or by U.S. corporations to issue debt abroad.[42] This has been superseded by the treaty's cancellation. The U.S. cancelled the treaty mainly out of frustration over the Netherlands Antilles' refusal to negotiate a new treaty with an anti-treaty shopping provision.

Portfolio Debt

In order to help U.S. MNCs tap foreign financial markets, particularly without the use of Netherlands Antilles intermediary companies, the 1984 tax law enacted an amendment permitting U.S. corporations to issue portfolio debt abroad with respect to which there is no U.S. withholding tax on the related interest payments.[43] Such debt has to be issued to unrelated parties, other than banks, and has to be carefully tailored to meet regulatory restrictions aimed at preventing their ownership by Americans.

"Permanent Establishment" (PE)

Most countries do not subject foreigners to income tax on business

329

activity unless they are somehow "engaged in business" in the host country. This tends to be a nebulous and varying standard. Under tax treaties, however, as exemplified in the OECD and U.S. model treaties, a relatively uniform standard has been established, in accordance with which a foreign MNC can conduct fairly extensive business activities in a host country without becoming subject to local tax. This is the so-called permanent establishment standard under which a foreign corporation is not taxed unless it carried on business locally through a permanent establishment.[44] The PE threshold is well defined, which creates certainty to the foreign investor.

Under the U.S. model treaty, an MNC can send salespeople into a treaty country (as long as they do not independently conclude sales), advertise, display goods, store goods, purchase goods, and use independent agents (who can conclude sales), without creating a PE. But if an MNC's sales employees work out of a "fixed place of business' (e.g., an "office"), such office will constitute a PE even if the salesmen cannot independently conclude sales. An important element of the PE concept is that a parent corporation (or other related corporation) is not deemed to have a PE in a country merely because it owns a locally incorporated subsidiary carrying on a business in that country.

To a certain extent, the local profits of a PE are to be determined as if the PE were an enterprise distinct and separate from its head office.[45] But this independent entity theory is not accepted totally. For example, if a financial institution (such as a bank) has funds advanced by its head office, few countries will allow the branch to claim a deduction for interest on loans from its home office or for home office charges for capital utilized. It would, of course, be entitled to a deduction for interest on third-party debt on the branch books (including debt owed other corporations in the MNC group) or an appropriate share of interest expense on the head office books. For some countries following the OECD model, interest charged on intracompany advances would be deductible.[46] The interest deduction of U.S. branches of non-U.S. corporations (including branches of foreign banks) is computed according to a variation[47] of the fungibility formula, discussed earlier, which U.S. corporations must adhere to in allocating interest expense in computing foreign-source taxable income.

Transfer of Assets to Foreign Corporations

Some countries permit their local taxpayers to transfer appreciated assets to controlled *domestic* corporations tax free because the assets remain within the country's taxing jurisdiction (the asset retains its original basis for depreciation and for computing gain if sold). Distributions in complete liquidations of wholly owned subsidiaries also are often tax free, with the assets passed to the parent on liquidation retaining a carryover basis (same as in the hands of the liquidated corporation).

However, there often are restrictions and limitations on tax-free transfers of assets to foreign corporations since any gain on a subsequent sale would be outside the originating country's tax net. The United States has a complex set of rules on the outbound transfer of assets, either by a U.S. MNC to its foreign subsidiary or by a liquidating U.S. subsidiary to its foreign parent.[48]

Except for five specific types of assets mentioned in the next paragraph, the U.S. rules (Section 367 of the Code) permit the tax-free transfer of assets to a foreign corporation if they are to be used by the transferee foreign corporation in the active conduct of a trade or business. Machinery, office equipment, transportation equipment, and foreign situs real property are often transferred to a foreign corporation under this provision. Other assets (that is, those not to be devoted to the active conduct of a business) will generally not be transferable abroad (to a foreign corporation) tax free. It should further be noted that on conversion of a foreign branch into a foreign corporation, gain is recognized if, and to the extent that, the branch had net accumulated taxable losses (for U.S. purposes) at the date of incorporation.

The "active conduct of a trade or business" exception does not apply to transfers of (1) inventory items, copyrights, and so forth, (2) installment obligations, accounts receivable, or similar property, (3) foreign currency or property denominated in foreign currency, (4) intangible property, and (5) property of which the transferor is a lessor (unless the transfer was the lessee).[49] When these assets are transferred, the gains inherent therein (i.e. excess of fair market value over basis), which was not previously recognized and/or reported, will be taxed.

Transfer of Intangibles Abroad

Intangibles (such as patents, technology, and know-how) have been subjected to increasingly harsh rules in recent years because the U.S. Congress believes their transfer to foreign subsidiaries, particularly the transfer of valuable technology to low-tax foreign locations, is a prime area of taxpayer abuse. In 1984 the statute was amended to, in effect, prohibit the transfer of intangibles abroad via tax-free transfer to controlled corporations. If such a transfer were made, it would be deemed to be a sale for continuing contingent payments based on productivity, use, or disposition of the property (that is, a standard-type arm's-length royalty), and such income would be deemed to be U.S. source income (rather than the more desirable foreign source income that royalties from abroad would otherwise constitute). This new rule was conceived to insure that U.S. taxpayers would not be able to accomplish transfers of intangibles through the tax-free contribution to capital route. The choices left were an actual sale of the intangible for an arm's-length consideration or a license of the intangible for an arm's-length periodic royalty.

The TRA of 1986 took the added step (as described in the transfer pricing discussion above) of granting the Internal Revenue Service carte blanche to adjust the transfer price of intangibles to reflect the income they produce for the transferee, even though the transfer price was arm's-length under the facts known at the time of the transfer. This is known as the superroyalty rule. Thus, such transfers remain open for tax purposes. As noted above, it is hoped that the IRS exercises judgment and discretion in its application of this new rule.

Foreign Sales Corporations (FSCs)

For many years, the DISC provisions provided the U.S. export incentive vehicle. Under the DISC, a U.S. manufacturer could reduce its current income tax on the income from export sales by routing the sale through these special U.S. subsidiary corporations or using such corporations as commission agents. Other industrial countries lodged complaints that the DISC provision violated the GATT[50] treaty rule that exports cannot be subsidized by lowering "direct" (that is, income) taxes. The United States denied that DISC was a GATT violation but replaced it, on January 1, 1985, with the FSC provisions. FSCs are intended to provide the same tax benefits as DISCs and are intended to negate the subsidy allegation by requiring the FSC to be incorporated abroad and to have certain substantive offshore activities (for example, by maintaining an office abroad and incurring a minimum threshold amount of export marketing expense abroad).[51] Incorporation and office sites must be in countries with which the United States has exchange of information agreements or tax treaties that contain acceptable (to the U.S. Treasury) exchange of information articles. FSCs can be set up and maintained at nominal cost. The foreign "office" and offshore record keeping requirements can be satisfied by agents who represent perhaps hundreds of FSCs or by related entities operating abroad. U.S. states and trade associations are sponsoring FSCs that can be used by up to 25 U.S. exporters; these are called "shared FSCs."

However, the interplay of the TRA of 1986 with a special source rule contained in the FSC legislation may well negate the value of an FSC to a U.S. manufacturer whenever the overall foreign-tax-credit basket, in which basket the income from an export sale by the manufacturer would fall, is in an excess credit position. MNCs' situations will vary, but with the new low rates (34 percent in 1988), excess credits will become much more commonplace. Exporters must analyze their foreign-tax-credit situation on a year-by-year basis to see if their export sales should be made using an FSC.

As discussed, the countries that tax the worldwide income of their MNCs mitigate double taxation by granting credits for foreign taxes actually incurred. Thus, where tax holidays are offered by a host country (usually the developing countries) to create incentives for foreign investors, these incentives are ineffective if the foreign investor merely increases its home country tax burdens by the amount of the host country tax incentive.

To encourage investment in developing countries, some industrial countries grant credit for the taxes forgiven by tax holidays, as if such forgiven taxes had actually been paid. This is called "tax sparing."

It has been long-standing U.S. policy not to grant tax-sparing credits to foreign countries. U.S. possessions have been the only exception to this policy. Section 936 grants a tax-sparing type credit to U.S. corporations on their possessions source operating income if they qualify as "possessions corporations" (that is, they derived 80 percent or more of their gross income from U.S. possessions over a three-year period and 65 percent or more of their income was derived from the active conduct of a trade or business within a possession). Such credit is equal to the U.S. tax that would otherwise have been payable on the qualified income and is tantamount to a tax-sparing credit (that is, credit for taxes whether or not actually paid).

Perils of Tax Reform

Over the past few years, U.S. tax reform has eliminated several widely used tax planning techniques. Three such items are briefly discussed below:

CAPTIVE INSURANCE COMPANIES

Over the past several years, case law and IRS policy were progressively limiting the use of captive insurance companies, but the TRA of 1986 has eliminated virtually all remaining income tax justifications for their use. Beginning in 1987, an offshore insurance company will be deemed a "controlled foreign corporation" if it is 25 percent or more U.S. owned, including ownership by any shareholders (not just 10 percent or more shareholders). Such CFCs will be taxed currently on their pro-rata share of the CFC's insurance income,[52] a class of tainted income that has been greatly expanded by the 1984 and 1986 legislations.

DUAL RESIDENT (OR "LINK") COMPANIES

U.S. MNCs have been able in the past to use U.S. corporations that are "resident" in the United Kingdom under U.K. law to hold the shares of

333

U.K. subsidiaries and to incur the debt used to acquire such subsidiaries. U.K. MNCs have used the same structure to acquire and hold U.S. subsidiaries. The purpose behind these structures is to make the interest on the acquisition indebtedness deductible in both countries. As discussed, a corporation is "resident" in the United States if it is incorporated in the United States and is "resident" in the United Kingdom if it is managed and controlled in the United Kingdom.

For the technique to work, the "link" company's losses must be passed to the U.S. operating companies via consolidated filing and to the U.K. operating companies via group relief. The TRA of 1986 denies use in consolidation of the losses of an affiliate that is subject to tax, by reason of residence, in another country.[53] Similar legislation has been announced in the United Kingdom, Australia, and New Zealand.

"STAPLED" OR "TANDEM" STOCK

Under a stapled stock arrangement, a U.S. corporation creates a tax haven corporation whose stock it distributes to its shareholders, generally on a share-for-share basis. By their terms, the shares cannot be traded separately from the U.S. company's shares (that is, the shares are "stapled"). Future non-U.S. business activity is assigned to the tax haven corporation. The purpose is to eliminate U.S. corporate income tax on offshore business activity.

This structure's tax advantage was eliminated in 1984 when the tax law was amended to provide that the stapled corporation will be deemed a subsidiary of the U.S. corporation. Thus, any dividends paid by the foreign corporation will be deemed to pass through (and be taxable to) the U.S. corporation.[54] However, the technique is being used by non-U.S. based MNCs (public companies) to pay dividends to local shareholders from local subsidiaries (rather than from the ultimate parent located offshore).

CONCLUSION

We repeat our opening caveat that MNC taxation is a complex and changing area. Wrong moves can be expensive. Action should not be taken without advice from professionals who specialize in the area.

NOTES

1. The United Kingdom and many Commonwealth countries deem corporate residence to be where the corporation is "managed and controlled." This generally is where the board of directors meets to make its decisions. It should be noted, though, that the United Kingdom's 1988 Budget provides that U.K. incorporated companies also will be considered U.K. residents.

2. The U.S. foreign tax credit limitation is at IRC, sec. 904. See also attendant regulations and Congressional Committee Reports.

3. The United States, France, Canada, Japan, and the United Kingdom tax domestic shareholders on the unremitted income of foreign subsidiaries deemed to be tax-haven corporations, although the method and manner of taxation vary.

4. For example, under the United Kingdom's Advance Corporation Tax (ACT) system, domestic individual shareholders get full credit for the ACT paid by resident corporations. Under the U.S.–U.K. income tax treaty (Article 10), U.S. parent companies get a refund of 50 percent of the ACT attributable to dividends they receive from the U.K. subsidiaries.

5. All twenty-four members of the OECD (the Organization for Economic Co-operation and Development) subscribe to the basis of the OECD model income tax treaty (Model Convention for the Avoidance of Double Taxation with Respect to Taxes on Income and Capital), although many member countries have taken exception to specific provisions of the model treaty.

6. Regulations attendant to IRC, sec. 482.

7. Ireland is the pioneer in tax holidays and incentives. Recent contenders for "clean" facilities include Belgium, the Netherlands, and France.

8. IRC, secs. 921–27.

9. Generally, worldwide taxable income is allocated by a three-factor formula. The allocation factor is the average of the ratios of (a) property in the state to worldwide property, (b) payroll in the state to worldwide payroll, and (c) sales in the state to worldwide sales.

10. Under the "water's-edge" approach, U.S. taxable income is allocated using U.S.-source allocation factors.

11. IRC, sec. 367 and attendant regulations.

12. IRC, sec. 1501–05 and attendant regulations.

13. IRC, sec. 1504.

14. For example, the United Kingdom has had group relief for some time. Australia adopted loss sharing by commonly controlled corporations in 1984.

15. IRC, secs. 901–02.

16. IRC, sec. 903.

17. IRC, sec. 907.

18. IRC, sec. 904(c). Special limitations apply to carrybacks of post-1986 excess credits to pre-1987 taxable years.

19. IRC, sec. 902.

20. IRC, sec. 964 and attendant regulations.

21. IRC, sec. 78.

22. See note 2 above.

23. IRC, sec. 902(a).

24. Source of income rules are at IRC, secs. 861–65.

25. IRC, sec. 882.

26. Treasury Reg., sec. 1.861-8

27. TRA of 1986, sec. 1216.

28. Treasury Reg., sec. 1.861-8. The rules for foreign corporations are at Treasury Reg., sec. 1.882-5.

29. IRC, sec. 864(e).
30. See note 3 above.
31. Subpart F of the IRC encompasses sec. 951–64.
32. IRC, sec. 954(a).
33. The banking and insurance exceptions of prior law were eliminated by the Tax Reform Act of 1986.
34. The Tax Reform Act of 1986 expanded shipping income to include any income derived from a space or ocean activity.
35. IRC, sec. 952(a).
36. IRC, sec. 482.
37. See the OECD and U.S. model income tax treaties at articles 11 and 12, respectively.
38. IRC, sec. 482. See also Committee Reports on the TRA of 1986.
39. IRC, sec. 1059A.
39A. Treasury Dept. News Release B-1033, June 29, 1987.
39B. Treasury Dept. News Release B-1046, July 10, 1987.
40. Article 16 of the U.S. Treasury's proposed model income tax treaty.
41. Rev. Rul. 84-152, 1984-2 C.B. 381.
42. Rev. Rul. 84–153, 1984-2 C.B. 383.
43. IRC, sec. 871(h), for payments to foreign individuals; IRC, sec. 881(c), for payments to foreign corporations.
44. Articles 5 of both the OECD model income tax treaty and the U.S. Treasury's proposed model income tax treaty.
45. Article 7 of both the OECD model income tax treaty and the U.S. Treasury's proposed model income tax treaty.
46. See Commentary on Article 7, paragraph 3, of the OECD model income tax treaty. "Double Taxation of Income and Capital," subtitled "Revised Texts of Certain Articles of the 1963 OECD Draft Convention and the Commentary thereon." Published by the OECD in 1974. The pertinent language of the current OECD model income tax treaty (1980) is identical to the language commented on.
47. Treasury Reg., sec. 1.885-5.
48. IRC, sec. 367 and attendant regulations.
49. IRC, sec. 367(a)(3)(B).
50. General Agreement on Tariffs and Trade, to which the industrial countries subscribe.
51. IRC, secs. 921–27.
52. IRC, sec. 953(c)
53. IRC, sec. 1503(d).
54. IRC, sec. 269B.

PART V

UTILIZING
CURRENCY SWAPS
AND OPTIONS

14 Currency Swaps

FRANK RIBEIRO

A SWAP is a financial transaction in which two counterparties agree to exchange streams of payments over time. The two main types are currency swaps and interest-rate swaps.

In a currency swap two counterparties exchange specific amounts of two different currencies at the beginning and repay according to a schedule that includes either fixed- or floating-rate interest payments and the repayment of principal. In some cases there is no exchange of currencies initially. Only on rare occasions is principal not exchanged at maturity.[1]

The interest-rate swap is a specialized form of currency swap in which a single currency is involved. Only the interest-rate structure of the two exchanged flows are different. The principal amounts, being in the same currency, are netted to zero and thus become only notional concepts. No actual principal is exchanged either initially or at maturity, but interest payments are exchanged calculated on the underlying notional principal amount. The main types of transactions are coupon swaps, where a party pays fixed interest-rate payments and receives floating-rate payments, and basis swaps, where the interest payments exchanged are calculated from two different floating-rate indexes (such as the three-month dollar LIBOR against the U.S. commercial-paper composite rate). This chapter will focus on the currency swap, but the concepts and principles also apply to interest-rate swaps.

BACKGROUND

The currency swap as we know it today was totally unknown to the financial markets as recently as the mid-1970s. Before that time companies unsophisticated in managing the foreign-exchange exposures created by the new system of floating exchange rates devoted their resources to building tools and strategies for the more immediate needs of managing their foreign-currency working capital. U.S. companies were also addressing the dilemmas created by foreign-currency accounting rules. For the rare company that did seek to hedge a long-term exposure, the forward foreign-exchange market offered little support. Forward contracts beyond one year were either unavailable or expensive. Nevertheless, the determined hedger could cover a long-term currency exposure by linking a series of one-year forward-exchange contracts and rolling them over each year-end.

The foreign-exchange rollover provides long-term protection against foreign-exchange-rate fluctuations but leaves the company exposed to changing interest rates. Therefore, the company could not lock in a complete hedge for the full term. Through the mid-1970s, however, interest rates moved in a relatively narrow band, and the interest-rate risk in a rollover was considered minor.

This view changed drastically in 1978 following Paul Volcker's appointment as chairman of the U.S. Federal Reserve System. He shifted the Fed's policy from targeting interest rates to targeting money supply growth. The resulting wide fluctuations in dollar as well as nondollar interest rates destroyed any notion that interest-rate risk was inconsequential.

In seeking to develop a more effective hedge, select companies bypassed bank foreign-exchange dealers and dealt directly with each other arranging long-term currency exchange contracts. These were simple one-time exchanges of currencies at dates far enough in the future to eliminate the need for rollovers; a company could therefore fix a hedge against both currency and interest rates.

Initially, this market was confined to a very small group of participants, all of which were high-quality credit risks. During 1981, however, the number and type of participants grew rapidly as commercial banks began to take on the role of credit intermediary. This allowed many borrowers to participate in currency swaps that had previously been excluded because they did not carry AAA or AA ratings from Standard & Poor's or Moody's on their senior debt. The resulting larger pool of participants made matching counterparties to transactions much easier and caused dramatic growth in the long-term swap market.

At about the same time, multinational companies were reaching advanced levels of sophistication in their use of foreign-exchange and Eurocurrency markets. Parallel loan structures, at the time a tool commonly used by multinationals to circumvent exchange controls, served as a basis for an entirely new way to structure a long-term hedge. The World Bank and IBM executed the first broadly publicized swap transaction of this type. In their swap IBM agreed, in effect, to service $175 million of the World Bank's long-term dollar debt (coupons and principal). Concomitantly the World Bank would service IBM's long-term Swiss franc debt (coupons and principal). This gave IBM a complete hedge against its Swiss exposure, while the World Bank created the Swiss franc debt it sought.[2]

This structure was revolutionary. The new configuration allowed two borrowers (or investors) to exchange entire currency repayment schedules. To the now sophisticated treasurer, the currency swap was no longer merely a defensive tool for hedging unwanted exposures. It became a creative financing tool enabling a company to raise capital at a cost not accessible to it without the swap. This evolution from a simple defensive tool to a vehicle for raising low-cost debt brought the currency swap into the spotlight in international finance.[3]

A CONCEPTUAL VIEW OF SWAPS

The concept of the swap (both interest rate and currency) has broad implications as well as applications in finance. Its most important implication is the ability to separate the funding aspect of a financing from the structure of the liability (that is, without altering the underlying lending structure, the swap can change its interest structure from, for example, a fixed to a variable rate; or it can change the currency denomination of the debt service—such as from repayment in dollars to repayment in sterling or marks). In the case of an asset, the swap can, in similar fashion, separate the investment or credit aspect from the asset's financial structure.

This ability of the swap to separate a financing from its repayment structure greatly increases the options available to the borrower or investor. Before the swap, funding was usually provided within a set liability framework where the borrower's choice of financing was limited to fairly inflexible instruments in which predetermined currency and interest-rate structures were inseparable.

The swap, on the other hand, assembles or "synthesizes" a financing. Identify the most attractive source of funding—regardless of its currency or interest structure—then engineer a swap to create the desired liability structure.

There are six rudimentary components of a financing:

1 *Credit*: The willingness of an investor to take the default risk of a company;
2 *Funding*: The provision of loan funds and the repayment of those funds;
3 *Tenor*: The repayment schedule;
4 *Currency*: The currency denomination(s) of the repayment;
5 *Interest rate*: The basis on which compensation for the loan is calculated;
6 *Duration*: Measure of the term interest-rate risk inherent in a financing.[4]

For some time, the capital markets have had the necessary instruments to synthesize a suitable credit structure for a financing. Letters of credit, debt guarantees, syndications, and other instruments allow flexibility in rearranging the credit aspects of a financing. With minor exceptions, the remaining components (funding, tenor, currency, interest-rate structure, and duration) were presented in a nonnegotiable all-or-nothing package.

Different financing options provide different benefits. Where one

341

option might be attractive on a funding basis, another would be attractive because of the currency denomination. Seldom, however, does a single financing proposal embody the most desirable in each category. With the emergence of the swap, and more recently the interest-rate option, the borrower is now able to assemble or synthesize a financing offering the best in terms of (1) duration, (2) currency denomination, and (3) interest-rate structure.

By facilitating the interchange of currency and interest-rate structures, swaps eliminate the currency and interest-rate risks that had represented a barrier between the world's capital markets. Borrowers and investors in those markets as a result have much freer access to one another, which benefits both sides: Borrowers lower their cost of capital because of a broader investor base; investors increase the diversity of their portfolios, at the same time reducing risk and enhancing the possibility of higher yields. Swaps in summary have improved the "Pareto efficiency" of the global capital market. All parties are made better off.[5]

THE MECHANICS OF THE CURRENCY SWAP

Definition

Currency swaps can imply a number of different transaction types. In the context of this chapter the currency swap will refer to a class of currency-exchange transactions designed to hedge a currency exposure for which the conventional foreign-exchange market is inadequate due to the length of the tenor and the size and structure of the transaction. The transaction may or may not involve a bank dealer but does not rely exclusively on the interbank foreign-exchange market for its pricing. Swap pricing is generally determined using one or more of the following market indicators, either explicitly or by reference: Domestic or international bond yields, money-market rates, interest-rate and cross-currency interest-rate swap yields, forward foreign-exchange points, financial futures prices, and so forth.

Although the structure of a currency swap may take a variety of forms, all have the following common characteristics. A swap

1 Exchanges one currency for another with specific or specifiable amounts at specified dates in the future;
2 Is recorded in the accounts as a contingent item and so does not inflate the balance sheet or alter a company's key financial ratios;
3 Provides a hedge in the case of an unwanted liability exposure, by synthetically creating an offsetting investment in the unwanted currency and a borrowing in the desired currency and, in the case of an undesired asset exposure, by synthetically creating a borrowing in the unwanted currency and an investment in the desired currency.

The currency swap can be applied most effectively in

1 *Risk restructuring*: As a hedging tool, the currency swap reduces, eliminates, or, if desired, creates long-term risk (currency and interest rate).
2 *Arbitrage*: The currency swap's central feature is the transfer of cost advantages from one capital market to another. For example, a borrower can use the favorable funding cost in Japanese yen to raise dollar debt through the use of a swap. Together the yen financing and the swap synthesize dollar debt while retaining the relative cost advantages realized in the yen borrowing.
3 *Availability creation*: The currency swap provides ready access to capital structures not directly accessible to the borrower or investor. For example, long-term fixed-rate Italian lira debt is often unavailable. But a dollar borrowing and a lira swap together can create something that does not exist in the cash markets alone: A term lira financing.

Swap Illustration

A simplified nonnumerical illustration of how the swap works is shown in Figure 14–1. There, a U.S. company borrows Swiss francs. The company receives the Swiss franc proceeds today and repays Swiss francs at maturity (for simplicity and clarity in this diagrammatic example, interest flows are not shown). The swap, we have suggested, is an exchange of currencies that hedges the currency exposure. To hedge our Swiss franc debt fully, a transaction would be arranged with a swap counterparty that would receive Swiss francs today and pay dollars to the U.S. company (see Figure 14–2). At maturity, this would be reversed, whereby the swap counterparty would receive dollars and pay Swiss francs.

By arranging the Swiss franc swap the company obtains a fully hedged position (see Figure 14–3). At drawdown it receives Swiss francs from the Swiss investor, immediately pays them out to the counterparty, and receives, in turn, dollars. At maturity, it pays dollars and receives Swiss

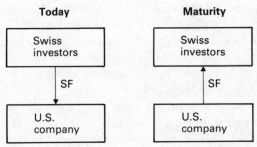

Figure 14–1. Foreign-Currency Borrowing.

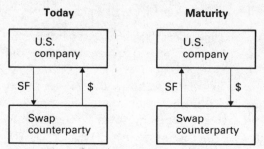

Figure 14–2. Currency Swap.

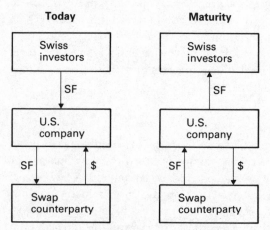

Figure 14–3. Borrowing through Currency Swap.

francs, which it uses to service its debt obligation. The net result is the elimination of all Swiss franc exposure as the Swiss franc flows offset each other. The new flows to the company become a dollar inflow today and a dollar outflow at maturity. Effectively, this could be described as a dollar drawdown and a dollar repayment—that is, we have created a synthetic dollar financing and have done so by sourcing the credit in a foreign capital market.

The initial exchange in Figure 14–3 is a simple spot transaction that might be arranged with a bank. As such, it can be executed separately from the currency swap and is therefore an optional feature of the swap. The critical feature of the swap is to arrange the forward exchange. In this way, long-term exposures that do not have a front-end exposure (such as project cash flows, long-term supply contracts, existing debt obligations, and so forth) can be hedged using these swaps.

Although currency swaps can be seen in a wide array of structures, conceptually they are derived from three fundamental structures: (1) Long-dated forward outright, (2) straight currency swap, and (3) debt swap.

The outright swap is based on the extension of the conventional bank forward contract. The exchange of currencies takes place at a single date in the future, with the rate of exchange being adjusted to reflect respective interest rate differentials. For example,

U.S. dollar borrower with Swiss franc 50 million debt at 4.0%, 5 years
Current SF 5-year yield = 5%
Current dollar 5-year yield = 8%
Spot rate = SF 2.00

$$\text{5-year forward rate} = \text{SF } 1.7372 = 2.00 \times \frac{(1.05)^5}{(1.08)^5}$$

Because most long-term swaps relate to term financing structures, the most glaring defect in this structure is that it does not lend itself to capital market transaction structures except for zero coupon bonds (a forward outright is essentially an exchange of zero coupon debt). In Table 14–1 the SF 50 million hedge inadequately covers the full exposure created by the debt as all the interest payments are unaltered. This may be remedied by entering into a series of forward outrights (see Table 14–2).

Table 14–1.
FORWARD OUTRIGHT SWAP.

Year	Debt Service	Buy SF	Outright Rate	Sell $	Net
1	(SF 2.0)	—	—	—	(SF 2.0)
2	(SF 2.0)	—	—	—	(SF 2.0)
3	(SF 2.0)	—	—	—	(SF 2.0)
4	(SF 2.0)	—	—	—	(SF 2.0)
5	(SF 2.0)	—	—	—	(SF 2.0)
Maturity	(SF 50.0)	SF 50.0	1.7372	($28.78)	($ 28.78)

Table 14–2.
FORWARD OUTRIGHT SWAP.

Year	Debt Service	Buy SF	Outright Rate[a]	Sell $	Net
1	(SF 2.0)	SF 2.0	1.9444	($ 1.03)	($ 1.03)
2	(SF 2.0)	SF 2.0	1.8904	($ 1.06)	($ 1.06)
3	(SF 2.0)	SF 2.0	1.8379	($ 1.09)	($ 1.09)
4	(SF 2.0)	SF 2.0	1.7869	($ 1.12)	($ 1.12)
5	(SF 2.0)	SF 2.0	1.7372	($ 1.15)	($ 1.15)
Maturity	(SF 50.0)	SF 50.0	1.7372	($28.78)	($28.78)

[a] $2.00 \times \dfrac{(1+.05)^t}{(1+.08)^t}$

In practice, however, the resultant net dollar payment schedule is so odd in structure that it would be very difficult to find a counterparty with an exactly matching cash flow. Only if a bank is willing to intermediate and restructure the deal for the other counterparty, taking on the risks, does this option become a viable structure for hedging debt.

A bank would be willing to take on these mismatches and the inherent interest-rate risks only if there is fair compensation for taking on these risks. The result is a more costly transaction to the borrower. Bid–offer spreads in the long-dated forward market can add fifty or more basis points to the borrowing cost. By comparison, bid–offer spreads in the straight currency swap markets (described in the following section) run ten to fifteen basis points.

Another major limitation to this structure is its inability to deal with floating-rate debt. This structure requires known cash flows in order to operate. It cannot be used to hedge floating-rate instruments.

Advantages:

1 Consistent with FX market conventions;
2 Consistent with existing bank foreign-exchange accounting methods;
3 Flexible, allowing partial hedges limited to specific payment dates.

Disadvantages:

1 Consistent with capital market structure;
2 Difficult to match with counterparty;
3 Tends to leave the intermediary bank with mismatches and gap risks;
4 Can result in tax and accounting anomalies;
5 Limited capital market applications;
6 Can be expensive.

Straight Currency Swap

In the outright exchange-rate pricing formula, the interest rates in both currencies were compounded (to reflect reinvestment) and, in effect, netted. In the straight currency swap, the reinvestment of interest is replaced by periodic interest payments producing a structure that begins to resemble more standard capital market configurations. The exchange at maturity is at today's spot rate (rather than forward exchange rate) with the interest rates and the differential reflected in explicit periodic payments of interest (see Table 14–3).

This structure addresses many of the difficulties faced with the forward outright. Its cash flows resemble those of a capital market instrument, making it much more likely that the dealing bank will be able to more exactly match the position with a third party. This structure also can be used to accommodate floating-rate debt. Because the periodic payments

Table 14–3.
STRAIGHT CURRENCY SWAP.

		Fixed-Rate Straight Currency Swap		
(A) Year	*(B)* Debt Service	*(C)* Receives[a]	*(D)* Pays[b]	*(E)* Net[c]
1	(SF 2.0)	SF 2.5	($ 2.0)	($2.0–SF 0.5)
2	(SF 2.0)	SF 2.5	($ 2.0)	($2.0–SF 0.5)
3	(SF 2.0)	SF 2.5	($ 2.0)	($2.0–SF 0.5)
4	(SF 2.0)	SF 2.5	($ 2.0)	($2.0–SF 0.5)
5	(SF 2.0)	SF 2.5	($ 2.0)	($2.0–SF 0.5)
Maturity	(SF 50.0)	SF 50.0	($25.0)	($25.0)

[a] 5% × SF 50 = SF 2.5
[b] 8% × $25 = $2.0
[c] Net flow (E) = (B) + (C) + (D).

are computed by multiplying the principal by the interest rate, we can create a floating-interest-rate series by specifying a floating index (such as 6 months LIBOR) in place of the fixed rate (see Table 14–4).

We have thus created a fixed foreign-currency swap versus floating U.S. dollars. This fixed/floating structure has become the standard structure in the international market for currency swaps. Most standard currency swaps are now quoted as an absolute fixed rate (such as 4.0 percent) against six-month LIBOR. The one exception would be Canadian dollar currency swaps in which the fixed rate is quoted as a spread over Canadian government bond yields, such as Canadian government yield plus 100 b.p. versus six-month U.S. LIBOR.

This fixed-rated versus LIBOR structure is also the convention in the U.S. dollar interest-rate swap market. Indeed the concept of the interest-rate swap developed as a specialized variation of the straight currency swap. Thus all currency and interest-rate swaps are conveniently quoted against a floating U.S. dollar LIBOR rate.

In both straight currency-swap examples there were some small unhedged residual Swiss francs. Often these are considered inconsequential because of their small size or are dealt with through the

Table 14–4.
STRAIGHT CURRENCY SWAP.

		Floating-Rate Straight Currency Swap		
Year	Debt Service	Receives	Pays	Net
0.5	—	—	(6 mo. LIBOR)	(LIBOR)
1.0	(SF 2.0)	SF 2.5	(6 mo. LIBOR)	(LIBOR–SF 0.5)
1.5	—	—	(6 mo. LIBOR)	(LIBOR)
2.0	(SF 2.0)	SF 2.5	(6 mo. LIBOR)	(LIBOR–SF 0.5)
2.5	—	—	(6 mo. LIBOR)	(LIBOR)
3.0	(SF 2.0)	SF 2.5	(6 mo. LIBOR)	(LIBOR–SF 0.5)
3.5	—	—	(6 mo. LIBOR)	(LIBOR)
4.0	(SF 2.0)	SF 2.5	(6 mo. LIBOR)	(LIBOR–SF 0.5)
4.5	—	—	(6 mo. LIBOR)	(LIBOR)
5.0	(SF 2.0)	SF 2.5	(6 mo. LIBOR)	(LIBOR–SF 0.5)
Maturity	(SF 50.0)	SF 50.0	($25.0)	($25.0)

347

long-dated foreign-exchange market. However, there have been times when it has been necessary to have a fully hedged exchange transaction with no residual exposure. To meet this requirement, a further refinement to the straight currency-swap structure is possible.

Debt Swap

The debt swap introduces the concept of exchanging entire streams of currency flows over time. Pricing adjustments are made, not by adjusting the coupon rates but rather by changing the principal amount. The single requirement of such an exchange is that the net present values of the two currency streams, when discounted at market interest rates for the respective currencies, must be equal at the prevailing spot exchange rate. Using the same example, various alternatives are possible, including a swap at market or off-market coupon rates and also floating rates. In all cases, the principal amounts, rather than the coupon levels, are adjusted to attain the same present value. This suggests that not just one but many different cash-flow configurations can be used to swap against a single exposure. A few examples are shown in Table 14–5.

In a straight currency swap the pricing is focused on the coupon rate. The principal amounts are established, so in order to arrive at a cash flow that equals in present value the foreign-currency forward flow, the coupon is adjusted. But there are instances, such as swaps linked to new issues, when the required coupon is predetermined by the new issue market. By adjusting the size of the issue (that is, the principal amount), we can still attain a workable swap with no unhedged coupon

Table 14–5.
DEBT SWAP.

			Debt Swap				
Year	Debt Service @ 4%	(1) Receives	(2) Pays @ 8.0% or	(3) Pays @ 5.2% or	(4) Pays @ LIBOR or		(5) Pays @ 15%
0.5	—	—	—	($ 0.7)	(6 mo. LIBOR)		($ 1.4)
1.0	(SF 2.0)	SF 2.5	($ 1.9)	($ 0.7)	(6 mo. LIBOR)		($ 1.4)
1.5	—	—	—	($ 0.7)	(6 mo. LIBOR)		($ 1.4)
2.0	(SF 2.0)	SF 2.5	($ 1.9)	($ 0.7)	(6 mo. LIBOR)		($ 1.4)
2.5	—	—	—	($ 0.7)	(6 mo. LIBOR)		($ 1.4)
3.0	(SF 2.0)	SF 2.5	($ 1.9)	($ 0.7)	(6 mo. LIBOR)		($ 1.4)
3.5	—	—	—	($ 0.7)	(6 mo. LIBOR)		($ 1.4)
4.0	(SF 2.0)	SF 2.5	($ 1.9)	($ 0.7)	(6 mo. LIBOR)		($ 1.4)
4.5	—	—	—	($ 0.7)	(6 mo. LIBOR)		($ 1.4)
5.0	(SF 2.0)	SF 2.5	($ 1.9)	($ 0.7)	(6 mo. LIBOR)		($ 1.4)
Maturity	(SF 50.0)	SF 50.0	($23.9)	($27.0)	($23.9)		($18.6)
Present value	SF 47.8[a]	SF 47.8[a]	$23.9	$23.9	$23.9		$23.9
Discount rate	5.0%	5.0%	8.0%	8.0%	LIBOR		8.0%

[a]SF 47.8 = $23.9 @ sot rate of SF 2.00/$.

residual. Thus our SF 47.8 million exposure can be hedged against an 8.0 percent annual dollar bond of $23.9 million (Table 14–5, column 2); a 5.2 percent semi-annual bond of $27 million (column 3); a $23.9 million floating-rate note paying LIBOR (column 4); or a 15 percent semi-annual bond of $18.6 million. All have the same present value as the Swiss franc exposure and can be swapped against it.

The debt swap is the most generic form of the swap. Both the outright and the par value forward structures fit within the debt swap structure and are but specialized cases of the debt swap. In both of these structures the discounted present value of the future cash flows in Swiss francs and dollars are equivalent at today's spot rate. The forward outright is a debt swap of zero coupon debt, while the straight current swap is a debt swap of coupon debt where the principal amounts are exchanged at par. The debt swap also allows exchanges at non-par levels and can accommodate different maturity structures.

Advantages:
1   Achieves complete hedge for both parties;
2   Facilitates the finding of matches;
3   Consistent with capital market convention;
4   Preserves advantages of a straight issue;
5   Easily understood and accepted by senior management, regulatory
        agencies, auditors, and rating agencies;
6   Can hedge both fixed-rate and floating-rate debt (and assets).

Disadvantages:
1   Not consistent with bank forward-market conventions.

COST AND PRICING

Market convention for quoting swaps is unique among traded financial products. It is the one traded item that is quoted not as a price but as a yield. Bond prices may be expressed as a yield, but the dealing quotation is always the bond price. Practical problems arise because while a security has but one price, it can have numerous yields, depending on the quotation basis: Annual, semi-annual, actual/360, 30/360, 365/365, and so forth.

Both interest-rate and cross-currency rates swaps are quoted in terms of the yields on the fixed-interest payments, either as an absolute rate or as a spread over some index yield.[6] Most nondollar interest rate swaps are quoted as an absolute fixed rate (for example, 10¾ percent) against a floating rate, typically U.S. six-month LIBOR. U.S. dollar interest-rate swaps (also Canadian swaps) are quoted as a spread over the yield of U.S. government notes, of similar maturity. For example, the price to a seven-year payor of fixed versus LIBOR might be quoted as "the current yield on the seven-year note plus 98 basis points versus six-month LIBOR." Under market convention, this is an "offer" swap price, while

349

Table 14–6.

SAMPLE SWAP QUOTE, January 12, 1987.

Maturity	US Dollars	Canadian Dollars	Swiss Francs
2 years	33/28	75/60	4.45–4.35
3 years	67/60	95/80	4.70–4.60
4 years	86/81	100/85	4.94–4.85
5 years	92/86	100/85	5.10–5.00
7 years	98/90	105/85	5.20–5.10
10 years	116/109	105/85	5.30–5.20

Maturity	Deutsche Marks	Yen	Guilders
2 years	5.07–4.97	4.67–4.58	6.25–5.95
3 years	5.43–5.35	5.08–4.98	6.50–6.20
4 years	5.73–5.65	5.23–5.13	6.65–6.35
5 years	5.90–5.82	5.35–5.28	6.80–6.50
7 years	6.38–6.28	5.60–5.50	6.85–6.35
10 years	6.70–6.61	5.76–5.66	6.95–6.65

the spread quoted to a floating-rate payer is the "bid" swap price. In such a swap, the intermediary receives six-month LIBOR flat and makes fixed payments. Swap prices are closely tied to the cost of hedging swap exposure. Swaps of shorter maturity are more likely to be hedged in the futures market. The price on a generic swap reflects arrangement fees, risk, the level of competition among swap dealers and the supply of and demand for fixed-rate funds.

All quotes in Table 14–6 are against six-month U.S. dollar LIBOR. U.S. dollar and Canadian dollar swaps are quoted as the basis point spread above the respective government bond yields for the same maturity. Thus if the five-year U.S. government note was yielding 7.00 percent, a swapper paying fixed-rate U.S. dollars would have a coupon of 7.92 percent (7.00 percent plus ninety-two basis points). If the five-year Canadian government bond was yielding 9.00 percent, a swapper paying fixed-rate Canadian dollars would have a coupon of 10.00 percent (9.00 percent plus 100 basis points). A five-year Swiss franc payer would pay 5.10 percent, 5.90 percent in deutsche marks, 5.35 percent in yen, or 6.80 in Dutch guilders. U.S., Canadian, and yen quotes are semi-annual bond basis; Swiss francs, marks, and guilders are on an annual bond basis.

Documentation

There are two ways a swap can be documented. In one method, a series of foreign-exchange telex confirmations is used. This is the simplest way but does not provide the safeguards of the second approach, which is a more detailed document resembling a loan agreement. This covers certain key matters:

1 Exchange of currencies, the dates, and the amounts;
2 Right of setoff;

3 Procedures for periodic settlements, including payment one day early if deemed necessary;
4 Representations and warranties;
5 Security, if necessary;
6 Events of default;
7 Method of determining damage compensation in the case of default;
8 Method of determining damage compensation in the case of an acceleration not resulting from a default (such as, illegality, imposition of withholding taxes, and so forth);
9 Contingency in case of cross-border withholding tax;
10 Governing law.[7]

The International Swap Dealers Association (ISDA) has developed a contract and accompanying code that goes a long way toward standardizing the documentation of swaps. The convention adopted by ISDA combines the advantages of the two methods. The master swap agreement is put in place between two counterparties. This master agreement provides the specifications and protection of all the items above except for the specifics of the transactions. When a transaction is executed, a confirmation detailing the exchanges and referencing the master agreement is exchanged. The deal execution document is thus much simplified while still retaining the protections afforded by the more detailed master document.

Rating Agency Views

Swaps, as they have been used by borrowers in the capital markets, reduce borrowing costs, eliminate risks, and generally improve the balance sheet of the borrower. This is reflected in views expressed by the major rating agencies, Moody's and Standard and Poor's. These agencies have said that swaps, as most often utilized, generally have no negative implications. At worst, the impact is neutral, and in many cases the impact is positive.

APPLICATIONS AND EXAMPLES

Key Features and Advantages

This section is designed to explain, through several examples, some of the new applications in which the currency swap can be and has been used advantageously by borrowers and investors. Because uses are evolving constantly, this is a sampling of applications and not a comprehensive list. The primary features of the currency swap are that it

1 Eliminates foreign currency exposures over time;
2 Creates the desired currency and interest-rate liability structure;

3 Locks in foreign-exchange gains accrued to date on existing
   liabilities;
4 Preserves relative interest-rate advantage enjoyed in the foreign
   borrowing.

Taken individually or together, these features provide the basic incentives underlying almost all currency-swap transactions.

Capital Market Arbitrage

The majority of all currency swaps are done as an arbitrage of capital markets.[8] Prior to the emergence of the swap, there had been no instrument to arbitrage these less-than-efficient long-term markets. The swap enables the long-term borrower to benefit from lower borrowing costs.

In this example, we look at two borrowers (see Figure 14–4):

1 Alpha Company seeks Swiss franc debt. It has been a frequent
   borrower in this market, and the cost of again issuing in the Swiss
   market will therefore be a relatively high 5½ percent for a
   borrower with a AAA credit rating on its senior debt.
2 Omega Company, a well-known U.S. consumer products company
   with a single A credit rating, seeks to raise dollar debt. Its
   borrowing cost in the dollar market would be 8.0 percent.

If these two borrowers proceeded with direct issues in their respective markets, total market investor requirement would be 13.50 percent (5.5 percent to the Swiss franc investors, 8.0 percent to the U.S. dollar investors).

Instead of issuing in the respective national markets, however, each could tap the other's market (see Figure 14–5). Alpha Company borrows in the Eurodollar market paying an AAA rate of 7.5 percent. Omega Company exploits its name recognition in Switzerland and pays an attractive 5.25 percent. The investor requirements are thereby reduced by seventy-five basis points, from 13.50 percent to 12.75 percent (5.25 percent to the Swiss franc investors, 7.50 percent to the U.S. dollar investor). This saving is a result of portfolio diversification advantages and investor idiosyncrasies. These seventy-five basis points

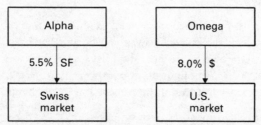

Figure 14–4. Capital Market Arbitrage, Direct Issues.

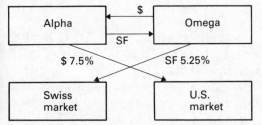

Figure 14–5. Capital Market Arbitrage, Swap.

are arbitrage earnings shared by the two borrowers. By swapping their liabilities, they both effectively borrow their desired currency but at a lower cost than could be attained with a direct issue.

In this swap application, the transfer of relative interest-rate advantage from one currency to another is the operative feature. The parties in the swap utilize each other's relative advantages: Alpha in the U.S. market, Omega in the Swiss market.

Subsidized Export Financing

A U.S. company wished to finance the purchase of machinery from Spain. Because swaps allowed this company's treasurer to look at financing opportunities beyond the dollar, he discovered an attractive alternative:

FINANCING DECISION: The equipment purchase qualified the company for a subsidized export loan in pesetas with a seven-year maturity and a 6 percent interest rate. This, compared with market peseta rates of 22 percent, represented a 16 percent interest rate subsidy.

CURRENCY DECISION: The company sought dollar debt to avoid foreign-currency exposure. Swapping into dollars preserved the company's 16 percent subsidy, thereby created dollar funding at a zero interest cost. The transfer and preservation of the interest-rate advantage from pesetas to dollars made the swap extremely attractive.

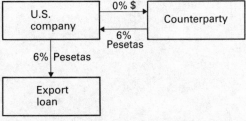

Figure 14–6. Export Financing.

Split-Exposure Debt Structure

Earlier we discussed the advantages of being able to choose the best components when assembling a financing. A good example of this is provided by a U.S. company in need of five-year funding for its French subsidiary at a time when interest rates were at high levels. The borrower perceives interest rates in France to be volatile and therefore risky. Interest rates in the United States, on the other hand, are expected to trend downward. Ideally, the borrower would like a borrowing denominated in French francs but an interest exposure in dollars. No cash instrument can provide this. But through the currency swap, such a structure is possible.

Selecting what was considered the most attractive financing among all of the available options, the company's treasurer raised funds in the U.S. commercial paper market and effectively routed them into France via an intercompany mechanism that avoided withholding taxes. The swap structure was quite unconventional.

FINANCING DECISIONS: Issue U.S. commercial paper.

CURRENCY DECISION: The treasurer, seeking French franc debt, entered into a five-year French franc/dollar currency swap (fixed for fixed). However, a mismatch results because his funding base is thirty-day U.S. dollar commercial paper.

The resulting French franc borrowing has an initial cost of 15.5 percent (18.5 percent – 3.0 percent yield curve advantage). This compares against a cash market cost of short-term francs of over 16 percent.

This swap strategy created the desired French franc funding, and although the cost of debt will float, it will not float with the volatile and unpredictable French rates but with dollar rates, which the borrower expected would fall.

Advantages:

1 French franc–denominated financing;
2 Beginning interest rate lower than French market rates because the swap transfers the relative advantage of dollar commercial paper funding to the French franc funding;

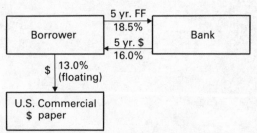

Figure 14–7. Split Exposure Swap.

3 Floating interest rate in line with U.S. interest rates;
4 Optimum financing achieved through a split exposure financing structure with currency exposure in French francs and interest exposure to U.S. dollar rates.

This technique makes any combination of currency and interest risk possible. It can, for example, hedge a U.S. currency risk by creating dollar liability at a cost linked to a stable interest rate, such as the yen, a managed interest rate historically characterized by relatively low volatility.

Availability Creation

Many borrowers prefer to raise funds at fixed rates in low coupon currencies, such as the Swiss franc. Often, however, borrowers from less developed countries lack the credit strength to tap the Swiss market and are limited primarily to dollar LIBOR financing.

FINANCING DECISION: A sovereign borrower accesses available funding by drawing down a LIBOR facility.

CURRENCY DECISION: The borrower swaps floating dollars for fixed-rate Swiss francs, synthetically creating a liability it otherwise could not obtain (see Figure 14–8).

Balance-Sheet Restructuring

A U.S. company has a Dutch subsidiary with low coupon dollar debt. Because of the new accounting conventions of FASB 52, the company now wants the subsidiary to refinance itself in guilders. It explores prepayment and refinancing options.

FINANCING DECISION: Explicit refinancing is not advisable for three reasons:

1 Loan terms have prepayment penalty;
2 Realization of accrued FX gain would involve a tax liability;
3 Company would lose attractive below-market dollar funding.

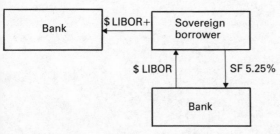

Figure 14–8. Availability Creation.

355

CURRENCY DECISION: To gain guilder liabilities, swap existing dollar
   debt for guilders:

1 No prepayment, so no penalty;
2 No prepayment, so no FX gain realization in the tax book;
3 Interest advantage not lost but transferred to guilder debt, producing below-market guilder cost.

Working-Capital Management

There are times when the cost of debt is not as important as the timing
and amount of debt service (that is, interest and amortization). A real
estate development company needed bridge financing for a five-year
period at the start of a building project. Because cash flows are low in
the early period, the company hoped to minimize the cash required for
debt servicing. The solution was reached in several stages:

1 A drawdown of a fixed-rate five-year bullet dollar loan at 13 percent;
2 A straight currency swap in which the borrower receives 13 percent
   dollars and pays 6 percent Swiss francs;
3 A series of forward outright transactions against the Swiss franc
   obligation. The result was about a 50 percent reduction in
   cash-flow requirements for interest (with a corresponding increase
   in the bullet repayment) (see Table 14–7).

Asset Swaps

The examples so far have been swaps on the liability side, but asset
swaps are also common. For example, Japanese investors wish to
diversify their yen portfolios geographically while enhancing their
yields.

INVESTMENT/CREDIT DECISION: They buy Mexican bonds yielding 15 percent (some 600 basis points over U.S. Treasury yields).
CURRENCY DECISION: They want yen assets. They swap the dollar
   income stream for a yen income stream. The resulting yen asset

Table 14.7.
CASH-FLOW MANAGEMENT.

Objective: Minimize early period cash requirement for debt service.

| 13% Debt | Straight Swap | | Forward Outright | |
Pays	Receives	Pays	Receives	Pays
($ 6.5)	$ 6.5	(SF 6.0)	SF 6.0	($ 3.2)
($ 6.5)	$ 6.5	(SF 6.0)	SF 6.0	($ 3.4)
($ 6.5)	$ 6.5	(SF 6.0)	SF 6.0	($ 3.6)
($ 6.5)	$ 6.5	(SF 6.0)	SF 6.0	($ 3.9)
($56.5)	$56.5	(SF 106.0)	SF 106.0	($73.9)

Result: Cash needs reduced in early periods some 50 percent ($3.2 versus $6.5).

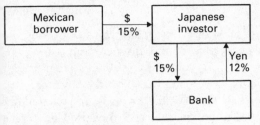

Figure 14–9. Investor Swap.

yields around 12 percent, a yield not available with a direct yen instrument (see Figure 14–9).

Cross-Currency Interest-Rate Swap

As already demonstrated, the currency swap allows for considerable flexibility in structuring. Most examples considered so far have been swaps converting fixed-rate instruments in one currency to fixed-rate structures in another. The swap can also convert rates from fixed in one currency to floating in another and vice versa, or from floating to floating. Borrowers therefore have the opportunity to optimize their relative cost advantages in both the fixed- and floating-rate markets.

Consider Alpha Corporation, which wants to borrow seven-year Japanese yen. A direct fixed-rate yen loan would cost 5.6 percent. To reduce the cost, Alpha issues U.S. commercial paper and swaps the floating-rate dollar liability into fixed-rate yen. The swap results in Alpha's receiving six-month dollar LIBOR and paying 5.25 percent yen.

Given the structure of the swap, Alpha's yen cost may even be lower than 5.25 percent. Alpha pays 5.25 percent yen and dollar commercial paper rate and, in turn, is paid dollar LIBOR and dollar commercial paper. LIBOR rates have historically been twenty to 100 basis points higher than commercial paper rates. Assuming that rate differential holds in this swap, Alpha has, at minimum, a twenty basis points (b.p.) arbitrage spread (relative advantage). This reduces the yen financing cost from 5.25 percent to 5.05 percent, 55 b.p. better than Alpha could achieve with a direct yen financing (see Figure 14–10).

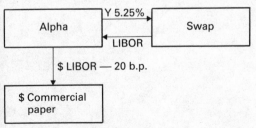

Figure 14–10. Cross-Currency Interest-Rate Swap.

CONCLUSION

This chapter has illustrated a few of the many innovative borrowing and investment opportunities generated by the currency swap. Basic to its versatility and effectiveness is the currency swap's ability to transfer cost advantages from one currency to another. For the investor, that translates into greater portfolio diversity, higher yields, and reduced risk levels. For the borrower, it provides access to worldwide capital markets, reduced interest-rate risks, increased structuring flexibility, and lower capital costs.

In all, the swap has proven itself to be a powerful tool in contemporary financial management. This is evidenced by a global swap market measured annually in the hundreds of billions of dollars. It is not a novelty transaction but has become a fundamental building block in the structuring of term financial transactions.

NOTES

1. Bank for International Settlements, *Innovations In International Banking* (Basle: BIS, 1986), Ch. 2, p. 37.

2. Simon Tait, "It Takes Two to Tango," *Euromoney* (February 1983): 75.

3. Rod Beckstrom, "The Development of the Swap Market," *Euromoney Swap Finance*, Volume I, Boris Antl, ed., (London: Euromoney Publications, 1986) p. 33.

4. Robert W. Kopprasch, "Understanding Duration and Volatility" (New York: Salomon Brothers, 1985).

5. John Price, "The Technical Evolution of the Currency Swap Product," *Euromoney Swap Finance*, Volume I, Boris Antl, ed., (London: Euromoney Publications, 1986), p. 53.

6. Kopprasch, MacFarlane, Ross, and Showers, "The Interest Rate Swap Market: Yield Mathematics, Terminology and Conventions," (New York: Salomon Brothers, June 1985).

7. Gray, Jurk, and Strupp, "Structuring and Documenting Interest Rate Swaps," *International Financial Law Review* (February 1984).

8. Coporate Finance Euromoney Supplement, "Why the Swaps Market Make Some Currencies Popular," *The Global Swaps Market* (June 1986): 27.

15 Currency Options

SCOTT N. DILLMAN

CURRENCY options have been in existence in subtle forms for centuries. Nevertheless, there was not a seriously conceived marketplace until 1982 when the over-the-counter (OTC) and exchange-traded markets blossomed. Although Amsterdam had limited activity in the late 1970s, it was not until 1982 that the Philadelphia Stock Exchange (PHLX) emerged with a viable trading, hedging, and investment tool in foreign-exchange options.

Since 1982 there has been remarkable growth in the foreign-exchange-options markets, yet the majority of the growth is yet to come. To date the market has been propelled by traders, arbitrageurs, and speculators with only a small portion of the volume coming from bona fide hedgers. Because currency options are not well understood in the United States, only a small portion of the *Fortune* 500 corporations have begun to use them.

Most corporate traders and treasurers know the basic terminology of options but cannot compare the merits of options in relation to other foreign-exchange-hedging products. When corporations finally establish a framework within which meaningful hedging decisions can be made, the foreign-exchange-options market will exhibit growth far greater than that of the past four years. This chapter gives step-by-step guidance on how to build a simple decision matrix from which corporate traders can decipher when best to use the spot, forward, futures, or options markets to hedge their currency exposures.

TERMINOLOGY

For the foreign-exchange-option novice, terminology used in discussing options may seem complicated. Dealing spot foreign exchange is a one-dimensional product, while dealing currency options is a four-dimensional product. Before one can discuss employing options in hedge management, the terminology of the options marketplace must be examined.

Definition

A currency option is the contractual right to buy or sell a currency against another currency, usually the U.S. dollar. A call denotes the right to buy a currency versus the U.S. dollar, and a put denotes the right to sell a currency versus the U.S. dollar. This right must be exercised before a specified date, which is known as the expiration date. The right, however, may be exercised only at a specific rate, referred to as the strike price. To acquire this right, the buyer of the option must pay a fee, called a premium. The important difference between the traditional spot or forward markets and the options market is that an option is a right while a spot or forward deal is an obligation.

Options are further differentiated according to whether they are "American" or "European". This does not indicate where the option is transacted. Instead, an American option can be exercised any day up to the final expiration date, whereas a European option can be exercised only on the expiration date. For this added degree of flexibility an American option usually trades at a premium vis-à-vis a European option.

Option traders also categorize options as either in-the-money, at-the-money, or out-of-the-money. An in-the-money option is where the spot price is above the strike price of a call or the spot price is below the strike price of a put. An at-the-money option is a call or put where the spot price is identical to the strike price, and an out-of-the-money option is where the spot price is below the strike price of a call or the spot price is above the strike price of a put. This classification is used to more specifically define puts and calls.

If spot sterling is trading at 1.44, the following options are classified as

1. In-the-money   1.45 put
                       1.40 call
2. At-the-money   1.44 put
                       1.44 call
3. Out-of-the-money   1.40 put
                       1.45 call

In the above example, the 1.40 call is profitable or in-the-money by the value of four cents because sterling is trading at 1.44 and one has the right to buy sterling at 1.40. The 1.45 call is out-of-the-money because if this were the expiration date the right to buy sterling at 1.45 has no worth because sterling is trading at 1.44.

MARKETS

The currency-options market provides two marketplaces in which to participate—the exchange markets and the over-the-counter market (OTC). The exchange markets have standardized contracts where the option contract size, strike price, and expiration date are predetermined by the exchange. OTC options, however, are nonstandardized contracts where the option's specifications are negotiated and fixed between the buyer and seller. See Figure 15–1.

Another important difference between the two marketplaces is that the exchange-traded market is subject to a regulatory body that enforces the rights and obligations of the buyer and seller and insures that the buyer and seller satisfy the required margins. In the United States the Option Clearing Corporation (OCC) serves as the regulator to insure the buyer and seller of their rights.

The OTC marketplace differs from the exchange-traded markets because there is no intermediary between the buyer and seller of an option. Because the OTC market is nonstandardized, corporations can buy "tailor-made" ,options. An OTC option provides the necessary maturities that a corporate trader needs, whereas an exchange-traded option cannot be structured to the exact expiration requirements because the exchanges have standardized expiration dates. An OTC option also can be of any tenor, while an exchange traded option can have a life of only twelve to eighteen months depending on the exchange. Another advantage is that OTC options have the flexibility of dealing options with any strike price the corporation desires.

OTC options can also be constructed as cross-rate or cross-currency options. For example, a deutsche mark call versus the Swiss franc is a cross-rate option that does not trade on an exchange. The exchanges offer options only in currencies in relation to the U.S. dollar.

Although the OTC marketplace is loosely defined as any place a buyer and seller mutually agree to an option's specifications and ultimately the dealing price, the exchange-traded marketplace is specifically defined. Today exchange-traded currency options are dealt in four different countries, England, Holland, Canada, and the United States. Because nearly 95 percent of the daily volume occurs on the U.S. exchanges, however, for our discussions we will refer to the U.S. exchanges.

As Table 15–1 illustrates, there are three U.S. exchanges where currency options are traded. There are material differences between these exchanges and the type of option contracts traded. On all three exchanges the currencies traded are the British pound, West German

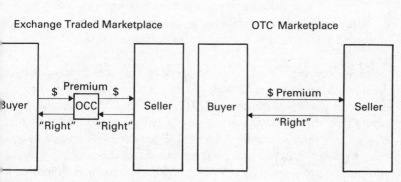

Exchange Traded Marketplace | OTC Marketplace

Figure 15–1. Option Marketplace.

Table 15–1.

CURRENCY OPTIONS, VOLUME AND OPEN INTEREST.

	November 1986 Volume	November 1986 Open Interest
CME:		
Deutsche mark	194,219	128,931
Swiss franc	82,263	55,815
French franc	NA	NA
Japanese yen	114,123	89,103
Canadian dollar	3,961	8,011
British pound	40,473	53,212
PHLX:		
Deutsche mark	269,028	262,334
Swiss franc	257,207	383,940
French franc	NA	NA
Japanese yen	114,637	164,001
Canadian dollar	10,597	23,561
British pound	63,665	145,957
European currency unit (ECU)	430	2,203
CBOE:		
Deutsche mark	9,022	9,302
Swiss franc	5,021	5,801
French franc	–	411
Japanese yen	8,641	11,376
Canadian dollar	3,446	10,043
British pound	2,317	4,713

Source: Futures and Options World (December 1986).

mark, Swiss franc, Japanese yen, and Canadian dollar. The Philadelphia Stock Exchange, however, offers the European Currency Unit (ECU) option contract, which the other two exchanges do not. Although they offer similar currencies, the exchanges differ in the following ways:

1. The International Monetary Market (IMM) trades options on the currency futures contract, whereas the CBOE and the PHLX deal options on currency spot.
2. The CBOE deals European currency options (that is, options exercisable only on the final expiration date), whereas the PHLX and IMM option contracts are U.S. currency options (that is, options exercisable anytime until the final expiration date).
3. The IMM option expires usually one week earlier than the PHLX and CBOE option within each expiration cycle.

Despite offering different option specifications the three exchanges provide the corporate trader with an additional tool to help manage his currency exposures. Although the OTC marketplace has many inherent advantages, the exchange markets offer a centralized secondary market where one's options can be liquidated. Both the OTC and exchange-traded markets have their advantages and disadvantages, and it is the corporation's responsibility to understand both markets in order that it can use both to their benefit.

What Is an Option Worth?

In the simplest form an option is worth what a buyer will pay for something else to assume his risks of hedging, or what a seller deems an acceptable premium for assuming the risks of the buyer. In an option trader's mind an option is composed of two major factors, the intrinsic value and the time value. The intrinsic value is the value of an option on expiration date. It can also be expressed as the amount by which the spot price is higher than the strike price in the case of a call or lower than the strike price in the case of a put. Intrinsic value cannot be referred to as a negative because no one would then exercise it and incur a loss.

The time value is the remaining value of an option. The term *time value* is a misnomer because it is composed of several items other than the time component of an option. It is composed of the effects of time to expiration, of volatility of the currency, and of the interrelationship of the domestic interest rate and foreign interest rate. For example,

December 17, 1986   Spot sterling = 1.44
March 15, 1987   1.40 call = 6.25 ¢
Intrinsic value of call = 4 ¢ (1.44 – 1.40)
Time value of call = 2.25 ¢ (6.25 ¢ – 4 ¢)

The "time to expiration" component of "time value" implies that the more time that an option has to expiration, the greater its chance to become profitable or gain intrinsic value. Therefore, the longer the time to expiration, the greater the value of an option. The volatility of the currency also plays an important role in determining the time value. A currency that has a high degree of volatility increases "time value" and the overall price of an option because the buyer will pay a higher price to the seller to assume the risk of hedging the currency with a higher volatility.

The third component of "time value" is the interest-rate differential between the two currencies involved over the life of the option. For example, forward premium currencies such as the deutsche mark have slightly higher values for their calls relative to their puts because German interest rates are lower than U.S. rates. The future value of the mark trades at a premium to the current spot, therefore biasing the model to assign a higher value for calls than puts that are struck at the spot price.

To properly assess the value of an option one must input the spot price, strike price, time to expiration, volatility, and the two currencies' corresponding interest rates into a computerized algorithm to generate an option's value. The value that is calculated is commonly referred to as the "fair value" or "theoretical value."

There are several models or algorithms used today by market participants to generate an option's theoretical or fair value, but all these models generate values with a small variance from each other. Although these models have slightly different specifications, they all employ the same variables to generate the theoretical value.

The most common pricing model for currency options is based on the Black–Scholes call option valuation formula, which was originally developed for the pricing of stock options. The model is the industry's standard and widely used with and without modifications by many traders to guide their trading decisions. It was the first option pricing model of an option assuming that no risk-free profits can be made by any combination of trading in options and the underlying securities. The formula is obtained by construction of a riskless hedge using the option and its underlying securities and then solving the equation for the option price.

EXPOSURE MANAGEMENT

Today the treasurer or corporate trader is presented with a growing number of investment tools to master. The treasurer's job is not simply that of spot trader, forward trader, futures traders or options trader, where the appropriate hat is quickly donned for the appropriate situation. Instead the treasurer must wear one hat entitled "Exposure Manager" and must be able to work with varying products as the situation demands.

The trader must be able to mix and match various hedging instruments to protect corporate concerns. There is no right or wrong method to hedge oneself, yet there are better or worse means of hedging. The better all the necessary hedging tools are understood, the better one will be able to perform as an "Exposure Manager."

There still remain a few die-hard corporations that will avoid the options markets. They claim that by employing good technical and fundamental analysis they can outperform corporate treasurers who try to use all available hedging tools. Nevertheless, if those same corporate treasurers understood options, they would be better able to perform their jobs.

Too often comments like, "options are too risky" or "options are too expensive," are uttered after a disgruntled corporation is confronted with a poor option hedge. It is only the naive or "seat of the pants" trader who throws options aside. Before starting to trade currency options, the corporate trader should build a well thought out decision matrix from which to derive hedging decisions. After the corporate trader builds a decision matrix from which to select the spot, forward, futures, or option market as a hedging tool, it becomes apparent that options are only a small part of hedge management. Such a disciplined corporate trader can decipher when an option strategy has the highest probability of producing the most desirable hedging results.

Options are a unique hedging tool, yet they are not the answer to all trading problems. Following a thorough assessment as described above, a corporate trader will realize that only 30 to 35 percent of all the hedging situations will result in using options as the preferred hedge solution.

The importance of constructing a detailed decision matrix before making a hedging decision cannot be underestimated. To construct the *simplest* decision matrix one must weigh the following factors: (1) The institution's risk tolerance or risk/reward ratio, (2) the nature of the exposure to be hedged (that is, contingent, future, or current), (3) the corporate trader's histogram on the price action of the currency to be hedged, (4) the duration that the currency needs to be managed, (5) the corporate trader's view of the interest-rate differential between the U.S. dollar and the managed currency's interest rate during the life of the exposure, and (6) the corporate trader's forecast of the future volatility of the managed currency.

`able 15–2.
)ECISION MATRIX.

actors	Description	Most Probable Hedge Instrument
stitutional risk tolerance	High risk/reward ratio	Spot, Forward, or Future
	Low to medium risk/reward ratio	Options
ype of exposure	Contingent exposure	Options
	Actual exposure	Spot, Forward, or Future
urrency outlook	70–100% confidence in direction of currency	Spot, Forward, or Future
	0–70% confidence in direction of currency	Options
xposure maturity	Definite date of exposure	Spot, Forward, or Future
	Indefinite date of exposure	Options
terest-rate differential	No change in differential	Spot, Forward, or Future
	Uncertainty of differential	Option
olatility outlook	Higher volatility expected	Options
	Lower volatility expected	Spot, Forward, or Future

Other factors are also important, but if these six points are considered one will avoid the common pitfalls in exposure management. If the corporate trader does not use these criteria or similar criteria, the job of exposure management will become a game of hit or miss.

Of the six criteria needed to develop a proper decision matrix, five are used by most corporations today. "The corporate trader's forecast of the future volatility of the managed currency" is the only criterion that most corporations did not include before options emerged. Surprisingly, the assessment of future volatility is often the most important criterion in deciding whether to use the spot, forward, futures, or options market as a hedge.

The most important and most often overlooked criterion is "the institution's risk tolerance or risk/reward ratio." Typical members of senior management vary in the level of risk tolerance and the risk/reward ratio that is acceptable to them. Few institutions have a documented and well-understood risk/reward ratio. Nevertheless, all management needs to understand whether the corporation has a moderate-risk/moderate-return or high-risk/high-return outlook and also understand what moderate risk or high risk means. It is surprising that few corporations have a good grasp of the concept of risk/return ratios and that few consciously adopt a risk/return approach. This shortcoming can take a prosperous corporation and sidetrack it financially.

The second criterion needed to build a proper decision matrix is understanding "the nature of the exposure." The corporate trader must know at the decision point whether the exposure is actual or contingent. If the exposure is contingent, there should be an assessment of the likelihood that the contingency will become an actual exposure. If a contingent exposure has a 70 percent or less chance of becoming an actual exposure, it is highly probable that purchasing an option to hedge the exposure is the preferred choice. When a corporate trader has a contingent exposure, it is usually a simple clear-cut decision to use options. This is the only criterion where it is often a simple process to decide on the best hedging tool.

"The corporate trader's histogram on the price action of the currency" is the third criterion and often erroneously thought of as the most important. The corporate trader spends much time using fundamental and technical analysis to decide a currency's future value. The preoccupation with "guessing" a currency's future value often dwarfs all other decision criteria so much that many corporations in reality are working with a one-dimensional decision matrix. If corporations spent more time on the other five decision criteria, they would find that their long-term results fared better.

A currency's price outlook is an important criterion, yet it should be given less weight then most corporations give it today. To properly evaluate this criterion in the decision matrix one must first establish a histogram for the exposed currency, over the life of the exposure. A histogram is a graph of an expected frequency distribution. Graphically going through this exercise, along with calculating profitability at all points along the histogram and weighing the results against the firm's risk/reward ratio, usually clarifies for the trader which hedging tool should be used.

For a moderate-risk/moderate-return corporation it is usually necessary to have a 70 to 75 percent confidence level of a particular outcome before the exposure is left unhedged or sold in the forward market depending whether the exposure is short or long. If a corporation is to be short deutsche marks in three months and the trader's histogram on December 17 indicates that there is a 70 percent probability that the mark will be stronger than current levels (2.0150), the purchase of spot,

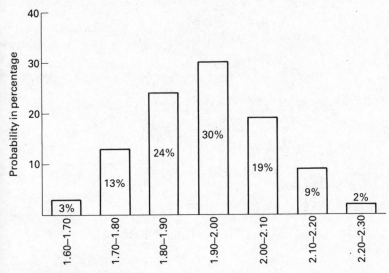

Note: December 17, 1986
   Spot deutsche mark = 2.0150

Figure 15–2. Histogram for Deutsche Mark Three-Month Horizon.

forward, or future marks would probably be the preferred hedge. If one does not have a 70 to 75 percent confidence level of a particular outcome, the decision matrix would normally point toward the options market as the preferred hedging vehicle.

The fourth criterion, "the duration that the currency needs to be managed," goes in tandem with the establishment of a histogram of the price outlook. The histogram should account for the duration of the exposure and not some arbitrary time period. This point becomes more significant if and when options are decided as the prescribed hedging tool.

The fifth criterion is "the corporate trader's view of the interest-rate differential between the U.S. dollar and the managed currency's interest rate." This is normally an inconsequential criterion, yet when dealing with currencies that have high or low interest rates relative to the United States, this factor has significance.

The sixth and final criterion needed to build a decision matrix is "the corporate trader's forecast of the future volatility of the managed currency." This criterion is new to most corporate traders and needs to be expounded. It often is the determining factor whether options, spot, or forwards are used to hedge. In the order of importance to the decision matrix, the traders' viewpoint of future volatility is second in importance only to understanding the corporation's risk/reward ratio.

VOLATILITY

Volatility is important in building a decision matrix and is also a key   **367**

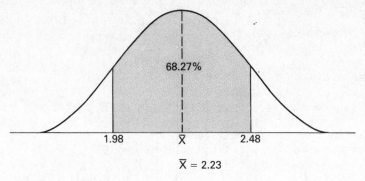

$\overline{X} = 2.23$

Note: In deutsche marks.

$\overline{X} \pm 1STD = 1.98$ and 2.48

Figure 15–3. Distribution Curve, January 1988–March 1988.

variable in determining the price of an option. To understand options and make hedging decisions one must understand volatility. Volatility measures the variability of a currency over a specified period of time. Statistically defined, volatility is the annual standard deviation of a currency. Mathematically, it can be defined as

$$\sqrt{\frac{N\Sigma_{a=1}^{N}(X_2 - \overline{X})^2}{N}}$$

N = Number of observations
$\overline{X}$ = Average price of N

For currencies that have a normal distribution, it follows statistically that 68.27 percent of all prices will fall between one standard deviation above and below the mean. Also 95.45 percent of all prices will fall between two standard deviations above and below the mean.

For example, if the deutsche mark had a standard deviation of 0.14 (that is, 14 percent volatility) it would be represented as shown in Figure 15–3, where 68.27 percent of the occurrences fall between 2.48 and 1.98. However, if the deutsche mark had a standard deviation of 0.07 (that is, 7 percent volatility) it would be represented as shown in Figure 15–4, where 68.27 percent of the occurrences fall between 2.36 and 2.10.

Both examples have identical means, yet because their standard deviations are different there is a difference in the variability of price. In Figure 15–4 there is a greater chance \$/DM is nearer to 2.23 than in Figure 15–3. However, in Figure 15–3 there is a wider range of possible outcomes. These simple properties are essential when deciding on hedging strategies and subsequently pricing an option. The importance will be apparent through various hedging examples.

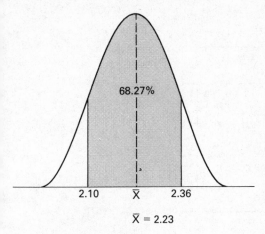

$\overline{X} = 2.23$

Note: In deutsche marks.

$\overline{X} \pm 1\,STD = 2.10$ and 2.36

Figure 15–4. Distribution Curve, January 1988–March 1988.

SIX TYPES OF VOLATILITIES

To understand volatility and its importance in exposure management one must dissect and expound it thoroughly. Within the concept of volatility there are six distinct types of volatility:

1 Historical
2 Implied
3 Seasonal
4 Range
5 Forecast
6 Future

Historical volatility is the most commonly discussed type. It is calculated by taking a given series of observations over a specific period of time and calculating the annualized standard deviation. Usually the option trader will take a fifty-, sixty-, or ninety-day series of observations and generate its standard deviation (that is, historical volatility). A time series of those durations is used because the average length of an option is two to three months. This is not to say that options do not trade with longer or shorter expiration dates, but the greatest volume of options traded is of the two to three months to expiration. Therefore, using the last fifty, sixty, or ninety days of price history of the spot currency should give the trader an idea of the possible next two to three months of price volatility. The past two to three months of price volatility is used as a starting point to forecast the future volatility. For instance, on December 17, 1986, the ten-, thirty-, fifty-, and 250-day historical volatilities are as shown in Table 15–3.

369

Table 15–3.
HISTORICAL VOLATILITIES.

	Days			
Currency	10	30	50	250
British pound	3.8	6.7	6.9	11.1
Deutsche mark	9.7	9.2	9.4	13.0
Yen	3.4	8.0	9.6	12.2
Swiss franc	17.3	13.7	12.7	14.5
Canadian dollar	4.8	2.9	2.4	4.7
Mexican peso	3.8	14.8	16.6	29.9
Dutch guilder	8.5	10.7	10.3	12.8
French franc	8.7	8.5	8.9	13.0
Belgian franc	15.2	11.0	10.5	14.1
Lire	9.0	8.7	9.1	13.1
ECU	8.0	7.9	8.3	N/A

Source: The Options Group (December 17, 1986).

Of the six types of volatilities, implied volatility is the most closely monitored. It is used as a predictor of volatility for pricing options. The implied volatility is the implicit level of volatility inherent in a particular call or put, assuming that all other option variables are held constant. It is calculated by taking a particular option's value and by iteration deriving the volatility level present in the option.

The implied volatility of options helps in determining relative worth. If a corporation intended to buy sterling calls to protect a short sterling position, the trader would pick the March 1.40 call as the cheapest option from an implied volatility standpoint. The corporate trader would also have to consider maturity and strike price. Nevertheless, the corporate realizes that all other factors being equal the March 1.40 calls are the cheapest call to purchase (see Table 15–4).

Table 15–4.
BRITISH POUND OPTIONS, PHILADELPHIA STOCK EXCHANGE.

Option Date/Strike Price	Call Bid	Call Ask	Call Last	Call Implied	
Mar 140	3.25	3.65	—	8.6	(Cheapest relative value)
Mar 145	1.05	1.25	—	8.9	
Mar 150	0.20	0.40	0.35	9.2	
Mar 155	0.05	0.25	—	11.1	
Mar 160	0.05	0.15	—	13.2	
Jun 140	3.75	4.15	4.05	9.1	
Jun 145	1.75	1.95	1.90	9.5	
Jun 150	0.70	0.90	—	9.8	
Jun 155	0.25	0.45	0.30	10.2	
Jun 160	0.10	0.20	—	10.6	
Sep 140	4.30	4.70	4.40	9.8	
Sep 145	2.20	2.60	—	9.9	
Sep 150	1.10	1.30	—	10.0	
Sep 155	0.50	0.70	—	10.2	
Sep 160	0.20	0.40	—	10.5	

Source: The Options Group (December 17, 1986).

Implied volatility coupled with historical volatility are used as predictive factors to forecast volatility. By understanding what the volatility of the spot currency has been in the past (that is, historical volatility) and using the volatility level that is implicit in options today (implied volatility) one can make a good approximation of future volatility and subsequently more accurately value options.

The better corporate option trader monitors the relationship between historical volatility and implied volatility. In most of the major currencies the implied and historical volatilities will not deviate from each other by more than 3 percent volatility (see Figure 15–5). As shown in Figure 15–5 sterling's historical and implied volatilities did not deviate more than 3 percent from each other except in one instance. From September 18 to 24 the implied volatility exceeded the historical volatility by more than 3 percent. This tells the corporation one of two things: (1) Implied volatility is too high relative to historical and the implied volatility will come down—that is, the relative option values will decline; or (2) the historical volatility will converge to implied volatility, in which case the British pound should become more volatile in the spot market.

A corporate treasurer who intended to buy an option for hedging purposes in late September would probably hold off the purchase and hedge in the spot market until the implied volatility traded closer in line with historical volatility. In delaying the purchase the corporate trader will likely be able to purchase a cheaper option from a volatility standpoint.

The third type of volatility is seasonal. Like spot rates of currencies volatility has similar seasonal pressures. Accordingly, the historical and implied volatilities have a tendency to be consistently higher at certain times of the year and lower at others (see Figure 15–6).

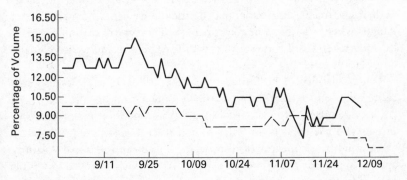

Note: A = Historical volatility
      B = Implied volatility

Source: The Options Group (December 17, 1986).

Figure 15–5. Historical and Implied Volatility, British Pound Sterling, September–December 1986.

371

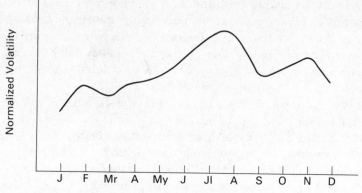

Note: No source to credit (December 17, 1986).

Figure 15–6. Seasonal Chart, Deutsche Mark, 1973–86.

Understanding the seasonal fluctuations of volatility can help the corporate trader. The trader gleans from this seasonal chart that August, December, and January usually display the lowest historical volatility levels, indicating the most opportune time to buy options, all other factors being equal. Remember that volatility is a major variable in the pricing of options and if the volatility component is lower the price will be lower.

The seasonal chart also illustrates that June and September are the months in which a corporation should avoid buying or instead sell options because those are the months that volatility is the highest. It is only the highly organized corporation who can take advantage of this knowledge. For example, if the corporate trader stays in close contact with his marketing/sales people and they indicate that they are perceiving a large September sales volume in Germany in September (invoiced in deutsche marks), the trader may decide to buy deutsche mark puts in August when volatility is at a seasonal low. This type of planning cannot be undertaken by all corporations, yet the aggressive and well-organized corporation can.

Range volatility is the fourth type of volatility. It is a more sophisticated version of volatility that usually only a bank or an investment bank trader uses. However, it is also important for the corporate to understand the concept in order to construct more efficient hedges.

Although the concepts of historical, implied, and seasonal volatility appear to provide the corporate or bank trader with the necessary tools to decide an option's relative worth, there are some shortcomings in those methods. The major shortcoming is in how historical volatility is calculated. To calculate historical volatility one records the closing spot price of a currency and from there calculates the standard deviation (that is, volatility). Suppose, for instance, that closing spot levels for the deutsche mark were as follows:

Day 1	1.9520
Day 2	1.9450
Day 3	1.9575
Day 4	1.9510
Day 5	1.9480

One would consider the deutsche mark to have relatively low volatility. Suppose, however, that on the same days the daily ranges of the deutsche mark were as follows:

	Range	*Close*
Day 1	(1.9380–1.9745)	1.9520
Day 2	(1.9295–1.9680)	1.9450
Day 3	(1.9460–1.9730)	1.9575
Day 4	(1.9265–1.9610)	1.9510
Day 5	(1.9275–1.9615)	1.9480

One then would consider the deutsche mark to be trading with a high degree of volatility and very difficult to hedge an exposure using the spot market during this five-day period. There is a fallacy in using the closing spot level to compute historical volatility. Using the aforementioned historical data, one would calculate the historical volatility as a relatively low figure. Using this as a forecasting tool where volatility will be over the life of the option, you will probably underestimate the volatility and also the value of an option. If you were to factor in the interday range of this five-day period, the deutsche mark would have a much higher volatility associated with it. Over the five-day period the mark had a daily range of 3 to 4 pfennigs, which is a relatively large range, yet all five of the daily closing spot prices were within $1\frac{1}{2}$ pfennigs, a relatively small difference on five daily closes.

For our purposes it is not important to show the different methods one could calculate "range" volatility (that is, a figure that takes into account the daily range of spot prices). However, it is important to point out that historical volatility may not be as viable a forecaster of volatility for the pricing and dealing of options as some banks and corporations think. A corporate trader should work with the banks and investment banks that understand the pitfalls of historical volatility and seek out those banks that can provide range volatility analysis before pricing an option.

The fifth type of volatility is "forecast." Through the analysis of historical, implied, seasonal, and range volatilities one "forecasts" where volatility should be over the life of an option. In the process of forecasting volatility one will estimate the optimum time to buy or sell an option and also the most appropriate price to deal an option. All market practitioners have subtle differences on how they forecast volatility, but most traders use historical, implied, seasonal, and some form of range volatility to make their forecasts.

The sixth and final volatility is "future" volatility. This measurement is the actual volatility that transpires over an option's life. It is important to track the actual historical and implied volatility of a currency over the life one has dealt an option. One should observe the future volatility of a currency in respect to the implied volatility that was paid for the option. In doing that a trader will be able to see how a forecast performs in relation to the future volatility and then perhaps be able to better hone forecasting skills.

It may appear that the concept of volatility has been overdone from a corporation's standpoint, but that is not the case. The corporate trader who is serious about using options to the fullest must have a good grasp of all six types of volatilities. Understanding volatility will enable the corporate trader to:

1 Choose the most appropriate hedging tool for a given situation;
2 Improve the timing of purchases and sales of options; and
3 Construct better option strategies for hedging purposes.

After understanding the basics of volatility one can also assess the proper worth of an option. In pricing an option one needs:

1 Current spot price;
2 Option's strike price;
3 Time to expiration;
4 Interest-rate differential between the U.S. dollar and foreign currency;
5 Forecast of future volatility of foreign currency.

The first four ingredients needed to price an option are known variables and can be readily obtained. The only variable that is not known is the "future" volatility. The option trader forecasts the figure by analyzing the historical, implied, seasonal, and range volatility.

After inputting all five variables into an algorithm, a "fair value" or "theoretical value" for the option is generated. This is not intended to be the exact or only price for the option. An option's "fair" value can come in many forms. For example, on December 17, 1986, we calculated the "fair value" for a deutsche mark option using the following variables:

1 Spot deutsche mark   = 2.0150
2 Strike price of call   = 2.000 European terms
                               0.5000 American terms
3 Time to expiration (June 17, 1987) = 176 days
4 Interest rate differential   = 6.500 U.S. dollar rate
                               5.1717 deutsche mark rate

5 Forecast of future volatility   = 10.6% annualized

The "fair value" generated from the options model was

1   2.8497%
2   142.49 U.S. points
3   5.74 pfennigs

All three answers are identical in dollar terms, yet they can be expressed in one of three ways. The first and most commonly quoted method in the over-the-counter (OTC) market is in percentage of nominal dollar amount bought or sold. If you were purchasing $1 million worth of calls, you would pay

$$\$1,000,000 \times 0.028497 = \$28,497$$

If this specific option were to deal on one of the exchange traded markets, however, it would be quoted as 142.49 U.S. points (0.014249). In actuality the price would be 142 U.S. points because the exchanges do not deal in fractions of points. Therefore, on the Philadelphia Stock Exchange, where each deutsche mark option contract has a nominal mark amount of DM 62,500, you would have to buy thirty-two contracts to equate to $1 million worth of deutsche mark options:

$$\frac{\text{Nominal dollar amount} \times \text{Strike price}}{\text{Size of option contract}} = \text{Number of PHLX contracts}$$

$$\frac{\$1,000,000 \times 2.00}{\text{DM } 62,500} = 32 \text{ contracts}$$

Then multiply the amount of contracts by the option price, and by the value of each U.S. point for the deutsche mark option:

$$(32 \text{ contracts}) \, (142.49) \, (\$6.25/\text{pt}) = \$28,498$$

If you bought the option from a German bank, you would pay in pfennigs and effectively pay

$$(\text{Price in pfennigs}) \times (\text{Dollar amount of option}) \div \text{Current spot price of deutsche mark}$$

$$\frac{(0.0574) \, (\$1,000,000)}{2.0150} = \$28,486.35$$

Using any one of the three methods of expressing the option value the dollar amount paid is the same other than a negligible rounding difference.

To calculate the "fair value" there are many systems that can be purchased or leased, with some systems being more sophisticated than others. Regardless of the system purchased or leased, it will approximate the same "fair value." No one system available today calculates a "fair value" superior to any other system.

HEDGING CASE

We have discussed option terminology, option pricing, the market-place, building a decision matrix, and volatility analysis. Using this knowledge one can approach currency exposure management in a professional manner. Nonetheless, it takes practice in working through the decision matrix and analyzing volatility before one can confidently make ultimate hedging decisions. To better understand how the decision matrix and volatility analysis are used in exposure management we will analyze the following situation.

On July 10, 1988, the ABC Company is attempting to sell machinery to a German company. The German company will assess all offers from several machine companies over the next three months, at which time the purchase order job will be awarded. All machine companies are required to submit their offering price in deutsche marks. If over the next three months the mark weakens relative to the U.S. dollar and the contract is awarded to the ABC Company, the machinery may be sold at a net loss due to the deterioration in the deutsche mark. To assess the situation properly the corporate trader should work through the decision matrix.

The ABC Company is an aggressive company that prides itself on taking risk. It has a treasurer's department that, besides managing hedging situations, trades foreign exchange and government securities. Senior management considers its risk profile as high risk/high return.

The exposure is considered contingent. Because the bidding is highly competitive and many machine companies are bidding, ABC cannot predict whether it will be awarded the deal. It normally is awarded 15 percent of the deals it bids on, but that does not help in weighing its possibilities in this particular deal. The duration of this exposure should be three months, but it could be shortened or lengthened depending on the response time of the German company.

The treasury department, through its use of fundamental and technical analysis, feels that the deutsche mark has an 80 percent chance of depreciating relative to the U.S. dollar over the next three months. ABC Company has no strong conviction about the interest-rate differential between Germany and the United States.

Because volatility is a major ingredient in pricing options, ABC Company should analyze the volatility of the deutsche mark in several ways. In the analysis of volatility the expected degree of difficulty in hedging in the spot market will be revealed.

To make the proper analysis ABC reviews five volatility figures. Studying the five volatility figures produced the following analysis.

Historical Volatility

In July 1988 historical volatility is near a one and one-half year high

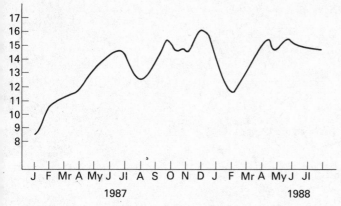

Figure 15–7. Historical Volatility (Sixty-Day), Deutsche Mark.

(Figure 15–7). From this figure alone there is a high probability that the volatility of the spot mark will decrease.

Implied Volatility

Implied in the three-month options there is 12.75 percent volatility on July 10 (Figure 15–8). Implied volatility is in the middle of the range that it has traded since 1987. From this figure alone it is difficult to say with any confidence which direction implied volatility will move.

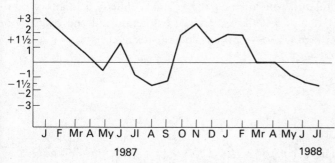

Figure 15–8. Implied Volatility (Three-Month Options), Deutsche Mark.

Volatility Differential

The volatility differential is $1\frac{1}{2}$ percent volatility on July 10 (Figure 15–9). Implied volatility is trading $1\frac{1}{2}$ percent less than historical volatility. This alone indicates that either option values are cheap or historical volatility will decrease (that is, the volatility in the spot mark will decrease) or a combination of the two. This figure indicates that this may be an opportunity to buy options because implied volatility is less than historical.

377

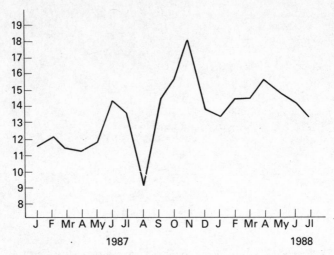

Figure 15–9. Volatility Differential (Implied, Historical), Deutsche Mark.

Range Volatility

For the past month the daily range (that is, difference between the high and low trades of the day) has been close to the average range of 1.9 pfennigs that the mark has shown for the past year and a half (Figure 15–10). This observation indicates that the historical volatility amount is meaningful and consequently the volatility differential figure is also meaningful. Range volatility therefore has reinforced the conclusion drawn from Figure 15–9—option values are relatively cheap on July 10.

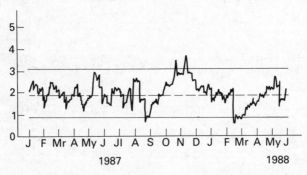

Figure 15–10. Daily Range (Pfennigs), Deutsche Mark.

Seasonal Volatility

The seasonal volatility chart indicates that for the remainder of July and half of August there probably will be a continual drop in historical volatility (Figure 15–8). However, before ABC determines whether it

won the deal in October, volatility will have risen close to its seasonal
highs for the year. Although the spot market (historical volatility) may
be quiet for another month, volatility seasonally will probably increase
during September and October. Therefore, the seasonal volatility chart
indicates that this is an ideal time to buy an option to cover an exposure
for three months.

The implied, differential, range, and seasonal volatility charts indicate
that the purchase of a deutsche mark put option would be an
appropriate hedge. The historical volatility chart, however, shows that
the spot market presently exhibits high volatility and may come down.
Nevertheless, weighing all volatility factors it is appropriate to buy a put
option to hedge the exposure. Through analysis of volatility we have
decided that the purchase of an option is appropriate, but there are five
other aspects to the decision matrix that also must be considered to
yield the best hedge:

1 Risk/reward ratio,
2 Nature of exposure,
3 Forecast of future volatility,
4 Duration of exposure,
5 Germany's and the United States' interest-rate differential, and
6 Outlook on the direction of the deutsche mark over the life of
     exposure.

After weighing all six factors the most appropriate hedge is the
purchase of a four-month deutsche mark put. Although ABC Company has a high-risk/high-return profile and it feels that the deutsche
mark has an 80 percent probability of depreciating relative to the dollar,
options were chosen as the hedging vehicle for this situation. Because of
the contingent nature of the exposure the risk profile and high
confidence level in anticipating the currency's direction did not have as
strong an influence as one might think. Despite its high-risk/high-
return profile, ABC cannot risk losing the deal, being incorrect on the
mark's direction, and consequently having a short mark position that
was established in July.

The interest-rate differential factor did not play a role in the decision.
However, as discussed the volatility factor indicated that the purchase
of an option would be appropriate. Also, the "duration of exposure"
was long enough that ABC, although having a high-risk profile, could
not risk leaving its potential exposure unhedged.

The "duration of exposure" factor also played a role in deciding to
buy a four-month option instead of a three-month option. Because the
German company cannot specify exactly when it will declare the
contract winner, it is in the best interest to buy an option contract with
an additional month. Indeed it will cost more, but it will help ABC
avoid having to make another hedge decision in three months if the
contract winner has not been decided. It also should be pointed out

that a three-month option and one-month option together cost substantially more than a four-month option.

A three-month put option with a strike price at the current spot costs 2.31 percent (assuming $12\frac{1}{2}$ percent volatility) and a one-month put option struck at the current spot costs 1.40 percent (assuming $12\frac{1}{2}$ percent volatility), together costing 3.71 percent. A four-month put option with a strike price at the current spot costs 2.64 percent (assuming $12\frac{1}{2}$ percent volatility). The four-month option is cheaper than the combination of the three- and one-month options by 1.07 percent. That is a feature of option-pricing dynamics that should be kept in mind when dealing with contingent situations.

CONCLUSION

This chapter describes currency options in terms of their basic characteristics and provides guidance for pricing. The importance of establishing a decision matrix to enhance "exposure management" is stressed. The matrix provides the corporate trader with a systematic method of deciding the most appropriate hedging tool given a series of hedging criteria. After currency options are worked through the decision matrix, only 30 to 35 percent of all situations should be hedged with options.

Currency options are a valuable hedge management tool, but if not used in the right context they can hurt the profitability of a corporation. The decision matrix, supported by thorough pricing and volatility analysis, will help the corporate trader provide responsible and profitable exposure management.

REFERENCES

BLACK, FISHER, and MAYRON SCHOLES, 'The Pricing of Options and Corporate Liabilities," *Journal of Political Economy* 81 (May 1973): 637–59.
GRABBE, J. ORLIN, "The Pricing of Call and Put Options on Foreign Exchange," *Journal of International Money and Finance* 2 (1983): 239–53.

PART VI

SUMMARY AND CONCLUSION

16 Closing Comments

HARVEY A. PONIACHEK

IN THE past decade, international financial markets and markets in the major industrial countries have expanded very rapidly and have undergone extensive structural changes in instruments, institutions and regulations. These trends are likely to continue, thereby resulting in greater international integration. This environment inherents significant implications for corporate financial management.

MNCs are the most important actors in the world economy. They are heavily engaged in international trade and capital flows, and account for the bulk of international direct investment. As the world economy becomes more integrated, MNCs' role is ever increasing, and new companies are joining the ranks. To date, a greater proportion of corporate operating functions are coordinated globally, including manufacturing, marketing, and all R&D activities, in order to obtain advantages of scale, scope, and earnings in a global market. In this context, financial management of MNCs and companies with large international business becomes global in its scope.

Corporate financial management of multinational corporations and corporations with substantial international business is more complex than that of domestic ones. In essence, the standard theory and principles of corporate finance are applicable, however, some adjustments are necessary because of complexities of the international environment, or due to problems associated with international operations that require new formulation or special attention. For example, there is a wide range of risk associated with international activities, particularly due to increased volatility of exchange rates and other major variables. While international activities increased companies exposure to currency volatility, various hedging techniques afford risk elimination to a great extent.

The financial markets' tremendous changes in recent years present both risk and opportunities for companies that participate in the international economy. A corporation's objectives, say, profitability performance, depend to a large extent on its financial executives' skills. In some cases, even corporate survival could depend on successful financial management. Ability to interpret correctly the market forces, and to size opportunities and diminish risk depends on the know-how and information of the financial managers.

383

APPENDIXES

Artificial Currencies

BRENDA BASKIN

THE ORIGIN of multicurrency valuation can be traced to the growth of international banking markets and the turbulence caused in these markets by floating exchange rates. Artificial composite currencies, or currency baskets, can limit the risk of floating rates. In pegging currencies to a composite currency such as the special drawing right (SDR) or the European currency unit (ECU), baskets of five and ten component currencies, respectively, the instability of the currency can be lessened.

Multicurrency valuation may be based on either existing baskets, such as the SDR or ECU, or on a hand-fashioned basket related to the pattern of trade. In this appendix, discussion is limited to the multi-currency SDR and ECU baskets. This appendix reviews the development, use, and applications of the SDR and ECU in official and private markets.

DEVELOPMENT OF THE COMPOSITE CURRENCIES

There are two types of multicurrency currency baskets: Fixed-currency unit and fixed weight. A fixed-currency unit basket, such as the SDR and ECU, is valued as the sum of amounts of each component currency. The fixed-weight basket is expressed as the sum of the value of the component currencies. In the latter, the value of each currency in the basket is maintained regardless of market fluctuations.

Compared to a single-peg system, two advantages arise from a basket valuation of currencies: (1) The relatively small impact of any one component currency in proportion to the entire basket; and (2) the stability gained because the currencies in the basket fluctuate in magnitude and direction only by coincidence. Theoretically, changes in the value of one component currency will be balanced by changes in another component currency. The basket also is a more stable alternative to a market-determined exchange rate.

Linking the value of one currency to the value of another contributes to financial market stability similar to what prevailed during the gold-dollar standard under the Bretton Woods system. Exchange rates **387** were pegged directly or indirectly to the U.S. dollar, and exchange-rate stability was assured in that the value of the dollar was fixed by the value of gold. But floating exchange rates meant that the numeraire currency, or the currency to which other currencies were pegged, could never be totally stable because its value was dictated by market forces. The second best solution for the choice of a currency peg therefore depends on the country's closest trading partner. Then the effects of events in the foreign-exchange markets on the country's external economic relationships will be minimized.

The efficiency of a single peg depends on the prosperity of the peg and the degree of compatibility between the economic and financial policies of the two countries. The usefulness of a single-currency peg depends on the volatility of foreign-exchange markets and the degree of divergence in economic policies. Such trade-related currency valuation ties can be a problem when, for example, the peg is based on geographical proximity or long historical links. The pegging country faces a tradeoff between (1) the stability gained in trading and the political benefits of maintaining an exchange-rate level and (2) the financial loss and turbulence caused by adjustment or the under- or overvaluation of the peg currency.

Use of a multicurrency peg in exchange-rate valuation began gradually following both the IMF's promotion of the special drawing right and the increasing use of trade-weighted baskets by various monetary authorities to reflect the degree of over- or undervaluation of their currencies. The obvious choices for currency valuation were the SDR and the ECU. The original official SDR was fixed in value against gold and was intended to supplement gold and currencies as reserve assets. Today, the typical multicurrency valuation standards are the SDR and the ECU. There are exceptions, however, such as the East Caribbean currency unit.

The purpose of multicurrency valuation is to stabilize purchasing power at an average level around which the component currencies fluctuate in response to market forces. The result is less volatility relative to the bilateral cross-rates between component currencies. The greatest benefits from a basket valuation come when a country's reserve currencies undergo a period of severe over- or undervaluation.

Gains in international trade result from a basket valuation because of greater exchange-rate stability and decreased probability of realignments, reducing the potential loss from uncovered trade-related transactions. Additional gains result because of a more stable cash flow and fewer repricing decisions. Finally, for multinational companies based in a single country, the geographical pattern of a basket serves as a proxy for the potential spread of business. For currency speculators, basket valuation suppresses the range of activity and thus reduces potential profits from market swings.

Valuation

At its inception in 1969 the SDR was valued the same as the dollar—one-thirty-fifth an ounce of gold. When floating exchange rates became widespread in 1973, the importance of gold in the international monetary system was reduced, and the valuation of the SDR in terms of gold became inappropriate. In 1974 a basket approach to the valuation of the SDR was adopted that based SDR value on the exchange value of fixed amounts of sixteen currencies. Stability in the value of the SDR results from the fact that movements of some currencies in the basket are balanced by opposite movements of other currencies in the basket. Thus, the SDR exhibits the properties of a diversified portfolio of currencies or financial instruments.

Currencies were originally selected for inclusion in the basket based on a number of criteria. The most important criterion was representativeness in terms of international trade and transmissions. Prior to 1978 inclusion of a currency in the basket depended on whether exports exceeded 1 percent of total world exports of goods and services. After 1978, as SDR became more widely used as a unit of account for transactions outside the Fund, a basket comprised of changing currencies was viewed negatively by institutions seeking financial stability. Therefore, in 1981 the basket was reduced to five currencies, which represented almost 50 percent of total world exports in the late 1970s. The sole reason for the change from a basket of sixteen currencies to a basket of five currencies was to make the value of the SDR more easily calculable. Informational costs of using the SDR as a numeraire were reduced with this simplification. Of the five currencies in the basket, the relative importance of each currency depends on a broad interpretation of representativeness, based on the overall importance of the currency in international trade and financial transactions. The percentage weights of the SDR component currencies has changed over time.

Table A−1.
CALCULATING THE U.S. DOLLAR VALUE
OF THE SDR, October 31, 1986.

SDR Currency Composition		US Dollar Exchange Rate	US Dollar Value of SDR
US dollar	0.54	1	0.54
Deutsche mark	0.46	0.48365	0.22
British pound	0.071	1.3998	0.1
French franc	0.74	0.151699	0.11
Yen	34	0.00619195	0.21
			1.18

The result of valuing the SDR in terms of a basket of fixed amounts means that the weight of each currency's value in the basket changes as the currency's value changes. An appreciating currency's fixed amount in the basket will increase its share in the total value of the SDR, and vice-versa. Table A–1 gives an example of how the U.S. dollar value of the SDR is calculated.

Official SDR

The official SDR was created in 1970 for use as a reserve asset when SDR 9.3 billion was allocated to the 105 Fund Members. Thus, the SDR supplemented existing reserve assets and could be used by countries when the need arose. It was designed to support increasing volumes of international trade and transactions by allowing for a planned growth in the value of international liquidity. Official SDRs may be held by IMF members and fourteen other official institutions. Since 1972 the SDR has been used as the IMF's unit of account, used to express its balance sheet and denominate its lending.

The Fund holds currency of its members and uses this currency to finance its lending operations. Subsequently, the member whose currency was used receives an SDR-denominated reserve position with the Fund. These countries earn a return on their reserve position that is denominated in SDRs and that may be paid in SDRs. Incidentally, if the Fund's lending were instead denominated in terms of a single currency, then countries would be subject to a greater exchange-rate risk.

Uses of SDRs include official Fund transactions (described above), voluntary purchases or sales of SDRs at daily exchange rates established by the Fund, and payment of interest and charges to the Fund. Exchange rates for the SDR are determined daily by the Fund on the basis of middle rates against the dollar of the component currencies of the SDR at noon in London. Other new uses of the SDR have emerged as restrictions on official SDR use have decreased. Although once the SDR was strictly a supplement to existing reserves, it now serves as a medium of exchange between countries. These transactions include spot transactions against currency by agreement, forward transactions, swaps, and the settlement of financial obligations between countries. In addition, they may also be lent or donated or used as security for the performance of financial obligations.

All 146 members of the IMF currently participate in the SDR allocation scheme. Decisions to allocate are made once every five years with approval of Fund governors representing 85 percent of the voting power and actual allocations, if agreed, are made yearly.

Participating in an SDR allocation scheme allows a country running a balance of payments deficit to convert its SDR holdings into a major currency necessary for transactions. The Fund then assigns a country whose balance of payments is relatively strong to provide one of the five

currencies in the basket in exchange for SDRs. SDR provision is
required of these countries up to the point that their SDR holdings are three times their allocations. The allocation scheme is self-financing because the interest that countries receive for holdings of SDRs equals the interest charges of the allocations.

The case for further SDR allocations hinges on more than just the immediate liquidity needs of poor countries. Developing countries are interested in the IMF creating more SDRs to boost their reserves and so improve their credit standing with Western banks. Richer countries fear that such allocations'cause debtors to use new SDRs to pay for more imports and thus postpone the need for economic adjustments. The purpose of each allocation is to meet long-term global liquidity needs. Decisions to allocate are therefore based on whether the allocation will avoid economic stagflation and deflation and excess demand and inflation in the world.

The interest paid on SDRs is based on a weighted basket of short-term high-quality debt obligations of the countries whose currency comprises the SDR basket. In this way, the effective yield, or interest plus expectations of appreciation or depreciation, is comparable with the holdings of major currencies as reserves. Consequently, the basket valuation of the SDR provides lower exchange risk due to unexpected movements in exchange rates than would any single currency valuation scheme. Likewise, the rate paid by the Fund on its borrowings is calculated as a weighted average of interest rates derived from the capital markets of the five component currencies.

Private SDR

The private-sector, or commercial, SDR is a basket of the same value as the official SDR. It is used to denominate borrowing and lending instruments traded in international capital markets. Today, the SDR's private role is limited to functions as a numeraire, for the use by organizations in pricing and accounting, and for countries in valuing their currency. Fifteen international and regional institutions use the SDR as the unit of account and a number of international legal conventions use the SDR to express monetary magnitudes, particularly liability limits in the international transport of goods and services. In addition, fifteen countries peg the value of their currency to the value of the SDR. The private SDR has also been used to denominate bonds, money-market accounts, fixed- and floating-rate CDs, and syndicated loans.

A chronological review of the development of the commercial SDR begins with the Eurobond market in 1975. SDR-denominated bonds were designed to supplement, rather than replace, single-currency debt instruments in the portfolio of investors and borrowers. As a hedge against changes in currency value, they perform a valuable function in any diversified portfolio and are especially important to risk-averse international organizations.

In 1981 when the basket was reduced to five currencies, pricing the bonds became simpler. The coupons of these bonds are set at up to half a percentage point below the weighted average of domestic instruments of the same maturity of each component currency in the basket because the theoretical weighted-average yield of the SDR is diversified for the lender, reducing the foreign-exchange risk.

In 1975 banks also began accepting deposits denominated in SDRs. The growth of an SDR money market has been slow, however, due to to the relatively low yield paid on these deposits and the high cost to banks of handling this type of transaction. In earlier years, because there was no demand for borrowing SDRs, the SDR deposit would have to be broken down into component currencies, or unbundled, and then hedged in the foreign-exchange market. The money market grew more rapidly after 1981, however, when the SDR bundle was reduced to five currencies because hedging became easier for the banks, new banks began to enter the field once the bundle was simplified, and the SDR became more attractive as a short-term investment. As a result, the deposit market became more competitive, and the minimum deposit time was reduced to as short as one week.

The first SDR-denominated CD was issued in 1980. The principal instrument used in this market is the short-term SDR CD, with a maturity of one to twelve months. It provides a vehicle for short-term investment in the SDR with the advantages of negotiability and liquidity and is therefore more flexible than the SDR deposit market. An SDR CD is usually purchased with one of the five component currencies, which creates an exchange-rate exposure against the other four currencies in the basket.

Forward covering can eliminate this exchange-rate risk if the CDs have short-term maturities. The issuing firm can enter into a set of forward contracts to purchase the component currencies in proportion to their true weights at the time of issuance. At maturity, the issuing firm can convert its covered position into the medium of exchange desired by the purchaser and thus overcome any exchange-rate risk due to exposure. However, by its nature, the SDR is a currency basket that minimizes the exchange-rate fluctuations relative to the fluctuations of the various component currencies. For the international investor, SDR CDs provide a hedge in any currency investment portfolio. There is very little secondary market trading because SDR CD investors did not insist on a high degree of market liquidity. Floating-rate SDR CDs (FRCDs) appeared in 1981 and were issued by four banks but disappeared from the market quickly due to the complexities in the calculation of rates and the lack of an interbank market for CDs.

In recent years, the fate of the SDR CD has been determined by the same forces that saw the demise of the SDR deposit market. Invest-

ments in SDR-denominated instruments could not match the rate of
return offered by the U.S. dollar. The result has been a decline in the
popularity and use of the new CD.

An SDR deposit market made SDR-denominated loans possible, but syndicated loans denominated in SDRs appeared only in 1981 when the SDR basket was reduced to five currencies. For investors trying to improve return over a U.S. dollar deposit, SDR deposits were found attractive as long as dollar interest rates were relatively low. When the opposite occurred in 1981, interest in SDR deposits lessened. Because SDR-denominated financial instruments were unattractive relative to dollar-denominated instruments, loans denominated in SDRs were also unattractive.

In addition, interest in SDR syndicated loans lessened in 1982 because those borrowers most attracted to this type of loan were developing countries in geographic regions where international bankers were beginning to moderate the extent of their exposure. Developing countries had the most to gain from this type of loan because it limited their exposure in any one currency from offshore borrowing. This type of stability is particularly important to developing-country borrowers without ready access to the hedging opportunities of international financial markets because these countries are geographically removed from the major financial centers like London and New York.

SDR Retrospective

SDR markets have been determined to a large extent by the hedging possibilities of its component currencies. The SDR market is unique, therefore, in the sense that its exchange rates and interest rates are determined by those of its component currencies in the basket, rather than by the market trading of the SDR itself. This is unlikely to change unless a method for clearing SDRs can be established, thus removing the need to unbundle the currencies themselves for hedging purposes. The necessary practice of hedging the component currencies may explain why many international banks issue SDR CDs only to use the funds raised, hedged into dollars, to supplement their dollar funding. Corporate exploitation of the SDR has been slow and interest has instead forcused on the ECU (discussed below).

The reasons for the slow growth of SDRs in the private market are many. The first is a general lack of familiarity with the SDR, at least partly due to investors' natural aversion to complexity and novelty. Second, there is an extra cost to investors stemming from the narrow spot and foreign-exchange markets, by difficult transfer, and by the specific contract clauses needed to accommodate the possibility that at a certain future point the value of one of the component currencies cannot be determined or that the composition of the SDR should be changed. Third, because no international clearing arrangements for

SDRs exist, international transactions must either be made in another currency or in one of the five component currencies. Finally, private SDRs have been slow to develop because many investors, particularly European institutions, have found that the unequal weights attached to the component currencies have not reduced exchange-rate risk sufficiently. Investors have found that the SDR, which most heavily weights the volatile U.S. dollar, does not afford a sufficient degree of diversification for non–dollar-based investors.

Relative to other reserve assets, the SDR has been in use only a short time. In an international monetary system of floating exchange rates, the SDR offers a means of portfolio diversification and, as a unit of account, offers stability in international financial transactions. Its use outside of the Fund has been limited as a unit of denomination in capital markets and by international organizations, but continued volatility of exchange rates implies that usage may broaden. Although the arguments for SDR-denominated financial instruments are plentiful, the actual demand for such services has depended on cost and yield differentials between the SDR and major international currencies, particularly the U.S. dollar.

A more stable international financial market condition for the official SDR could foreshadow an increased role in international transactions for the commercial SDR, giving it a more important role beside the strong currencies. The SDR CD could be an important source of liquidity necessary for efficient market operation.

The future use of the SDR as a world currency depends on several factors, such as the achievement of more stable exchange rates than have existed in the world, development of SDR-denominated assets and liabilities in private capital markets, and the acceptance by national authorities of an enhanced central banking role for the IMF. If the SDR was the world's main reserve asset, it would be possible for the IMF, acting on behalf of its member governments, to influence the world supply of reserves. IMF control of reserves could provide for greater overall domestic stability. If governments agreed to planned increases or decreases in international reserves, the risks of excessive inflation or deflation could be reduced.

THE EUROPEAN CURRENCY UNIT

At the heart of the European Monetary System (EMS) is a system of fixed but flexible exchange rates. The purpose of the EMS is to establish greater monetary stability between EEC member states. Each currency has a central rate expressed in terms of the European currency unit (ECU) (see Table 3–8). The ECU consists of a basket of fixed amounts of the ten currencies of EEC countries. As part of the EEC's new exchange-rate arrangements in 1979, the ECU replaced the European unit of account (EUA) as the linchpin of the EMS. The EUA was established in 1974 as an attempt to integrate Europe's financial and currency systems. The ECU is a fixed-weight basket of currencies, but the EUA was a closed-currency basket indicator that was used as a reference point and not as a payments mechanism. A closed-currency basket is one that has to be completely separated into its constituent currencies every time it is used in a transaction. Until 1981 most transactions were carried out in closed ECU.

The crucial difference between the EUA and ECU is that the ECU has become an open basket and can be used as a normal currency for transactions and investment. As an open currency, the structure of the component currencies can change. Development of the ECU was a reaction to wide daily variations in exchange rates and the need to overcome the instability of a system based on any single currency in a system of floating exchange rates. The ECU offers several advantages over a single currency, including (1) stability in volatile exchange markets, thus offering less foreign-exchange risk and eliminating the need to hedge and to make frequent price conversions; (2) lower exchange rates than many of Europe's weaker currencies; (3) a useful means for simplifying and standardizing accounting systems; and (4) a neutral currency that is not dependant on the economic policies of one government trying to control the value of its currency.

Valuation

The value of the ECU in terms of any currency of the basket is equal to the sum of the amount of that currency and the amounts of the other currencies converted into that currency. Originally, the ECU was defined by fixed amounts of the currencies of the nine countries that in 1979 constituted the EC. Each currency is not a set percentage part of an ECU, but a component itself is a set sum. Due to movements in the bilateral exchange rates, the percentage of each set sum will continuously change as each currency appreciates or depreciates in value relative to other currencies in the basket. Because of interest-rate differentials that affect the changes in the bilateral exchange rates, the currency percentages will be different for each forward date calculated. Therefore, in the calculation of the ECU rate, the current weighting for the maturity date being calculated is used for the quotation. Daily exchange rates are calculated for each component currency by the Commission of the European Communities. Any difference between quoted official and commercial rates stems from the fact that the Commission calculates its dollar rate based on the rates recorded at 2:30 P.M. on each of the exchange markets of the basket currencies, while a private bank must consider the rates of the component currencies in its own national market.

The composition of the ECU basket may be revised either by adjusting the amounts of the basket currencies or by introducing **395** another currency into the basket. A revision of the ECU basket brings the percentage weights of the currencies in the basket more in line with the relative economic importance of EC countries. The respective relative economic weights are based on GNP, share in intra-EEC trade, and share in the short-term monetary support mechanism of the EMS. Any change in the weights by the Commission would be made to reflect changes in these economic criteria. A revision of the basket changes the amount of national currency in the basket but does not affect the external value of the ECU at the time of the transition. The weight of a currency in the basket is the ratio between the number of units of that currency and the value of the basket in terms of that particular currency. A currency will gain or lose weight in the basket according to whether it appreciates or depreciates relative to other basket currencies.

Official ECU

The ECU plays a central role in the EMS. The ECU is used in two official areas: Within the EMS and in other Community activities. The ECU was established to function as a means of settlement, a reserve asset, and as a unit of account for official transactions. Within the EMS, there are three main roles of the ECU. First, the ECU serves as a denominator for exchange-rate valuation within the EEC with each currency expressed as an amount of currency per ECU. By comparing these ECU central rates one obtains bilateral central rates. Bilateral intervention limits exist within fluctuation margins of plus and minus 2.25 percent of the bilateral central rates (except the Italian lira, which is within 6 percent). The formula for calculating the maximum divergence for each ECU component currency is shown in Table 3–8. The ECU central rates can be adjusted, based on mutual agreement of the EMS participant countries. By nature, then, a change in the central rate of one country's currency implies a change in the central rates of the other countries.

The second official role of the ECU within the EMS is as a divergence indicator, measuring the exchange-rate performance of each EMS currency in relation to the EEC average, as represented in the ECU. Exchange-rate performance is determined by comparing each currency's ratio between actual appreciation (depreciation) of its ECU market rate against its ECU central rate, and the maximum appreciation (depreciation) that the ECU market rate of the currency may show against its ECU central rate. The maximum deviation is reached for a currency when its bilateral central rate has reached its fluctuation margin of 2.25 percent against the other currencies in the ECU basket. A currency is said to reach its divergence threshold when the appreciation (depreciation) of the ECU market rate for the currency reaches 75 percent of the ECU market rate. The effect of a divergence threshold is to reduce currency movements to within reasonably assessable parameters.

The third purpose of the official ECU is as the denominator for intervention and credit operations of the EMS. In the framework of currency transactions between EEC members, the ECU rate on the day of the intervention is the conversion rate used, as calculated by the Commission. There are institutional limitations placed on the use of the ECU for intervention purposes, however, in that it cannot be used directly for intervention and can be used only within the specified limits for the settlement of intervention debts within the EMS. The ECU is also used as a denominator in the short-term monetary support mechanism and the currency of the medium-term financial assistance loans through the European Monetary Cooperation Fund to provide for balance of payments financing. When the credit is granted, however, the choice of currency is part of the agreement and need not be made in ECUs.

Finally, the official ECU serves an important role as a reserve asset for EMS countries. The ECU acquired as reserves are used primarily as a means for settling debts that result from central bank intervention in EEC currencies to maintain currency values within the 2.25 percent fluctuation margins. As remuneration for the use of short- or medium-term ECU funds, a net user of ECU funds is required to pay interest to a net holder of ECUs at an interest rate equal to the average of the official discount rates of all EEC central banks, weighted according to the respective currency weights in the currency basket. No interest payments are required on the amount of outstanding ECUs issued against a deposit of reserves.

Outside of the EMS, the official ECU is used in the operation of the EEC budget, the European Development Fund, the European Coal and Steel Community, and the European Investment Bank. As an example, since 1981 the ECU has been used by the Community's development bank, the European Investment Bank, as the unit in which EIB borrows in the international bond market, services such borrowings, and on-lends to borrowers in member countries. In turn, this official ECU use has produced a growing volume of ECU assets and liabilities in financial markets to provide a nucleus of real demand for ECU accounts. Over the years, the ECU has become more than just a unit of account; it is increasingly used as a means of denomination and settlement for intra-EEC activity.

Private ECU

Floating exchange rates made it risky for European countries to borrow in dollars. European commercial organizations therefore needed a currency outside the limitations of national controls and at the same time one that possessed limited exchange-rate risk. Although no provision is officially made for the use of ECUs in private transactions, the ECU fits the description and is therefore appealing to financial markets. By definition, the ECU is outside of national or supranational monetary control, and exchange-rate changes can take place only in the form of negotiated settlements between EEC members. Thus, the private ECU market is completely independent of official ECU creation. The use of the ECU in private markets has grown because the ECU has gradually developed into a unit of account that possesses the characteristics of a convertible currency: Exchange-rate quotations, time deposits, a bond market, and an interbank market. Further financial innovations are quickly following; for example, ECU-denominated traveler's checks recently hit the market. More than 350 European banks provide a full range of ECU-denominated financial services. The ECU is essentially book money, however; the ECU is not officially issued to the public because there are no coins or bank notes. Private banks simply create a book value for ECUs by crediting an ECU account.

The ECU has developed its own interest-rate structure and foreign-exchange behavior, both determined by market forces. As a result, major financial instruments available for national currencies are also available for the ECU. There are several reasons for this development. The most important is the exchange-rate stability that stems from using the ECU, rather than any one of its component currencies, to denominate international transactions. In addition, the ECU has become a viable alternative to the U.S. dollar because the dollar is not a part of the ECU basket. Second, the ECU has developed in private markets due to the very nature of a basket currency that is made even more attractive by the fact that financial intermediaries can balance their ECU position in assets and liabilities by borrowing or lending in any one of the component currencies. The difference between the market's ECU assets and ECU liabilities can be maintained in the component currency proportions of the ECU. The markets for the component currencies of the ECU act as lenders of last resort for the ECU. Finally, the use of ECUs in private markets has benefited from the patronage of the EMS, which provides the ECU with a great deal of respectability. This means that the ECU is perceived as an important instrument for promoting the financial integration of Europe, a characteristic not shared by other artificial, or composite, currencies.

Commercial use of ECUs is expanding rapidly, as demonstrated by the increasing number of trade contracts, export credits, and other commercial transactions denominated in ECUs. In fact, the ECU has become the third most sought after currency, following U.S. dollars and deutsche marks. ECU loans have been raised by MNCs, EEC governments, East European banks, and even a Japanese supermarket chain. There are many reasons for borrowing and investing in ECUs. Borrowing and investing in ECUs eliminates the risk of sharp exchange-rate movements that financing in single currencies always involves. In addition, it provides access to many currencies otherwise unobtainable and offers the possibility of wide market diversification. For institutional investors with liabilities in various EMS currencies, it is attractive to have counterbalancing assets also denominated in ECUs. Because the ECU is composed of strong and weak currencies, it is stronger than the weak currencies and weaker than the strong currencies. Therefore, an ECU-denominated investment is particularly appealing to someone wishing to invest in strong currencies. In addition, because the ECU does not contain a dollar component, individuals wishing to diversify their dollar holdings find the ECU a good investment.

The choice of the appropriate borrowing currency is important to the financial management of a corporation with foreign trade business. When the currency's trade exchanges are geographically and monetarily diversified, characteristics of the ECU such as interest-rate and exchange-rate risk may make the ECU the appropriate borrowing currency.

Determination of interest rates on the first ECU-denominated bonds was a difficult task due to the problem of knowing which interest rate to apply to the instrument. The first issues carried a coupon based on both an estimate of the average rate of the component currencies and considerations of the rate needed to place an issue given the rates offered in other currencies. As soon as a secondary market developed and the number of issues increased, however, a market rate could be determined, as for any component currency bond issue. Today, the prevailing rates on the secondary market are the most reliable indicator of the interest rate to be offered on new issues.

Borrowers find ECUs attractive because ECU bonds offer lower coupons than U.S. dollar bonds. Some U.S. companies, such as the Chrysler Financial Corporation, have tapped the ECU Eurobond market and then swapped the proceeds back into U.S. dollars. In the long run, issuing bonds to raise ECUs is likely to be more attractive to companies that do not need U.S. dollars but instead need one or more of its component currencies. Those wishing to hedge portfolios against international exchange-rate movements would find that a portfolio composed of equal amounts of U.S. dollars and ECUs affords a higher return than an SDR investment.

The plan for a formal clearing system for ECUs was finalized in March 1984. The explosive growth in the use of ECUs necessitated the development of a full-fledged clearing system, or secondary market, and has meant that the transfer of ECUs can be conducted in the same manner as transfers of other currencies. Prior to the development of a clearing system, ECU funds were unbundled and transferred-in their component currencies. The clearing system that developed as a result of the inconvenience of this unbundling became similar to a normal currency settlement system. There do exist some differences. Because there is no domestic central bank for the ECU, the lack of a formalized clearing system once meant that the final balancing settlement of daily

currency transactions between the few clearing agents may have to be
settled in the individual component currencies. The result of the
development of a secondary market has increased market liquidity.
Although once ECU issues were concentrated in Benelux countries and
France, they have now become common in Germany, Switzerland, and
the United Kingdom and are rapidly developing in the United States
and Japan.

Exchange risk is better diversified when funds are denominated in a
currency basket. For the ECU this is particularly true in that the
component currencies are interlinked by the monetary agreement that
is formalized by the EMS and that contains currency fluctuations within
the divergence thresholds. For multinationals that import and export to
and from Europe, such exchange-rate stability can be highly beneficial.
ECU indebtedness is particularly attractive to residents of weak-
currency countries because the interest rate on ECU bonds is lower
than their own currency rates. Note that when a national currency
appreciates against the currency of indebtedness, the result is a yield,
rather than a cost, of indebtedness.

Floating-rate notes (FRNs) denominated in ECUs were first issued in
1982 and today are relatively rare although their numbers are increasing. The growing number of FRNs will help to develop the liquidity of
ECU-denominated bonds, a market previously hindered by the limited
number of market managers in the secondary market. This sophisticated and computationally difficult instrument is being geared toward
large-scale institutional investors rather than toward a retail market.

There are several reasons for the expansion of the ECU bond market.
The first reason lies in the direct financial benefit it gives its borrowers
and investors. Second, as a basket, it offers relative exchange-rate
stability at a reasonable level of interest. Third, it gives corporate
treasurers the opportunity to tap into new sources of funding and
diversify their debt. Finally, ECU bonds give fund raisers access to
currencies that might otherwise be difficult to raise because of exchange
controls or foreign-exchange restrictions. In particular, investors in
ECU bonds like their relatively high rate of return and the fact that an
ECU-denominated portfolio effectively spreads risk over ten currencies.
Recent innovations in the bond market include zero coupon ECU
bonds (attractive to investors who are subject to a tax regime that
differentiates between capital gains and interest income) and ECU
convertibles.

ECU-denominated syndicated loans were developed in 1980 following the wider private use of the ECU and private-sector familiarization
with the new monetary instrument. Since 1980 there have been
significant yearly increases in the number and size of ECU loans issued,
both by credit organizations and by medium-sized industrial and
commercial companies.

A futures contract is an agreement to buy or sell a specific commodity at a set price. Unhedged futures trading can be very risky because the investor can lose much more than was initially invested. Spreading exchange-rate risk through the use of a composite currency can lessen risk because the investor simultaneously buys and sells related contracts. The absolute price levels are not important, yet the differences in their prices matter a great deal because spreads change less abruptly than absolute prices. Therefore, trading spreads are attractive to the conservative investor.

Put and call warrants entitle the holder to purchase or sell ECUs at a fixed rate against the U.S. dollar. Currency options are proving particularly interesting in this market because the U.S. dollar and the ECU usually fluctuate in opposite directions, thereby opening up attractive speculative opportunities to investors. Such instruments also indicate that the market views the ECU as an attractive investment alternative to the U.S. dollar.

In 1985 the first ECU option started trading on the European Options Exchange in Amsterdam and at New York's Cotton Exchange. The ECU contract was more difficult to popularize than the U.S. dollar contract because the ECU is not well known in the United States. The success of a futures contract depends on whether professional and speculative investors are willing to assume risk in return for the opportunity to profit. Without wide use of the ECU futures contract, there is some doubt as to whether there is enough liquidity in the market. Because of the opportunities for cash and futures arbitrage, the ECU futures contract should lead to narrower bid-offer spreads in the cash market and therefore fuel growth. The chances for the success of the ECU futures contract should be further enhanced by the spreading opportunities available between the U.S. dollar index futures contract and ECU futures contracts because of the high inverse correlation between the two.

Commercial uses of the ECU are growing. Billing is currently being studied by several European associations for the collection and settlement of dues for their multinational members. Increasingly, the ECU is being used in the payment of goods and services. For the importer/exporter trading with parties in EEC countries, the ECU-denominated financial instrument provides a uniform pricing mechanism and a transferable unit with a store of value. In project finance, a company may be eligible for a loan from the EEC that may be paid in ECUs.

ECU Retrospective

Explaining the success of the ECU requires hints of the complexities of handling ECU-denominated currencies. The initial use of the currency by the EEC obliged banks to open accounts in the new currency. To a large extent, banks tried to handle the composite as a bundled currency rather than go through the burdensome and costly process of unbundling the basket. With ECU deposits in hand, the banks then tried to develop an ECU market by lending, borrowing, and charging interest in the unit. Thus a private interbank market emerged. Private banks were encouraged in their efforts to create an active secondary market in the ECU by the European Commission. The Commission considered increased private use of the currency as a welcome development facilitating its policy of European financial integration.

The biggest reason for the success of the ECU stems from the direct financial benefits that the use of a composite currency can bring to its borrowers and lenders. The currency basket gives its holders relative exchange-rate stability at a reasonable and predictable level of interest, which is certainly important in our world of volatile exchange rates. The ECU basket effectively spreads exchange-rate risk over its ten component currencies.

The ECU is attractive to investors because it generally earns a higher rate of interest than strong currencies such as the deutsche mark, Swiss franc, and U.S. dollar. The rate is higher because the ECU yield is a weighted average of its components and the weaker currencies, such as the lira, have higher interest rates. In addition, some investors, like the Japanese, find the ECU attractive because it allows diversification of currency resources without increasing dollar exposure. Corporations are drawn to the use of the ECU as an opportunity to tap new sources of funding and diversify their debt. Because the ECU market is not subject to national currency regulations, corporations are given access to foreign currency, like the lira and French franc, that might otherwise be unavailable because of foreign-exchange restrictions.

In a nutshell, the success of the ECU for investors can be traced to four primary reasons. The first is the marketing efforts of the pioneer banks. The second is the stability of the system. Because the ECU is composed of fixed amounts of both strong and weak currencies of the EMS, an appreciation of one of more of its strong component currencies is automatically offset by a depreciation of one or more of its weaker component currencies. Third, the most important stabilizing influence in the basket is that the component currencies of the ECU are linked to each other in value and can fluctuate only within defined limits. Finally, the composition of the ECU means that it commands higher interest rates than those for the stronger currencies in the EMS.

CONCLUSIONS

The instability of the international monetary system suggests that one alternative to ensure greater financial stability is increased reliance on artificial currencies like the SDR and ECU in exchange-rate valuation and international pricing of financial instruments and goods. An increased role in international monetary transactions for the SDR and

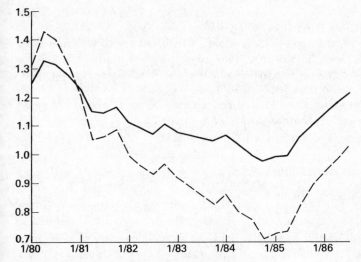

Figure A–1. U.S. Dollar Exchange Rates.

ECU would reduce, but not eliminate, the exchange-rate risks of
multinational business payments, billing, and funding operations. Since
the SDR and ECU are composed of currencies that are floating, they
are, in turn, floating too. Their volatility in the 1980s is shown in
Figure A–1.

To date, the strong dollar has deterred many U.S. companies from
entering the ECU market. Should the dollar weaken significantly,
thereby exposing U.S. corporations with European subsidiaries to
exchange-rate risks, the ECU could become increasingly attractive to
U.S. investors. Among EEC member countries, the expected stability
of the monetary system caused by transactions denominated in ECUs
implies a future convergence of pricing developments across country
borders. Some economists suggest that the ECU may become the
EEC's official monetary unit and thus oust the national currencies.
Similar development of the SDR as a world currency depends on the
achievement of more stable exchange rates, greater development of
SDR-denominated assets and liabilities in private capital markets, and
finally, acceptance by national authorities of an enhanced central
banking role for the IMF.

REFERENCES

VAN DEN BOORAERDE. P. "The Private SDR: An Assessment of its Risk and
    Return," *International Monetary Fund Staff Papers* 31 (March 1984): 25–61.
CANTERBERY. E. R. "Commercial Use of the SDR," *Columbia Journal of
    International Business* 17 (Winter 1982): 11–16.
COATS, WARREN L. "The SDR as a Means of Payment," *International
    Monetary Fund Staff Papers* 29 (September 1984): 422–36.

International Corporate Finance

DE V. WRAGG, L. *Composite Currencies: SDRs, ECUs and Other Instruments* (London: Euromoney Publications Limited, 1984).

HOOD, W. C. "International Money, Credit and the SDR," *Finance and Development* 20 (September 1983): 6–9.

POZO, S. "Composition and Variability of the SDR," *Review of Economics and Statistics* 66 (May 1984): 308–14.

UNGERER, HORST. "Main Developments in the European Monetary System," *Finance and Development* (June 1983).

Assessing Country Risk: A Practical Approach

HARVEY A. PONIACHEK

THIS appendix defines country risk, reviews some of the theoretical and empirical issues, and outlines a quantitative model for country risk assessment. The model is simple, cost effective and easy to adopt by a finance department in a corporation.

DEFINITIONS

There are several types of risk in doing business abroad, as shown in Table B–1, of which country risk is the most significant. Country risk measures a country's ability, either through earnings or international reserves, to provide its resident corporations and government entities with sufficient foreign exchange to service international obligations denominated in foreign currency. High country risk could reduce the ability, for example, of a creditworthy corporation located abroad or of a foreign subsidiary of a U.S. corporation, to purchase from the local commercial banks and monetary authorities foreign currency to pay foreign obligations.

Country risk can be defined in narrow and broad terms. The narrow definition measures the creditworthiness of a country, or its ability or capacity to payback external debt denominated in foreign exchange. We commonly refer to this capacity as convertibility, or ability to facilitate a

Table B–1.
INTERNATIONAL RISK.

1	CURRENCY RISK
	TRANSACTION
	TRANSLATION
	ECONOMICS
2	COUNTRY RISK
	INCONVERTIBILITY
	BLOCKED FUNDS
3	COMMERCIAL RISK
4	CREDIT RISK

transfer payment. Country risk is often erroneously interchanged with sovereign risk, which addresses transactions vis-à-vis the public sector or its entities. Broadly defined country risk includes the narrowly defined measure plus political risk. The latter measures the risk due to political instability, expropriation, nationalization, revolution and war.

THEORETICAL ISSUES

There are a variety of theoretical explanations and models for country risk assessment, but there is no consensus which theory or model is best. One approach, known as the two gap theory, considers the balance of payments and external debt problems arising because of inadequate domestic savings and insufficient foreign exchange earnings.

An alternative interpretation of country risk is based on the cash flow or the balance of payments approach. It analyzes the external debt problem of a country analogously to a firm that faces a cash flow or liquidity difficulty. Accordingly, country risk arises from the economic, social and political environment of the country. These factors, in turn, have potential adverse effects on foreign debt, equity investment, or on various other types of foreign exposure in that country. Due to balance of payments deficits, there is sometimes insufficient foreign exchange reserve or liquidity to service foreign debt. The government might occasionally ration foreign exchange to the most critical needs, like import of food and fuel, by imposing currency controls.

There is large variety of statistical models that address country risk assessment, and provide early warning information. These models provide medium- or long-term projections about the international financial conditions of the country.

APPLICATIONS

The liquidity model uses several variables to measure the country's ability to service its external debt. The model described in Table B–2 includes financial, economic and political variables. Each variable is weighted or multiplied by a fixed weight, or coefficient, and the results are then aggregated to form the index or composite score. Factors that adversely influence the country's creditworthiness, or ability to payback, have negative weights or coefficients. The indexes of the various countries, or of the same country over a period of time, can then be standardized. The higher the score, the better off is the country. This approach has some shortcomings, however.

For individuals trained in econometrics and statistical methods, multiple regression analysis could be an effective approach deriving country risk ratings. Nowadays, the widespread availability of personal computers and statistical programs (such as Lotus 1–2–3), make the applications of regression analysis rather simple. While this approach eliminates the discretion of choosing the coefficients of the explanatory variables, it could introduce other complexities that need to be addressed (such as statistically insignificant variables).

We have gathered the data for the independent (that are listed in the check list method) and dependent variables from publicly available sources. Then we estimated multiple regressions and simulated the estimated function for in-the-sample and out-of-sample data. The results for in-sample simulation are reported in Table B–3. These have to be compared with ratings provided by the *Institutional Investor*. The model was sensitive and was able to identify countries that have either defaulted on their international obligations or required rescheduling or other external debt relief.

SUMMARY

The adoption of an elaborated country risk rating system is expensive and beyond the means and needs of the average corporation. Modeling

Table B–2.
COUNTRY RISK RATING; CHECK LIST METHOD (Data are in Percentages).

Variables	(a) Weights	(b) Country I	(c) (a) × (b)	(d) Country II	(e) (a) × (d)	(f) Country III	(g) (a) × (f)
Domestic:							
GNP Growth	5	0.05	0.25	0.03	0.15	0.02	0.10
GNP/Population Rank	10	30	3	60	6	100	10
Inflation	−5	0.15	−0.75	0.08	−0.04	0.05	−0.25
International:							
Reserves/(Imports/12) Rank	10	75	7.5	87.5	8.75	100	10
Current Account Balance/GNP	15	−15	2.25	−3	−0.45	2	0.3
Debt Service Ratio	−25	0.25	−6.25	0.12	−3.00	0.075	−1.875
Debt/GNP	−15	0.30	−5.25	0.15	−2.25	0.10	−1.5
Political:							
Political Stability	15	0.50	7.5	0.57	8.5	0.80	12
	100%		7.75		16.80		48.85

Source: Harvey A. Poniachek
Notes:
1) Country I-LDC
   Country II-NICs
   Country III-Industrial
2) All the variables are percentages and are entered as decimal points.
3) Rescaling the above results, by using country III as the base:

   Country III $\left(\dfrac{48.85}{48.85}\right) 100 = 100$

   Country II $\left(\dfrac{16.80}{48.85}\right) 100 = 34.39$

   Country I $\left(\dfrac{7.75}{48.85}\right) 100 = 15.86$

4) Alternative methods are Z-scrore approach by applying MDA or regression analysis.
5) GNP/Population is ranked by determining the percent of country I figure to III, and country II figure as a ratio of country I.
6) International reserves/(imports/12) is ranked in relationship to country I, in a similar way shown in note 5 above.

Table B-3.

COUNTRY RISK RATING; APPLICATION OF 1987 MODEL FOR 1987 DATA.

Country	Real GDP/GNP Growth (%)	GNP/GDP per capita	Rate of Inflation (%)	Current Account Deficit (% of GDP)
Algeria	2.0	2,933	7.5	1.2
Egypt	(2.0)	1,235	19.7	3.0
Gabon	(3.8)	3,190	5.3	14.0
Ivory Coast	(1.5)	1,035	7.0	8.3
Kenya	5.0	342	5.2	5.4
Morocco	1.0	747	2.7	1.8
Nigeria	(4.0)	205	11.5	8.4
South Africa	2.5	2,494	16.1	-3.3
Tunisia	5.5	1,306	7.2	3.7
Zimbabwe	1.8	1,204	12.5	1.7
Australia	2.6	10,698	9.3	5.0
China	9.3	229	7.3	0.4
India	1.4	304	10.0	2.1
Indonesia	3.5	373	9.3	2.6
South Korea	11.2	2,881	3.0	-8.1
Malaysia	4.7	1,797	1.1	-7.8
New Zealand	0.2	11,184	15.7	4.0
Pakistan	7.7	343	3.7	0.9
Philippines	5.7	615	3.8	2.0
Singapore	8.8	7,490	0.5	-2.7
Taiwan	11.2	4,946	0.6	-18.7
Thailand	6.3	890	2.5	0.5
Costa Rica	3.0	1,558	16.8	6.9
Dominican Republic	8.0	753	30.1	5.9
Jamaica	5.1	1,187	6.7	3.2
Trinidad and Tobago	(6.1)	4,447	11.4	4.2
Israel	4.5	7,480	19.8	3.1
Kuwait	(3.0)	10,909	0.6	-21.6
Saudi Arabia	0.0	6,016	(1.0)	12.4
Turkey	7.3	1,134	32.1	1.7
Canada	3.9	15,881	4.4	3.5
United States	2.9	18,401	3.6	5.0
Argentina	2.0	2,569	174.8	5.4
Bolivia	2.2	620	14.6	11.7
Brazil	2.9	2,211	229.7	0.4
Chile	5.7	1,491	19.9	4.3
Colombia	5.5	1,176	23.3	-0.1
Ecuador	(3.1)	1,067	29.5	10.4
Mexico	1.4	1,730	131.8	-3.2
Peru	7.0	1,785	85.9	5.4
Uruguay	4.5	2,349	63.6	2.9
Venezuela	1.3	1,931	28.1	0.9
Austria	1.3	15,542	1.4	0.3
Belgium	1.8	14,271	1.5	-1.8
Denmark	(0.9)	19,029	4.0	3.3
Finland	3.6	17,203	3.7	2.5
France	1.9	15,428	3.3	0.4
Germany	1.7	18,438	0.2	-4.0
Greece	(0.5)	5,146	16.4	2.5
Ireland	2.5	7,983	3.1	-1.4
Italy	3.1	12,651	4.7	0.1
Netherlands	2.5	14,649	(0.5)	-1.5
Norway	1.3	19,806	8.7	5.1
Portugal	5.0	3,380	9.3	-1.9
Spain	5.2	7,214	5.3	0.0
Sweden	2.8	18,972	4.2	0.6
Switzerland	2.5	25,093	1.4	-4.3
United Kingdom	3.6	11,768	4.2	0.5

Source: Harvey Poniachek, July 1988.

Total Debt-service Ratio (%)	Ratio of Foreign Debt to GNP (%)	Ratio of Reserves to Imports (months)	Political Factor	Standardized Country Risk (US = 100)	Institutional Investor Standardized Credit Rating (US = 100)
53.7	32.7	6.4	75	55	47
32.2	55.1	3.8	50	28	25
10.9	53.6	1.1	75	44	37
45.8	71.9	0.2	70	36	29
41.6	75.4	2.1	70	45	32
37.7	115.1	2.2	70	33	24
30.2	140.0	3.0	70	22	22
18.0	27.2	2.7	85	56	34
24.8	77.0	2.6	75	50−	37
40.0	26.2	3.8	75	51−	23
28.7	46.0	6.2	100	81	79
10.9	14.7	7.6	90	72	70
34.3	23.5	7.4	75	52	54
38.2	82.1	8.3	75	47	47
17.6	29.3	2.9	75	66+	66
14.0	84.8	8.6	80	52+	59
45.0	74.0	5.9	85	66	71
26.6	44.3	3.7	55	47	32
33.8	88.0	3.9	45	34	25
7.0	96.3	6.1	100	77+	80
4.8	23.4	30.0	90	93	81
21.8	41.4	5.2	80	59+	58
29.3	104.9	4.4	75	43	18
26.7	78.6	1.5	55	41	17
39.4	146.2	2.0	60	31	16
27.1	33.2	2.3	75	43	43
26.0	97.9	6.0	80	60	36
5.0	16.7	13.3	80	66	63
5.0	19.9	17.0	90	78+	66
38.8	65.8	2.9	85	56	43
19.0	30.0	2.1	100	93	93
32.0	13.8	4.4	100	100	100
68.4	66.6	7.9	60	28	27
57.5	122.5	12.1	50	33−	9
87.0	38.7	5.9	75	32	34
32.1	116.5	9.6	75	48+	28
39.4	48.9	10.7	70	54	42
51.0	101.9	4.0	70	30	26
48.0	75.4	13.4	80	40	29
42.9	46.5	5.1	50	40−	15
49.0	78.6	17.9	80	57	41
37.0	94.3	15.7	80	50+	39
7.9	9.6	6.5	100	93	90
22.8	43.0	4.1	100	85	83
45.1	77.0	5.3	90	81	78
26.2	51.2	4.9	100	93	85
6.0	7.7	5.7	100	94	92
9.3	16.0	7.0	100	98	102
29.0	41.6	4.6	75	53	49
24.9	106.2	4.6	80	56+	67
16.3	13.9	6.2	90	85	83
9.0	8.5	5.3	100	93	93
24.0	60.2	8.0	90	91	88
23.1	54.7	12.2	85	65	59
14.1	16.8	9.1	85	77+	78
31.1	40.8	3.3	90	90	87
5.0	15.2	15.3	100	117	101
26.9	30.3	4.1	100	85	93

of country risk would have been redundant if we could have forecast the balance of payments over the medium and long term accurately and cost effectively. The weights or coefficient assigned to the various variables can determine on the basis of experience, as we have done in the model listed in Table B–2, or they can be estimated empirically by applying econometric methods, or by using multiple discriminate analysis. If, however, structural relationships in the economy are changing substantially and frequently, then the model is not likely to provide efficient predictors of country risk.

In practice, the application of the model is done as follows: (1) Select the variables, (2) assign weights to each variable, whereas total should be 100 percent (in absolute value), (3) obtain the data for the variables, (4) multiply the weights column by the data column for the country, (5) add the product to obtain the summary index, finally, (6) standardize the summary index. The model could be maintained and updated by utilizing a Lotus 1–2–3 spread sheet, or comparable software programs utilizing a Z-score approach and by using a stepwise regression. The weights must be applied consistently over time and for different countries. (See Table B–3.)

Subject Index

413

414

416